M000236148

THE COMPANION GUIDE TO
BERLIN

THE COMPANION GUIDES

*It is the aim of these guides to provide a Companion
in the person of the author, who knows
intimately the places and people of whom he writes, and is able to
communicate this knowledge and affection to his readers.
It is hoped that the text and pictures will aid them
in their preparations and in their travels, and will
help them remember on their return.*

BURGUNDY · THE COUNTRY ROUND PARIS
DEVON · EDINBURGH AND THE BORDERS
FLORENCE · GASCONY AND THE DORDOGNE
GREECE · GREEK ISLANDS · IRELAND · ISTANBUL
KENT AND SUSSEX · LAKE DISTRICT · LONDON
MADRID AND CENTRAL SPAIN · NEW YORK
PARIS · ROME · SICILY · SOUTH OF SPAIN
ST PETERSBURG · VENICE

THE COMPANION GUIDE TO

BERLIN

BRIAN LADD

COMPANION GUIDES

First published 2004

Companion Guides

ISBN 1 900639 28 9

*The publishers and author have done their best to ensure
the accuracy and currency of all the information in*
The Companion Guide to Berlin.
*However, they can accept no responsibility for any loss, injury,
or inconvenience sustained by any traveller as a result
of information or advice contained in the guide.*

Companion Guides is an imprint of Boydell & Brewer Ltd.
PO Box 9, Woodbridge, Suffolk IP12 3DF, UK
and of Boydell & Brewer Inc.
PO Box 41026, Rochester, NY 14604–4126, USA
website: www.companionguides.com

A BIC catalogue record for this book is available
from the British Library

Printed and bound in Finland by WS Bookwell

Contents

Orientation

Old Berlin guidebooks make fascinating reading, but, unlike old guides to Paris or Venice, they only confuse the novice visitor. Any description of Berlin written in the twentieth century, even at its very end, requires significant revision: so much has been destroyed, and so much has been built. For all the turmoil of the past century in Berlin, its final decade wrought more visible change than any other, excepting only the 1940s. Early in the new millennium, however, things seemed to be slowing down. The government had arrived from Bonn and settled in; the most visible signs of the city's former division had been erased; and the real estate market had crashed, leaving a bankrupt municipality, unable to pay for ambitious new projects. All of which might mean that Berlin can now be appreciated with more leisure, and with a greater detachment, than has been possible for some time.

This is not to say that Berlin has lost its edge. During the Cold War, the divided city attracted many people – Germans and foreigners – who sought a *frisson* of excitement on the dividing line between East and West. After the Berlin Wall came down, another sort of young person – less rebellious, more entrepreneurial – came to help build a new metropolis. Many of the migrants from both groups remain, along with unprecedented numbers from the fringes of Europe and beyond, who bring their hopes and their energy, their diverse cultures and the inevitable tensions that accompany that diversity. Berlin, no longer protected from the economic hurricanes of international capital, is becoming more like any other big city, but it remains a refuge from some aspects of Western normality. Much as some Berliners might wish it, their city is in no danger of becoming a normal place anytime soon. What makes Berlin exciting is the tangible presence of history. This is a city where the present is suffused with the past, in often startling juxtapositions. It is filled with people who saw and survived decisive events of the twentieth century, and as that century recedes, those events seem to attract more, not less, attention. Berlin is also filled with visible traces of history: resonant buildings, ruins, even empty spaces. The history of some places is common knowledge (although the common knowledge is not always accurate); every month new memorials spring up to mark others; for the rest, you need this book.

A century ago, when Berlin emerged as one of the world's great metropolises, it struck visitors as a raw and unfinished city – the German Chicago, some said, whether admiring its energy or scorning its tawdriness. Despite all efforts to civilize the city and its uncouth natives, Berlin still seems incomplete and uncultivated, by European standards, and certainly when compared to Germany's smaller and more refined metropolises, Frankfurt and Hamburg, Munich and Düsseldorf. The streets are shabbier and dirtier, and so are the people – by German standards, Berlin is, measurably, a poor city. Informality reigns in social intercourse: a refreshing cheekiness, when you are in the mood for it; an appalling rudeness, when you are not. Beneath their big-city insolence, Berliners reveal a subversive humor. New Yorkers recognize a familiar in-your-face quality. (Germans tend to feel the same way about Berliners that Americans feel about New Yorkers.) Berlin dialect, a mixture of Saxon and Low German, is said to be best suited to fast talking and witty retorts. (More and more, however, you can expect to be addressed in a halfway competent English.) This is not the home of warm south-German *Gemütlichkeit*. This is a city, one might say, where Kafka could feel at home – as he apparently did in the last year of his life, much of which he spent here.

In some ways Berlin is a pale shadow of the early-twentieth-century boom town that formed its character. That is as it should be: the excitement of those days was built on desperate poverty, ideological extremism, vicious hatreds and uncontainable aggression. The cold war that followed Hitler's defeat was disquieting enough, with its looming threat of nuclear annihilation, but it permitted decades of peaceful development. What remains after reunification in 1990 is a city that straddles eastern and western Europe, by far the most diverse in Germany as well as the most open-minded. By conventional standards, Berlin is not a beautiful city, and it never has been. Fine specimens of classical order and serenity can be found here, to be sure, but if Berlin is a work of art, it is the kind of modern art that unsettles you, and forces you to confront the demons that lurk within and without. A tour of Berlin must therefore strike some very different notes from a tour of Paris or Rome.

Berlin is a relative newcomer to the front ranks of European capitals. The twin towns of Berlin and Cölln, later to be united under the former name, were founded around 1200 on opposite banks of the Spree river (Cölln was an island), an inauspicious part of the eastward settlement of Germans during the Middle Ages. The year 1237 has been celebrated as the towns' founding only because that is the date of the oldest known document mentioning either one. In the fifteenth century, the towns and the surrounding territory of Brandenburg came under control of the Hohenzollern dynasty from southern Germany, which suppressed their independence and, a century later, embraced the Protestant liturgy. The fact that Berlin was the seat of one of the electors of the Holy Roman Empire did nothing to protect it from the ravaging armies of the Thirty Years' War (1618–48). It was the 'Great Elector'

Frederick William (ruled 1640–88) who directed the reconstruction of Berlin, acquired new territories and made his state a military power to be reckoned with. He laid out Friedrichswerder, Dorotheenstadt (including the boulevard Unter den Linden) and Friedrichstadt, new towns attached to the western side of Berlin and Cölln. His son crowned (literally) the father's achievements by obtaining a royal title, which, however, was named after the remote duchy of Prussia because that territory lay outside the titular domains of the Holy Roman Emperor. Henceforth Berlin's name would be bound up with that of distant Prussia. King Frederick I, as he was now known, otherwise devoted his reign to cultivating the arts and sciences and to building grand palaces in Berlin and Charlottenburg. His son, in turn, the thrifty, shrewd, pious and cruel King Frederick William I (ruled 1713–40) ceased to squander money on such extravagances and instead devoted his energy and treasury to a greatly expanded army, which he used to extract diplomatic advantage but not (for the most part) to draw blood. The next king also despised his father: Frederick II loved music and philosophy, not religion – but he welcomed the potent army and full treasury he inherited, and his wars nearly destroyed Prussia. It is remarkable, therefore, that he became known as Frederick the Great.

In the early 1800s, the Prussian army proved no match for Napoleon's France, but the humiliation spurred military and administrative reforms, as well as growing anti-French nationalism among intellectuals, leading, after Napoleon's defeat, to a deceptive stability in the era sometimes called Biedermeier, under Frederick William III (to 1840) and Frederick William IV. The latter, as crown prince, became the patron of Karl Friedrich Schinkel, whose Romantic and neoclassical architecture reshaped both Berlin and Potsdam. After the abortive revolution of 1848, in which the people of Berlin demanded economic and political reforms, the king grew to distrust his capital city. When his brother succeeded him as William I in 1861, he faced a constitutional crisis as the parliament (a post–1848 creation) demanded powers he refused to grant. Salvation came in the form of his new prime minister, Otto von Bismarck, who re-established royal authority by giving the liberals the other thing they wanted, a unified Germany, something achieved through a series of wars ending in 1871, when King William acquired the additional title of German Emperor (or Kaiser). By this time Berlin had changed beyond recognition. A major European city of 150,000 at the beginning of the century, its population reached a million in the 1870s, as the massive apartment blocks that still characterize much of the city spread outward. William himself, born in 1797, lived to see vast changes before his death in 1888. By that time his son, Frederick III, was himself dying, and Frederick's mildly liberal tendencies, abetted by his British wife, Queen Victoria's daughter and namesake, could no longer change Prussia. Their son, the charming and foolish William II (that is, the second Kaiser Wilhelm), cared as little for his capital city as for his parents, especially as more and more of its burgeoning proletariat voted for the socialists. When war came in 1914 (to the emperor's consternation – he didn't think he was being belligerent) the workers rallied to the flag, but as the war dragged on and the British blockade left the workers starving, they drifted away.

Late 1918 and early 1919 were a time of chaos in Berlin, as communists and right-wing nationalists tried to turn defeat into revolution. The new republic, founded in and named after the town of Weimar, but ruled from Berlin, never managed to stop the political violence in the streets, especially when a devastating depression played into the hands of the growing National Socialist (Nazi) party. Against that backdrop, however, Berlin in the 1920s became synonymous with the cutting edge of culture.

As the playwright Carl Zuckmayer recalled, 'Berlin tasted of the future, and that is why we gladly took the crap and the coldness'. The darkest episode in German (if not world) history came after the Nazis took power in 1933 and directed world war and genocide from Berlin. Berlin did not vote for the Nazis as strongly as most of Germany. Until 1933 it remained a Red stronghold, where the Communists and the Social Democrats fought for primacy. When it suited them, the Nazis could portray Berlin as a foreign body that had to be conquered, but enthusiastic Berlin Nazis were not hard to find, and after they took control of the capital the Nazis set out to make Berlin their own, something they accomplished most thoroughly by letting the city be destroyed. Anglo-American bombing raids and then Red Army artillery left large parts of the city in ruins by the time Hitler killed himself in his bunker. In 1945 Berlin lay defeated and destroyed – a new Carthage, some thought – yet even then it did not cease to matter, as the division of Europe was completed here with the Berlin blockade and airlift in 1948–49, and seething tensions culminated in the construction of the Berlin Wall in 1961, which inaugurated a period of uneasy stability that lasted until 1989. The fall of the Wall that November permitted the reunification of Berlin and of Germany and the capital's return to Berlin.

Like so many cities, Berlin grew westward, with the fashionable districts spreading around and beyond the Tiergarten, the great park that stood west of the old town. In 1920, the city annexed a vast area, including its rapidly growing suburbs, doubling the city's population overnight, from two to four million, which ranked it third in the world after London and New York. (By comparison, its current population is under three and a half million, which puts it far down the list of world cities.) The twenty districts established then remained basic reference points for the rest of the century. In the inner city, these included such new names as Kreuzberg and Prenzlauer Berg, which up to then had only denoted minor hills. Farther out, the districts largely coincided with the boundaries of substantial cities that had grown up, including Charlottenburg, Schöneberg, Wilmersdorf and Lichtenberg. In the outermost districts, local identities remain to this day linked to former villages engulfed by the city. The four allies kept the districts intact in 1945; the eight claimed by the Russians became East Berlin. In 2001, an administrative reorganization reduced the number of districts to twelve. The newly consolidated districts, many with hyphenated names, have barely penetrated public consciousness, while the old ones are no longer marked on new maps, so district boundaries will not serve as reference points in these pages.

The decades-long division of the city forced it to grow in peculiar ways: it was, for most purposes, two cities, where two separate worlds coexisted. East Berlin was the capital of the German Democratic Republic (GDR), the Soviet Union's most loyal ally, while West Berlin was a subsidized outpost of the distant Federal Republic. The divided city was also an unfinished one, where the Wall kept memories of the war alive by standing in the way of reconstruction. Since 1990, however, a wave of new construction has engulfed Berlin's historical center. Only in a few places will the casual observer recognize traces of the hundred-mile-long wall that once encircled West Berlin, although much of the border guards' patrol road remains in place, open to bicyclists. Despite the growing resemblance between East and West, however, a mental distance – the 'wall inside the head' – can still be felt.

More than a few street names have changed since reunification. After lively debates, some communists honored by the East – but not all – disappeared from the map, while the arguments mounted in defense of these 'antifascists' led to some soul-searching in the West that caused a few people with Nazi pasts to be purged from West Berlin street signs. A new street map is thus a good thing to have, but when you are searching for a particular address, be aware that most streets are numbered up one side and down the other, so that number 7 might be opposite number 237. Then, just when you get used to that system, you will discover that a few streets – you can never tell which ones – are numbered in the more familiar manner, with odd numbers on one side and even ones on the other. Things may have improved a little since Mark Twain visited in 1892: 'There are a good many suicides in Berlin; I have seen six reported in a single day. There is always a deal of learned and laborious arguing and ciphering going on as to the cause of this state of things. If they will set to work and number their houses in a rational way perhaps they will find out what was the matter.'

This book is intended to encourage you to walk for miles through Berlin, but the city is too vast for you to rely on your feet alone. A bicycle can also be very useful (and can be rented), especially since you can take it on the U-Bahn and S-Bahn. The tours that follow are arranged for convenient access to and from Berlin's superb public transportation system – rapid rail above all, with trams and buses for shorter trips. If you have a car (or use taxis), in most cases things will be simpler, except that parking can be hard to find in some parts of the inner city. Visitors from London, Paris and New York often marvel at how easy it is to navigate Berlin by car: they forget that Berlin, for all its cosmopolitan attractions, is a much less populous urban area.

Public transport, good as it is, does have its complications. There are two rail networks, the U-Bahn and S-Bahn, and some of the transfers between them are long and inconvenient. The U-Bahn (which means Untergrundbahn, or underground railway, and in fact most but not all of it is underground) was first private and later municipal. The

S-Bahn (originally the Stadtbahn, or city railway) was built by the state, and in most places runs above ground, often next to the intercity tracks. Until the 1980s, the East Germans ran the S-Bahn even in West Berlin, so only since then has much been done to coordinate the two systems. Transit maps are readily available in stations and elsewhere, also from the World Wide Web: www.bvg.de (the Berlin main transit authority), www.s-bahn-berlin.de (the separate administrator of the S-Bahn), or www.vbbonline.de (the association of Berlin and suburban transit systems). On weekends most lines run all night. Otherwise trains stop running around 1 a.m., after which special night buses ply the city. A single ticket enables you to transfer freely among U-Bahn, S-Bahn, trams (which are confined mainly to eastern Berlin) and buses. You can buy your ticket in the rail stations, from bus drivers or from machines on rail platforms and at some bus stops. You can save trouble by buying a daily pass, and a weekly or monthly one is a real bargain. Note that the standard ticket covers zones A and B, which encompass all of Berlin. If you are traveling to Potsdam or elsewhere beyond the city, you need to buy an ABC ticket for a few cents more (and will thus be able to use Potsdam's own trams and buses). Everything operates on the honor system (that is, you only show your ticket when an inspector pops up out of nowhere – and fines you if you don't have one) except that you might have to show your ticket to your bus driver. Unless your ticket comes out of the machine with a printed date and time, you must insert it into a stamping machine on the bus or the platform when you first use it.

The transit system is good not only for going places, but also for sightseeing. The east–west S-Bahn line, which runs elevated through the city center, affords some good views. Many of the buses are double-deckers, and the front seat upstairs, if you are lucky enough to find it free, turns the passing street into a movie. Particularly popular among tourists (and thus all the more crowded upstairs) are the 100 and 200 lines that run from Zoo station through the Tiergarten to the Reichstag and Unter den Linden. Tour boats on the rivers and canals offer a different view. And for a unique ride, in a few central locations you can find Velotaxis, modern bicycle rickshaws.

Berlin weather is unpredictable – rain can be followed by sunshine several times in the course of a day – but is often marvelous, especially on the long summer evenings. In the colder months, however, the clouds, short days and damp chill make it hard to sustain a long day's sightseeing. In warm (and even not-so-warm) weather, the outdoor cafés make life pleasant; in the cold, the indoor ones make it bearable. You are rarely far from a café or pub, and there is no clear distinction between the two types, if you leave aside the dwindling numbers of bakeries-cum-cafés, on the one hand, and old corner pubs with their dark wood and lace curtains, on the other. Many of them also serve substantial meals – again, although some establishments are clearly identifiable as restaurants, distinctions matter little. And you can eat and drink at any hour. You have to look more carefully to find late-night establishments, but Berlin nightlife runs until morning. The early subway runs carry a remarkable mixture of the working class and the partying class, and some cafés specialize in afternoon breakfasts. Nearly everywhere you will find neighborhood bakeries, with their reliably wonderful bread and reliably mediocre pastries.

When the Wall was up, both East and West Berlin were, for different reasons, preternaturally safe cities, nearly free (as they no longer are) of the usual urban scourges of pickpockets and con artists. Keep that in mind if you hear laments about how dangerous the city has become. You may also have heard that Berlin and Brandenburg are crawling with neo-Nazis and racist skinheads. Chances are, you won't even see any. However, foreigners – or rather, those who do not look German – are sometimes the objects of unwanted attention in the eastern suburbs and, especially at night, they might do well to avoid empty streets or long S-Bahn rides in the the drearier parts of the east that they probably won't visit anyway.

Newspapers and magazines, including the long-established bi-weekly *Tip* and *Zitty*, publish listings of daily events including concerts, films, and plays as well as museum shows and hours. They also list the walking tours (some in English) offered by many different, mostly small operations – which can often be very informative. Listings of upcoming plays, concerts, and operas are also posted all over town – in subway stations, for example, and on the street, on the stout pillars known as Litfasssäulen after their nineteenth-century Berlin inventor, Ernst Litfass.

Berlin is enormous, spread out over some 300 square miles that offer rural attractions like forests and lakes as well as urban ones. It offers plenty to occupy you. This book also covers Potsdam, the adjacent second city of Brandenburg, which offers some sights that Berlin cannot match, especially houses and palaces from the eighteenth century. If you exhaust the attractions described in this book, you will be well prepared to find more on your own.

I
Center

1

Unter den Linden and the Museum Island

FROM THE FIFTEENTH CENTURY to the twentieth, Berlin was ruled from Schlossplatz (palace square). Modern Berlin is too big and diverse to have a single center, but in some ways this spot remains the city's heart – and the heart is hollow. In 1411 the Holy Roman Emperor granted control of the twin towns of Berlin and Cölln to Count Frederick of the south German Hohenzollern family, who became Elector of Brandenburg. The burghers, accustomed to self-government, chafed under noble control, and in the 1440s the next elector, Frederick II, took personal control of the town's affairs and seized the northern part of the Cölln island for the construction of a fortress. In the sixteenth century this medieval castle was rebuilt as a Renaissance palace which, in its greatly expanded Baroque form, stood until 1950. The new Berlin does not long for a king but, oddly, it does long for a palace to bind up its many wounds.

If there were a palace here, it would be the place to start. Under the circumstances, it is best to pick your way around the edges of the vacant Schlossplatz, beginning at **Werderscher Markt,** just west of the Spree arm that separates Cölln island from the mainland. (The nearest U-Bahn stop is Hausvogteiplatz.) The major building here is the foreign ministry, with its large glass surfaces intended to project democratic transparency. The front part of the building is in fact open to the public and includes a 'Coffee Shop', a first hint of how pervasive

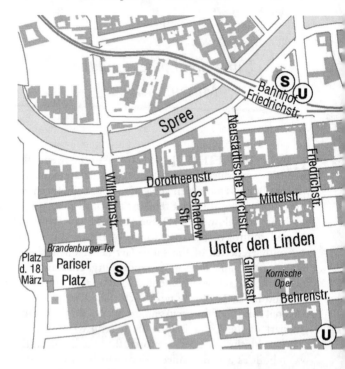

English (if often bad English) has become here. This wing fills what had been an empty space since the war. Behind it, the bulk of the foreign ministry is housed in the immense former Reichsbank, the Third Reich's first major government building. This project was already in the works when the Nazis took power in 1933. They held a design competition, which attracted prominent modern architects who were willing to work for their new masters, notably Walter Gropius and Ludwig Mies van der Rohe. Mies's dramatic modern design was a finalist, but in the end the Nazis rejected it, and all modernist designs, as insufficiently monumental. The architect they chose,

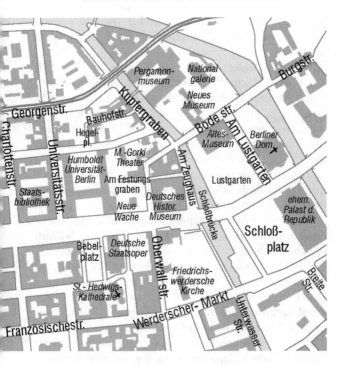

Heinrich Wolff, gave them the kind of overscaled, stripped classicism that came to signify power, here as in other lands. The monumental front is obscured by the new wing, but on the long curving façade facing the river you can see the stone cladding, deep window openings, and simplified classical columns. The building is even larger than it appears: it has three cellar stories, built for the national bank's vaults and soon thereafter filled with stolen gold from all over Europe. The foreign ministry archives are now housed there. From 1958 to 1990, the building retained its forbidding aura by serving as headquarters for East Germany's ruling Communist Party, the place where

Walter Ulbricht and Erich Honecker tried to pretend that they were fully sovereign 'brothers' of their Russian 'allies'.

The only older building on Werderscher Markt is Karl Friedrich Schinkel's **Friedrichswerder church** (1830) across the street. It is one of Schinkel's stylistic experiments, intended to provide a focal point for Friedrichswerder, the narrow district created on this bank of the river when the mid-seventeenth-century fortifications extended the town a short distance to the west. While Schinkel is known for his neoclassical architecture, he shared with many of his Romantic contemporaries a fascination with the Gothic. This church, however, is a peculiar hybrid. Schinkel was asked to prepare both classical and Gothic designs, and the crown prince (the later Frederick William IV) chose the latter. The arched front window, high ceiling, and buttresses are clearly Gothic, but the horizontal and cubic forms of the exterior betray classical rather than Gothic proportions. Schinkel based the design of the simple interior space on English collegiate chapels. It was Berlin's first brick neo-Gothic building, reviving a local tradition that subsequently became the norm for new churches. When Heinrich Heine saw the new building, however, he thought it 'could have been put there among the modern buildings only from a sense of irony, to show, in allegorical fashion, how silly and ridiculous it would be if we were to reestablish the ancient, long-defunct institutions of the Middle Ages in the very midst of the new creations of a new age'. Since its restoration in the 1980s it has housed the Schinkel Museum, devoted to nineteenth-century sculpture. A plaque in the vestibule recalls that in 1937 the leaders of the anti-Nazi Confessing Church were arrested by the Gestapo during a meeting here. Their most famous colleague, Martin Niemöller, was captured a few days later, and he spent the rest of the Third Reich in concentration camps.

The space between the church and the river was occupied by the German Democratic Republic's foreign ministry building until its demolition in 1995. Before that, it was the site of one of Schinkel's most celebrated buildings, the Bauakademie, built in 1831–36 for the Prussian architectural academy. Despite its rich terracotta decoration, this simple cube became a model for modern architecture. Its brick construction owed less to the classical orders than to the structural systems of the factories that Schinkel observed in his travels in England – buildings that appalled Schinkel but also suggested to him new possibilities for design. Unfortunately the East Germans demolished the Bauakademie in 1962 to make way for their foreign ministry. With that building, too, now gone, many people would like to rebuild the Bauakademie. In 2000, a corner of it was in fact reconstructed on what is now called Schinkelplatz.

On the bridge that takes you over the river, the iron railing with decorative bronze reliefs dates to the celebration of Berlin's 700th anniversary in 1937. The reliefs portray the vicinity of the bridge in the seventeenth and eighteenth centuries. The two inner reliefs are the work of Kurt Schumacher (1905–42), later executed for his resistance work. Directly across the river from Schinkelplatz is the larger open space of **Schlossplatz**. Extending into the river on that side is a large platform. This was the base of the bombastic National Monument built by Emperor William II in the 1890s in honor of his grandfather and of German unification. It, too, was leveled by the East Germans. Unlike the palace, it is not missed, but some people want to replace it with a new monument to the second German unification of 1990. They face resistance from the many Germans averse to any hint of nationalist triumphalism.

The memorial once flanked the western façade of the palace. On the south side of Schlossplatz stands the Staatsrat building. This was East Germany's first new structure in the area, completed in 1964 to house the Council of State, the more ceremonial institution of its government (with real power lurking in Communist Party headquarters across the river). In the 1950s the GDR had planned to declare a new beginning in the old city center with grand Stalinist monuments and skyscrapers; this building marked the beginning of a new architectural modesty. Its façade incorporates one of the portals from the Eosander wing of the Baroque palace – the only substantial intact remnant of the palace. The portal originally faced the same direction but stood farther north, near Unter den Linden. It was chosen for preservation because it was from this balcony that the Communist leader Karl Liebknecht proclaimed the socialist republic of Germany on 9 November 1918, as the emperor abdicated. The portal gives you a hint of the scale and style of the palace, with its Baroque statuary and the muscular atlantes supporting the balcony. If you are able to enter the main entrance hall behind the portal, you can see, on the opposite wall, a large and bright glass mural by Walter Womacka with images from the workers' movement – a typical piece of late socialist realism.

The far end of the Staatsrat building faces Breite Strasse. Between it and the main channel of the Spree (separating the original twin towns of Berlin and Cölln) stands the Marstall, the royal stables. The massive Neuer Marstall (1902) has a grand façade facing Schlossplatz and a long front along the river. Its most dramatic days came at the end of 1918, as the mutinous sailors who helped topple the emperor barricaded themselves here. On its Breite Strasse side, it incorporates two buildings that, uniquely, document the transition from Renaissance to Baroque in Berlin. The first is the remaining section of the old Marstall, completed in 1670, with an early Baroque roofline, as distinguished from the similar Ribbeck house beside it. The latter was originally constructed for a court official in

1624 out of two earlier buildings. A third story was added in 1804, with the house's most distinctive features, its high and ornate gables, reattached to the new roof. These buildings were put to use as East Berlin's central public library, along with the adjoining glass-fronted structure, one of the East's more innovative, if not necessarily beautiful, modern buildings (1966).

Schlossplatz was originally the name of the narrow space between the royal palace and the mouth of Breite Strasse. Most of the open space you now see was covered by the palace. The Renaissance palace stood on the riverbank. In the 1690s Elector Frederick III (soon to be King Frederick I) commissioned Andreas Schlüter with a massive Baroque extension to the west. Thereafter the most prized part of the building was the Schlüter wing and especially its large courtyard, richly decorated with sculpture and usually open to the public. Little is known about the life of Schlüter, a gifted sculptor who was less prepared for the architectural duties he also had to assume. He lost his job because his buildings didn't always stand up. Johann Friedrich Eosander von Göthe then added a matching extension, and a second large courtyard, to the west. Following Frederick's death in 1713, the frugal new king, Frederick William I, canceled all further expenditure on architectural extravagance. The only substantial later addition was a large dome atop the western entrance, commissioned by Frederick William IV shortly after he regained full control of Prussia in the wake of the abortive 1848 revolution. Although some Prussian kings (Frederick the Great, William I) spent little time here, this was the primary home of the Prussian monarchy until its demise in 1918. It was the place where rebels managed to gain the king's temporary submission in 1848, and where revolutionary soldiers and sailors briefly seized control in 1918, just four years after huge crowds had cheered the emperor at the outbreak of war. Parts of the palace were badly damaged in World War II, but no more than most other major buildings around it. Despite international protest, the East Germans leveled it in 1950 to make way for an enormous Red Square where the masses could salute their new rulers. In recent years archaeological excavations have exposed the palace's foundations.

This space has been in limbo since 1990. Most people want to fill the void with a new building in the precise dimensions of the old palace, a building that would then be used by museums and a library. More controversial is the question of whether that building should be a replica of the old palace. Many Berliners think it is not only feasible but necessary to reconstruct Schlüter's Baroque masterpiece in order to restore Berlin's heart. By the time you arrive, perhaps the new (or old) building will be under construction. Perhaps, too, the existing building here will be gone. On the eastern part of the old palace's site, along the main channel of the Spree, a structure of white marble and bronze glass, long but not overly tall, was put up in the 1970s. This **Palast der Republik** (palace of the republic) was the home of the powerless East German parliament and of mass meetings such as party congresses. More important, it housed theaters, restaurants and even a bowling alley, and it became East Berlin's most popular gathering spot, a genuine place of popular entertainment in a city (and country) where such places were in short supply. In 1990, it briefly attracted a different kind of attention, as the GDR's first and only democratically elected parliament met here and voted to unite Germany. Within weeks, however, the building was declared to be dangerously contaminated with asbestos (a typical hazard of 1970s buildings) and closed. In the following years, Westerners demanded that the ugly building be demolished to make way for a reconstructed palace, while many Easterners recalled pleasant hours spent here. The Palast der Republik became a rallying point for Easterners (led by the reorganized former Communist party) who resented Western tutelage and who accused Westerners of trying to pretend that German division and the GDR never happened. However, asbestos removal left little more than its frame by 2002, scarcely enough to bolster Easterners' fading memories.

Across Unter den Linden is the expanse of the **Lustgarten**, the former royal 'pleasure garden' that was once the largest open space in central Berlin. (If you want to avoid crossing the busy street, a more pleasant option is to climb down to the riverside path and cross under the bridge to the river side of the cathedral.) The Great Elector had the palace's kitchen garden landscaped in the Dutch style in the1640s; his son redid it in the newly fashionable French manner. When the next king, Frederick William I, ascended the throne in 1713, he had the 'pleasure garden' cleared for use as a parade ground, marching soldiers being the only sight that pleased his eyes. ('But where is the garden?' Heinrich Heine asked his readers in 1822. With tongue in cheek, he explained that Berlin is a place of irony – advice still worth keeping in mind, even if both pleasure and a garden have finally returned to the 'pleasure garden'.) In 1829, Schinkel was charged with new plantings. His redesign included the enormous granite bowl, carved from a single boulder, that sits in front of the museum. Later the Lustgarten became a favorite place for Nazi rallies. In 1935 the Nazis cleared it once again and paved the garden. In many newsreels and propaganda films you can see Hitler addressing rallies from the front of the museum (not from the palace, which he avoided). The Communists outdid the Nazis by demolishing the palace to stage even larger rallies, keeping the Nazis' pavement. Only at the end of the 1990s was the Lustgarten replanted with vegetation, in a design based on, but not identical with, Schinkel's.

A stone cube near Unter den Linden and the cathedral commemorates one of the more spectacular acts of internal resistance against the Third Reich. In 1942, as the savage war on the eastern front entered its second year, the Lustgarten was the scene of an official exhibition with the sardonic title 'the Soviet paradise', intended to reinforce the official Nazi view of the Communist enemy. An underground Jewish communist cell led by Herbert Baum firebombed the exhibition. In short order its members were captured and executed. The memorial, put up by East Berlin in 1981, does not explain the historical circumstances, instead merely honoring the group's 'brave deeds' and affirming 'eternal friendship with the Soviet Union'. This was typical for the GDR, which saw its identity in an alliance of 'antifascist' Germans with their Soviet liberators. In a gesture characteristic of the new Berlin, a plexiglass cover added in 2000 provides (in four languages) the names of the other conspirators as well as further explanation of what happened in 1942 as well as 1981, thus creating a new kind of layered memorial. The fact that the conspirators were Jews threatened by Nazi racial policy may deserve mention in connection with their politically motivated resistance; of unquestionable significance is the fact that in retaliation the Gestapo arrested 500 randomly selected Jews and executed 250 of them.

It is a shame that the loss of the palace leaves the Lustgarten dominated by its ugliest building, the **cathedral**. It was long uncertain whether the cathedral would be restored from wartime damage, but with funding from the West German Protestant church, work began in the 1970s and continued until the 1990s. The result is somewhat altered from the original – believe it or not, the church was once even more laden with ornament – but certainly restores any glory the building might have had. In its scale and form it is very much a product of the era of Kaiser Wilhelm II, who considered the previous building far too modest since he, as the protector of Protestants in Germany and beyond, needed a cathedral that would rival St Peter's in Rome and St Paul's in London. The original court church had actually predated the court, since the medieval castle took over the site of the thirteenth-century Dominican monastery. In the eighteenth century, Frederick the Great had a Baroque church built here, which Schinkel remodeled in neoclassical style. It was razed in the 1890s to make way for Julius Raschdorff's new building, completed in 1905. Its style as well as its scale is borrowed from Rome. Contemporary critics, embracing the new architectural simplicity of the twentieth century, saw in it nothing but pointless extravagance. It is dominated by an enormous dome, flanked by four corner towers. The main entrance, facing the Lustgarten, takes the form of a triumphal arch. The interior, too, is vast and ornate, and has been beautifully restored. The main church is a spacious octagon under the dome, with an apse facing the river, and a chapel for weddings and baptisms on the south side. The building is now used for concerts and theater performances as well as church services. Worth a visit is the crypt, with the tombs of ninety Hohenzollerns from the sixteenth to the twentieth century. The oldest is that of Elector Johann Cicero, a bronze tomb from the 1520s by Peter Vischer. Sarcophagi from the sixteenth to the eighteenth century display first Renaissance and later Baroque forms. They include the graves of Frederick William the Great Elector (d. 1688) and his second wife. The most important Baroque tombs, however, are those by Schlüter for King Frederick I and his wife, Sophie Charlotte. Tombs from the reign of their son, the 'soldier king' Frederick William I (1713–40), are mostly wooden. That of the penultimate emperor, Frederick III (d. 1888), is marble.

The **museum island** is not an island, merely one end of old Cölln. It began with Schinkel's museum (1828) facing the Lustgarten; over the next century, four more museums filled the remaining space behind it, forming one of Europe's most distinguished museum complexes, now on

UNESCO's World Heritage list. After 1945 it housed East Berlin's share of the great collections. Plans to renovate each museum and connect them with a network of underground passages have proceeded slowly since 1990. As work continues, expect some collections to be moved.

With his museum (called the **Old [Altes] Museum** since others were built behind it) Schinkel completed an ensemble that framed the Lustgarten with the institutions of the monarchy (the vanished palace), the church (his cathedral), the army (the Arsenal) and, with the museum, the achievements of culture that permitted commoners to claim a place of respect. The building's colonnade reinterpreted ancient temples; in turn, it has been imitated so many times that its appearance will be familiar even to first-time visitors. The staircase and roof are decorated with neoclassical sculptures, while Prussian frugality is apparent in the side and rear façades, which are not stone, but rather stuccoed to resemble stone. In front, stone steps extending the entire width of the building lead up to a double row of Ionic columns. Behind them, Schinkel's open staircase established the model for neoclassical entries. (Even if you have no interest in the exhibition upstairs, you should climb the stairs for the view of the Lustgarten.) Behind the entry, you enter a beautiful rotunda modeled on the Roman Pantheon, lined with Roman copies of Greek statutes, a pantheon of stone gods.

The exhibition rooms surround the rotunda. The main floor has been tastefully renovated to house Berlin's magnificent collection of Greek antiquities. You can encounter the entire glorious history of Greek stone sculpture and even see rare works in bronze and wood. Two treasure chambers display gold and silver. Most impressive is the pottery, including an unequaled collection of vases from the golden age. Extensive wall texts in German and English accompany the exhibition all the way around the perimeter. Only in the final room do you get a peek at the Roman collection, most of which is in storage, but this room is not to be missed, with its carved sarcophagi, expressive stone bust of Julius Caesar, friezes and mosaics, and especially the extraordinary wax portraits from Egypt. Apart from the interior of that floor, the building awaits its planned renovation. Meanwhile, the upper floor houses temporary exhibitions, and the colonnade remains sheathed in glass put up by the East Germans.

Just behind, the opulent **New (Neues) Museum** by August Stüler dates to the 1840s, after Frederick William IV had ascended the throne and loosened the purse strings. It has stood as a ruin since the war: the East Germans always intended to restore it, and so does unified Germany. It is designated to house the collection of Egyptian antiquities now in Charlottenburg (see Chapter 15) after its reconstruction.

Next to it, the Nationalgalerie was designed in the 1860s by Stüler and completed in the 1870s by Heinrich Strack, based on sketches by Frederick William IV, whose equestrian statue dominates the front. It takes the form of a Roman temple perched on a high pedestal behind a spacious forecourt framed by a colonnade (where films are shown in the summer). The iconography of its friezes and sculptural decoration reflects its purpose as a temple of the German nation, as imagined by the Romantic nationalist king. It was opened as a museum of contemporary German art; now, as the **Old National Gallery** (to distinguish it from Mies's New National Gallery) it houses nineteenth-century art, with its strengths clearly in German art and its display skewed toward Prussian and Berlin artists. The collection of French Impressionists is marvelous, for example, but is smaller and no better than you will find in many other museums, whereas the Friedrichs and Menzels are unmatched. It was the first of the museums here to be fully renovated for the new century. The grand external staircase (based on earlier designs by Schinkel and Friedrich

Gilly) is purely decorative: you enter below it, into the white marble vestibule. Little wall text describes the newly reinstalled collection; instead, recorded audio guides are available in English as well as German. The logical place to begin is on the third (top) floor, where you pass neoclassical paintings and sculpture from the 'age of Goethe' on your way to some of the high points of German Romantic painting. A central room is devoted to Schinkel, an accomplished painter as well as an architect, who created imaginary medieval scenes complete with fantasy Gothic churches. Beyond it is a roomful of works by the greatest of the Romantic painters, Caspar David Friedrich, with his characteristic portrayals of human figures gazing away from the viewer toward the moon or the shore, overwhelmed by the elements, and surrounded by a Gothic world that, unlike Schinkel's, is in ruins.

Other rooms on the floor are categorized by the label 'Biedermeier' and include scenes of Berlin by Eduard Gaertner and others. The second floor covers the mid-to-late nineteenth century and includes 'realist' works with domestic themes, portraits by Wilhelm Leibl and Franz von Lenbach, French impressionists, and German realist-impressionist paintings by Lesser Ury and Max Liebermann. On the first floor, a small central room devoted to the history of the building has been left with unrenovated walls and ceiling. Elsewhere are more neoclassical sculptures by Schadow and Rauch, some notable French and English realist paintings (Courbet, Constable), turn-of-the-century Secession works including Lovis Corinth portraits and early Max Beckmanns, and a large selection of paintings displaying the prodigious talents of Adolph Menzel, who produced enormous royal and historical panoramas as well as bucolic rural scenes and innovative views of industrial Berlin. He managed to please everyone: realists and impressionists cherished his smaller works, but when the elfin Menzel died in 1905 at the age of ninety, the Kaiser, sworn enemy of modern art, walked behind his coffin.

Until internal connections are built, you have to exit the island to reach the other two museums, passing (for at least a few more years) bullet-pocked façades. Cross the bridge by the New Museum and follow Am Kupfergraben (past number 7, one of the few surviving eighteenth-century houses in the center) to a pedestrian bridge that leads back across the water. This is the shabby but pictur-esque route to the **Pergamon Museum**, begun in 1909 to a design by Alfred Messel. Construction continued to 1930 but the building remains unfinished, the colonnade intended to enclose its forecourt never having been built. Current plans call for a new entry as well as a renovated interior. The museum was built to house the enormous architectural fragments hauled home by German archae-ologists, and you can still see them as they have long stood (although some were carted off by the Russians and later returned). The centerpiece is the most acclaimed late Hellenistic artifact anywhere, the enormous altar brought from Pergamon in Turkey. The frieze around the second-century BC structure, the largest surviving piece of ancient Greek sculpture after the Parthenon marbles, dramatically illustrates a battle between gods and giants. Around to the left is an entire wing filled with other extraordinary Greek and Roman antiquities, notably early Greek statues – large pieces are displayed here rather than in the Old Museum. On the other side is the enormous market gate (120 AD) from Miletus, a Roman town in Asia Minor. Past it you enter the wing devoted to Near Eastern antiqui-ties, notably the stunning blue Ishtar Gate and proces-sional way from Nebuchadnezzar II's Babylon (6th century BC) and even older interiors from an Assyrian palace. Upstairs, the collection of Islamic art features ceramics, calligraphy and many gorgeous small objects, as well as the façade of an eighth-century caliph's palace from

Mschatta in Jordan, given to William II by the Ottoman sultan.

Beyond the elevated rail line is the neo-Baroque **Bode Museum** (1904), which presents an impressive silhouette from downstream, where its copper dome marks the lower end of Cölln island. When its renovation is complete, it will house coins and Byzantine art as well as Berlin's outstanding collection of European sculpture, but will also include its original period rooms, in each of which a variety of objects from an era are displayed amid architecture modeled on that of the same period. These rooms were the brainchild of the man after whom the museum is named, Wilhelm von Bode, who more than anyone else was responsible for assembling the great Berlin museum collections.

Back at the Lustgarten, another of Schinkel's contributions is the **Palace Bridge** (Schlossbrücke) from 1824, replacing the simple 'dogs' bridge', which dated to the time when the royal hounds were gathered here in preparation for hunting parties in the Tiergarten. The bridge features an elegant cast-iron railing between high pillars of red granite and white marble. Schinkel also planned the sculptures that decorate the bridge, which were carved only after his death. They portray goddesses advising young warriors. During the war they were removed for safekeeping, and they were stored in West Berlin until an international agreement permitted their return in 1981.

Just across the bridge is the **Arsenal** (Zeughaus), Berlin's finest Baroque building since the demise of the palace, and a splendid monument to Prussian military might. It was built between 1695 and 1706 to give the Prussian army a worthy home for its arms. It had four supervising architects in succession: Arnold Nering, Martin Grünberg, Andreas Schlüter and Jean de Bodt. Nering died; both Grünberg and Schlüter faced disfavor after partial collapses of their work (Grünberg's at the

Parochialkirche, Schlüter's here). De Bodt, who completed the job, was one of Berlin's many distinguished Huguenot refugees from Louis XIV's France, and the original design may have come from François Blondel, de Bodt's teacher in Paris. Among the rich façade sculpture, perhaps the most notable works are Schlüter's helmets in the keystones of the ground-floor arches. More impressive is the interior courtyard (which has recently been glassed over), with Schlüter's twenty-two heads of dying warriors carved over the portals. They powerfully convey images of war at odds with any simplistic slogans either promoting or denouncing militarism.

After 1877 the building was converted from a storehouse for weaponry to a museum of it. Later the East Germans used it as their national history museum, organized to tell the Marxist story of class struggle and proletarian revolution. The past now appears in a different light in the **German Historical Museum**. The arsenal has recently been remodeled (restoring its original pink color) and given an angular addition at the rear by I. M. Pei. The venerable American celebrity architect Pei was personally chosen by the chancellor, Helmut Kohl, in a rare and controversial exception to the German practice of open architectural competitions. The stark stone surfaces of Pei's design recall his 1978 annex to Washington's National Gallery, but its most spectacular element is a glass-sheathed spiral staircase. An underground passage leads you from the old building to the new one, and its airy spaces and startling angles open up before you. The expanded museum will soon offer permanent displays and special exhibitions on all periods of German history.

Any venerable boulevard displays the skills of the restorer along with, and indistinguishable from, those of its architects. **Unter den Linden** is an extreme case, a distinguished row of counterfeits. Opposite the arsenal, in fact, the old building next to the river is – a new building.

Here stood the home of Johann Gregor Memhardt, built in the 1650s after the Great Elector gave him this choice property as a reward for his work constructing the new town fortifications. After the 1790s it served as the Kommandantur, home of the city's garrison commander. A remodeling in the 1870s gave it a rusticated Florentine façade. The East Germans demolished it in the 1960s for their foreign ministry, but a replica (of the 1870s version) has just been built. The city sold the land to the Bertelsmann media conglomerate, which thus acquired the prestigious address Unter den Linden 1, agreeing in return to restore the Kommandantur's old façade (but not the interior, for which no plans exist).

Next to it stands another replica with a different history. The Kronprinzenpalais (crown prince's palace) also dates to the seventeenth century, and also was given its current appearance in the nineteenth. After the 1770s it was the residence of Prussia's crown princes. Frederick William III chose to remain here while king. His grandson, the later Frederick III, had it rebuilt by Heinrich Strack, a Schinkel pupil, in the 1850s. It was badly damaged in the war and its ruins were subsequently leveled. The building you see, a slightly altered replica of Strack's design, was put up by the East Germans in the 1960s and used as an official guest house. In the rear is a door salvaged from Schinkel's Bauakademie. The interior is modern but includes a frieze from the 1790s, salvaged from a Potsdam theater. During the 1920s the National Gallery displayed its collection of modern art here, before the Nazis declared much of it to be 'degenerate'. Recently the building has again been used as exhibition space, by the German Historical Museum.

An arched bridge across narrow Oberwallstrasse connects it to the Prinzessinnenpalais (princesses' palace), which retains more of its Baroque appearance. It dates to the 1730s, when two adjoining houses on Oberwallstrasse were joined. Frederick William III acquired it (for his daughters, hence its name) and commissioned Heinrich Gentz with an extension in 1809, of which only the end facing Unter den Linden was built, plus the bridge, the design of which is attributed to Schinkel. The French poet Jules Laforgue lived here in the 1880s while he worked as a reader for the Francophile and crypto-Catholic Empress Augusta, whom he pitied for having to live in such a rude and uncultivated town. This building, too, was destroyed in the war, and what you see is another replica from the 1960s. Since its reconstruction the building has served as a café, which spills out onto the open space on its western side. Here stand Schinkel's and Rauch's elegant marble statues of Generals Bülow and Scharnhorst, heroes of the Napoleonic wars; farther back are Rauch's bronzes of three more generals, Blücher, Yorck and Gneisenau.

Directly across the street, a small chestnut grove (Kastanienwäldchen) frames the stately classical cube of Schinkel's **Neue Wache** (new guardhouse), his first major commission (1818). A portico of Doric columns supports a sculptural frieze and pediment with allegorical figures decorating an otherwise simple building with massive corner towers, inspired by Roman military architecture and carefully placed to harmonize with the old buildings all around it. Schinkel had other plans to transform the eighteenth-century boulevard, but, as it turned out, this small building completed the great ensemble. For a century it housed the palace guard. After the First World War it was converted to a war memorial by Heinrich Tessenow, who transformed the interior into an austere room framing a simple memorial consisting of a wreath resting on a stone cube. The Nazis continued to use the memorial, adding a Christian cross to the wall. After severe wartime damage, the East Germans restored an altered version of the interior for their 'memorial to the victims of fascism and militarism'. What made it a tourist attraction in those years was the ceremonial changing of the guard, at which the East German soldiers goose-stepped into position. This display at a monument honor-ing the victims of militarism puzzled many visitors who thought the goosestep – a traditional Prussian parade step that had otherwise fallen out of use – was itself a symbol of Prussian militarism.

After 1990 the unified Federal Republic decided to rechristen the building as the 'memorial to the victims of war and tyranny' – shorn of goosestepping guards, but otherwise surprisingly little changed from the Communist shrine. In another of his few but decisive interventions in the planning of the new capital, however, Chancellor Helmut Kohl chose a statue by Käthe Kollwitz for the center of the room. To the dismay of many artists, Kohl believed that Kollwitz's statue of a mother mourn-ing her dead son better expressed the horrors of war than would any abstract design. Since Kollwitz's original statue was only fifteen inches high, however, it had to be re-created in a life-sized version. Kollwitz's private expression of grief (she had been shattered by the loss of a son in the First World War) was thus transformed into a public statement. Critics also complained that a *pietà* (based on depictions of Mary mourning Jesus) seemed to exclude Jewish victims. The enlarged version of Kollwitz's statue now stands at the center of the austere room, which has otherwise been largely restored to Tessenow's elegant design. A small opening overhead lets limited light (and rain) into the cool, dim, soothing space, as visitors come and go, some quickly, others at a pace that lets them absorb the pathos of the memorial. Neither this design nor any other could begin to encompass the horrors of twentieth-century German history, however. It is intended above all for official ceremonies – it is, as Berliners labeled it, a 'wreath-dumping place'. A brass plaque at the entrance offers a long list of categories of victims worthy of remembrance. It offers an impressive litany of suffering, but its presence is an attempt to mollify critics who complained that a memorial to all victims unacceptably lumped SS concentration camp guards together with the prisoners they murdered. (The plaque does not mention Nazi officials or SS soldiers.) Also controversial was the plan to re-erect the statues of Scharnhorst and Bülow, which had originally stood in front. This, too, smacked of militarism to critics, and so the generals ended up across the street.

Instead, in 2002 a bronze statue of the poet Heinrich Heine was erected outside. This was where the GDR planned a Heine monument in 1956, but Communist leaders deemed Waldemar Grzimek's statue insufficiently heroic (one shudders to imagine what they wanted Heine to look like), so it was banished to the Volkspark am Weinberg. This new cast is a humble and rather old-fashioned tribute to the great poet, a passionate German patriot whose critical views forced him to live in exile and whose Jewish ancestry led the Nazis to reprint his song 'Lorelei' (a classic too popular to banish) as the work of an 'anonymous' poet. Heine wrote of Unter den Linden with great affection and gentle irony, admiring the well-built soldiers on the street and the luscious pastries in the bakeries. But he also observed that 'no city has less local patriotism than Berlin' and predicted that his praises of it would cause the Berliners to 'shrug their shoulders and whisper to one another, "That man has become very shallow; he actually praises us."' In Heine's time, Berlin appeared as a very new city, where 'it is difficult to see spirits': 'As a matter of fact, you need several bottles of poetry before you can see something beside dead houses and Berliners in Berlin.' Now the spirits are everywhere (although those bottles of poetry might yet help), but you still risk being thought shallow if you praise the city too fulsomely.

Two buildings stand behind the Neue Wache. The one on the right is the Palais am Festungsgraben, which dates to the 1750s but was rebuilt in the 1860s. It was long the home of the Prussian finance minister, then the House of Soviet Culture (which is why it includes a Tajik tea room). Inside is a complete room probably designed by Schinkel, which was salvaged from another building, and a Baroque ceiling attributed to Schlüter, originally from yet another long-vanished palace. The building now houses both a small theater and a district history museum. Adjoining it is the former Singakademie from 1827, an important center of choral music thanks to the remarkable talents of Carl Friedrich Zelter, a mason by training who became a close friend of Goethe and a great musical teacher. His star pupil was Felix Mendelssohn-Bartholdy, and together they revived the works of Johann Sebastian Bach, whose music (hard as it may be to believe) had been all but forgotten by 1800. Heine attended their premiere of Bach's *St Matthew Passion* in 1829. The building's interior was destroyed in the war and rebuilt in the Stalinist neoclassical style, using marble from Hitler's chancellery. Since then it has been the Maxim Gorki Theater.

Just past the grove surrounding the Neue Wache stands a large palace built in the 1750s by Johann Boumann for Frederick the Great's brother Heinrich. Its main entrance sits back from the street, with two wings extending forward to frame a forecourt. Berlin University has had its home here since its establishment in 1809. After the war it was renamed **Humboldt University** in honor of the two men whose late-nineteenth-century marble statues flank the entrance to the forecourt (but are covered in winter to protect them). Wilhelm von Humboldt, a political philosopher and government reformer, helped create the university; his brother Alexander was one of the world's most renowned naturalists and explorers. Other marble statues from the same period honor the physicist Hermann

Helmholtz and the historian Theodor Mommsen, two of the professors who helped make this the world's most distinguished center of scholarship by the end of its first century. (The philosopher G.W.F. Hegel, perhaps the university's most famous professor, is honored on Hegelplatz, behind the building.) The front of the university is usually lined with booksellers' tables, which offer bargains comparable to (but no better than) Berlin's many used-book stores. At the base of the stairway inside the main entrance, a quotation from Karl Marx, carved in red granite, is the most famous of his 'Theses on Feuerbach': 'Until now the philosophers have only interpreted the world; the point is to change it.' It has not been removed, as some demanded in the 1990s; instead, it is now accompanied by a small plaque identifying the source of the quotation and explaining that the GDR put it here in 1953. In the rear garden is a 1976 GDR memorial to anti-Nazi resisters. On the side streets stand numerous other university buildings, often recognizable by their dinginess, the university's budget having left it unable to undertake the renovations that have transformed the neighborhood.

In the 1740s the young King Frederick the Great and his favorite architect, Georg Wenzeslaus von Knobelsdorff, planned a grand ceremonial square at this spot. Originally they envisioned a new royal palace at its northern end, but Prince Heinrich's palace was built instead, with its forecourt enclosing the northern end of the Forum Fridericianum, as it became known (it is now Bebelplatz, after the nineteenth-century socialist leader August Bebel). The ensemble was not completed for decades, with a more diverse architecture than originally planned. The first building constructed, and the only one Knobelsdorff designed, is the **State Opera** (Staatsoper), the former royal opera house from 1743. It was an innovative design, since up to then all German theaters had been housed within palaces. Its modest classical façade is largely intact, but its Rococo interior has been much altered. The main floor could originally be winched up to the level of the stage so that grand masked balls could be held there. Heine, visiting when the university had just been opened, pitied the poor students who had to endure dull lectures in rooms from which they could see the excited crowds gathering across the street. (It would be nice to report that German professors' lectures have in the meantime become scintillating, but some things haven't changed.) From its beginning this has been a center of musical life, attaining particular fame a century ago under the leadership of Richard Strauss, whose revolutionary operas put him in repeated conflict with the emperor's conservative tastes, and then of Erich Kleiber, who thrived in the emperor-free 1920s. All the twentieth-century German regimes treasured the state opera, even the Nazis, who hastily repaired the building after bombs damaged it in 1943. It was destroyed a second time before the war ended, and subsequently restored by the GDR.

Behind the opera house, at the corner of Bebelplatz, stands **St Hedwig's**, Berlin's Roman Catholic cathedral. In several respects it owes its existence to Frederick the Great. When this young lover of music and philosophy ascended the throne in 1740, he was finally free of his austere father, Frederick William I, who had cared for nothing but his soldiers. Along with the throne, however, Frederick inherited a full treasury and a formidable army, which he promptly used to seize Silesia from Maria Theresa's Austria. Silesia, unlike the rest of Prussia, was a largely Catholic region, and the new church, dedicated to Silesia's patron saint, was Frederick's gesture of reconciliation with his new subjects. Frederick was an eighteenth-century rationalist whose lack of religious faith made it easy for him to view religion simply as a political instrument. The happy result of his belief that all religions were 'more or less absurd' was an unprecedented religious toleration. Prussia had benefited enormously from his predecessors' offers of asylum to persecuted Protestants, and he broadened the policy: 'If Turks and heathens came and wanted to populate the country, we would build them mosques and churches.' For St Hedwig's, Frederick wanted a circular design modeled on the Roman Pantheon, which was sketched by Knobelsdorff and built by Boumann, with a portico set diagonally to the square. Financial problems delayed its completion until 1773. It looks even odder now than it did when Thomas Carlyle compared it to 'a huge wash-bowl set bottom uppermost on the top of a narrow-ish tub'. It was reconstructed after the war with a flattened and simplified dome (now made of reinforced concrete) and a modern interior, with an opening to the crypt in the center of the main floor. Also inside is a display honoring Bernhard Lichtenberg, a priest who, unlike nearly all his colleagues, openly preached against the Nazi persecution of Jews as well as Christians. He was arrested in 1941 and died in captivity. He is buried in the crypt, surrounded by Berlin's bishops.

Across the square from the opera, home of the arts, stands the former royal library, representing the sciences. The king insisted on borrowing an unbuilt Baroque design by Johann Emanuel Fischer von Erlach for an extension of Vienna's Hofburg palace. This 1725 design was completed here in 1780, after the Baroque was out of fashion elsewhere. Paradoxically, however, Fischer von Erlach's wing of the Hofburg was actually built in the 1890s, amid the neo-Baroque revival, so the Berlin library can claim to be the original building. Despite its Viennese elegance, Berliners remarked on the curved façade's resemblance to a chest of drawers. Since the completion of the new state library across the street, the building has been used by the university. Little more than its façade survived the war. In the law library (above the main entrance) an extraordinary stained-glass window depicts

Lenin with unmistakably Christian iconography. The other building on the square, at the southern end, is a later addition, built as the headquarters of Dresdner Bank in 1889. In 1923 its owners added two stories to the building's original three, leaving it painfully out of proportion to its neighbors. Fortunately, the GDR postwar restoration removed the top stories, restoring harmony to the Baroque square. The building may soon be converted to a luxury hotel, with its old vault turned into a swimming pool.

Bebelplatz itself, extending south from the boulevard, is a vacant paved space – but it only appears empty. It was here, on the night of 10 May 1933, that spirited Nazi students piled up twenty thousand 'un-German' books looted from the library and set them ablaze. Watching from the shadows was Erich Kästner, best known for his children's book *Emil and the Detectives*, who saw the ashes of his own books mingle with those of Thomas Mann, Albert Einstein, Sigmund Freud, Helen Keller, Marcel Proust and other literary luminaries. The East Germans, no paragons of free expression, commemorated the event with a plaque on the wall of the library. In 1995, reunified Berlin installed a more substantial memorial by the Israeli artist Micha Ullman – but it can easily be overlooked. In the center of the square, a small plate of glass set in the ground offers the only view of it: an empty underground room, lined with bare white bookshelves that invite the viewer to recall everything that was lost in the bonfire here. Your attention is called to it by pairs of bronze plaques on either side. One explains what happened here in 1933. On the other are the words of Heine, who wrote in 1820: 'That was only a prologue: where books are burned, in the end people are burned too.'

Completing the ensemble of the Forum Fridericianum is the equestrian statue of Old Fritz himself, standing in the center of Unter den Linden. Christian Daniel Rauch's enormous 1851 masterpiece is scaled to the wide street. Below the figure of the philosopher-king, its crowded pedestal portrays scenes from Frederick's life amid allegorical and historical figures, including generals and state officials as well as scholars and artists. The portrayal of commoners such as Kant and Lessing on an equestrian statue was unprecedented, even if they are conversing under the horse's posterior. The statue survived the war, but the East Germans chose not to re-erect this symbol of Prussian militarism in its original spot. It stood instead in an obscure corner of Potsdam until 1980, when, shortly after an officially approved biography described Frederick as a promoter of progressive bourgeois tendencies, the statue was returned to Unter den Linden.

Unter den Linden means 'under the linden trees': the Great Elector created it in the seventeenth century as a tree-lined boulevard (the only one in the city) for riding and strolling. Only here, west of Bebelplatz, is it lined with trees. That was always the case: the eastern end was not considered part of Unter den Linden until after the war. It was, instead, identified as a series of connected squares, dominated by the soldiers of the palace guard. From here to the Brandenburg Gate, however, the shady median offers a pleasant place to sit or stroll, unless you would rather rent a carriage – bicycles rather than horses now being the means of locomotion, in a recent Berlin adaptation of the Asian rickshaw. (These 'velotaxis' are available here and at a few other busy spots.) This has always been a place of leisure and display, slower and quieter than neighboring streets – downright dull, if you are in the mood for action. Generations of kings and aristocrats rode through on their way to the Tiergarten or paraded here with their soldiers. In later years, ordinary folk came for Sunday strolls or rented chairs for a few pfennigs. Until 1918 Unter den Linden was the place where visitors were either awed or appalled by the dominance of royalty and army in Berlin. Today, however, you will see fewer uniforms in Germany than almost anywhere else, and unlike George Eliot in 1855, you do not have to worry that 'the swords of officers threaten one's legs at every turn in the streets'.

Attached to the corner of the old library is the modest Altes Palais, built in the 1830s for Prince William, the later King and Emperor William I, one of those Hohenzollerns whose only real love was his army. He lived here to the end of his long life in 1888, by then the ruler of the greatest power in Europe, and this became a place of momentous decisions, mainly when Bismarck came to bend the old man to his will. But his palace, sniffed an English visitor, 'might pass for a respectable club-house, or, were it a few storeys higher, for a modern grand hotel'. Henry Adams, who found Berlin in 1858 to be 'a poor, keen-witted, provincial town, simple, dirty, uncivilized, and in most respects disgusting', offered as evidence of the town's dreariness the fact that its ruler 'seemed to pass his time looking at the passers-by from the window of his modest palace on the Linden'. The emperor's main interest was the noon parade of the palace guard, but children on family strolls were instructed to watch for curtains moving in the corner window, a sign that the old man might have taken notice of them.

The adjoining Gouverneurshaus was built next to the town hall in 1721 but moved here in the 1960s. Next come two renovated bank buildings. Their ground floors house the austere exhibition space of the **Guggenheim Berlin**, a modest affiliate of the New York and Bilbao museums, with rotating displays from its enormous collection of modern art. Directly across the boulevard is the enormous **State Library** (Staatsbibliothek, 1914), designed by the royal architect Ernst von Ihne. The Prussian library was founded by the Great Elector in 1661 in the royal palace, later moving to its own building on Bebelplatz, which this one replaced. By that time it was one of the world's great libraries, but it suffered substantial losses in the war (some of its former holdings are probably still in Russia), and the remaining collection was subsequently divided between this building and Scharoun's new library in West Berlin. The cavernous building is being renovated piecemeal. The interior remains disorienting, since its grand central reading room was destroyed in the war. You enter the library after crossing the enclosed forecourt, past one of the finer examples of East German socialist-realist sculpture, Werner Stötzer's *Reading Worker* (1961), which takes its theme from the poem inscribed on a bronze tablet here, Bertolt Brecht's 'Questions of a Reading Worker', in which Brecht muses on a history that attributes all great achievements to the leaders who demanded them, not the men and women who did the actual work. Brecht would, with good reason, challenge guidebook entries that describe a building as having been constructed by its architect. Let the reader beware.

Across Charlottenstrasse to the west of the library are elegant stone commercial buildings from the early twentieth century. The one on the corner replaced the nineteenth-century Hotel de Rome. Because William I's palace down the street lacked any bathing facilities, he had his baths, complete with bathtub, delivered from the hotel. Between here and the Brandenburg Gate are enough century-old buildings to maintain the old boulevard's grace. (In several cases, however, everything behind the façade has been replaced.) Now catering to tourists, many of the old storefronts have been taken over by shops and cafés, most of which are relatively tasteful while some offer surprisingly good selections of books on Berlin, even in English.

The next corner is Friedrichstrasse (see Chapter 4), where the nineteenth century's main commercial corridor crossed its aristocratic promenade. The next cross street on the right side is Neustädtische Kirchstrasse. One block up that street, on the right side (facing a vanished square and a vanished church that gave the street its name) is the United States embassy. This neo-Renaissance building (1887) housed Berlin's first department store, which was (this being Prussia) a state institution run exclusively for army and navy officers. It became the embassy when the United States established diplomatic relations with the GDR in 1974 but is to be replaced by a long-delayed new building on Pariser Platz.

On the other side of Unter den Linden, the side street is named Glinkastrasse. Turn left into Behrenstrasse and you will be facing the Komische Oper. Many old façades in Berlin conceal new interiors. The **Komische Oper** is the opposite: inside the white cube from 1967 is the former home of a popular revue theater, in the rich neo-Baroque style of the 1890s. 'Comic opera' is not an accurate name: this is the home of serious opera, with a repertory company known for more innovative productions than the nearby Staatsoper or the Deutsche Oper in Charlottenburg. And this is a town where opera is taken very seriously. The way Berliners dress for gala occasions – black leather has long been the norm – evinces a studied irreverence, but do not mistake it for insouciance.

Dominating the next block on the south side of Unter den Linden is the **Russian embassy**. The site has been home to the Russian embassy since the eighteenth century. After the war, the triumphant Soviet Union hastened to impose its visible presence on the destroyed city. Inside and out, the 1952 building displays the richly decorated neoclassicism then prevailing in Stalin's Soviet Union, and thus offered a model for East German architects to follow. After the breakup of the Soviet Union, the Russian Federation took over most of the building, and a Lenin bust disappeared from the forecourt. Opposite the embassy, a few steps up Schadowstrasse, the neighborhood's oldest building is number 10–11, the 1805 neoclassical home of the sculptor Gottfried Schadow, with ground-floor stucco reliefs by Schadow or his workshop, and a third story added later.

At the next corner, you reach Wilhelmstrasse (see Chapter 5). Visible to your left, on the far side of Wilhelmstrasse, is the new **British embassy**, designed by Michael Wilford. The prewar British embassy stood here after 1872, when the British bought a nearly new mansion from the bankrupt railroad magnate Bethel Henry Strousberg. The U.K. reacquired the vacant site after 1990. Wilford's playful postmodern classicism (his late partner was James Stirling) maintains the horizontal sandstone lines of neighboring buildings, but breaks up the monotony of the façade with startling colors and angles.

Wilford's façade largely follows the architectural guidelines applied to all the new buildings on Pariser Platz, including the **Hotel Adlon**, which abuts it. The original Adlon (for which a Schinkel palace was demolished) was Berlin's grandest hotel from its opening in 1907 through the chaos of the Second World War. Its halls and balls swarmed with the rich, the well-connected and the notorious during the 1920s inflation and the intrigues of the Third Reich. It was reputed to have the city's largest wine cellar (a million bottles!) and safest air-raid shelter. By 1989 the building was long gone, however. The idea of rebuilding it was one of many hare-brained schemes hatched in the intoxicating days after the Wall came down; but this one was carried out. What you see is an approximate copy of the original with its proportions altered in order to cram one additional story into the same height. If the result looks old to you, you will not be impressed by the architectural establishment's outcry against this cheap knockoff. The original building did not extend all the way to Wilhelmstrasse; you can gauge its extent by the arched ground-floor windows. The interior is also intended to capture the luxurious ambience of yesteryear (just like Las Vegas hotels), and celebrities once again stay here (Michael Jackson made headlines for dangling his infant son over a balcony railing), but if you are a lingering tourist rather than a paying guest, you may be made unwelcome by muscular young men in black jackets.

Once past the Adlon, you are on **Pariser Platz**, the square that since 1735 has marked the outer end of Unter den Linden. In the nineteenth century it was the most elegant address in town. After the war, however, its location on the East–West dividing line left it empty and neglected. Since 1990 there has been a determined effort to restore the old elegance, with the return of venerable institutions and the establishment of strict architectural guidelines for new buildings – and all the buildings you see are new. It is perhaps fitting that the major challenge to the guidelines came from the **Academy of Arts** (Akademie der Künste), which has reclaimed its old site adjoining the Adlon. The architect of its new home, Günter Behnisch, is a master of glass and steel best known for his parliament building in Bonn. The city objected to his proposed glass façade, but in the end required only that it be more articulated. Through it you can see the only surviving prewar structure on the square other than the Brandenburg Gate. This storied wing of the old academy building was built in 1907 as an exhibition hall, used in its early years to display controversial modern paintings. During the Third Reich, with Albert Speer in charge of the academy, it housed a model of the new Berlin envisioned by Speer and Hitler, who spent hours absorbed in their fantasies. After 1945, East German artists were given studio space here, but when the Wall was built, border guards took it over.

The façade of the adjoining building, a bank, adheres more closely to the architectural guidelines, with unornamented stone pilasters punctuated by simple rectangular windows. Its most unusual feature is the angle of the window glass, which makes life difficult for window wash-ers. (The rear of the building contains apartments, and the undulating façade facing Behrenstrasse is less restrained.) The work of this architect is generally thought to be unmistakable, but until you step through the door (the lobby is open to the public) you might not recognize it as a **Frank Gehry** building. Gehry has conformed to the rules for the front façade, but in the large atrium he lets loose, filling his rectangular box with swelling curves of glass and steel that make this building entirely unlike its neigh-bors. His forms are usually described as organic: here the roof has been compared to a fish, with its triangular glass panels resembling scales. The central feature below it is a conference room framed with steel plates vaguely resem-bling a horse's head.

Next to it will be the last building constructed on the square. The land was reclaimed by the United States, whose embassy stood on the site until 1941, in a palace it had acquired only a few years before. Plans for a new embassy became stalled as new American security rules threatened to unleash a diplomatic row over access to the square and adjoining streets. Amid the sober office buildings on the north side of the square, the French embassy has reclaimed its prewar site. Like Gehry, Christian de Portzamparc tried to stretch the architectural rules. Here the result is very peculiar. On the west side of the square, the Brandenburg Gate is flanked by a matched pair of buildings. They are entirely new, but the architect Josef Kleihues restored the exact dimensions and approximate façades of their destroyed 1840s predecessors. The one on the north side is known as Haus Liebermann because its predecessor was the home of Max Liebermann, Berlin's finest impressionist painter. Liebermann was said to instruct prospective vis-itors, 'Enter Berlin and turn left'. He resigned as president of the Academy of Arts in 1933, two years before his death and just before the Nazis would have expelled him.

Once again the **Brandenburg Gate** faces an enclosed square, after standing alone for years. After Frederick William I built his customs wall in the 1730s, to regulate commerce and prevent soldiers from deserting, this western gate led to the Tiergarten and on to the old cathedral town of Brandenburg. The original gate was replaced by this grander one in 1791. Until Frederick the Great's death in 1786, curly Rococo ornament had been standard in Berlin. Carl Gotthard Langhans's design for the new gate, modeled on the Propylaea of Athens, brought the more severe lines of neoclassicism to Berlin. The frieze and attica reliefs illustrate the victorious wars of Frederick the Great and the peace that followed. They rest on a double row of Doric columns framing five openings that long filtered east–west traffic (although a recent closure to motor vehicles may become permanent). Until 1918 the wider central passage was reserved for the king's carriage. On that 9 November, Lorenz Adlon, owner of the the hotel, knew that William II was out of town and did not bother to look as he crossed the central passage. But William's abdication ended the old rule, and a truck ran down and nearly killed poor Adlon.

Crowning the gate is Gottfried Schadow's copper quadriga, a goddess driving a chariot drawn by four galloping horses. When Napoleon entered Berlin through the gate in 1806, fresh from his defeat of the Prussian army at Jena, his eyes are said to have been drawn upward. Clearly he admired the quadriga – enough to have it taken down and shipped to Paris. The denuded gate became the symbol of resistance to 'the horse thief of Berlin', and following Napoleon's defeat in 1814, a triumphant procession returned the quadriga to Berlin. The square was named after prostrate Paris, and the gate was on its way to becoming the preeminent symbol of Berlin, Prussia and Germany. The goddess was also given a new staff, designed by Schinkel: a Prussian eagle perched on a wreath surrounding the new Schinkel-designed military medal, the Iron Cross. Thereafter the gate became the traditional backdrop for military parades and diplomatic ceremonies. After the customs wall was pulled down in the 1860s the gate became a pure monument, site of glorious military parades in 1871 and 1914 – and on 30 January 1933, when thousands of torch-bearing stormtroopers celebrated the appointment of Hitler as chancellor. Crusty old Max Liebermann, watching from his window, is said to have remarked: 'Too bad one can't eat as much as one wants to vomit.'

After 1945 the grievously damaged gate and quadriga marked the border between the Russian and British sectors. A rare example of East–West cooperation permitted their restoration. Though the gate stood within East Berlin, the West was in possession of the plaster casts (made during the war as a precaution) necessary for restoration of the quadriga. As the East restored the gate, the West recreated the quadriga. The West deposited the reconstructed quadriga at the demarcation line in 1958, but the East put it up only after sawing the eagle off the top of the staff and the Iron Cross out of the wreath – it had banned these symbols of Prussian militarism. (In 1991, after heated debate, Schinkel's complete staff was restored.) In those years, traffic still flowed through the gate; that ceased with the construction of the Berlin Wall in 1961. (Billy Wilder's film *One, Two, Three*, a hilarious farce about the intrigues of the Coca-Cola Company's Berlin representative, features a car chase through the gate. The film was a commercial flop because the very unfunny Wall went up before it was released.)

According to a persistent myth, the quadriga once faced the other direction and was later turned around. An 1860 guidebook tells us that this happened when it was returned from Paris; twentieth-century versions blamed the communists. In fact, the quadriga has always faced east, toward the city: its intended audience was the towns-people, not outsiders. The outer side of the gate, facing the Tiergarten, has recently been renamed Platz des 18. März in honor of the democratic rebels of 1848 who, on 18 March of that year, marched into the city and on to the palace to demand reforms.

It was a remarkable coincidence that the more notorious twentieth-century wall followed the same course as its eighteenth-century predecessor. The famous gate that was never open offered an irresistible symbol to Western politicians, especially American presidents from John F. Kennedy, who stopped here before proceeding to the Schöneberg Rathaus to deliver his famous speech, to Ronald Reagan, who stood here in 1987 (after bulletproof glass had been erected to preserve the view but protect him from any communist snipers) and demanded, 'Mr. Gorbachev, open this gate! Mr. Gorbachev, tear down this wall!' The Wall has indeed been torn down, but its course is marked in the street by a double row of paving stones: a semicircle bowing outward from the gate, and a line north toward the Reichstag and south toward Potsdamer Platz. The East Germans never made this semicircular section of Wall as tall as the rest, in order not to spoil the view of the gate from Unter den Linden – that is, from the far end of Pariser Platz, which was as near as ordinary people were permitted. (VIP guests were escorted to one of the gatehouses, which housed an exhibition devoted to the brave deeds of the border guards.) Here the Wall was also broader and it lacked the rounded top used elsewhere. That was why the crowds on 9 November 1989 were able to dance atop it, perfectly positioned so that television cameras could capture them in front of the Brandenburg Gate.

The 1990s architectural guidelines restoring visual unity to Pariser Platz (a unity that had never actually existed before) required all façades to approximate the sandstone color of the gate. However, that has not always been the gate's color. The gate was designed with the white marble of its Greek models in mind, but with typical Prussian frugality, it was built of sandstone and painted white. After about 1804, it was painted a brownish color; in the 1860s, that was changed to grey. Only since the 1920s has the sandstone been permitted to display its natural color. In 2001, the public was asked to choose its favorite shade for the newly restored gate. If the familiar sandstone color had not been the favorite (as, not surprisingly, it was) the rest of the rebuilt square might have required a coat of paint as well.

2

Alexanderplatz and the Old Town

WHETHER YOU THINK Alexanderplatz has character depends, as Marxist intellectuals used to say, on your class position. Or it might simply depend on how you react to aromas of grilled sausage and beer. 'Alex', as Berliners call it, has long been the hub of Berlin's proletarian east, the point where U-Bahn, S-Bahn and streetcar lines from the south (Kreuzberg and Neukölln), the east (Friedrichshain, Lichtenberg), and the north (Prenzlauer Berg, Wedding) converge. Alfred Döblin's *Berlin Alexanderplatz* (1929), the most evocative of Berlin novels, portrays the underside of that churning world: plucky people grubbing for survival and pleasure amid an urban cacophony that threatened at every moment to drown out their very consciousness. Dr. Döblin, a health-service physician, knew his Berliners' language and obsessions. 'Aschinger has a big café and restaurant. People who have no belly can get one there; people who have one already can make it as big as they please.' Aschinger, the original fast-food chain, is gone, but its successors – German, Turkish and American – remain, and so do the bellies. In the self-proclaimed proletarian state that ruled the eastern half of divided Berlin, Alex was shorn of its petty crime, most of its bustle and indeed most of its buildings, but it retained a working-class identity. Although little remained of the prewar square, Alex was still the place for downscale shopping – in a dreary socialist department store – as well as meeting friends.

More than a decade after reunification, Alex preserved its East German appearance and identity. Since the early

1990s plans have called for its complete transformation into a more respectable center of offices and shops, but investors' reluctance has delayed any substantial changes. Meanwhile, Alex remains a slightly shabby place, offering little to please the tasteful Western visitor – a place best appreciated through Eastern eyes. This former army drill ground has always had an Eastern aura: it was named on the occasion of a visit by Tsar Alexander I in 1805. The one anchor of its identity is the elevated rail line that separates Alex from central Berlin. The station's recent restoration uncovered parts of the original building while giving it a new steel-and-glass skin and creating space for new shops on two levels below the platforms. The three U-Bahn lines can also be reached from here, but they actually run under different parts of the square, and are linked by a dingy underground labyrinth with more character than most Westerners will appreciate.

The only other prewar structures are a pair of buildings by Peter Behrens that frame one side of the square and separate it from the rail line. These concrete-framed buildings from 1932 – one a simple slab, the other bent at an angle – were the only completed parts of the Weimar Republic's ambitious plans to rebuild the square. (Even in Döblin's time the square was a huge construction site and a muddy mess.) Behrens's starkly modern structures fit easily into the East German reconstruction of the square, featuring a department store covered by a peculiar aluminum screen and the 37-story slab of a thousand-room hotel, still one of Berlin's tallest structures.

These buildings and the 'international friendship fountain' (1969), an East Berlin icon, frame a perfectly adequate public space, even if those who meet and linger here are distinctly less bourgeois than the crowds you see farther west at Gendarmenmarkt or Hackescher Markt. The problem with Alex, as a matter of urban design, is apparent when you look toward its far end: it is simply

too vast. Westerners sniff that the steppe begins here. Many Easterners, however, like the open space, too, and argue that the square justified its existence on a single day, 4 November 1989, when a million people gathered to demand reforms in their regime. (The Wall was opened five days later.) If current plans are carried out, Alex will shrink to a quarter of its present size.

The more distant sides of the square are lined with buildings that were intended to display East Germany's technological and stylistic modernity in the 1960s. They are neither particularly Eastern nor particularly interesting, and they, like the hotel and department store, are to be replaced with new ones likely to be neither Western nor interesting. One façade has recently been enlivened by large letters spelling out an excerpt from Döblin's *Berlin Alexanderplatz*. At the far end stands the one complex (apart from the Behrens buildings) guaranteed to remain. Hermann Henselmann's twelve-story Teachers' Building (1964), with its attached, domed Congress Hall, was the GDR's first contribution to a rebuilt Alex as well as its first steel-framed building with a curtain wall. Its most striking feature is the two-story-high mural that extends all around the exterior. Walter Womacka's colorful glass, ceramic and metal composition, inspired by Diego Rivera's murals, is entitled 'The Victory of the Human Being in Socialism'. Beyond the building stretches Karl-Marx-Allee (see Chapter 18).

If you cross under the rail line between the two Behrens buildings, you pass another East German landmark, a crude circular clock (1969) that gives the time anywhere in the world. The rail line follows the course of the wall that surrounded medieval Berlin, so when you pass the station, you enter the medieval town. A historical map will tell you that; your eyes will not. Nearly all medieval remnants had vanished long before the war, amid the city's explosive growth, as this became a densely packed commercial district. The East Germans chose to rebuild it in a very different form. In the 1950s plans called for an enormous government tower to stand alone here, flanked by vast decorative pools. In the 1960s, however, plans changed. The dominant structure, by far the tallest in the city, is the 1200-foot-high **television tower** (1969), a monument to modern technology rather than political power. Elevators take you up to the glass sphere containing a revolving restaurant, café and observation deck affording a panoramic view. From afar, sunshine reflects off this globe in a horizontal and a vertical line, creating a glittering cross. When the Communist monument was new, this unexpected phenomenon became an object of great mirth (and, presumably, secret shame), giving the tower such nicknames as 'Saint Walter' (after the Communist boss Walter Ulbricht) and 'the pope's revenge'.

The war and GDR planning left the broad band of open space extending beyond the tower. This central axis, framed by 1960s buildings on each side, links Alexanderplatz and Karl-Marx-Allee (behind you) with the palace square and Unter den Linden. Beyond the television tower, the neo-Baroque Neptune fountain by Reinhold Begas (1886), obviously inspired by Bernini's Fountain of the Four Rivers in Rome, portrays the sea god surrounded by female figures representing four main German rivers, the Rhine, Elbe, Oder and Vistula. It originally stood beside the royal palace.

This open space was once a densely built-up neighborhood. The only reminder of that history is the battered and forlorn Gothic parish church that sits alone, aligned with the heavens but not with the surrounding streets. For centuries the **Marienkirche** (Church of St Mary) stood amid narrow and bustling lanes. It dates to the late thirteenth century and was rebuilt in its current form a century later. Its tower was built in the fifteenth century, with a neo-Gothic crown added by Langhans in 1790. (When lightning set the tower on fire in 1661, a quick-thinking general is said to have hauled out a cannon and shot off the burning crown.) It is a simple three-aisle building of brick and stone, still well supplied with medieval paintings and carvings, some of which were brought here after the war from the ruined Nikolai and Franciscan churches. Most famous is the Dance of Death, a fresco painted on the wall of the tower in the 1480s, probably just after an outbreak of plague. It shows human figures dancing with corpses, in a long procession led by a preaching Franciscan, followed by representatives of all ranks of the clergy up to the pope, and then by figures representing all the strata of lay society, from the fool to the emperor. Underneath are moralizing rhymes written in Low German dialect. Another large fresco from the same era, only recently uncovered at the west end of the nave, depicts a ten-foot-high Madonna and child, with the pope, the emperor and others seeking shelter under her blue cape. In addition to other late medieval paintings and carvings, the church also contains many Baroque pieces remaining from an eighteenth-century remodeling. These include the altar and, most notably, an alabaster pulpit from 1703 by Andreas Schlüter.

The busy Karl-Liebknecht-Strasse next to the church dates to the 1880s, when it was torn through the neighborhood to carry the growing volume of traffic from Unter den Linden past the palace. The northern wing of the palace, in fact, was demolished to make way for Kaiser-Wilhelm-Strasse, as it was originally named. Just across it from the church is the corner of Rosenstrasse, which is closed to cars. A few steps up Rosenstrasse, stone sculptures commemorate the **Rosenstrasse protest**, a singular event in the history of the Third Reich. Here stood an administrative building of the Jewish community, next to Berlin's oldest synagogue. In February 1943 the

SS chose the former as a collection point for several hundred Jewish men. They had been kept at work in armaments factories and protected from earlier deportations because they had 'Aryan' wives. Now, however, the Nazis, determined to make Berlin 'Jew-free', arrested the men at their workplaces and brought them here. Word spread of the arrests, and hundreds of wives and relatives gathered outside the building to inquire and perhaps even to protest. The SS threatened to shoot, but without effect. After several days and nights, the men were released, and twenty-five who had already been sent to Auschwitz were even retrieved. This rare episode of open defiance of the Nazis raises the question: might ordinary Germans have been able to stop other Nazi atrocities? The purpose of Ingeborg Hunzinger's memorial, however, is to celebrate the women protesters. Her sculptures of them and the imprisoned men include carved slogans such as 'Give us back our men!' They were put up in 1995, but the project dates to the final months of the GDR, when it was finally beginning to acknowledge the events of the Holocaust. If the Jewish community builds a proposed old-age home here, the sculptures will be integrated into its garden.

On Spandauer Strasse, parallel to Rosenstrasse, stands another rare remnant of medieval Berlin, the Chapel of the Holy Ghost (Heiliggeistkapelle), once part of a medieval hospital. After the rest of the hospital was demolished, the chapel was attached to a new business school (1906), now part of the Humboldt University. The exterior of the chapel is a good example of north German red-brick Gothic, as is the fifteenth-century vaulted interior, which has long been used as a university cafeteria. Up Spandauer Strasse is Hackescher Markt (see Chapter 7); just around the corner is the museum island (see Chapter 1). Spandauer Strasse will also return you to the open space around the television tower, past a new hotel with its 'Sea-Life-Centre', a flashy aquarium. On the right side of the street, the vast open square is occupied only by a few sculptures loosely arranged in a large circle.

This is the official GDR monument to **Karl Marx and Friedrich Engels**, the creators of 'scientific socialism'. It dates to 1986, having been delayed for decades as plans for the central axis were repeatedly changed. By the 1970s, when this project was approved, East German sculptors had prevailed in their wish to create a low, modest, approachable monument, rather than a soaring Soviet-style one. The memorial was originally supposed to stand across the river, on the former palace square, but was shunted to this less prominent location. It is the collective work of a group of artists and is arranged to illustrate historical progress. At the far end, near the river, reliefs on a white marble wall portray the suffering of the oppressed workers under capitalism. Bronze reliefs at the near end show the happiness of life under socialism. The paths to the center are framed by steel pillars into which photographs illustrating the history of the workers' movement have been etched. The central statue of Marx and Engels (by Ludwig Engelhardt) marks the passage from suffering to triumph. Marx (sitting) and Engels (standing) gaze eastward toward the future. Although their bronze figures are twice life size, they are approachable on their low pedestal. Indeed, visitors approach them all the time, and children often climb onto Marx's lap. Their static postures and unruffled clothing lend them an aura of passivity. The absence of monumentality was supposed to represent a confident and secure East German state, but three years later that state collapsed, so Marx and Engels now seem to embody the helplessness of East European socialism. Indeed, when the statues were new, many East German communists were outraged at their lack of heroic militancy, and they soon acquired the nickname 'the pensioners'. After the Wall came down, the pedestal long bore spray-painted graffiti reading 'we're not guilty' and 'next time everything will be better'.

The major building on the Rathausstrasse side of the television tower is, of course, the **Rathaus**, the town hall. In the 1860s this building replaced its medieval predecessor on the same site. Its nickname, 'red town hall', comes from its red-brick construction, not the political tendencies of its occupants. During the years of division it was indeed the home of the Communist administration of East Berlin, while West Berlin was governed from Schöneberg Town Hall. Since 1991 the mayor of the unified city (which is also a federal state) has once again worked here. Hermann Waesemann's design, influenced by the Schinkel school as well as the Italian Renaissance, is rarely praised for its grace or beauty, but is unmistakable, especially its high tower. The terracotta façade sculpture includes a 36-part frieze that extends all the way around, depicting events in the city's history from its founding up to German unification in 1871. Facing the building are a pair of 1950s statues by Fritz Cremer, depicting a man and a woman rebuilding the city. Their human forms clearly met the criteria of the then-reigning socialist realism, but their unheroic modesty avoids the superhuman grotesqueness of much of that genre.

Across Spandauer Strasse from the town hall you reach the heart of medieval Berlin, as the GDR has reinterpreted it for you. This is the **Nikolai quarter**, where Berlin began around 1200 – the Marienkirche belonged to the New Town extension begun a half century later. Like that area, the Nikolai quarter did not survive the war, and for decades it was mostly empty space, with a few scattered buildings and ruins. However, the GDR rebuilt the neighborhood as its major contribution to the competing celebrations of the city's 750th anniversary in 1987. High above the Spandauer Strasse corner, a frieze depicts a large dove and the slogan, 'Berlin – City of Peace'. This was standard Soviet-bloc language at the time. (Recently the dove has been covered by a more up-to-date symbol of international harmony: the

McDonald's arches.) Lining Spandauer Strasse and Rathausstrasse are GDR prefab buildings, typical except for the addition of historicizing gables intended to evoke old Berlin – although they look more like Lübeck than Berlin. The narrow lane Am Nussbaum leads you into the quiet interior of the neighborhood, lined with craft shops and restaurants. The café Zum Nussbaum, in a squat freestanding house, became well known primarily because the celebrated caricaturist Heinrich Zille was a regular visitor a century ago. However, the building stood on the Fishermen's island, across the river, and was demolished decades ago. The East Germans reconstructed it here, largely from Zille's drawings, and reestablished the café. This was, in any case, the typical form of sixteenth-century Berlin houses, of which none are extant.

It faces the **Nikolai (St Nicholas) church**, Berlin's original parish church from the early thirteenth century. The fortress-like lower wall of the west front remains from that era. The rest of the church took its Gothic form in the late fourteenth century. The church stood in ruins for decades after the war, until, in the 1980s, the East Germans carefully restored it in its original form – or rather, in its nineteenth-century form: until then it had one tall spire and one older, stumpy tower. In the 1870s the tower was reconstructed with two matched spires, as you now see it. The interior, too, was restored in the 1980s to an approximation of its late medieval appearance, its bright colors based on recovered paint samples. It is a three-aisle church with a semicircular apse but no transept. The redbrick vaulting is typical of the north German adaptation of Gothic forms to the local building material. Near the west entrance are Baroque burial vaults of prominent Berliners. Not surprisingly, the Communists did not restore the building's use as a church. It now belongs to the Berlin city museum and serves as an exhibition space for medieval artifacts.

The church is pleasantly hemmed in by narrow, winding pedestrian lanes. Visitors to German towns expect to find an Altstadt – the old town with its church and market square. Those West German towns that found themselves without one after the war typically recreated it in some form; and that is precisely what the East Germans obligingly did here in the 1980s. The row of narrow old houses on the south side of the church is particularly attractive. None are the seventeenth-century originals; their façades were reconstructed to match old photographs. Some of the other old-looking houses, such as those facing Mühlendamm, were reconstructed from extant plans of destroyed houses that originally stood elsewhere in central Berlin.

On Poststrasse, which bisects the neighborhood, the Gothic loggia to the right is a copy of one from the old town hall. Nearby are the extant buildings that were incorporated into the rebuilt neighborhood, including an elegant one from 1907 on the right as well as one on the left (1896) that extends through the block and boasts an ornate German Renaissance façade facing the river. Propststrasse, the main cross street, takes you from the church to the riverbank and a bronze statue of St George fighting his dragon, which dates to the 1850s and originally stood in the courtyard of the royal palace. Propststrasse 8 is the newest location of the Zille museum, dedicated to the artist's works. Between the church and Poststrasse is the oldest extant house in the neighborhood: unlike its neighbors, Poststrasse 23 is not a reconstruction. It dates to 1760, its neoclassical façade to about 1800. It was the home of the prominent Knoblauch family and houses, in addition to a restaurant, an exhibition on life in the Biedermeier period.

At the corner where Poststrasse opens out onto the wide Mühlendamm stands the **Ephraim palace**. The rounded corner is the distinctive characteristic of its four-story stone façade with intricate Rococo windows and balconies.

It was completed in 1766 for the court jeweler Veitel Heine Ephraim, a Jew who had become one of Berlin's wealthiest men. The building stands near its original site. It was taken down in 1935 in order to widen the street. The stones of its façade were put in storage, and they ended up in West Berlin, which in the 1980s hatched a plan to re-erect the building in Kreuzberg. The East Germans were determined to rebuild it here, set back just a few feet from its original site. Berlin was spared the sight of two competing replicas when an agreement was reached to hand the stones over to the East as the Nikolai quarter was being rebuilt. The building now houses rotating exhibits of eighteenth-century arts and crafts.

Mühlendamm, as widened in the 1930s and 1960s, has obliterated Berlin's oldest market square, **Molkenmarkt** (milk market) in all but name. Across the street, the Baroque Palais Schwerin has faced the square since Jean de Bodt completed it in 1702. However, in the 1930s it was moved back to make way for the widened street and incorporated into the new complex of the Mint (Münze), whose long curved façade extends to the river in the ponderous neoclassical forms typical of the Third Reich, but with a copy of a frieze from 1800 that once graced an earlier Mint building. Across the open space left by the 1935 clearance looms the tower of the Stadthaus, the grandest of the many public buildings designed by the municipal architect Ludwig Hoffmann, built in 1902–11 as a town hall annex. This enormous pile of rusticated stone and Renaissance pillars actually represents a step toward architectural simplification, since it was not designed in the neo-Baroque style then mandatory for Prussian and Imperial buildings. Its high tower echoes those of the churches on Gendarmenmarkt. The GDR prime minister's office was formerly here.

The street on the near side of the building, leading to the Red Town Hall, is named Jüdenstrasse (Jew Street).

This was once the medieval Jewish quarter, as the Nazis well knew when they completed long-delayed plans to clear the area between Stralauer Strasse and the Spree. The Krögel had become a notorious slum with a jumble of ancient buildings, dark alleys, and dead ends that horrified the official guardians of public health and public order. At the turn of the century plans had been made to level it, which attracted photographers eager to record last images of the old slum, and they discovered its picturesque qualities.

Since the thirteenth century the twin towns of Berlin and Cölln have been connected by the Mühlendamm (mill dam). The lock and dam just upstream is still much used by barges and pleasure boats. Cross the bridge from the Nikolai quarter and you are in **Cölln**, the island enclosed by the main Spree here and its western arm on the other side. Old Cölln has been even more thoroughly obliterated than old Berlin. Its northern end is now the museum island, and its center was taken over by the now-vanished royal palace. The area to your left, the southern end of Cölln, was known as the **Fischerinsel** (fishermen's island). (Like the museum island at the other end, it was, despite its name, a peninsula.) Most of its closely packed old houses survived the war, but in the 1960s the GDR deemed them deteriorated beyond repair and leveled them. (Attitudes toward old buildings changed rapidly in the few years before the resurrection of the Nikolai quarter.) In their place came six 25-story apartment towers surrounded by green space, eliminating (in typical modernist fashion) any streetscape. Recent proposals to surround them with new low-rise buildings, including luxury housing on the riverbank, have been applauded as attempts to reurbanize the area but also decried by current residents, descendants of Zille's brash proletarians, who treasure their open space and resent being pushed into the backyards of rich Western interlopers.

Gertraudenstrasse takes you past Breite Strasse (which leads to Schlossplatz – see Chapter 1) to an open space that has recently regained its old name, Petriplatz, and may soon gain some new buildings, but St Petri, Cölln's main church, is long gone. A few old buildings do line Brüderstrasse, which leads off to the right. Past the corner of Scharrenstrasse, marked by the remaining wing of a 1909 department store, Brüderstrasse 13, built about 1670, assumed its current neoclassical appearance after the publisher **Friedrich Nicolai** made it his home in 1787. Nicolai was the central figure in the Berlin Enlightenment, and his home was one of the city's intellectual centers (several plaques commemorate important visitors). It is now a branch of the city museum, used for special exhibitions, as is number 10, which dates to the 1680s and was renovated in neoclassical form around 1800, with stucco decoration in sinuous acanthus forms inside and out. If you turn left at the next corner, you are in Sperlingsgasse, which leads down to the left branch of the Spree. The street was called Spreegasse in the mid-nineteenth century, when Wilhelm Raabe lived here while writing his touching fictional account of an urban neighborhood, *The Chronicle of Sperlingsgasse*. The street was later renamed in its honor. Now, however, it would take a powerful imagination to conjure up the ancient houses and intimate neighborhood Raabe described.

Across the river is the massive stone façade of the former Reichsbank, now the foreign ministry (see Chapter 1). If you turn left and follow the quay (Friedrichsgracht), you pass Berlin's oldest bridge, Jungfernbrücke, a Dutch-style drawbridge from 1798. A few more fragments of the past remain near Gertraudenstrasse, notably a neo-Gothic commercial building from 1898. Next to the wide modern Gertraud bridge stands an old bridge (1895) open to pedestrians, decorated with an 1896 bronze statue of the nun St Gertraud giving a drink to a poor boy. The statue comes from the St Gertraud hospital that once stood across the river on Spittelmarkt, a name that, like its English cousin, comes from a corruption of the word hospital. Nothing remains of old Spittelmarkt or of old Leipziger Strasse beyond it.

A pedestrian walkway on the riverbank leads under the Gertraud bridge and permits you to follow the bank into the Fischerinsel. Three graceful early-twentieth-century stone bridges cross the Spree branch between here and the upper tip of the Fischerinsel. If you cross the first of the bridges, you reach the pleasant Wallstrasse, which parallels the river and is lined with elegant commercial buildings from the early twentieth century. (Its name recalls the seventeenth-century town rampart.) A left turn at the next corner (Neue Rossstrasse) brings you back to the river at the quay of **Märkisches Ufer**. Numbers 6 and 8 are old buildings that have been incorporated into the new Australian embassy, which faces Wallstrasse. The narrow band of land between Wallstrasse and the water was added to the city when its new fortifications were built around 1680. The new quarter was called Neucölln or Neukölln (not to be confused with the outlying district that appropriated the name much later). On Märkisches Ufer are the only remaining traces of its early days – and some of them are actually from elsewhere. In the 1960s the GDR designated Märkisches Ufer as an 'island of tradition', a refuge for old buildings that stood in the way of urban renewal. Number 10, the Ermeler house, stood on Breite Strasse from 1770 until that street was widened in the 1960s. Its façade was decorated in neoclassical form in 1804, with a balustrade and friezes. Its generous proportions contrast with its more modestly proportioned neighbor, number 12, built in 1740 on the opposite bank of the river. These houses have been incorporated into a hotel belonging to the Art'otel chain, which features modern art in its rooms, in this case works of Georg Baselitz. It also operates, in season, a café on a barge moored on the river in front, a pleasant spot to watch the boats on the working river. The rest of the houses in the row were built here. Number 14, from 1890, with its doorway flanked by caryatids, is typical of its era. Number 16 dates to about 1780; number 18, to 1741; number 20, to 1874. By the time you reach the next corner, Inselstrasse, you are facing the upper end of Cölln island, and you can see all the way across the Spree to the new Dutch embassy.

Either the quay or Wallstrasse will take you past the new Brazilian embassy to Köllnischer Park, on an irregular site once occupied by a bastion of the seventeenth-century fortifications. The building standing in the park is not a red-brick Gothic church, nor a medieval Rathaus, nor a Renaissance palace, although even its interior spaces might fool you. The **Märkisches Museum** was founded to display the history of Berlin and the Mark Brandenburg (the original territory of the margrave, or Markgraf), and Ludwig Hoffmann took the opportunity to design a building (1907) inspired by regional models, with several wings arranged in picturesque fashion. (The entry hall was destroyed in the war.) Since reunification the museum has come under new management, but it has not been systematically renovated, so its displays are certain to change in the coming years. This somewhat dingy, little visited museum is a treasure trove for anyone interested in the social and cultural history of Berlin. Many old photographs are on display, as are maps, and sculptural fragments from vanished buildings, including medieval houses as well as Schinkel's Bauakademie. There are three wooden models of the city at different phases in its early development: 1450, 1688, and 1750. There is a great deal of furniture, clothing, jewelry, and porcelain, including an 1830 vase with a panoramic view of Unter den Linden painted on it. Two ornate eighteenth-century tile ovens recall a long Berlin tradition that has only just died out: apartments were long dependent on these ovens for their heat, and until the 1990s their coal smoke turned the winter air brown. There are old weapons, and a collection of late-medieval wooden religious statues. There are many paintings, especially from the nineteenth century. A pair of extremely wide ones by Eduard Gaertner give an incomparable 360-degree panorama of the city as seen from the tower of Friedrichswerder church in 1832. Grandiose royalist paintings include one of the 1878 Congress of Berlin, by the court painter Anton von Werner, and an 1888 work by Ferdinand Keller of 'Kaiser Wilhelm the Victorious', stuffed with all kinds of allegorical figures. A large bronze portrays Bismarck as a blacksmith, 'the smith of the German Reich'. There are also early twentieth-century paintings and graphic works, including Lovis Corinth's portrait of the critic Alfred Kerr; a set of terrifying Otto Dix etchings of scenes from the First World War; several of Hans Baluschek's paintings of workers; and delightful lithographs by Heinrich Zille. Small displays document the Third Reich and the GDR, which are likely to receive more attention in the future.

The park outside serves as an extension of the museum as well as a lapidarium filled with fragments of statuary salvaged from many places. Since the 1930s an enclosure at the rear has housed live bears. The name Berlin is of Slavic origin and refers to the marshy ground, but a swamp makes neither a vivid nor an inspiring symbol, so the similarity of the name to the German word for bear (Bär) made the animal an irresistible choice for the city's emblem. Inanimate objects in the park include segments of the Berlin Wall as well as a brick tower that originally stood nearby as part of the seventeenth-century city fortifications. Also visible is the stone foundation of a windmill that was built here around 1700. A sandstone statue of Hercules conquering the Nemean lion is a 1787 work of Gottfried Schadow. Next to the museum entrance is a 1905 copy of a large fifteenth-century Roland statue that still stands in the city of Brandenburg. A newer work at the edge of the park is a 1965 bronze statue of Heinrich Zille, a sentimental image of the artist at work as a boy peeks over his shoulder.

The park is lined with early twentieth-century buildings. Most notable is Am Köllnischen Park 3 by Alfred Messel (1903). Messel chose brick and stone colors to blend with his friend Hoffmann's museum, then under construction. He subordinated the obligatory Baroque decoration to simplified brick pillars that dispense with the horizontal distinctions between stories. This is a style Messel had already displayed a few years before in his now-destroyed Wertheim department store on Leipziger Platz; a few years later, Peter Behrens would develop it further. Around the corner, Rungestrasse 3–6 is a monumental insurance office from 1932 in which the vertical emphasis has been taken much farther, with expressionist accents added in the glazed-brick front.

As you continue along the river, the large building on your right, which faces the busy corner of Brückenstrasse, was a GDR showcase from the 1980s, built for the official trade unions. It is now the Chinese embassy. The Chinese communists are probably not trying to rekindle German communist traditions here, but there is a long history of international communist interaction in Berlin. Zhou Enlai lived here from 1922 to 1924, working in the communist movement. In 1954, as the premier of one new communist state, he returned on a state visit to another one. A surviving photo from the 1920s shows Zhou rowing a small boat on a Berlin lake. In the published photo, he is alone; in the original, other communists sat beside him, but as they were later purged, they were airbrushed from the photo, a practice notoriously associated with Stalin's Soviet Union and its allies.

Brückenstrasse, as its name (bridge street) implies, connects to Jannowitz bridge. From the bridge you can see some of the recent redevelopment upriver, including a 1990s office building at the corner of Brückenstrasse with a riverfront façade that does everything possible to call attention to itself. Under the S-Bahn, turn left on the river-bank and you are back within the confines of medieval Berlin. Here at its southern end are a few remnants of ear-lier centuries, but most of the fine-grained scale of the old city vanished even before the war. Along the river, for example, you pass a large 1911 Ludwig Hoffmann office building, then an even more massive municipal building from the 1930s in the characteristic style of Third Reich bureaucracy. Past it, across Klosterstrasse, is the new **Dutch embassy**, the only recent Berlin building by the influential Dutch architect Rem Koolhaas, whose denunciation of the conservative Berlin architectural guidelines made him unpopular with the local authorities. It can be expected to make a splash when it is completed.

Follow Klosterstrasse across Stralauer Strasse, and Hoffmann's Stadthaus is on your left. Facing it is a build-ing with the inscription 'Gebr. Tietz' (Tietz brothers). This 1906 structure, which displays a mixture of Baroque and Jugendstil forms, housed administrative offices of the once powerful Tietz department-store chain, 'Aryanized' in the 1930s. Just beyond is one of Berlin's few Baroque churches, the Parochialkirche, designed by Arnold Nering and completed in 1703, with the entry hall and bell tower added a decade later. It is a square building with four semicircular apses, a form apparently borrowed from Holland and otherwise unknown here. In 1944 the church was gutted by fire and the top portion of the tower collapsed. Restoration began only in the 1990s. The crypt, recently opened to visitors, contains eighteenth- and nineteenth-century tombs with mummified remains.

One of the city's oldest subway lines, the U2, runs under Klosterstrasse. The Klosterstrasse station at the next corner is one of the best examples of the austere elegance achieved by Alfred Grenander, who designed many stations. On the underground platform, note the iron pillars with scrolled Ionic capitals, a synthesis of classical and machine-age aesthetics. Also at the corner of Parochialstrasse are a Third Reich building with oppressively grandiose stairwells that has served as an annex to the Stadthaus; and a rare Baroque house, Palais Podewils, built by Jean de Bodt for a Prussian minister in the first years of the eighteenth century. Parochialstrasse between the Baroque church and the Baroque house takes you to Waisenstrasse and the only extant section of the **medieval town wall**. The brick and stone wall, dating to the fourteenth century, was replaced by new fortifications in the seventeenth, with this section remaining intact because it was incorporated into houses built along it. The four houses that remain are among Berlin's oldest. One claims to be Berlin's oldest pub. Its name, Zur letzten Instanz (At the last resort), is a judicial term, inspired by the proximity of the city courts. It is no longer the proletarian dive it was when the caricaturist Heinrich Zille came here to sketch ordinary people. Although its kitchen serves up uncompromisingly German fare, heavy on pork and cabbage, Napoleon is said to have dined here, and, much more recently, it became a favorite of Jacques Chirac, who, unlike his illustrious predecessor, came to Berlin as an invited state guest.

Follow Waisenstrasse to the left and you reach the shell of the destroyed **Klosterkirche**, a vivid relic both of medieval Berlin and of World War II. The Franciscans built their simple but elegant Gothic church in the thirteenth century at the eastern edge of town. The solid walls of the nave contrast with the more airy and soaring choir, which was probably built a few decades later. After the building was destroyed by bombs, the East Germans shored up its exterior walls as a memorial to the war. The open space that was once the church's interior, plus the small park that surrounds it, now form a quiet oasis in the city. Two carved stone capitals that lie in the grass are from Eosander's wing of the destroyed royal palace. The friars' quarters were once attached to the north side of the church. After the Reformation they were converted to a school, and until its destruction in the war the Gymnasium zum Grauen Kloster (At the Grey Cloister) was considered the city's finest. Its ruins now lie under the widened street that disturbs the quiet of the churchyard.

Across the side street Littenstrasse stands a massive Wilhelmine court building from 1905, notable for its grandiose neo-Baroque staircase. Turn the corner of the building, and you cross under the S-Bahn to the vicinity of Alexanderplatz. The open area on the right has long hosted the largest of Berlin's outdoor Christmas markets, but a new shopping mall is planned here. In the median of Grunerstrasse, as you cross back to Alex, a GDR memorial in the form of a cracked bronze plaque recalls that police headquarters once stood here, giving Alex its identity in the minds of the marginal citizens chronicled in Döblin's novel. It is hard to know what, if anything, will lend Alex character in the future.

3

The Reichstag

THE BRANDENBURG GATE may be the symbol of Berlin, but it is the nearby Reichstag building that bears the most scars of German history. A visit here can reveal traces of the troubled birth of modern Germany; of war, defeat, and abortive revolution; of a struggling democracy; of a fateful 1933 fire that sealed the democracy's fate; of the Nazi dictatorship's birth, as well as its death at the hands of Red Army soldiers in the halls; of the Wall that was built just outside; and of the new beginning that followed that Wall's demise.

The Reichstag, as an institution, was created by the constitution of the new German Empire (Deutsches Reich) in 1871. It was the democratic element of the empire, answering demands for inclusion of the people in the decisions of government. Members were elected by direct and universal suffrage – universal, that is, to males over the age of 25. Recall that Britain, the model of parliamentary government for German liberals at the time, did not yet have universal male suffrage then. However, suffrage did not make Germany a democracy, since Bismarck's carefully crafted constitution left the most crucial powers in the hands of either the emperor (and thus those of his trusted servant, Bismarck) or the twenty-five states, most of which (including the dominant Prussia) had far less democratic institutions. Nor did Bismarck think the Reichstag would be his enemy. His main opponents were the middle-class liberals, and the system of universal suffrage left them outvoted by the far more numerous peasants, who (Bismarck thought) would remain loyal to the throne. What he failed to account for was the rapid industrialization that changed Germany from a nation of peasants to one of restive urban workers.

From its beginning, then, the institution occupied an uneasy place in the new German empire. And its place in the new capital was also uncertain. The former royal porcelain factory on Leipziger Strasse was hastily remodeled as a temporary home – for, as it turned out, twenty-three years. An architectural competition in 1872 chose a design for a new Reichstag building, but it was never built, in part because of opposition to the design and in part because of the parliament's inability to acquire the property it had selected (which says something about its powers). A second competition, a decade later, was more successful, as the chosen site was finally obtained: the eastern side of Königsplatz (King's Square), a former army drill ground between the Tiergarten and the recently demolished customs wall. By 1873 the new Victory Column stood in the center of the square (in 1938 it was moved to its present home in the Tiergarten). Among the many new buildings around it, the most important housed the Army General Staff.

The chosen architect, Paul Wallot, had to modify his design repeatedly, even after construction began in 1884, and the building was not finished until 1894. It might perhaps be best to say that its architecture has not been universally condemned. Its ponderous monumentality soon went out of fashion, but the scars of history have tempered our view of it. Hitler seems to have liked the building – a fact unlikely to draw our sympathies to it, but it is possible that Nazi planners would have demolished it otherwise. Wallot lamented that 'we are building a national edifice without having a national style'. Some architects envisioned Gothic as the German national style, but Wallot followed the classical tradition, drawing

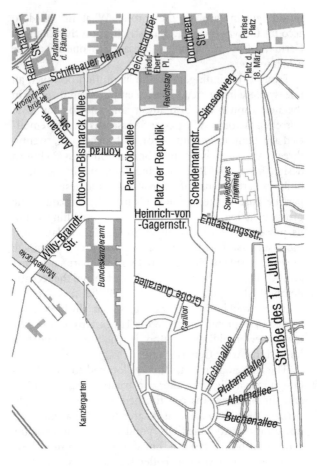

his forms mainly from the Italian Renaissance: massive pillars and pilasters, porticos and pediments, arched windows, corner towers, and abundant statuary. The most innovative part of his building was its dome (now gone), made of iron and glass instead of stone – materials hitherto associated with railway stations and exhibition pavilions, not palaces or government buildings.

By the time the building was completed, Bismarck was gone, as was his patron, Emperor William I. The young Emperor William II (better known as Kaiser Wilhelm) resented the Reichstag's opposition to his whims, and his outbursts against the 'imperial monkey house' extended to the 'height of tastelessness' that was its home. His inability to work with the parliament, encouraged by aristocratic opponents of liberal reform, brought Germany to the brink of governmental paralysis before 1914. The precarious constitutional balance between imperial autocracy and democratic representation, crafted by Bismarck to place the decisive power in his own hands, left Germany too dependent on its impulsive emperor. The prominent inscription above the west entrance, 'Dem Deutschen Volke' (To the German People), only went up in 1916 (with lettering designed by Peter Behrens in a modernized version of the old German style), when the miseries of World War I demanded at least a symbolic acknowledgment of popular sovereignty.

The most important change in the composition of the Reichstag up to 1914 was the growth of the avowedly Marxist (but increasingly reformist) Social Democratic Party, which became the largest single party in the 1912 elections. The Social Democrats rallied to the flag in 1914, to the great relief of German leaders and to the disgust of radical foreign admirers like Vladimir Lenin. However, the long war eventually split the party. As the army and monarchy collapsed, on 9 November 1918, one of the more conservative Social Democratic leaders, Philipp

Scheidemann, stepped to a window of this building (the second one to the left of the west entrance, between the bases of the massive pilasters) to proclaim the German Republic. He acted because he had heard that the radical Karl Liebknecht was about to proclaim a socialist republic from the balcony of the royal palace.

Thereafter the Reichstag was the true center of power in Germany's first republic, although it was founded at (and informally named after) a constitutional convention in Weimar, convened away from the revolutionary tension in the capital. Its leaders struggled with enormous problems, including defeat, inflation, depression, and large communist and nationalist parties determined to destroy it. The end came in 1933. The schemers around President Paul von Hindenburg, who appointed Hitler chancellor on 30 January of that year, certainly intended to bury democracy, but their plan was to manipulate the Nazis for their own purposes. Hitler proved too clever for them, and the event that turned the tide in his favor occurred, ironically, in the home of the parliament for which neither he nor Hindenburg's aristocratic friends had any use. On the night of 27 February, a suspicious fire broke out in the building, gutting the parliamentary chamber. The police – newly under Nazi control – immediately arrested a Dutchman, Marinus van der Lubbe, who professed vaguely anarchist sympathies and showed signs of mental illness. The Nazis proclaimed that they had uncovered a communist conspiracy to undermine the state, and they declared a state of emergency, suspended civil liberties and arrested thousands of communists and other political opponents. Soon the Nazi-dominated parliament handed all its powers to Hitler, and the Reichstag ceased to function. The Nazis' fantasy of a communist conspiracy was rejected even by the courts of the Third Reich, but historians still argue whether the Nazis set the fire or van der Lubbe acted on his own.

During the next twelve years, the Reichstag, now a body of compliant Nazis, met occasionally in the Kroll opera house (now gone) across Königsplatz to applaud a Hitler speech – for example on 30 January 1939, when he announced that the coming war would be the Jews' fault and would result in their annihilation. Parts of the damaged Reichstag building remained in use, and Allied bombing inflicted little additional damage. Its crucial role was restricted to the very beginning of the Third Reich, and its very end in 1945. For some reason Stalin identified it as the very heart of the Nazi capital, and the Soviet armies that fought their way into the city from different sides competed to take the building. Finally they did, in bloody hand-to-hand fighting through dark hallways. A Red Army photographer captured the climactic unfurling of the hammer-and-sickle flag on one of the corner towers.

The battered stone shell of a building ended up in West Berlin, just barely: after 1961 the Berlin Wall stood just a few feet from its rear entrance. Its sagging dome was demolished in 1954. A few years later, the building was restored, stripping much of the ornamentation. (You will still find plenty of sculptural decoration, but it is a fraction of the original.) Visitors were told that the building would one day house the parliament of a reunified Germany, but a glance out of the east windows told them that this was the wildest fantasy. Fantasy became reality in 1991, when the Bundestag narrowly chose Berlin over Bonn as the future seat of government.

While the Wall stood, the artist Christo, becoming known for his projects that temporarily 'wrapped' prominent structures, conceived the idea of wrapping the lonely and battered Reichstag. Politicians repeatedly turned him down, but after the Wall crumbled, the idea found high-level support, and ultimately was debated and approved by the Bundestag. So, for two weeks in 1995, the building was wrapped in shimmering silver fabric, an immense and ghostly package flapping in the summer breeze. Crowds came to gawk, mingle and share the experience. When the wrapping came off, there was a feeling that the building had been reborn – that it could now be the home of a democratic Germany that knew but did not fear its failed predecessors. Meanwhile, an architectural competition had sought plans to remodel the building. Sir Norman Foster came out the winner, although his original design, calling for a vast canopy covering the building, had to be changed. Renovation began after Christo's wrapping came off. The sandstone walls have been cleaned and patched; the numerous patches are the most visible evidence of the building's troubled history.

Above the battered walls rises Foster's gleaming glass **dome** (which bears little resemblance to the old one), the part of the building most accessible to visitors. The view from the top is not to be missed, as, unfortunately, nearly everyone seems to think. It is open daily from 8 a.m. to 10 p.m., but expect a long wait. Visitors queue up at the main west entrance, at the top of the grand staircase (with wheelchair access to the side). You are permitted a glance into the west lobby before being whisked to the top in an elevator. As the forest of construction cranes thins in the early 2000s, you can see the new parliamentary buildings and the chancellery, the new rail station to the north, Potsdamer Platz to the south, Unter den Linden to the east, with Pariser Platz at its near end, and the Holocaust memorial behind it. On the south side of Pariser Platz, the organic curves of Frank Gehry's bank building extrude from the roof behind its prim stone façade.

You can stroll all over the Reichstag's roof, under the dome and outside it, around the two courtyards that flank the plenary chamber and up to the old corner towers with their allegorical depictions of industry, agriculture, law, defense, education and the arts. A reservation at the rooftop café, if you can get one, permits you to bypass the queue outside. Two ramps, one leading up, the other down, carry you through the air between the base of the dome and its top, eighty feet above. The ramps spiral around the inverted glass cone that reaches downward. This is the dome's functional part. Foster proclaimed his lack of interest in an ornamental dome, but agreed to design one that counted as technologically innovative construction. The cone's open top and bottom permit stale air to be sucked upward from the plenary chamber. Its mirrored surface also reflects daylight into the chamber. Whether you can see into the chamber from above depends on light conditions.

The expanded plenary chamber extends from the bottom to the top of the building and to the courtyards on either side. Ordinary visitors are permitted in the galleries, by reservation, when the house is not in session. The largest decoration is a large aluminum eagle. A similar eagle designed for the Bundestag in Bonn had been dubbed 'the fat hen', thanks to its distinctly unthreatening mien. A typical German controversy broke out over the question of whether the new Berlin eagle might take on a slimmer, more imposing appearance. The result was a compromise, slimmer than the Bonn eagle but still nothing like Imperial or Nazi forebears.

The rest of the building is usually off limits to visitors. The interior is almost entirely new, but in a few places the old, battered walls have been left bare. During renovation, graffiti scrawled by Russian soldiers in 1945 were found on the walls. In most cases, they simply carved their names. The decision was made to leave them visible as a reminder of the building's history, even if they include 'death to the Germans' and praise of Stalin. A few samples can be seen on the roof, along the parapet. The lobbies are decorated with artworks that were commissioned for the building. They include works by Katharina Sieverding and Christian Boltanski recalling the dark episodes in

German parliamentary history, and two large Georg Baselitz paintings in the south lobby. On one wall of the north lobby are five light boxes by Sigmar Polke; opposite them are three color panels (variations on the German flag) by Gerhard Richter; and in the center is a floor-to-ceiling stela by Jenny Holzer. Its digital letters display, in constant upward motion, a selection of speeches given in the Reichstag and Bundestag. They are visible from the outside, and if you can read German, the reading gets tedious very quickly. The most controversial work is in the north courtyard, and is visible from the roof. Here Hans Haacke arranged earth to form the words 'Der Deutschen Bevölkerung', a dedication 'to the German population' rather than the German 'people' or 'nation' (Volk), thus calling attention to the tensions between Germany's identity as an ethnic nation and its millions of residents who are not ethnic Germans. Haacke's gesture was decried by conservatives (perhaps accurately) as an insult to German national pride, but – and this is also typically German – it was installed nevertheless.

The west entrance faces the open space of the **Platz der Republik**. Königsplatz was thus renamed in 1926; the Nazis restored the old name, and the new one returned with the new republic, after 1945. For decades the Reichstag stood alone here. The Nazis moved the Victory Column and its attendant statues in 1938, and began clearing the buildings from the Spree bend to the north. Hitler and Speer intended this to be the ceremonial center of the new capital, Germania, as the reshaped Berlin was to be known. The entire Spree bend was to be taken up by the largest building in the world, an enormous domed hall where 170,000 people would hear Hitler's speeches. This would also be the northern end of the North–South Axis extending three miles south to a similarly oversized triumphal arch. An expanded Königsplatz was to be lined with ceremonial buildings. The Reichstag, dwarfed by its neighbor, was the one old building designated to remain. Preliminary work continued as late as 1942 before yielding to pressing wartime needs. Allied bombers provided additional clearance, which Speer's office sardonically described at the time as 'valuable preparation for the goal of reorganization'. (It was Robert Harris's inspired whim to set his otherwise unremarkable detective novel *Fatherland* in a 1964 Berlin rebuilt after Hitler's victory in the war.) In the postwar decades, poverty, political uncertainty and the nearby Wall discouraged new plans, and this open space became an extension of the Tiergarten, suitable for soccer games and outdoor rock concerts (to which East German youths huddled behind the Wall could listen, until the police chased them away). Christo's 'wrapping' was the last such mass gathering before the government returned.

Ghosts linger all around. On the Scheidemannstrasse side, an array of irregularly shaped bronze plaques, dedicated in 1992, recalls the 96 members of the Weimar-era Reichstag who were murdered by the Nazis. Nearby, south of the Reichstag, stands a row of white crosses that commemorate victims of the Berlin Wall. These long stood on the north side, next to where the Spree marked the border and where many people tried to swim to freedom. The area across Scheidemannstrasse from the Platz der Republik has been proposed as a site for a central memorial to the Sinti and Roma (or Gypsies) murdered by the Nazis. Since the decision to build a central memorial exclusively to the Nazis' Jewish victims, painful and sometimes nasty debates have raged about the relative status of other victim groups and the memorials to which they might be entitled; after the Jews, the Sinti and Roma have the strongest claim to total persecution on the basis of Nazi racial policies.

A wide roadway formerly led southward from the Victory Column. In the 1890s the emperor lined this Victory Avenue (Siegesallee) with grand marble statues depicting all the rulers of Brandenburg-Prussia, each flanked by important personages of his time. In an age of changing artistic tastes, modern artists saw the project as a declaration of imperial opposition to their work. Even the broader populace recognized the overblown propaganda of the 'puppet avenue' (Puppenallee), as it was known. The Nazis moved the statues to the center of the Tiergarten along with the Victory Column; their splintered remains now rest at the Lapidarium (see Chapter 5).

The Nazis intended to replace the Siegesallee with their North–South Axis. Astride it stands instead the **Soviet war memorial**, which faces south onto the Strasse des 17. Juni. The remains of 2500 Red Army soldiers claim the spot where this East–West Axis was to intersect the new North–South Axis at the heart of the Nazi capital. Work began here only days after the German surrender in 1945 and was completed within months, using stone stockpiled for Hitler's projects. Ungrateful Berliners called it the 'tomb of the unknown plunderer'. It may be bombastic – clearly a product of the Stalin era – but it is not without a certain grandeur. The two arms of the symmetrical colonnade curve forward from the central pillar, which serves as a high pedestal for an enormous bronze statue of a burly Red Army soldier. On each side T34 tanks and artillery pieces are mounted on pedestals. During the decades of division this memorial puzzled visitors, since it was located on the West Berlin side of the Brandenburg Gate. By Allied agreement it was maintained by the Russians, who posted an honor guard. After the Wall went up, it became too visible a target of West Berliners' hatred, so the British authorities closed the street in front and kept all passers-by at a distance – which did not prevent a neo-Nazi from shooting one of the Soviet guards in 1970. In the 1990 treaty permitting German reunification, Germany pledged to maintain in perpetuity this and all Soviet memorials on its soil.

The GDR renamed the street leading east from the Reichstag after Clara Zetkin (1857–1933), a prominent Jewish feminist and politician. The decision to restore its old name, Dorotheenstrasse, after the Great Elector's wife, was controversial, but after World War I Zetkin had joined the Communist Party and denounced the Weimar Republic, and officials declared that the street linking the city center to the parliament should not carry the name of an enemy of parliamentary democracy. (Princess Dorothea's views on the subject were spared any such scrutiny.) The street is lined with new parliamentary buildings. Directly across from the Reichstag's eastern entrance (the one intended for, but almost never used by, the emperor, and now used by MPs), the old building facing the Spree was built by Wallot as the Reichstag president's residence. This office was held by some distinguished parliamentarians in the Weimar years, but by 1932 was in the hands of the head of the largest party delegation, the Nazi Hermann Göring. The riverbank here may be the best ground-level spot to get a sense of the ambitious spatial plan that guided the rebuilding of the Reichstag quarter. In a 1993 international design competition that drew 835 entries, the winner was Axel Schultes's plan for an east–west band of buildings that linked the former East and West Berlin across the river and the empty spaces left by Hitler and the Wall. The eastern end of the band is marked by the parliamentary buildings that face each other across the river, Paul-Löbe-Haus and Marie-Elisabeth-Luders-Haus. They are linked by a two-level bridge, one part open to the public, the other for parliamentarians. Both buildings, designed by Stephan Braunfels, manage to combine simple elegance with great size.

If you cross the Spree here and follow it downstream past Marie-Elisabeth-Luders-Haus, you reach an open area. The river once marked the border here, and this bank was the free-fire zone of no-man's-land. A portion of the wall that marked the eastern edge of that zone remains. (That is, it was a part of the Berlin Wall, but it wasn't the massive wall that faced West Berlin.) During the chaotic months after the Wall was abandoned, the environmental artists Ben Wargin and Volker Martin established a 'parliament of trees' here, an installation of trees, sculpture and slogans painted on the wall, dedicated to victims of violence and war. Wargin's banal installations (another is at the Savignyplatz S-Bahn station) have proved effective in capturing public attention. The government eventually agreed to leave this 'parliament' in place.

Just beyond, Reinhardtstrasse leads to the right, under the S-Bahn and into the old Friedrich-Wilhelm-Stadt (see Chapter 8). To the left, a new bridge crosses the Spree. This 'crown prince's bridge', taking the name of its long-vanished predecessor, is an elegant composition of curved white steel tubes, designed by the famed Spanish engineer-architect Santiago Calatrava and completed in 1997. Across the bridge, the diagonal street named after Chancellor Konrad Adenauer leads past a small building of a striking blue color, a kindergarten specially built for the children of Bundestag employees. Its construction and its exclusivity displeased many Berliners facing funding cuts to existing kindergartens across the city.

Past the kindergarten, you are back on the northern side of Schultes's east–west band. Paul-Löbe-Haus faces west onto what Schultes intended as its centerpiece, a public forum, but security concerns have so far prevented this from becoming anything but a useless open space. (Long-term plans also foresee underground S-Bahn and U-Bahn stations here.) To the north, the wide space enclosed by a bend in the Spree has been nearly empty since the war, and Schultes's plan leaves it that way, thus emphasizing the east–west band of buildings next to it.

This was where Hitler's great domed hall would have stood; in fact, a buried and forgotten part of its foundation had to be removed to build Paul-Löbe-Haus. One building stands alone amid the empty space, as it has for decades, despite all the changes around it. This is the Swiss embassy, the one building that Hitler's planners did not have the authority to remove. It was built in 1870, given its current form in 1910, and taken over by the Swiss in 1919. In 1945 Russian troops stormed the Reichstag from here. Now, with a new addition, it again serves Switzerland as a centrally located embassy. Past it, the diagonal Willy-Brandt-Strasse (named after another former chancellor) leads to another remnant of the vanished prewar neighborhood: the ornately carved sandstone Moltke bridge (1891) which crosses the Spree to Moabit and the new rail station.

The view from the forum is, however, dominated by the new **chancellery** (Bundeskanzleramt). In addition to winning the design competition for the government quarter, Schultes (with Charlotte Frank) was also given the commission for this, its largest building. During the course of planning, the chancellery was much enlarged, so that in the end it dominates, more than it fits into, the east–west band of buildings. Germany is a large country, with a large government, and as elsewhere the head of government has gathered greater powers in recent years. Nevertheless, when the building was completed in 2001, foreign observers tried to divine a message about a return to the assertiveness of Bismarck's (if not Hitler's) day, scrutinizing the building's style as well as its size for a political message. It is inevitably compared to Albert Speer's designs, but it displays anything but traditional classicism. Indeed, it is quite odd looking. Its irregularly shaped front columns evoke organic forms (a message reinforced by the actual trees planted atop some of them) and enhance an open and transparent appearance. A walk along the side wings, with their enormous round windows (which suggested the irreverent nickname 'chancellor's washing machine'), will give you a sense of the building's dimensions. It extends westward all the way to the Spree. The westernmost portion of Schultes's federal band, the raised chancellery garden, lies across the river.

A few steps downstream from the rear of the chancellery is the back of an older building. It faces south toward John-Foster-Dulles-Allee and is best approached from there. The **Haus der Kulturen der Welt** (House of World Cultures) was built in 1957 as the Berlin Congress Hall, an American gift to the city's international building exhibition that year. The wide curve of its roof makes the building, the work of the American architect Hugh Stubbins, a distinctive sight, and soon gave it the curious nickname 'pregnant oyster'. The roof was designed as an act of bravado modernism, resting its entire weight on only two points. In 1980 it collapsed. The repaired building reopened in 1987 as a showcase for exhibits and performances featuring non-European cultures. The same year, a Henry Moore sculpture, *Large Butterfly*, was installed in front. The nearby 68-bell carillon was added in 1988, when this was still a quiet place far from the center of government.

Long before that, however, this was part of the bustling city. In the 1740s Frederick the Great opened the Tiergarten to the public and granted two Huguenot immigrants the right to sell refreshments in tents. The lane along the river, from here to where the chancellery now stands, was named In den Zelten ('in the tents'). Over the years, their establishments grew into large pleasure gardens and amusement parks, and stone buildings supplanted the tents. From 1919 to 1933, one of them was home to Magnus Hirschfeld's famous Institute of Sexual Science. Hirschfeld was a scholar who believed that sexual behavior, and homosexuality in particular, deserved serious attention, but it was the sensational aspects of his work that attracted the most attention. In his memoir, Christopher Isherwood recalled viewing the institute's collection of bizarre sexual paraphernalia not long before the Nazis sacked it. From here you can wander south into the Tiergarten or catch a bus west toward Zoo or east to the Reichstag and Unter den Linden.

4

Friedrichstrasse and the Newspaper Quarter

FRIEDRICHSTRASSE has always been the main axis of Friedrichstadt, the largest of the seventeenth-century town extensions. It extends for two miles from the Oranienburg Gate south to the Halle Gate. In the eighteenth century it was a residential street, but in the second half of the nineteenth century nearly all the old houses were replaced by four- and five-story commercial buildings and it became Berlin's main commercial artery. At the end of that century, however, the fashionable shops moved elsewhere, first to nearby Leipziger Strasse and soon far to the west around Kurfürstendamm. Narrow Friedrichstrasse became associated with the demimonde, a place of mysterious doorways, dark passages, dubious commercial transactions and the illicit pleasures of the night. (It will only reinforce your German stereotypes to tell you that this underworld was actually well organized, with guilds protecting the interests of upstanding criminals – the portrayal of them in Fritz Lang's great film *M* is not far from reality.) That reputation remained until the Second World War, and was enhanced by some of Berlin's most celebrated art, such as Ernst Ludwig Kirchner's dramatically colored expressionist portraits of women on the street and George Grosz's sharply satirical drawings of debauched profiteers. Kirchner's pictures, like the apocalyptic scenes of his contemporary Ludwig Meidner, have often been seen as expressing a horror at the city's decadence, but they exude the fascination that drew the

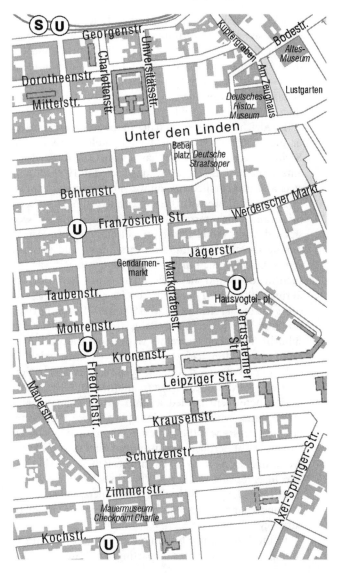

Brücke expressionists to this inexhaustible source of sensory excitement and primitive energy. Wartime bombing and the Communist takeover left Friedrichstrasse a shadow of its former shadowy self. Only in the 1980s did the GDR begin a major redevelopment here, little of which had been completed by the time the regime collapsed. Since then the street has been born anew.

Friedrichstrasse station dates to the Stadtbahn project of the 1880s, when a rail line was built across central Berlin. A recent renovation has restored the finest elements of the station as it was reconstructed in 1919, with its steel and glass arched hall above and the muted expressionism of its lower structure, decorated with dark glazed brick and black terracotta. The interior is now well stocked with shops aimed at commuters transferring among U-Bahn, S-Bahn, streetcars, buses, and regional trains. During much of the twentieth century it was not such an open and airy place. The construction of the Berlin Wall in 1961 marked a decisive break in the station's history. From then until 1990 the GDR authorities carefully segregated the S-Bahn trains to the eastern suburbs from those traveling west across the Wall. As a result the station had to be extensively subdivided in order to prevent visual contact – and even the penetration of sound – from one section to another. Travelers transferring here were herded around corners and up and down stairs, without knowing quite where they were. Friedrichstrasse was the busiest border crossing between East and West Berlin, the only one not directly at the Wall. Westerners arriving by U-Bahn or S-Bahn were shunted into lines leading to enclosed booths where uncommunicative border guards checked their papers, collected visa fees and changed the mandatory minimum amount of currency.

In the 1960s a new building was put up north of the station to process those departing the 'capital of the

German Democratic Republic'. It still stands; after unification it was turned into a nightclub, which took the name informally given to the departure hall: **Tränenpalast**, or 'Palace of Tears'. This was a place of leave-takings, whether by Westerners hurrying back before their day visas expired, or by Easterners departing on rare – and perhaps permanent – westward journeys. The building's large glass façade gave it a hint of transparency, but once inside visitors were funneled into the warrens of the station. The Palace of Tears may yet yield to some grand new project, but this triangular site between the station, the river, and Friedrichstrasse has a long history of failed development plans. Most famous was an architectural competition just after the First World War, organized by an eager developer. The winning design, which remained unbuilt amid Germany's subsequent economic troubles, has been forgotten. Not so one of the losing entries, a revolutionary glass skyscraper sketched by Ludwig Mies van der Rohe, which made its way into every history of modern architecture.

Not to be forgotten at Friedrichstrasse station are the underground connections. A long-planned north–south S-Bahn line to complement the east–west one was finally completed underground during the Third Reich. Also connecting here is an older U-Bahn line, the U6. Both of these remained in use, in a limited way, during the years of division. As with the elevated S-Bahn line, visitors could travel into East Berlin on the underground lines before officially crossing the border at Friedrichstrasse. Since the underground lines crossed into West Berlin both north and south of here, they were operated by the Western transit authority and passed across Eastern territory on their way from West to West. They stopped at Friedrichstrasse but not at the other stations under East Berlin. (Another subway line, the U8, passed from West to West without stopping in the East at all.) These were the so-called 'ghost stations' that Western passengers could view through their train windows, stations where no trains stopped and no one set foot except the border guards who could be seen patrolling the platforms. There was one exception, and that was even odder. In the early 1970s, after Walter Ulbricht was deposed as East German leader, his name no longer merited official mention. The only public facility in Berlin that bore his name, Walter Ulbricht Stadium, was renamed World Youth Stadium (Stadium der Weltjugend). Unfortunately, a subway stop – one of the ghost stations – had been named after the stadium. Workers entered the closed station, changed the signs visible only to passing Westerners, and then sealed it up again. (The stadium itself is now gone, and the station is called Schwartzkopffstrasse – all of these icons of divided Berlin are entirely normal stations again.)

Passengers disembarking from S-Bahn or U-Bahn at Friedrichstrasse found their way to the border crossing – there was, of course, no other way out. However, the intersection of the different Western lines meant that it was possible, and often convenient, for Westerners to change trains at Friedrichstrasse on their way from one point in the West to another (no border crossing was necessary). The GDR's unending thirst for hard currency led it to exploit this peculiarity by establishing 'Intershops' on the rail platforms, where Western goods, notably liquor, coffee and chocolate, were sold for West German marks at prices typically just below those available in West Berlin. (Lenin, after all, had predicted that the communists would be able to sell the capitalists the rope with which they would hang themselves.) It was technically illegal, but not at all difficult, for Westerners not actually traveling from the East to buy these goods. Western alcoholics were regular visitors here, along with others willing to violate the taboo of supporting the Communist regime.

An earlier and darker history is recalled by a plaque mounted on the exterior wall of the station where the tracks pass over the street (on the west side of Friedrichstrasse). It reads: 'Shortly before the end of Hitler's criminal war two young German soldiers were hanged here by inhuman SS bandits.' This is typical GDR language (the plaque was first put up in 1952); the facts, however, are accurate. Roving SS fanatics executed many deserters in the final days of Hitler's Reich. The GDR embraced deserters as antifascists; the West was hesitant to view them as anything but deserters. Soon after the fall of the Wall the GDR plaque vanished, and since then it has been replaced more than once by a private initiative.

Across the street, facing the Palace of Tears, stands the Admiralspalast. Behind its bold 1910 neoclassical façade, with ornate white marble reliefs, parts of the building date to 1874, when it was built as a luxurious bathhouse. It was later converted to a theater, best known in the 1920s for its revues featuring the chorus line of the English 'Tiller Girls', which a critic later recalled as 'a remarkable combination of ecstatic Prussian drilling, French carnality and English cleanliness', whereas some intellectuals likened the synchronization of bodies to the American assembly lines of Henry Ford. During the GDR years this was the home of Die Distel (The Thistle) cabaret, whose shows became required viewing for the politically astute in East and West because they tested the limits of permitted political speech. The crumbling building's future is uncertain.

For better or worse, **Friedrichstrasse** is now a showcase of the policy of 'critical reconstruction' that guided Berlin's redevelopment after 1990. In order to bring back urban density and variety (and also to maximize available real estate for development) planners decided to restore the prewar width of the street, and to fill every meter of street frontage with buildings – limited, however, to a cornice height of 22 meters, the typical size of buildings a century ago. Architectural guidelines for the inner city required masonry façades, rectangular windows and identifiable entrances, all in the interest of preserving a traditional streetscape – a good thing for pedestrians, since you pass lively rows of shops, not endless blank walls. The prevailing architectural style of the new Berlin is, however, not nostalgic: geometric forms prevail, not fussy decoration. You are likely to find it cold, monotonous or generic, but it might be judged a success in its goal of turning ravaged central Berlin into an ordinary European city. Those who hoped that the new Berlin would be anything but ordinary are disappointed, but after decades of disruption we should not begrudge the Berliners a little European normality.

Certainly the area just south of the rail station has become much more normal. After the buildings on its south side were destroyed in the war, the East Germans left the area as a park. Taking the policy of critical reconstruction to its logical extreme, post-reunification planners decreed that since this was, historically, built-up space, it would once again be just that, and in the early 2000s new commercial buildings replaced the park. A comparable story played out on the other side of the street. Here, in 1978, the East Germans had completed one of their showcase buildings, the 300-foot-high black and white International Trade Center, visible from far away (including from West Berlin). Its presence was intended to symbolize the economic power of the little East German state; in hindsight, it might rather be seen as symbolizing the bankrupt state's desperate search for hard currency. It is still there, but well concealed. Its lower two stories originally extended far forward, forming a complex of cafés and shops that were among the most-frequented public spaces of East Berlin. That front wing was torn down in 1999 to make way for new buildings that hide the East German tower.

In the next block, new buildings encroach on the street to recreate a pedestrian arcade. The building on the right side conceals a hotel, built as one of the GDR's hard-currency hotels for Western visitors. Ordinary East Germans were not welcome in this hothouse of financial and political intrigue, hard-currency prostitutes, and poorly kept secrets. It still stands, behind a new façade. The next block on the right side contains the only stretch of covered arcade that survived the war. The first building, on the corner of Mittelstrasse (Friedrichstrasse 153) was opened in 1900 for the 'Polish Pharmacy' (Polnische Apotheke), which obtained a royal patent and established itself on this site in 1682. Number 155–156, extending to the corner of Unter den Linden, is the 'Swiss House' (Haus der Schweiz), built in 1936 by a Swiss architect and effectively blending into the neighborhood's grand stone architecture while also displaying the simpler grandiosity of the Third Reich.

At the corner of Friedrichstrasse and Unter den Linden, the nineteenth-century commercial corridor met the eighteenth-century royal promenade. Elegant gathering places included the original Café Kranzler, on the southwest corner, Café Bauer, on the southeast, and Café Victoria, on the northeast. For all the attempts to recreate vanished Berlin attractions, this corner has not attracted cafés again since 1990. Shoppers are drawn indoors on Friedrichstrasse, strollers to other parts of Unter den Linden (see Chapter 1). The covered sidewalk arcade continues south from Unter den Linden, lined on both sides of Friedrichstrasse with square stone-faced pillars. Those on the left side are a product of 1990s postmodernism, but that building echoes the bland pomposity of its neighbor on the right side of Friedrichstrasse, built by the GDR in 1987. This Grand Hotel was the last of East Berlin's hard-currency hotels, intended as an oasis of pampered comfort in the hard-edged socialist capital and

also as the anchor of a revived Friedrichstrasse. Its rusticated ground-floor sandstone facing and vaguely historicist decoration tried to echo the early twentieth-century
commercial buildings that remain nearby.

After German unification in 1871, German finance
increasingly centralized its operations in Berlin.
Behrenstrasse became the center of the banking quarter
and is still lined with imposing stone buildings. To the
west, past Glinkastrasse, a complex of connected buildings housed the biggest bank of all, Deutsche Bank. Like
its surviving competitors, it took its wartime profits to the
safer confines of the American occupation zone after
1945; since then, most big German banks have been
headquartered in Frankfurt. Beyond Behrenstrasse,
Friedrichstrasse 165, on the right side, was built in 1888
for the Munich brewery Pschorr. In 1990 it was taken over
by East German opposition groups and, as the 'House of
Democracy', hosted many lively discussions before and
after German reunification. The scruffy democrats were
later eased out to make way for higher-rent uses. Number
166, next door, was built in 1899 in a different idiom, with
a red sandstone façade richly carved in Gothic forms. The
next building, number 167–168, by Bruno Schmitz, has
another heavily laden stone façade and is only a little
newer (1905), but is noticeably more modern with the
vertical thrust of its massive pillars supporting relatively
wide bays. It was also built for a modern use: an automat
restaurant – not quite the fast food we know and hate, but
a proud contribution to speedy, industrialized life along
the bustling street. The food was prepared in an upstairs
kitchen and loaded into vending machines in an elegant
vaulted hall at the rear of the ground floor.

The block on the other side of Friedrichstrasse, from
Behrenstrasse to Französische Strasse, offers a good
example of the officially encouraged new mixed-use
architecture. (The city prescribed minimum percentages

of floor space devoted to office, commercial and residential use; in most cases developers kept the residential portion as small, and invisible, as possible, but there are indeed apartments atop most of the new buildings.) Old buildings at the corner of Behrenstrasse were incorporated into the new project, which was planned by Josef Kleihues, the most important architect of the new Berlin school, who, however, shared the work with three other exponents of this severe, conservative modern architecture. Kleihues designed the Four Seasons hotel at the back of the block, facing Charlottenstrasse; Max Dudler, the apartment house on Behrenstrasse; Hans Kollhoff, the office building at Friedrichstrasse and Französische Strasse; and Jürgen Sawade, the black office building on Französische Strasse.

Although the new construction is supposed to rekindle Friedrichstrasse's urban flair, there was no intention of reviving the prewar tawdriness that is actually the street's most storied past. On the contrary, the goal was to create an elegant shopping quarter in short order, and the next three blocks on the left side of the street were the core of the 1990s redevelopment. They are connected internally through an underground passage lined with shops. Thus the appearance of traditional city blocks is to some extent deceptive; from the inside, it looks more like a mall. At the corner of Französische Strasse is the most striking of the 1990s buildings, Jean Nouvel's glass-clad Galeries Lafayette department store. Inside, inverted glass cones bring in light from above. One reason the building stands out is that the developers managed to circumvent the rules requiring masonry façades. When it was only a few years old, it seemed to clinch the arguments of the opponents of glass architecture: panes were frequently shattering and raining glass on passers-by; all the windows had to be replaced. Next to Nouvel's building is one by the American architect Henry Cobb, which combines horizontal lines with angular protrusions from the façade. Only when lit up at night does it convincingly evoke 1920s expressionist architecture. Its neighbor displays the square forms typical of its architect, Oswald Matthias Ungers.

The rear of the Ungers building faces Gendarmenmarkt. Before coming this far, however, you might take Französische Strasse to the northern end of Gendarmenmarkt. Adjoining Sawade's new office building is an old structure at Französische Strasse 47, its red sandstone façade and black stone doorway pillars incorporated into the new complex. It was built in 1895 as a wine shop and delicatessen by the proprietors of the adjoining Borchardt restaurant, long the favorite of diplomats and nobles. The original restaurant building is gone, but the name has been revived for a new restaurant in the old shop. Gendarmenmarkt has in fact become the center for elegant dining in Berlin, including other restaurants that have revived old names, notably Lutter und Wegner, once the haunt of E.T.A. Hoffmann (who lived on the square), Heinrich Heine and other writers.

Gendarmenmarkt was originally the central market of Friedrichstadt. It was named after the army regiment 'Gens d'Armes', whose stables surrounded the square. In the late eighteenth century, Frederick the Great had the stables moved elsewhere and decreed that the square would display his capital at its most elegant. He sponsored the expansion of the two churches here, the construction of a theater, and the erection of imposing buildings all around the square. The churches are all that remain from the eighteenth century, however, and little more remains from the following century and a half. Nearly every building here was grievously damaged in the war and those that were not leveled stood in ruins for decades. Only in the 1970s did the GDR begin restoration. With the return of capitalism, this has once again become a center of wealth and elegance – or, as some would persist in seeing it, of ostentation and pretense. Although the ghosts of communism would seem to have been entirely banished, the GDR's restoration has left its mark. Facing both sides of the square at its northern end are buildings left from the GDR's attempt to adapt its prefabricated construction to the neo-historicist styles fashionable in East and West in the 1980s. The building at the corner of Französische Strasse and Charlottenstrasse is a particularly gaudy example.

Facing the north end of the square is the former headquarters of a major bank, the Berliner Handelsgesellschaft; later it housed the GDR State Bank. Französische Strasse 42 was designed by Alfred Messel in 1899 and is in many ways a typical stone bank building of its age, with its stone façade with a rusticated lower story, very high ceilings, and massive pilasters. This is actually the rear of the building; it faces Behrenstrasse (number 32–33), the banking street, rather than the square. The building has recently been renovated for yet another bank, with new wings on Behrenstrasse intended to synthesize modern architecture and Messel's classicism by setting a vaguely classical concrete grid in front of a glass façade.

Gendarmenmarkt covers three Friedrichstadt blocks, with one building on each. Here at the north end stands the **French church**. It, like the so-called German church, comprises two distinct parts. The original church, entered from the west side, was completed in 1705 for the French Reformed community. Its design was based on the destroyed main church of the French Protestants (known as Huguenots) in Charenton, near Paris. Its most recent restoration leaves its external appearance close to the original; the interior is less thoroughly restored. After 1685, when Louis XIV revoked the Edict of Nantes, which had permitted Protestants to practice their faith in France, the Great Elector invited many to settle in remote and sparsely populated Brandenburg. Of the 20,000 who came, six thousand settled in Berlin, making them nearly a quarter of the city's population. As the Great Elector had hoped, their commercial and technical skills contributed a great deal to Brandenburg's economy. They and their descendants also loomed large in the city's cultural life for centuries to come, and their influence is apparent in the many corrupted French words in Berlin dialect. In a 'Budike' (boutique), for example, a Berliner might seek to ease his 'Deez' (tête) during hard times by purchasing some 'Muckefuck' (mocca faux, or ersatz coffee).

After 1780, when Frederick the Great demanded a grander square, his architect Karl von Gontard added the east wings to both churches. They were intended purely for display, comprising narrow domes set on bases high enough to make them visible from afar. Their height and distinctive form established the pair of domes among Berlin's iconic symbols. The dome end of the French church houses a small museum displaying the history of Berlin's French community. Upstairs, at the base of the dome, a café offers a comfortable view of the area. Up more steps are a grander view as well as a working carillon.

Frederick the Great's theater in the center of the square was replaced in 1801 by a new building by Langhans, which burned down in 1817. Karl Friedrich Schinkel was given the job of replacing it with the state theater (**Schauspielhaus**) you now see, completed in 1821. The foundation, some walls, and the six Ionic columns of Langhans's front portico survived the fire and, with typical Prussian frugality, Schinkel was required to fit his structure into those existing pieces. Within those constraints, Schinkel adapted classical forms to a flow of interconnected spaces that justify the label 'Romantic classicism'. He reinforced the east–west axis fronted by the portico with a raised central section of the building, which contains the auditorium and stage. Schinkel was an important stage designer as well as an architect, and he worked with the writer Johann Wolfgang von Goethe to develop an intimate theater, with a thrust stage and dramatic painted backdrops. (The GDR's renovation altered the interior, and it reopened in 1984 as the Konzerthaus, a concert hall.) The grand external staircase became the focal point of the square, but it was intended only for use by bourgeois patrons. Nobles drove their carriages under the stairway, and the king used a special side entrance. A later addition, in the axis of the theater entrance, is Reinhold Begas's 1871 monument to the dramatist Friedrich Schiller, which the GDR returned to its original spot in 1988 – Schiller having proved to be suitable fare for all theatrical ideologies. The great leftist director Leopold Jessner had declared a new direction for the Schauspielhaus with his 1919 production of Schiller's *Wilhelm Tell* drenched in revolutionary symbolism. The theater remained a prominent institution even into the Third Reich, with Hermann Göring putting the great actor Gustav Gründgens in charge of it in 1934. Gründgens's work here is variously remembered for extraordinary productions and abject collaboration – the latter view of him fictionalized in Klaus Mann's *Mephisto*.

Because the north church was the French church, its counterpart has always been known as the **German Church**, serving the fusion of Lutheran and Calvinist Protestantism that was the state religion of Prussia. (The churches are usually called 'Französischer Dom' and 'Deutscher Dom'. The German word 'Dom' usually means cathedral, but in this case it refers to the domes.) The church was designed in 1701 by Martin Grünberg in an unusual pentagonal form with five round bays. Restoration of the ruin was begun by the East Germans in 1983 but was not completed until 1996. In the interior, the scars of wartime damage have been left visible. The building now houses a permanent exhibition, 'Questions Put to German

History', which documents the difficult history of democracy in Germany over the past two centuries.

Various stories give the 'authentic' origin of the name Mohrenstrasse ('Moor Street'), as the street on the south side of the square has always been called. All the versions credit one or more Africans who lived here as either soldiers (in a musical corps) or servants. Facing this end of the square is another ostentatious late-GDR building, a hotel opened just after reunification. A short distance to the east along Mohrenstrasse are the **Mohren colonnades**, a remnant of a much older Berlin. Here was the seventeenth-century fortification wall, which was surrounded by a watery moat. The bridge across the moat was rebuilt in 1787 with a decorative colonnade on each side, framing a grand entrance into the city. (Two other such colonnades have been re-erected on new sites; this is the only one in its original location.) It was designed by Carl Gotthard Langhans, with sculpture by Gottfried Schadow and his workshop, a few years before Langhans and Schadow collaborated on the Brandenburg Gate. After the moat was filled in the nineteenth century, the colonnades remained, and still remain, as the entrances to newer buildings. Behind the colonnade on the south side now resides the federal justice ministry, in a row of restored buildings. Just beyond, the typical zigzag form of the seventeenth-century wall is still apparent in the angular form of Hausvogteiplatz, named after the city jail that once stood here. In the nineteenth century this became the center of the Berlin clothing industry, which was dominated by Jewish entrepreneurs.

Jerusalemer Strasse leads from Hausvogteiplatz south to **Leipziger Strasse**. Here you encounter urban development on a very different scale. The GDR cleared away what little remained along this stretch of Leipziger Strasse, formerly a busy commercial street, and after 1969 lined it with high-rise apartment buildings. In typical modernist fashion (and that of Soviet bloc modernism in particular) the greatly widened street was lined with two-story buildings for shops and other non-residential uses. Here this showcase project had a special function: it provided a spatial and visual screen between the city center and the Berlin Wall, and more particularly obscured the view of the Axel Springer tower (see below). The high-rises have been renovated and given new 'skins' since 1990. In line with the prevailing policy of urban reconstruction, a more drastic modification of the streetscape is planned. As you look to the west, you will see that the street has been much narrowed by new buildings near the intersection of Friedrichstrasse. Something similar may eventually happen here as well, leaving the high-rise towers in the courtyards of new buildings. Across the street and a short distance east (left) stands a reconstruction of another of the colonnades that once marked the entrance to the fortified town. This is a replica of the southern half of the 1776 original. Next to it is another replica: of a milepost in the form of an obelisk, which was originally erected near here in 1730.

Make your way south, away from Leipziger Strasse, to where the eastern end of Krausenstrasse (the next street south) meets the diagonal Axel-Springer-Strasse. On the east side of Axel-Springer-Strasse, at the corner of Kommandantenstrasse you reach the former course of the Berlin Wall. It turned the corner here, as you can see from the double row of paving stones that marks its course. A few steps farther down Axel-Springer-Strasse – you are now in the former West Berlin – number 44–50 is the headquarters of the insurance company Barmer Ersatzkasse, a renovated 1912 office building and a 1993 annex. A plaque in the entryway of the newer building gives some information (in German) about the memorial behind. Here stood a grand 1800-seat synagogue opened in 1891. As was typical, the synagogue stood in the courtyard and was only partly visible from the street. After a fire gutted it on Kristallnacht in 1938, it was confiscated for use as a grain warehouse. It was badly damaged in the war, razed in 1956, and long forgotten. The courtyard memorial by the Israeli artists Zvi Hecker, Micha Ullman and Eyal Weizman is conceptually complex but visually simple. It is intended both to resemble a page from the Talmud and to incorporate reminders of different periods in the history of the site. Thus the main elements of the memorial, the rows of white benches standing in the grass, represent the original building – they stand where benches stood in the synagogue – as well as graves. The trees and bushes around them grew up during the decades of postwar neglect, thus they represent the destruction and its aftermath, while at the same time they have been arranged to form parts of a Hebrew prayer text. The present is represented by the entry itself, the emergency access required by fire regulations.

If you cross the street back to Schützenstrasse and head west, you enter the former **newspaper district**, home to the press syndicates that dominated German journalism until the Nazis removed their editorial independence as well as the Jewish families that headed the best of them. In 1929 the city's fifty-one dailies, with their screaming headlines, thunderous editorials, vehement reviews, trenchant social commentary, lively sports coverage and sensational crime reports, were the essential currency of politics and culture in the streetcars and cafés. Berlin papers lack the national clout they once had, but this remains a newspaper town, with several dailies as well as a small army of vendors who hawk the next morning's editions late at night in the pubs. One remnant of the vanished world stands at the corner of Jerusalemer Strasse. After 1871 Rudolf Mosse made the *Berliner Tageblatt* a respected and successful newspaper, housed in a 1903 sandstone building, of which the Schützenstrasse wing still stands. After its corner was damaged in street fighting during the abortive 1919 revolution – the Communists knew the importance of seizing the presses – Mosse hired Erich Mendelsohn and Richard Neutra to renovate it. Their dramatic tower-like corner (recently restored) was an early trend-setting example of modern commercial architecture. Mendelsohn later used similar curved fronts and horizontal bands of windows for entire commercial buildings, establishing a style of corporate modernism that has conquered the world.

This was a forgotten corner of East Berlin, since visitors were discouraged from coming so close to the Wall. However, it was one of the places where the GDR permitted itself a display of pride in its 'antifascist protective rampart'. Across Jerusalemer Strasse from the Mosse building stood a memorial to the border guards killed in shootouts at the Wall. After 1989 it was vandalized, neglected and finally removed. From 1966 to 1991 Schützenstrasse (ironically, the old Prussian name means 'sharpshooter street') was named Reinhold-Huhn-Strasse after a border guard killed near here in 1962. A glance south on Jerusalemer Strasse shows you what the GDR feared. Just across the former no-man's-land looms the tower of the Axel Springer press syndicate. The golden tower, oriented north to south, has stood here since 1966; the darker east–west high-rise was attached to it in the 1990s. Across the top of the older tower, an electronic band ran news headlines visible in East Berlin. After the war Axel Springer built up West Germany's largest newspaper chain, best known for the tabloid *Bild*. Passionately committed to reunification – for decades he required his newspapers to refer to 'the so-called German Democratic Republic' – his decision to build a large complex here was at once a vote of confidence in walled-in West Berlin, a defiant gesture in the direction of the communist East and a commitment to the historical continuity of the divided Berlin newspaper quarter. The Springer tabloids' vicious verbal attacks on the political left (which still continue, in an attenuated form) made their headquarters the target of demonstrators, particularly after an assassination attempt against the student leader Rudi Dutschke in 1968, when the building was firebombed.

If you remain on the former East Berlin side, a long block west brings you to Markgrafenstrasse. The entire block enclosed by Markgrafenstrasse, Schützenstrasse, Charlottenstrasse and Zimmerstrasse was rebuilt according to a design by the Italian architect Aldo Rossi (who died in 1997, before it was completed). The project incorporates the one extant building and adds eleven new ones of greatly varied proportions, decor and especially color. As an architectural theorist, Rossi's musings about the symbolic elements and spatial forms of the traditional European city greatly influenced recent Berlin architects, notably Josef Kleihues, although Rossi's work is bolder and more playful than that of his German followers. Some of the façades here recall the Italian rationalism of the earlier Rossi; others, a more ornate historicism drawing on old Berlin buildings; and, oddest of all, there is (facing Schützenstrasse) a copy of the courtyard façade of Rome's Palazzo Farnese, its Renaissance details extending even to its rear elevation. Rossi arranged the interior of the block in ways that recall the unplanned density of nineteenth-century Berlin neighborhoods, with several irregular courtyards scattered among wings of the new buildings.

The Berlin Wall ran down Zimmerstrasse, on the south side of the Rossi block. One of the Wall's most agonizing crises occurred here. On 17 August 1962, 18-year-old **Peter Fechter** tried to flee across the succession of crude barriers that the Wall then consisted of. A guard shot him, and he fell just short of the final barrier, bleeding and crying for help. American soldiers and West

Berlin policemen did not dare step across the line to help him; they threw first-aid packets, but he was too weak to pick them up. Photographers snapped his picture, which flashed around the world, but too late to help him. After an hour East German guards, who up to then had not stirred, carried away his lifeless body. On the south side of the street, West Berliners put up a wooden cross as a crude memorial to Fechter. The memorial stood for three decades, until post-unification development claimed the site. The cross is now in the nearby Checkpoint Charlie museum; a red stone marks its location. A short distance away stands a new memorial, a rusted-steel pillar set into the sidewalk.

South along Charlottenstrasse, the restoration of the eighteenth-century block structure of Friedrichstadt, and of its early twentieth-century scale of construction, is apparent all around. Here on the former West Berlin side of the Wall, it began in the 1980s. Many of the projects of the International Building Exhibition (Internationale Bauaustellung, or IBA) were built in this area, which had been neglected after the Wall went up. An example of restoration of the streetscape that, however, breaks with the standard 22-meter building height, is the headquarters of the GSW housing company on the south side of **Kochstrasse**. In the 1960s plans called for widening Kochstrasse into an urban highway that would have obliterated the old Friedrichstadt. A square 19-story tower, set far back from the street and now barely visible from it, was built in 1961 with those plans in mind. Three new wings were added in 1998 by the Anglo-German architectural team of Matthias Sauerbruch and Louisa Hutton. Above a dark, slightly curved three-story dark building facing Kochstrasse rises a squat but colorful oval tower as well as a curved 22-story slab, oriented north–south like the older Springer and Leipziger Strasse towers nearby. The building is a prominent example of energy-efficient 'green' architecture. The west side of the tower has a double glass skin, leaving an open shaft for interior air to be carried upward and vented through the roof, whose curved shape is not merely a sculptural gesture but also designed to pull the air upward. The west side is also fitted with individually adjustable metal shades in bright and varied colors. When the afternoon sun shines on them, they seem to reflect a spectacular sunset.

Across Charlottenstrasse to the west are the offices of the leftist newspaper *tageszeitung* (or *taz*) in a new building attached to an old one. The grand office building from 1909 (Kochstrasse 18) is premodern in its ornate decoration but modern in its verticality and especially its large windows. The traditional importance of the next corner west, where Kochstrasse meets Friedrichstrasse, is apparent in the stone façades of the two surviving old commercial buildings on the western side. Just south (left) on Friedrichstrasse is a stone building with a tall tower, an unmistakably Third Reich version of modern architecture, with a stone eagle still perched on top. It was built for the employment office (which it has housed since the war) but upon completion in 1940, it was turned over to the new minister of munitions, Fritz Todt. Next to it, number 32–33 is a 1987 IBA building by the Austrian architect Raimund Abraham (now best known in New York for his Austrian Cultural Forum) with bold sculptural angles across the façade and a semicircular courtyard elevation. Kochstrasse 62–63, at Friedrichstrasse, is a design by Peter Eisenman and Jaquelin Robertson from 1986. The two slightly different vertical planes juxtaposed on the façade display an intellectual game typical of Eisenman. The rectangular grid of the eighteenth-century Friedrichstadt is aligned approximately, but not exactly, north–south and east–west. One of the planes of the façade corresponds to history – the Friedrichstadt block – while the other displays geography by lining up true east and west. Even if you understand the building, it is difficult to love it.

Part of this building is an extension of the **Museum Haus am Checkpoint Charlie**, a private institution founded in 1963 by a human-rights campaigner, Rainer Hildebrandt, to publicize the injustice of the Wall and other oppression in East Germany and beyond. It quickly became a tourist attraction, a cluttered and sensational contrast to staid public museums and memorials. Since the disappearance of the Wall, it has if anything become more popular, since tourists can no longer look at the functioning Wall. The museum is chock full of documents, film clips and historical artifacts of German division – including, since 1990, a collection of objects salvaged from the defunct Wall and GDR border security apparatus, among them segments of brightly painted Wall. The most popular exhibits are the paraphernalia of spectacular escapes across the Wall, acquired after their use, such as hand-stitched Red Army uniforms, cars with secret compartments and homemade hot-air balloons. The museum shop does a lively business in Wall literature and souvenirs.

The famous **Checkpoint Charlie** was at the corner of Friedrichstrasse and Zimmerstrasse. The name is simply U.S. armyspeak for Checkpoint C (checkpoint Alpha having been the crossing between West and East Germany, and Bravo marking the entrance into the far side of West Berlin), contrary to the Russian poet Yevgeny Yevtushenko's assertion (in a poem) that it was 'named in honor of a black soldier'. This was the official crossing point into East Berlin for foreigners. (West Berliners and West Germans crossed elsewhere.) In the early days of the Wall it was the scene of confrontations that drew the world's rapt attention, notably in October 1961, when, in one of the tensest moments of the Cold War, American and Soviet tanks faced each other, barrel to barrel, across the demarcation line painted on Friedrichstrasse. It was by no means inconceivable that World War III might have started here, although many diplomats agreed with U.S. Secretary of State Dean Rusk, who fumed about 'the silly confrontation at Checkpoint Charlie brought on by the macho inclinations of General Clay', the hardline American commander.

On the American side (this having been the U.S. sector) the central feature of the checkpoint was a wooden guard hut in the middle of Friedrichstrasse. In a 1990 ceremony crawling with foreign ministers, it was lifted away (and given to the Allied Museum out in Dahlem) but a replica has since replaced it. The Checkpoint Charlie museum has also put some historic artifacts on outdoor display, notably the once-ubiquitous four-language signs warning that 'you are now leaving the American sector'. Across Zimmerstrasse, in East Berlin, a large area was devoted to guard houses and bays where cars were searched. The foreigners who crossed the border passed through a sluice of corridors and doorways in dingy temporary buildings, their papers scrutinized repeatedly before they were (if all went well) permitted to step onto the soil of 'Berlin, capital of the German Democratic Republic'. (There was no such thing as East Berlin on that side of the Wall.) All that has been torn down and replaced by new office buildings. With the Wall entirely gone here, it is difficult to imagine the mixture of drabness, tension and coal smoke that pervaded the atmosphere, as evoked in many spy novels. Nevertheless, coaches arrive frequently to discharge tourists seeking to absorb a little of the historic ambience, while eager entrepreneurs of various ethnicities offer to sell them pieces of concrete purporting to be from the Wall, along with other authentic detritus of the Soviet empire.

The block on the west side of Friedrichstrasse in West Berlin, across from the museum, was redeveloped in the

1980s as part of IBA. Rem Koolhaas designed the most striking building here, with a diagonal overhanging cornice. It was intended to provide extra space for the U.S. army, but by the time it was completed in 1990, the Americans were pulling out, and the building was remodeled for commercial use. Take Zimmerstrasse to the left, following the former course of the Wall, and you pass between old buildings that for decades were blighted by the presence of the Wall. Those in West Berlin faced it only a few feet away; those on the other side were used exclusively by security forces. The restored brick and terracotta entry of number 90–91 takes you into a vaulted vestibule, all that remains of a municipal market hall from 1886. After its interior was rebuilt, it reopened in 1910 as Konzerthaus Clou, Berlin's largest dance hall, with room for four thousand people. In the late 1920s, the growing Nazi Party began to rent it for mass meetings. On May Day, 1927, as socialists and communists were demonstrating nearby, Hitler gave his first Berlin speech here, introduced by the new Berlin Gauleiter, Joseph Goebbels. In February 1943, as the last Jewish forced laborers were rounded up for deportation to the death camps, many were first brought here. The dance hall was destroyed soon after. However, you can walk through the courtyard, past industrial lofts, and emerge at Mauerstrasse 81.

Mauerstrasse runs diagonally northward from Checkpoint Charlie. Its name, 'Wall Street', has nothing to do with *that* wall, however. Berlin has seen many walls in its history. The one referred to in this name, its course still apparent in the irregular course of the street through the rectangles of Friedrichstadt, was the original western wall of seventeenth-century Friedrichstadt. On the east side of Mauerstrasse is an open space called Bethlehemkirchplatz. Here stood a round eighteenth-century church built for the community of Bohemian Protestants who found refuge from persecution in Berlin. The church's ruins were leveled in 1963, but in 1994, the foundations were excavated, then reburied, with the outline of the church now marked in red bricks and black and white stones paving the square. The enormous Claes Oldenburg sculpture, a colorful ball, is supposed to evoke the few possessions of a refugee.

The adjoining building is by the aged American celebrity architect Philip Johnson, who studied in Berlin in 1929 and variously revered both Mies van der Rohe and the Nazis. The developers used Johnson to advertise their project, erecting a billboard with a twelve-foot-high portrait of Johnson extending above it. Berliners take architects very seriously, but in this case matters took a bizarre turn: one night in 1995, persons unknown 'kidnapped' the Johnson figure, and later sawed off one ear and sent it to a local newspaper. Johnson's granite and glass building (which not even he seems to have admired much) covers an entire (albeit small) block. Its eastern side faces Friedrichstrasse, at about the point where a pre–1989 visitor would have stepped from the checkpoint onto the grey and forlorn street and surveyed its neglected buildings and vacant lots. In its final years, however, the GDR began to spruce up Friedrichstrasse, even at this end. Cross Krausenstrasse to the north, and across Friedrichstrasse is one of the best examples of the GDR's redevelopment. Between two renovated buildings (the 1909 structure at the corner of Leipziger Strasse is especially notable) was inserted a new one, designed by Peter Meyer and completed in 1988. Among architects who retain some sympathy for the conditions under which their GDR colleagues worked, this building has been widely praised for avoiding both gaudy historicist decoration and the mindless application of prefabricated panels. Meyer had to use the standardized, prefabricated panels for the upper residential stories, but he varied them with his liberal use of glass surfaces and of color. Without resorting to historicist decoration, he adapted his forms to the dimensions of the adjoining old buildings. Back across the street, the entire block is fronted by the largest building that survived the war in this area, a Third Reich office building from 1935, which in most respects resembles 1920s modernist structures but was also built with an air-raid bunker in its cellar as well as a specially hardened roof.

A century ago, the corner of Friedrichstrasse and Leipziger Strasse was Berlin's major commercial intersection. That claim was staked in the name of the subway station, Stadtmitte (city center), where the east–west U2 and the north–south U6 cross. Otherwise, few traces of that era remain here, although the dimensions of the old streets (their widths as well as building heights) are being restored. While Friedrichstrasse has been made a shopping street again, Leipziger Strasse's future is less clear.

5

Wilhelmstrasse: from Bismarck to Hitler

WHEN FRIEDRICHSTADT was expanded in the early eighteenth century, the newly created Wilhelmstrasse became a favored address for nobles' town palaces. In the nineteenth century, Prussian government ministries took over most of the palaces, and Wilhelmstrasse became synonymous with government, especially the foreign ministry. If you walk south along Wilhelmstrasse from Unter den Linden and the Adlon hotel, past the new British embassy, you reach the area where the ministries stood. The most important – the chancellery, the foreign ministry, the Weimar presidential palace – were on the right side, and they are all gone. Only two old buildings of lesser importance remain, the former Prussian ministry of education (1903) at Behrenstrasse, and, farther down, the former home of the imperial civil cabinet (1898). Explanatory signs along the street (in German) identify the sites of former ministries and important events connected with them. This street echoes with ghosts of Germany's era as a Great Power, from Bismarck in 1871 to Hitler in 1945.

The first cross street south of Unter den Linden is Behrenstrasse, which was extended west of Wilhelmstrasse after 1990 to relieve the crush of traffic at the Brandenburg Gate. The entire area west of Wilhelmstrasse, down to Potsdamer Platz, was long known as the ministerial gardens: the gardens of the old palaces extended back to the town wall at what is now Ebertstrasse. In his memoirs, Albert Speer recalled that Hitler often walked across the gardens from his chancellery and residence to the

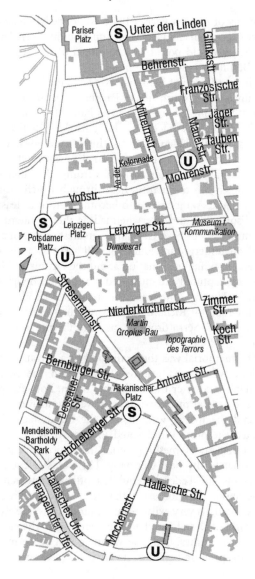

Academy of Arts on Pariser Platz, where he had installed Speer's agency in charge of replanning Berlin. There Hitler and Speer would pore over the model of the grotesque new Berlin they planned to build.

The north side of Behrenstrasse faces the backs of the buildings on the south side of Pariser Platz, including the apartment wing of Frank Gehry's bank. The south side of the street is something else entirely: the five-acre expanse of the **Memorial to the Murdered Jews of Europe**. Construction began in 2003 on its 2700 rough concrete pillars, ranging in height from half a meter to four meters, an undulating field through which visitors are invited to wander, and to become lost, or at least to feel disoriented and overwhelmed as they contemplate the immensity of Nazi Germany's greatest crime. In addition, an underground building will serve as a visitors' center, providing information about the victims and how they were captured and murdered. The original design was developed by two Americans, the architect Peter Eisenman and the sculptor Richard Serra. Amid the heated debates that followed, Serra dropped out, and Eisenman revised the design alone.

The memorial was the brainchild of a private organization, which was granted this site in the former no-man's-land after the Wall came down. Both the project and several proposed designs were controversial. In the end the matter went before the Bundestag, which debated the project and voted to approve it in 1999 – a step that says something about the importance of the memorial to the new Germany. This colossal endeavor represents the Federal Republic's official statement in stone about the Holocaust that its predecessor regime perpetrated. Its very existence is remarkable: where else in the world has a state built a huge memorial to the victims of its own crimes? But one wonders if it is Germany's place to speak on behalf of its victims. Quite apart from the unsurprising reluctance of some Germans to recall the Holocaust, it is hard to see how an overwhelming memorial serves as an answer to an overwhelming crime. You must judge for yourself whether the memorial carries the emotional power expected of it. Its location on valuable land in the heart of Berlin is certainly significant, but it is also arbitrary, unlike many memorials that have been placed on historically burdened sites (notably the Topography of Terror, see p. 126). It has been claimed that the memorial sits atop Hitler's bunker, but it doesn't. However, preliminary work on the site accidentally uncovered another bunker, which turned out to be Joseph Goebbels's personal command post, at the northeast corner of the site, behind what had been his official residence, where Hitler witnessed Diana Mitford's marriage to the British Fascist leader, Sir Oswald Mosley, in 1936. The bunker remains intact under the memorial, unmarked and inaccessible.

Most of the remaining space in the former ministerial gardens was set aside for the Berlin offices of the federal states. Five buildings representing seven states have been built along the new east–west street In den Ministergärten. Some have ground floors open to the public with exhibitions related to the host states. The other states chose to move elsewhere, leaving unused space, so the fate of the southern end of the gardens, between the new buildings and Vossstrasse, remains uncertain. This was the site of Hitler's chancellery, the bombastic structure intended to intimidate state visitors, built for him by Albert Speer in 1938–39 along the north side of Vossstrasse, extending from Ebertstrasse nearly to Wilhelmstrasse, where it was attached to the rear of the existing chancellery that had served Bismarck and his successors. The war-damaged building was leveled in 1949, but its large underground bunker remained in place. The eastern half of the bunker was obliterated by the East Germans in the 1980s to make way for the foundations of the apartment buildings that now stand there. The western half was then under no-man's-land and remains untouched. A small rise near the corner of Ebertstrasse, long visible all by itself in no-man's-land (and perhaps visible still) marked the covered entrance to that bunker.

Contrary to what you often hear, however, this was not the famous **Führerbunker**, Hitler's personal command bunker, constructed deep underground in 1943. Its unmarked site lies near the eastern end of the street In den Ministergärten – more precisely, under the land-scaped parking area behind the apartment building An der Kolonnade 8. A long shelf of books has been written about the banal events here in the days leading up to Hitler's suicide in 1945, as the Red Army closed in: the comings and goings of loyal and disloyal satraps, the Führer's endless, self-pitying diatribes (delivered to his loyal secretaries and anyone else who was available), his marriage to Eva Braun before their joint suicide, Joseph and Magda Goebbels' suicide after they took care to murder their six children. Hitler's biography and person-ality were taboo in the GDR, and after the Wall went up in 1961 all information about the bunker was kept strictly secret. In the late 1980s, however, the East Germans began constructing apartment buildings on the long-neglected site, and excavation for their foundations required demolishing much of what was underground. How much of the original bunker remains is unclear. Road construc-tion in 1999 accidentally uncovered a portion of it, nearer the surface than anyone expected to find anything. (It was promptly covered up again.) Just as East Germany never acknowledged its presence, current officials decline to permit any designation of the site, declaring that they do not want to create a pilgrimage site for neo-Nazis. It seems unlikely that the lack of a sign will deter neo-Nazis. (Please keep this book out of their hands.) At the same time, it is fair to ask whether attention to the site (even in guidebooks) serves any purpose other than the glorification of Hitler's evil genius.

Perhaps it is fitting that the site of Hitler's chancellery is now occupied by a kindergarten. These buildings present the GDR's standardized, prefabricated construction at its most elegant. Apartments this close to the Wall were only available to the privileged and politically reliable; it was said (plausibly) that clearance from the Stasi was required to live here. The notorious East German secret police has now given way to a special government office in charge of its records, which maintains a permanent exhibition just off Wilhelmstrasse, accessible from the vacant lot at number 55, and also from the corner of Mauerstrasse and Französische Strasse. This 'Informations und Dokumentationszentrum der Bundesbeauftragten' (free admission) offers a thoroughly documented exhibit (in German) that also displays artifacts of the Wall and the pervasive domestic spy network.

Across Wilhelmstrasse from Vossstrasse was Wilhelmplatz, once the heart of the government quarter, now vanished under the 1970s Czech embassy and a 1980s apartment house. On its east side was the Kaiserhof hotel, also gone. When it opened in 1875 it was considered Berlin's first hotel up to modern European standards. In 1878 it hosted Bismarck's 'beer evenings' during the Congress of Berlin, when more refined prime ministers were shocked at the gluttony of their host, stuffing shrimps into his mouth with one hand and cherries with the other. Bismarck and Britain's Disraeli hit it off famously, however. By the 1920s the Kaiserhof was less fashionable than newer hotels such as the Adlon and the Esplanade, but it served as Hitler's Berlin headquarters until he was able to move across the street into the chancellery. The Mohrenstrasse subway station was originally called Kaiserhof, a measure of the hotel's importance. The station was rebuilt after the war with richly colored marble carried from the ruins of Hitler's chancellery. Go down to the station platform to get the closest thing to a visit to Hitler's office.

Just north of Wilhelmplatz was one of the many vanished palaces that once housed government offices. This one, which had been renovated by Schinkel for a Prussian prince, was taken over in 1933 by the **Ministry of Popular Enlightenment and Propaganda**, newly created for the diabolical Joseph Goebbels. Goebbels sponsored two major extensions of his ministry, which still stand as typical examples of the stripped classical style used for Third Reich public buildings. One wing faces the former Wilhelmplatz at its northeast corner. A more substantial façade faces Mauerstrasse; take Mohrenstrasse to Mauerstrasse and turn left. The GDR, seemingly oblivious to fears of ideological contamination, placed its press office here. Now it is the federal labor ministry. The long Mauerstrasse façade is little changed except that the massive walls at each end were originally topped by huge stone eagles.

You will find the only extant eighteenth-century houses in Friedrichstadt by taking Taubenstrasse (across Mauerstrasse from the labor ministry) a block east to the corner of Glinkastrasse. This pair of pastors' homes built in 1739 gives you a sense of the old city that disappeared in the boom years around 1900. This was the Friedrichstadt of, for example, the intellectually sparkling salons run by the Jewish women Henriette Herz and Rahel Levin two centuries ago. If you follow Glinkastrasse (or Mauerstrasse; they merge) south, back across Mohrenstrasse and on to Leipziger Strasse, on your left at the corner is a 1905 building with an oval tower, a fine product of that later age. A mosaic over the entrance preserves the name and logo (including an emu) of the firm that built it, the Württembergische Metallwaren

Fabrik. Across the intersection is the **Museum für Kommunikation**, in a massive building constructed in the 1890s for both the imperial postal authority and the postal museum, which has now acquired a broader name and mission. Its exhibits on the history of activities that were long the preserve of the post office – mail and telecommunications – will interest aficionados of stamps and of old gadgets, but, this being Berlin, more earnest matters are available for contemplation as well. A recent exhibit documented the East German government's use of the mail and telephones to spy on its citizens. Admission is free, and the rotunda is itself worth a visit.

Leipziger Strasse leads back to Wilhelmstrasse and the grand entry of Hermann Göring's **Reich Ministry of Aviation** (1936), one of the Third Reich's largest government buildings. Göring, like his rival Goebbels, was a bureaucratic empire builder keenly interested in self-aggrandizement. His ministry was in charge of civil aviation as well as the newly created air force he headed, and the building included grand ceremonial spaces for the ostentatious social events he liked to preside over in his many splendid uniforms. Göring chose Ernst Sagebiel to design it. Until 1933, Sagebiel was the chief assistant to the great modernist architect Erich Mendelsohn. Unlike Mendelsohn, he was not Jewish, and so he had the option of accommodating himself to the new regime. Here he has clearly turned his back on the concrete-and-glass modernism so hated by the Nazis. The façade is, instead, clad in stone, with recessed windows, an overhanging cornice, and stout window frames to give an impression of solidity. Nevertheless, by Third Reich standards this is a very modern building, steel framed and sparsely adorned. It is also enormous, with four miles of corridors connecting two thousand rooms.

At the end of the war it was largely intact, unlike most of the government quarter (partly by luck and partly thanks to its bomb-resistant construction), so it was quickly pressed into use by the new Communist regime. In fact, the ceremony officially establishing the German Democratic Republic was held here in 1949. In the early 1990s it was home to another important institution, the Treuhand, the agency charged with the difficult task of liquidating East Germany's state-owned property. (During that time the head of the Treuhand was assassinated by left-wing terrorists; in his memory the building is now named Detlev-Rohwedder-Haus.) Subsequently it was renovated for the finance ministry, preserving, however, much of its original appearance inside and out.

The building's origins are no secret, but, despite complaints from local activists, no memorial recalls its role as the headquarters for the bombers that destroyed Guernica, Warsaw, Rotterdam and Coventry. Instead, it is the GDR that is recalled here. Inside the pillared loggia facing the corner, a mosaic mural from 1950 commemorates the founding of the GDR (replacing an original mural portraying soldiers). Its portraits of happy and vigorous workers offer a classic example of socialist realism. Despite its unfashionable style and content, it will be preserved. However, in front of the loggia, a newer memorial recalls the GDR in a different way. On 17 June 1953, twelve thousand East Germans assembled here to demand higher wages, free elections and German reunification. Violence followed and the nationwide uprising was crushed by Soviet tanks. The day left dozens dead, and it shattered the Communist leaders' hopes of winning the people's hearts and minds. Brecht, no hero, protected his privileges with a pro forma endorsement of the repression, but party hacks' justifications of it provoked him to write a sarcastic poem wondering that if the people had lost the confidence of the government, 'would it not be easier for the government to dissolve the people and elect another?' West Germany made 17 June a national holiday (superseded after 1990 by 3 October, the day of German reunification). Berlin's official memorial to the 17 June uprising is the long pool of water here, designed by Wolfgang Rüppel and dedicated in 2000. Under the water is an enormous photograph of the protesting workers. The lines in the stone pavement run from the pool to the building's pillars, thus linking the memorial and the older mural – that is, two contrasting views of the defunct German workers' state.

In the next building on Leipziger Strasse sits the **Bundesrat** (federal council), the lesser but far from powerless upper house of parliament, which represents the sixteen federal states. It was originally supposed to get a new building opposite the Reichstag, but was placed here instead to save money. This building was completed in 1904 for the upper house of the Prussian parliament, which comprised nobles and high officials named by the king. The rich sculptural decoration of the stone façade was intended to reinforce the upper house's status relative to the lower house, which is behind it. In December 1918, amid the postwar turmoil of revolution, a national assembly of workers' and soldiers' councils met here. The new buildings of Leipziger Platz extend westward from here (see Chapter 6).

If you return to Wilhelmstrasse, you can walk the full length of the former aviation ministry, including the recessed court of honor halfway down. Its square travertine pillars were once topped by stone eagles clutching swastikas, but otherwise the building looks much as it did when Göring came and went. At its far end you reach one of the few pieces of the Berlin Wall left in place – battered by souvenir hunters in 1989, but still standing. The spray paint on the near side is also from 1989: this was the East Berlin side of the Wall, which remained pristine until the Wall was abandoned. To the left, the Wall formerly followed Zimmerstrasse toward Checkpoint Charlie (see Chapter 4). At the corner of Wilhelmstrasse and Kochstrasse, one block down, is a striking 1988 red-brick building by Aldo Rossi, with green highlights, tiny gables, and a massive corner pillar.

On the right side of Wilhelmstrasse, behind the segment of Wall, is an apparently neglected lot, but its neglect has been carefully planned. This is the grounds of the exhibition with the significant name **Topography of Terror**. Here, at the southern edge of the Wilhelmstrasse government quarter, the Nazis established their center of terror. Facing Wilhelmstrasse was an eighteenth-century palace that Schinkel had renovated for a Hohenzollern prince, after whom it became known as the Prinz-Albrecht-Palais. In 1934 it became the headquarters of the Security Service (Sicherheitsdienst, or SD), a powerful division of the SS headed by Reinhard Heydrich. The extension of Zimmerstrasse beside the palace, now Niederkirchnerstrasse, was then called Prinz-Albrecht-Strasse, a name that became feared after 1933, when the newly established national police force, the Gestapo (short for Geheime Staatspolizei, or Secret State Police) moved into the former school of applied art at Prinz-Albrecht-Strasse 8. The next year, the Gestapo came under the control of Heinrich Himmler, head of the elite party guard, the SS (Schutzstaffel), which ultimately controlled all German police forces as well as programs aimed at establishing racial purity, including the concentration camps. In 1934 Himmler moved SS headquarters from Munich to a former hotel next to Gestapo headquarters. The Gestapo converted sculptors' studios in the basement of the art school into jail cells. Suspected dissidents were brought here for questioning and, often, torture, before being released or sent on to one of the new concentration camps.

After the war, West Berlin leveled the badly damaged buildings, including the architecturally distinguished palace. When the Wall went up, this became one of those quiet and forgotten corners of the divided city. Part of the land was leased to a dealer in construction debris, which left the piles of dirt that still remain. Next to it was a business that permitted people to drive cars without a license; the rutted paths are still visible in places. In the early 1980s, as West Berlin began to redevelop this neglected corner of the city, a few citizens called attention to the site's forgotten history. Their pressure led the city to authorize excavations and then a temporary exhibition that opened during the city's 750th anniversary celebrations in 1987. A small building, erected over the excavated foundations of an SS kitchen, first housed the exhibition Topography of Terror, which soberly documented the espionage, repression, and terror directed from here, and explained their links to all of Berlin and all of Europe. Outdoor signs scattered over the remainder of the site identified the structures and authorities once found here.

The exhibit quickly became too popular, and too critically acclaimed, to be simply closed, and it remained unchanged for a decade amid uncertainty about further plans. In 1997 it was replaced by an even more provisional exhibit, as work began on a permanent building by the Swiss architect Peter Zumthor. Its construction was accompanied by more controversy, as costs grew out of hand. The second temporary exhibition may, therefore, last another decade, with its documentary signs lined up against the excavated foundation walls along Niederkirchnerstrasse. Here you can read about the Gestapo and SS and about many prisoners – some famous, most not – who suffered here. (The texts are all in German; however, you can buy on site an inexpensive but substantial English version of the catalog.) Those broken walls will remain in place, as will the paradoxically preserved neglect across much of the site – the idea being to recall the postwar decades of willful forgetting along with the Nazis' crimes. Zumthor's elegantly simple building, extending east–west across the site, will provide much better facilities for a permanent exhibition, but it may give the exhibit more of the formality of a traditional museum at the expense of the deliberately maintained 'open wound' that attracts accidental visitors.

Next to the Topography of Terror stands the only old building remaining on this side of Niederkirchnerstrasse, the **Martin-Gropius-Bau** exhibition hall, built as a museum of applied art in 1877–81 by Martin Gropius and Heino Schmieden. Its delicately detailed brick and terracotta façade resembles Schinkel's Bauakademie. It was a ruin until its restoration was completed in 1981; since then, it has housed large temporary exhibitions. The interior rooms, only partly restored in full detail, surround a large central court. In 1981, the main entrance was placed at the south, the former rear of the building, since the original entrance stood an arm's length from the Berlin Wall, its course now marked by a copper band in the street.

Directly across Niederkirchnerstrasse stands the building completed in 1899 for the lower house of the Prussian Parliament, which was popularly elected, but by an unequal franchise (limited to male taxpayers, with more weight given to the votes of those who paid more taxes). Since 1993 the parliament of the city-state of Berlin (**Abgeordnetenhaus**) has met here. Some members were unhappy that their address would be a street that the East Germans had renamed after Käte Niederkirchner, a Communist agent captured and killed by the Nazis. They failed to get the street's name changed, but the more conservative parties left the street address off their letterheads.

Niederkirchnerstrasse ends at Stresemannstrasse. Here the Wall turned right toward Potsdamer Platz. If you turn left, however, across the street, at the corner of Dessauer

Strasse, you will see a greenish building twisted at unusual angles. This design by the deconstructivist architect Zaha Hadid was completed in 1994 but is a product of the 1980s IBA redevelopment; such radical architecture was not welcomed in 1990s Berlin. On the near side of Stresemannstrasse stands a 1931 modernist tower. When it was new, this Europahaus dominated the view toward central Berlin from Askanischer Platz, which served mainly as a forecourt for **Anhalter Bahnhof** (Anhalt station), one of Berlin's busiest rail terminals. The station was damaged in the war but remained in use until it was razed in 1959. A small piece was left standing and has become a symbol of postwar Berlin's broken connection to its past. The name now designates only this mute fragment, plus an underground S-Bahn station. Little trace remains of the bustle that once prevailed here. Across Stresemannstrasse stood the Excelsior, Berlin's largest hotel, with 600 rooms. A tunnel under Möckernstrasse connected the station with a building that still stands, an enormous 1930s post office built in a hybrid of modernist functionalism and the monumental architecture typical of the Third Reich.

Anhalter Bahnhof, like the other terminals, stood just outside the eighteenth-century wall, which ran down Stresemannstrasse. A small section has been excavated and restored in the middle of the street, a little farther down. On the area once covered by the train shed stands a new tentlike structure. The Tempodrom, a large venue for alternative music and theater, long occupied improvised quarters in the Tiergarten, where the chancellery now stands. This permanent building retains the appearance of a tent as well as the fluid connection between indoor and outdoor spaces. It was designed as an ecologically sensitive structure by Frei Otto, best known for his lightweight buildings for the 1972 Munich Olympics. One of its facilities is the Liquidrom, where bathers can relax to carefully coordinated sound, light and water, including underwater music.

Near Schöneberger Strasse, and visible from here, stands a 1943 above-ground concrete bunker, built as an air-raid shelter. Too costly to remove, it stands, ugly and graffiti-laden, as a reminder of the past. Its interior has been turned into a 'Gruselkabinett' (chamber of horrors), which includes an exhibit about bunkers. Schöneberger Strasse takes you from Askanischer Platz to the Landwehrkanal. Just to the left on Hallesches Ufer stands a pumping station from 1876, one of the original structures from the city's first comprehensive sewage-disposal system – an engineering project of enormous significance, since it replaced open street sewers and cesspools, rescued the Spree from the stinking mess it had become, and drastically reduced deaths from cholera and typhoid. The station was replaced by a new one, next door, in 1972, but it retains its original equipment. It serves another function as well, one that has given it the name **Lapidarium**. The battered remnants of the last emperor's monumental row of marble statues, the Siegesalle from the Tiergarten, now rest inside. Brandenburg's rulers back to the twelfth-century Margrave Albrecht the Bear huddle here, deprived of the dignity of their smooth finish, high pedestals, and generous spacing. Each figure was originally flanked by smaller statues of distinguished personages from their eras; many of those statues rest outside. Also here are several Tiergarten statues that have been replaced by copies.

Cross the canal at Schöneberger Strasse and you enter an area dominated by the former rail yards of the Potsdam and Anhalt stations. In the 1990s they became the staging ground for the massive construction project at Potsdamer Platz. The new north–south rail tunnel emerges here as well. Above your head, just down Schöneberger Strasse, are intersecting U-Bahn lines.

(Yes, U-Bahn means subway; no, neither line is underground here.) The station name Gleisdreieck means 'track triangle'. It's not a triangle, but it originally was: an intersection was built into Berlin's first U-Bahn line so that some trains coming from the west could turn north here into the city center, while others continued east. However, in 1908 the spectacular project failed in a spectacular accident, and the triangle was subsequently rebuilt as an ordinary crossing.

Follow Tempelhofer Ufer (the quay) left to Trebbiner Strasse, under the elevated U-Bahn, and you reach the **Deutsches Technikmuseum**, an institution devoted largely to the technology of the railway age. The new wing facing the canal, however, features the twentieth-century technology of aviation: mounted on top is one of the American 'raisin bombers' that brought food rather than destruction during the 1948 Berlin airlift. Behind it, in older buildings, you will find displays suitable for children and adults alike. Many large rooms are devoted to manufacturing technologies and to nineteenth- and twentieth-century electronics, displaying, explaining and permitting experiments with a vast array of machines. One small building houses a reconstructed brewery; outdoor displays include windmills and water pumps. The largest part of the museum, however, is devoted to the railroads. In the former locomotive roundhouses of the Anhalter Bahnhof's freight depot you will find locomotives and other rail cars from all eras, including the Third Reich.

6

Potsdamer Platz and the Kulturforum

POTSDAMER PLATZ is one of the most storied places in Berlin, where the vicissitudes of the twentieth century have been most dramatic: from prewar bustle, to postwar desolation and division, to renewed commercial vigor. Whereas the past is visible and palpable in so many sites across the city, however, the layers of history are not on display here. You need to bring along your memories of the old days – memories that will be secondhand, for nearly all of you, courtesy of film, photographs, and text. The new masters of Potsdamer Platz invoke the past, but not in the subversive and provocative ways it is done elsewhere in Berlin. This history is much closer to the Disney version. Nevertheless, it is a place not to be missed, even as you take account of the ghosts that have been banished from sight but not from mind.

This is actually a double square, and the older and more clearly defined space is **Leipziger Platz**, which marks the western end of Leipziger Strasse. It is another of those old places in Berlin where everything is new. While the Wall stood, it belonged to no-man's-land. And even during the 1990s little was built here, while Potsdamer Platz proper, across the street, was perhaps the world's most famous construction site. From 1995 to 2000 Leipziger Platz was occupied by a large temporary building, the Info Box, devoted to telling the story of Potsdamer Platz's new construction. Construction was a tourist attraction, and the Info Box rivaled the Brandenburg Gate as the city's most visited site. At the turn of the millennium, however, the Info Box came

132

down, and construction began on its site. Leipziger Platz finally took shape – and that shape is an octagon. This was the outline of the original drill ground laid out in the eighteenth century just inside the Potsdam Gate, a counterpart to the square by the Brandenburg Gate and the circle at the Halle Gate. By the early nineteenth century it was the home of elegant townhouses; a century later, it had become a commercial hub. The most famous building here, at the northeast corner, was Alfred Messel's flagship department store for the Wertheim chain, a landmark of modern commercial architecture. That building, like its neighbors, is gone, although its subterranean vault has become the techno music club Tresor.

The array of new buildings (including the Canadian embassy at the northwest corner) has restored the octagonal shape. Perhaps you will find that some of the long-lost elegance has been restored as well – that would be a pleasant surprise. Just beyond the octagon ran the eighteenth-century customs wall (and the twentieth-century Wall too), along what is now Ebertstrasse (heading north toward the Brandenburg Gate) and Stresemannstrasse (to the south). In the nineteenth century, many wealthy Berliners built their villas on the streets beyond – the Grimm brothers, for example, on Lennéstrasse. By the end of that century, however, this became a busy commercial district, centered on the intersection of several streets outside the former Potsdam Gate (framed by Schinkel's guardhouses until their destruction in the war), where the royal highway to Potsdam began. This intersection – and it was always just an intersection, not a proper square – became known as **Potsdamer Platz**. Much of the traffic between the old city center and the emerging western hub around Kurfürstendamm passed through this bottleneck, as did many people and vehicles on their way to and from the Potsdam and Anhalt rail stations. By the 1920s this was famous as the busiest

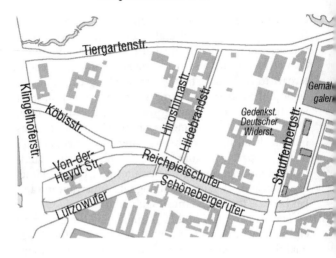

intersection in Europe. Traffic statistics do not bear out that claim, but the legend has overpowered mere numbers. The fame rests not on numbers but on the quality of the reporting: photographers and filmmakers captured the scene in memorable images; Berlin's clever journalists and essayists painted word pictures of a new metropolitan mentality; and the painters themselves did their part as well. Ernst Ludwig Kirchner's *Potsdamer Platz*, recently acquired by the New National Gallery, is the most famous of the Brücke expressionists' attempts to render the swirl of urban encounters in vivid blues and reds.

Now you, too, have the opportunity to join the crowds that again fight their way across the intersection. It's all quite well ordered, but don't look for guidance from the reproduction of Europe's first traffic light (from 1924, borrowing an American invention) – it is just for show, to remind you that you're not merely crossing a street: you're continuing a tradition. Also at the corner are the

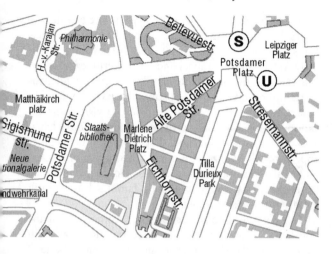

main entrances to the underground S-Bahn station. (There is an underground connection from here to the U-Bahn, but its platform is located farther east, under Leipziger Platz.) During the 1990s, platforms were also built for additional rail lines that may one day connect here. A great deal of the new Potsdamer Platz, in fact, is invisible under the ground, including parking garages and delivery streets as well as road and rail tunnels. Berlin's high water table made the first phase of construction here a special challenge. Divers, working deep underwater, affixed the footings of the complex.

Once again streets fan out from here. Between them stand several new office towers. The one on your right, between Ebertstrasse and Bellevuestrasse, was designed by Hans Kollhoff and Helga Timmermann and adjoins the Ritz-Carlton Hotel. Across Bellevuestrasse from it stands the curved glass tower of Helmut Jahn's Sony Center. Next to it are two more towers, both roughly triangular, with dramatic points facing the square. They belong to the Quartier DaimlerChrysler. The one next to Jahn's building is the square's most striking presence. Hans Kollhoff's design, with its dark brick facing, recalls early American skyscrapers and 1920s Berlin expressionism as well as the shiplike form of Fritz Höger's Chilehaus in Hamburg. Like many a postmodern pastiche, it looks best at twilight. For a small fee, you can visit an observation platform at the top of the building. To its left is a tower of similar size and shape, but a much lighter appearance, by Renzo Piano and Christoph Kohlbecker. Its angular form as well as its glass façade are intended to evoke Mies van der Rohe's famous but unbuilt Friedrichstrasse skyscraper.

The park next to it occupies the former site of the Potsdam rail station. Berlin's first rail line was built from here to Potsdam in 1838, and this remained one of the city's major stations until 1945. Across the park is another new office complex, the Park Kolonnaden. Its curved front recalls a famous building that once stood at this very site next to the rail station. Potsdamer Platz was known as a place of mass entertainment, and its most famous institution was Haus Vaterland, with a cinema and a ballroom as well as several themed restaurants, enabling Berliners to wander from Vienna to Bavaria to the Rhine, from Hungary to Turkey to Spain, from the Garden of Eden to the Wild West. Across Stresemannstrasse is an old Prussian government building that long stood alone on the East German side of no-man's-land. Next to it was (and possibly still is, depending on the course of development) the last remnant of the Berlin Wall at Potsdamer Platz. This was a piece of the eastern wall separating East Berlin from the death strip, not the wall that faced West Berlin – so its gaily painted surfaces date only to 1990, a reminder of the exhilarating chaos that shattered the eerie silence of no-man's-land.

Quartier DaimlerChrysler, stretching back from the Piano and Kollhoff towers, is the largest of the Potsdamer Platz projects. It comprises a large wedge of land between the park and Neue (new) Potsdamer Strasse – so called because the street was realigned after the war. However, the Alte (old) Potsdamer Strasse still runs a short distance back from the intersection (between the two office towers) and functions as the main axis of the complex. Daimler agreed to keep this relic of the old city, even saving (at great expense) the mature trees that line it. Facing it is the one surviving prewar building, Haus Huth from 1910. It was built on a small plot amid the dense fabric of old Potsdamer Platz, then later stood for decades alone. Its stone façade has been preserved as a tenuous link to the old days.

Renzo Piano drew up Daimler's master plan, which divides the complex into several small blocks, separated by narrow streets, with the intention of re-creating a traditional urban milieu. The plan is a product of compromises between the developer, which sought corporate signature towers, and the city, which demanded a pedestrian-friendly, mixed-use complex. There are in fact a substantial number of apartments here, tucked into the quieter corners, including some courtyards clearly intended to bring to Berlin the labyrinthine ambience of towns in Piano's native Italy. Most of the space is devoted to offices, however, and the office workers are in turn outnumbered by those who come here for shopping and entertainment. The heart of the complex is found not in the narrow streets but in the enclosed shopping mall that extends across several blocks on three levels (below, at and above the ground). It attracts crowds of, especially, East Berliners, but in most respects is quite an ordinary mall, with well-known American chains. Other familiar attractions are the multiplex cinema, behind the Kollhoff tower, and the domed IMAX cinema in a Piano building off Marlene-Dietrich-Platz.

Marlene-Dietrich-Platz, the open area at the dead end of Alte Potsdamer Strasse, is the focal point of the Daimler complex (if you view the complex from outdoors, that is; otherwise it might appear to be centered on the mall or the underground tunnels). Its name implies a connection between this new entertainment center and its vanished prewar predecessor, even as it honors the Berlin native who rose to cinematic stardom during those years. The irregularly shaped, sloped space can accommodate concerts and other outdoor events. Piano's musical theater encloses this end of the Daimler complex. A small opening offers a glimpse of the rear of Hans Scharoun's State Library (see below). Piano's metallic façade is intended as a visual transition to Scharoun's gold-roofed building. The opening creates the possibility of a connection to a new rear entrance to the library, which, however, does not yet exist. For now, the new unified Berlin and Scharoun's old West Berlin turn their backs on each other.

Other than Kollhoff's tower, none of these buildings particularly stand out from their neighbors, and many critics lamented the lack of stunning new buildings here, despite the talents of famous architects. The starkly modern interior of José Rafael Moneo's Hyatt hotel, just off Marlene-Dietrich-Platz, a striking contrast to the ostentatious Adlon on Pariser Platz, is tastefully understated – or is it merely bleak? Moneo also designed the Mercedes office building between the hotel and Neue Potsdamer Strasse. Three buildings on the Linkstrasse side, facing the park, are the work of Richard Rogers (Piano's erstwhile partner in the design of the Centre Pompidou in Paris). Each of Rogers's buildings features curved and twisted shapes on the upper stories, with glass façades lacking any of Piano's earth tones. Farther down Linkstrasse are two connected office buildings with odd trapezoidal windows, by Arata Isozaki.

Back to back with Isozaki's buildings, also at the Landwehrkanal end of the complex, is Piano's other tower, which serves as the headquarters of DaimlerChrysler Services. Like Piano's other buildings in the complex, this one is faced with the terracotta tiles that lend the area its dominant color. It is centered around a large and light atrium, open to the public and furnished with artworks: Jean Tinguely's busy sculpture *Meta-Maxi*, François Morellet's *Light Blue*, a lighted tube that meanders across the floor and walls; and Nam June Paik's *Nam Sat*. (Among the outdoor sculptures in the area are works by Robert Rauschenberg, Keith Haring, and Jeff Koons.) The glass and ochre structure is designed as a 'green' building, with a double skin and natural ventilating system that reduces the need for heating and cooling. The roof, like all others in the complex, collects rainwater, which is used to flush toilets and water plants. Outdoors, at ground level, water has also been made a central feature of the landscaping, with a channel running from Marlene-Dietrich-Platz to a large pool by Piano's tower. One odd result is the further isolation of the only other old building remaining here, a massive stone edifice from 1913 that faces the Landwehrkanal. Once it was surrounded by similar buildings; then, for decades, it stood alone in empty space; now it stands alone in a pool of water.

Viewed from the canal, the new buildings loom as an alien imposition separated from the city around them. Here, too, is the main entrance to the automobile tunnel that swallows cars in search of parking or passage to the north, as well as trucks making deliveries – thus keeping the side streets open for old-fashioned strolling. The U-Bahn also emerges from underground to cross the canal. (It's confusing: this is the 'underground' U-Bahn, not the normally elevated S-Bahn, which in this area runs underground.) The new station here, Mendelssohn-Bartholdy-Park (named after an older park on the other side of the station), is a convenient debarkation point for visitors to the Daimler complex, but it does not show the new development from its best vantage point.

If you return to Neue Potsdamer Strasse and cross it, either at Potsdamer Platz itself or near Marlene-Dietrich-Platz, you enter the gleaming expanse of the **Sony Center**, designed by the German-born and Chicago-based Helmut Jahn. This, too, is a wedge-shaped plot extending outward from the Potsdamer Platz intersection, but as urban design, it is the antithesis of Piano's Daimler complex: glass and steel, not earth tones; a monostructure, not architectural variety; soaring open spaces, not intimate streets and lanes. Critics of the Daimler project complain that it fails to achieve the intimacy and variety of the old city, whereas even Jahn's critics agree that he achieved what he set out to build. The Daimler complex may feel like a single entertainment center, with the interior streets as mere stage sets to accompany the mall, but in fact the streets are public property. The large open atrium of Sony Center, by contrast, is private property, where begging and even unauthorized filming are prohibited. Beyond the office tower at one end, the Sony Center consists of a ring of buildings surrounding a large oval space, covered by a soaring canopy roof but open at several points around the perimeter. It offers the ambience of a spacious shopping mall, but it is really something different: a combination of corporate billboard and entertainment center. There is little retail space, except for showrooms displaying Sony products. In addition to cinemas, there are numerous restaurants and cafés that invoke and market the old image of the *flâneur*. One is named Café Josty, after the best known café on the old Potsdamer Platz, where writers and artists observed the tides of humanity and machines in the 1920s. Another is called Billy Wilder's, after the Austrian native who got his start in journalism and film in 1920s Berlin but who made his name as a Hollywood screenwriter and director.

A more substantial recollection of the past is also here: the **Filmmuseum Berlin**, dedicated to the history of the German cinema in all its eras, although it also takes note of Berlin's links to Hollywood. The most famous of those links is of course Marlene Dietrich, and items from her estate are among those on display. Before Hitler, German cinema, whose Hollywood was Babelsberg (see Chapter 25), was Hollywood's strongest competitor. Even in the Third Reich, Babelsberg, under Goebbels's control, produced high-quality entertainment as well as high-quality propaganda. Since the war the highlight of cinematic life has been the Berlin Film Festival, now held here every February.

The disdain for history evinced by Jahn's high-tech design extends to the treatment of historic remnants. Sony was required to keep the one extant building on the site, a wing of the Hotel Esplanade, which was one of Berlin's grandest after it opened on Bellevuestrasse in 1911 – even the emperor frequented it. Its façade remains, but it is sheathed in glass and visually crushed by the several stories of new construction suspended over it. Two historic interior rooms were disassembled and moved to new locations in the complex, where they have been incorporated into new restaurants, but they look as if they are still on wheels. Nor will you find any sign of another historic building that once stood on Bellevuestrasse, the Third Reich's notorious People's Court (Volksgerichtshof), known for its brutal and summary treatment of dissenters. Its site remains unmarked.

On the other side of Bellevuestrasse, the block enclosed by Lennéstrasse and Ebertstrasse was known as the Lenné triangle. The corner of Bellevuestrasse and Ebertstrasse was briefly but memorably occupied by the elegant curved façade of Erich Mendelsohn's Columbushaus, completed in 1932, damaged in the war, further damaged in the 1953 uprising, and razed afterward. By that time, the triangle belonged to East Berlin, although it protruded awkwardly into the West. When the East put up the Wall in 1961, it did not bother to enclose the useless triangle, instead building its barrier along Ebertstrasse. The triangle thus ended up on the Western side of the Wall, but the West had no jurisdiction over it, so it was utterly neglected. In a land swap in 1988, West Berlin acquired the triangle, intending to complete a long-planned highway, but in the weeks before the official handover, Green-minded West Berliners occupied the land in protest and began counting rare plant and butterfly species that thrived in the renaturalized site. They were joined by anarchists who clashed repeatedly with the helpless West Berlin police along the borders of the sanctuary. When title to the land finally passed to West Berlin, police stormed the property, but the protesters scaled the Wall in the only mass escape from West to East. Eastern border guards escorted them away, served them breakfast, asked them to use a regular border crossing for their next visit to the German Democratic Republic, and released them to slip home on the S-Bahn. The next year, of course, the Wall was opened to everyone, and the open space was doomed.

Next to, but largely separate from, all the new commercial development are the scattered buildings of the **Kulturforum**, one of West Berlin's most important projects. The idea for the project, which was never fully realized, goes back to Scharoun's leading role in immediate postwar planning for the destroyed but not yet definitively divided city. He envisioned a decentralized 'urban landscape' spread out along the valley of the Spree, a concept which gave rise to West Berlin's more modest plan for a landscape of cultural facilities between the eastern and western nodes of commerce. The one visual acknowledgment of the Kulturforum in the new Potsdamer Platz is the roof of the Sony Center, which resembles the gold canopy of Scharoun's **Philharmonie** and that of the smaller Chamber Music Hall, which was completed in 1988 by his former assistant Edgar Wisniewski, based on a sketch by Scharoun. Also attached to the Philharmonie, and also based on Scharoun's design, is the Musical Instrument Museum (1984), a modest repository of beautiful objects.

Scharoun was a prominent modern architect already in the 1920s, known for his belief in organic architecture and his unusual curved forms – visible in Siemensstadt, for example (see Chapter 16). The roof of the famed Berlin Philharmonic Orchestra's home, completed in 1963, is distinctive in its color as well as its indescribable shape, which reflects the arrangement of the interior spaces. And the interior is the real treasure, best appreciated, of course, by obtaining tickets to a Philharmonic concert. The hall is spacious, with its airiness reinforced by white tiles and blonde wood, but its informal arrangement of spaces, combined with its extraordinary acoustics, dissolves the traditional separation between performers and audience and lends it a pleasant intimacy. It is formed from three superimposed pentagons, creating an arrangement of forms that defies all conventional geometry. The sections of seats (2200 in all) are arrayed at many different heights and angles in an architectural landscape of 'vineyard mountains'. They extend all around the stage, in Scharoun's adaptation of the theater-in-the-round to a concert hall.

The Philharmonic, which played until 1945 in a converted roller-skating rink on the other side of Potsdamer Platz, has ranked as one of the world's great orchestras since the 1880s, when it attained its first fame under Hans von Bülow, who was closely associated with Johannes Brahms as well as the young Richard Strauss.

(Bülow's connection to Brahms's great rival Richard Wagner was of a different sort, his wife Cosima having left him for Wagner.) Its later conductors, from Artur Nikisch and Wilhelm Furtwängler to Claudio Abbado and Simon Rattle, have generally ranked among the world's most influential musicians. The Philharmonie faces away from the Sony Center, toward Tiergartenstrasse. The side street here is named after Herbert von Karajan, the Philharmonic's longtime postwar conductor, revered by many as a great master, reviled by others as a great butcher of music. Karajan was also controversial because of his early and apparently enthusiastic membership of the Nazi party, which didn't hurt his thriving career during the Third Reich.

What is now the plaza in front of the concert hall was the site of a converted villa with the address Tiergartenstrasse 4. The code name T4, based on the address, designated the activities carried out here in the 1930s and early 1940s, when SS experts organized Nazi Germany's euthanasia program. During the 1930s the Nazi government inveighed ceaselessly against the burden of useless people housed in asylums and confidently asserted that their mental defects were hereditary, thus justifying their sterilization. After war broke out, T4 secretly began to murder mental patients across Germany, using carbon monoxide and then other poison gases. Word leaked out, and there were a few protests, resulting in the official (but not complete) suspension of the program. Meanwhile, by 1941 the T4 experts had moved on, applying their skills to the mass killings of Jews in the new extermination camps in Poland. In 1988, a large Richard Serra sculpture, *Berlin Junction*, comprising two curved steel plates with a narrow passage between them, was erected here. Local activists called attention to the history of the site, and, with Serra's approval, the sculpture was declared to be a memorial to the victims of T4. A plaque set in the ground explains the history of the site.

Across Herbert-von-Karajan-Strasse stands the **Museum of Applied Art** (Kunstgewerbemuseum), which displays a large collection of European crafts from the Middle Ages to the present: textiles, clothing, and tapestries; furniture, glass, and porcelain; gold and silver. The building was designed by Rolf Gutbrod, who was commissioned in 1968 to develop a master plan for a new museum complex on this largely vacant site. After years of controversy, however, this was the only one of his buildings to be completed. The architects Heinz Hilmer and Christoph Sattler were entrusted with a new master plan in 1988, with the goal of moving West Berlin's main collections of European art here from Dahlem. (Since then, of course, the East and West Berlin collections have been administratively – and in some cases physically – reunited, and the continued rearrangements will change the functions of some of these buildings in the coming years.) The new architects completed the buildings around the open 'piazzetta' that was the centerpiece of Gutbrod's plan. These include a central entrance hall as well as the Kunstbibliothek (an important art research library) and the **Kupferstichkabinett**, the enormous collections of prints and drawings, where a rotating selection of the finest works from many centuries is on display. Dürer, Rembrandt and Brueghel are only a few of the artists represented with numerous works.

Hilmer and Sattler's main contribution is the **Gemäldegalerie** (picture gallery), which, when it opened in 1998, reunited Berlin's great collection of European painting from the late Middle Ages through the eighteenth century. When the city was divided, so was the collection, although the West ended up with the lion's share, which was long displayed in Dahlem. Most visitors find the new building a pleasant enough place to view it; some architectural critics, less charitable, find it mediocre and nondescript. But the paintings are neither of those things. They are hung in two rows of connected galleries. On the right side are the northern European holdings, beginning with the great collection of early Netherlandish paintings, including three van Eycks: two portraits plus the glittering *Madonna in the Church*. Robert Campion and Petrus Christus are represented with several portraits, Hugo van der Goes and Rogier van der Weyden with important altarpieces. There is an odd double-sided painting by the mysterious Hieronymous Bosch, and one of Pieter Brueghel's crowded village scenes, this famous one portraying, in a deliberately and amusingly literal manner, many traditional proverbs. Also worth seeing is his portrait of two chained monkeys.

Early German painting is well represented, including much late medieval religious painting as well as Renaissance masterpieces. Among a variety of Lucas Cranach's works is his witty painting of the transformations wrought by the Fountain of Youth. There are several marvelous Dürer portraits and Madonnas as well as numerous works by Altdorfer, Hans Baldung Grien and Holbein. Seventeenth-century Flemish and Dutch painting is also richly represented, with many Rubens works, several van Dyck portraits as well as many by Frans Hals, and one of the world's largest collections of Rembrandts. (What was long Berlin's best known painting, however, the luminous *Man with the Golden Helmet*, was deemed a few years ago to be the work of a follower, not of Rembrandt himself.) The many Dutch landscapes and genre scenes include two Vermeers.

The galleries on the left side are not to be neglected. They contain mostly Italian works, an extraordinary collection, beginning with medieval altarpieces and two Giottos. There are Masaccio experiments in perspective, a Giorgione portrait of a young man, several Fra Angelicos and Botticellis, several Raphael Madonnas, works of Giovanni Bellini as well as portraits by Bronzino, Titian and Tintoretto, a striking Caravaggio and several Canalettos, among many others. Seventeenth- and eighteenth-century Spain, France and England are represented with a much smaller number of works, but they offer a brief, high quality glimpse of the likes of Velázquez, Watteau, Poussin, Gainsborough and Reynolds.

Outside the gallery you see the one old building that remains here: the small St Matthäus church by August Stüler (1846), an elegant example of the Schinkel school's neoclassicism, notable for its yellow and red bands of brick. It was gutted by fire in 1945; the exterior was carefully restored, but the interior is modern. Even before the bombers came, the church stood nearly alone. This area was designated the core of Hitler's North–South Axis, terminating near the Reichstag, so most of the buildings here were demolished around 1940. The one completed building on the new axis was the House of German Tourism. Its ruins remained until the 1960s, when they were razed to make way for Scharoun's **State Library** (Staatsbibliothek), which stands on the other side of Neue Potsdamer Strasse. The library, in fact, sits astride the old Potsdamer Strasse, which was rerouted.

This ungainly colossus is worth a trip across the street (or around from Marlene-Dietrich-Platz behind it). It was completed in 1976, after Scharoun's death. The mountain-like gold tower in the rear contains the book stacks (closed to the public), with the bright and spacious reading rooms arrayed in front. The qualities of the extraordinary interior spaces, which flow into one another at different heights and are connected by ramps and stairs, were shown to best effect in Wim Wenders's 1987 film *Wings of Desire*. They are a popular place to read and study, even for students who don't need the library's books. Since reunification, a seat in the reading room has been hard to come by. The cafeteria, at the rear, is also a legendary student hangout. It once commanded a broad but grim panorama of no-man's-land and East Berlin. The building was put up to house West Berlin's share of the great Prussian state library. Its books and manuscripts were stored in several places during the war, with roughly a third ending up in Western hands (and thus in this building), a third in the East, and a third lost. During the decades of division, neither side ever managed entirely to catalog its own holdings. Librarians in the West sometimes had to place discreet telephone calls to their colleagues across the Wall, asking them to check a prewar catalog for a collection in Western hands. Since 1990, the two buildings have been administratively reunited, but reintegration of the collections has proceeded at a snail's pace.

Back across Neue Potsdamer Strasse is the last of the Kulturforum's great buildings: the **New National Gallery** (Neue Nationalgalerie), so called because it was West Berlin's substitute for the old National Gallery on the museum island. Ludwig Mies van der Rohe, the master modernist architect, spent his formative years working in Berlin, until he emigrated to the United States in 1937, having tried but failed to secure commissions from the Nazi regime. This is his only major Berlin building, and the only one he designed for Berlin after leaving the city. It ranks with a handful of other famous monuments of Mies's mature style of glass framed by black, geometrically ordered steel – a style sublime in its purity, if lacking in warmth. It was completed in 1968, the year before Mies's death. The building takes advantage of its open site, but it is in no way an example of contextual architecture, and critics like to point out its similarity to Mies's earlier, unbuilt design for a Cuban rum company's headquarters. It sits on a broad granite platform, which encloses a large lower floor. The flat roof is supported only by a few thin steel pillars, leaving the sides of the building enclosed by little other than glass, so that the distinction between interior and exterior is visually dissolved and the roof appears to float in the air. The interior of the main floor is entirely free of pillars, interrupted only by two green granite slabs that are purely decorative. The open space is marvelously suited to certain kinds of special exhibitions – but only to certain kinds. The uncontrolled sunlight makes it unsuitable for the museum's permanent collection, which resides downstairs. After the museum island is fully renovated, in fact, this building may serve only as a hall for special exhibitions.

Two stairways lead down to the lower floor, which opens onto a terrace on the western side. Here you find the normal museum facilities (shop and café) as well as the paintings. Its holdings span the early to mid-twentieth century and include a great collection of German expressionist art (Nolde and Kirchner, for example) as well as expressionism's 1920s successor movements, Bauhaus and New Objectivity: savagely satirical works by George Grosz and Otto Dix, experiments in abstraction by Paul Klee and Lyonel Feininger, Hannah Höch and Kurt Schwitters collages, and geometric designs by Moholy-Nagy, Mondrian and El Lissitsky, along with European art from the immediate post–World War II years. Unfortunately, limited space means that only a small portion of the collection is on display at any one time.

The broad terrace outside is home to many sculptures, most from the time the museum was built. They include works by Henry Moore, Alexander Calder, Richard Serra and George Rickey. From the museum you can look across the Landwehrkanal down Potsdamer Strasse, where much of the prewar street remains intact. Directly across the canal, on the corner, is the battered façade of a 1929 office building, with its elegantly curved horizontal lines. At Potsdamer Strasse 96, just beyond, the

Wintergarten theater claims to continue the 1920s tradition of variety shows, with its dinner performances of
music, dance and circus acts. If you remain on the north
side of the canal, however, and follow it to your right,
behind the museum you reach a complex of one old
building and several newer ones, varied in form but not
in color. This is the Wissenschaftszentrum Berlin, a
research institute. The old Prussian building, facing the
canal, was built in the 1890s to house the administration
of the pioneering social insurance programs established
by Bismarck. In the 1980s the British postmodernist
architect James Stirling integrated it into his complex of
new buildings. Their bands of pastel color and stout
window frames are striking, as is the variety of shapes.
Each of the separate structures recalls an ancient form: a
basilica, a semicircular amphitheater, a stoa and a hexagonal tower resembling a bastion.

The next building along the canal, the **Shell-Haus**, fills
a highly visible site with what has long been one of the
city's most distinctive silhouettes. Emil Fahrenkamp's
office building, completed in 1931, is a steel-frame building with horizontal window bands and a travertine-clad
façade. What makes the building striking are the wavelike
curves, along which the building's height steps up from
five to ten stories.

Across the next side street, Stauffenbergstrasse, the
ministry of defense has embraced its own traditions by
occupying the former headquarters of the Wehrmacht.
The building facing the canal, built just before World War
I as the headquarters of the imperial naval office, was
extended back along Stauffenbergstrasse when Hitler tore
up the Versailles Treaty and rebuilt the German military
during the 1930s. Here played out one of the most
dramatic events in the history of the Third Reich, the
attempted coup against Hitler on 20 July 1944. After
Colonel Claus Schenk von Stauffenberg planted his bomb

under the conference table at Hitler's East Prussian head-quarters, he left the room, heard the explosion, assumed Hitler was dead, and flew back to his office here, where his allies had begun to seize the levers of power. After Hitler's voice on the radio proved he had survived, the tide turned against the conspirators, and Hitler loyalists seized them. Stauffenberg and several comrades were shot in the courtyard, and war and genocide raged on for many more terrible months.

You can enter that courtyard from the street that now bears Stauffenberg's name. (It was then called Bendlerstrasse, and the complex of Third Reich buildings is still sometimes called the Bendlerblock.) A statue of a shackled young man, by Richard Scheibe, was erected in the courtyard in 1953 as the first memorial to the resisters, whom many Germans then still viewed as traitors. Only in 1967 did this site become the **German Resistance Memorial Center** (Gedenkstätte Deutscher Widerstand). It served as a kind of shrine, holding great importance for the identity of the Federal Republic, as Stauffenberg's group, along with a few other tiny bands of conspirators, were honored as the better Germans who offered a moral basis on which the postwar republic could build. The exhibition about the German resistance was revised and expanded in the 1980s in an attempt to give an improved sense of the entire spectrum of groups that resisted Hitler. After it reopened it was denounced by some conservatives for devoting space to communists, including the later founders of the German Democratic Republic. Leftists replied that the communists had at least resisted Hitler from the beginning, whereas Stauffenberg and most of his aristocratic fellow-officers had at first welcomed the Nazis. You can draw your own conclusions from the sober and scholarly exhibit, which teaches about many different resistance groups, without losing sight of the fact that resistance to the Nazis was limited to a tiny minority of Germans. Amid the carefully documented reminders of the horrors of Hitler's Reich and the courage of those who opposed it are echoes of the history of these rooms, especially, as a sign informs you, the place where General Ludwig Beck, the highest ranking 1944 conspirator, was given the chance to shoot himself rather than face the firing squad outside.

A little farther up Stauffenbergstrasse, you pass the rear of the Gemäldegalerie. The museum complex has incorporated two of the grand villas that remain from the days when this was the city's most exclusive residential neighborhood, the 'privy councillor quarter', home to high state officials of noble origin. After the First World War, several embassies acquired villas, and this became a secondary **diplomatic quarter**. Hitler and Speer accelerated that change when they encouraged embassies to move here from the Spree bend near the Reichstag, which they had designated for their megalomaniacal monuments. The second war left this area largely in ruins, and little was built here until recently. Now it has again become a diplomatic quarter. At the corner of Tiergartenstrasse, for example, stands Austria's new embassy, designed by Hans Hollein. It combines a conservative consular building facing Stauffenbergstrasse, intended to fit in with its neighbors, with a more flamboyant wing at the corner.

If you follow Tiergartenstrasse to the left, the park will be on your right. If you choose to escape into it here, just ahead you will find two of the Tiergarten's many monuments: a statue of Prussia's beloved Queen Luise, from 1880, and one of her husband, Frederick William III, a concrete cast of the 1849 original. A short distance farther down Tiergartenstrasse is a statue of Richard Wagner, a grandiose Wilhelmine marble from 1903, which shows the composer flanked by groups of figures from several of his operas: Tannhäuser, the Götterdämmerung, Rheingold and Parsifal.

The left side of Tiergartenstrasse is lined with new embassies. The Italian embassy is not new, however. This huge building with wings extending down both Hildebrandstrasse and Hiroshimastrasse was completed in 1942 for Nazi Germany's most important ally, with monumental colonnades, travertine and red stucco intended to echo the grandeur of ancient Rome and the Italian Renaissance. For decades after the war it was largely in ruins, as were several other embassies in the area (including some much farther west – see Chapter 12). Whereas embassies were needed in Bonn and East Berlin, West Berlin remained in diplomatic limbo. Italy did, however, maintain a consulate in one wing of the sprawling ruin. Now the building has been restored to serve its original function.

Just beyond Hiroshimastrasse (formerly Hohenzollernstrasse) was the slightly less monumental embassy of the other Axis ally, completed in 1940 and crowned by the rising-sun symbol of imperial Japan. It, too, was long a ruin. In the 1980s, as West Berlin sought to revive the area, the city reached an agreement with Japan to restore the building as a Japanese cultural center, stipulating that the exterior be preserved as an important example of Third Reich diplomatic architecture. However, the Japanese decided the building had deteriorated beyond repair, and they demolished it, erecting an exact copy in its place, to the horror of German preservationists. Now the building has been renovated to serve as the Japanese embassy. Another Third Reich relic stands just beyond at Tiergartenstrasse 30, the former Berlin office and residence of the Krupp steel concern, Ruhr industrialists who felt entitled to their own home in the diplomatic quarter.

Past the Italian embassy on the left side of Hiroshimastrasse is a 1911 villa that became Greece's embassy before the war and then stood in ruins until its recent renovation. Behind it, facing Hildebrandstrasse, is an 1870 villa once again serving as the Estonian embassy, as it did before Estonia lost its independence to the Soviet Union in 1940. Hiroshimastrasse leads you past more new embassies and back to the Landwehrkanal. Turn right into Von-der-Heydt-Strasse and you pass number 18, the grandest remaining villa in the neighborhood, built in neoclassical style in 1860 for August von der Heydt, Prussian minister of trade.

Next to it stands the **Bauhaus Archive**. The famous and controversial Bauhaus was founded as a reorganized design school in Weimar in 1919. Under pressure from a right-wing provincial government, it moved to Dessau in 1925, then, after the Nazis took control of the local government there, to Berlin in 1932, before the Nazis shut it down entirely in 1933. After the war its doctrines and alumni exerted great influence on architecture and design, and it became the exemplar of a pure modernist idiom in an era when politicians and architects agreed that a modern city like Berlin should cast off its historicist froufrou and proudly embrace its industrial identity. The building was originally designed in 1964 by Walter Gropius, the Bauhaus's founding director, for a steep slope in the city of Darmstadt. After Gropius's death, his design was adapted to this site and completed in 1979. It had to be turned 180 degrees, which required that its most prominent feature, the factory-like skylights, be turned around as well. (In the end, natural light was not used at all in the galleries.) In addition to its valuable research holdings, the building serves as a museum of Bauhaus-related art and design, with changing exhibits of drawings, sculpture, furniture and other items, mainly displaying the simplified, industrially inspired styles associated with the school and its teachers, who included, in addition to Gropius, the architects Ludwig Mies van der Rohe, Hannes Meyer and Marcel Breuer, and the painters Vassily Kandinsky, Paul Klee, Josef Albers, Oskar

Schlemmer, Lyonel Feininger and Laszlo Moholy-Nagy. Their collective influence can be measured by the frequency with which they have been vilified. First the Nazis, then the Stalinists denounced their decadent cosmopolitanism; later they personified the European contamination of wholesome American comfort as well as the ruthless annihilation of traditional art and architecture.

The new buildings across Klingelhöferstrasse include the national headquarters of the Christian Democratic Union (CDU) and the new Mexican embassy. (For this area and beyond, see Chapter 12.) From here you can cross the canal to Lützowplatz and follow Einemstrasse to the U-Bahn at Nollendorfplatz, or take one of the frequent buses, either west toward Wittenbergplatz and Kurfürstendamm, or back east along the canal to the Kulturforum and Potsdamer Platz.

II
North of the Center

7

Spandauer Vorstadt

FOR CENTURIES, SPANDAUER STRASSE began the route to nearby Spandau. The suburb that grew up on this edge of town, the Spandauer Vorstadt, is the best-preserved section of old Berlin. Already in the last years of the East German regime, its warren of crumbling buildings had begun to attract attention and a little redevelopment. In the 1990s the area boomed, so its secrets are not so well hidden as they once were. However, the oldest buildings are often disguised by newer façades, and much of the life of the quarter still goes on in its many and diverse courtyards. Increasingly, though, the mysteries of the city are those of exotic cuisine and the murky finances of art galleries – an astonishing number of them have sprung up here.

Among the many ethnic, occupational and religious groups that settled here over the centuries, Jews have been particularly important. The medieval Jewish population was expelled from Berlin, as from most European cities. Some Jews returned in 1671: fifty wealthy Jewish families, expelled from Vienna, were invited by the Great Elector to bring their skills and capital to Berlin. Despite much discrimination, their descendants were able to establish a small but thriving community over the next two hundred years, which then grew rapidly during the industrial boom. This neighborhood is filled with memories of that once-thriving community as well as with recent Jewish immigrants (most from the former Soviet Union) who are building a new one.

Hackescher Markt is the best starting point. Its restored S-Bahn station is the finest remaining piece of the original Stadtbahn project from the 1880s, with its richly decorated wall of glazed brick and terracotta. Here, too, are some fine examples of the recent redevelopment of the arched vaults underneath the tracks: directly below the station, facing Hackescher Markt, and also west toward the Spree, bars and restaurants have moved in. On this side of the river, the Stadtbahn was built over the filled-in moat that once encircled the landward side of old Berlin. In the late seventeenth century, artisans and merchants began settling in this area just beyond the town walls. The square is named after the city's army commandant, Count von Hacke, who laid it out in 1751. Most of what you see is much newer, but opposite the station, on Neue Promenade, a restaurant now advertises its eighteenth-century cellar. To the right, across the short side of the triangular open space, the curved intersection of An der Spandauer Brücke (named after the bridge that once crossed the moat here) and Dircksenstrasse (which follows the rail line toward Alexanderplatz) is lined with varied and colorful new façades that in fact were all constructed as a single project during the 1990s in an attempt to create an impression of architectural diversity. This is a fairly good example of the recent return to the scale of the city of a century ago: here, where several old buildings were destroyed in the war, any postwar reconstruction would have created a single megastructure. But this remained a vacant lot for half a century – a fact reminding us that Hackescher Markt has only recently awakened from a long slumber.

The intersection where Neue Promenade and An der Spandauer Brücke squeeze into Oranienburger Strasse (to the left) and Rosenthaler Strasse (to the right) offers a more authentic (and thus more harrowing) experience of Berlin bustle than the all-new Potsdamer Platz. Here the crowds (and people do flock here, day and night) must dodge streetcars as well as autos. A century ago, this

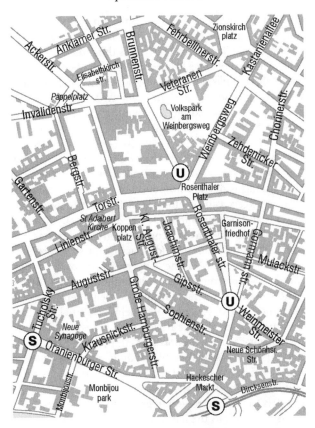

neighborhood, shabbier than Potsdamer Platz, was the setting for much of Alfred Döblin's *Berlin Alexanderplatz*. Döblin's novel turns the city into its main character, thrusting the reader into the jumble of shop signs, street-car bells, newspaper headlines and fragments of conversation. Rosenthaler Strasse from here to Rosenthaler Platz was a tangle of cheap bars and street vendors, filled with people like Döblin's fictional Franz Biberkopf, struggling for fortune and pleasure, sometimes on one side of the law, sometimes on the other. Now the bustle is distinctly more upscale. If you make it across the intersection, you will be at the entrance to the **Hackesche Höfe**, the center-piece of what has become Berlin's liveliest entertainment district. This series of eight connected courtyards was carved out of the old block a century ago. The architect August Endell's Jugendstil decoration from 1906 is best seen in the first courtyard, with its Gothic windows and colorful glazed tile intended to simulate a market square. The courtyards are lined with restaurants, galleries and shops catering to the young and tasteful.

If you keep going (not in a straight line: the courtyards are not all lined up and some are dead ends) you reach the other entrance to the complex, on Sophienstrasse, a quieter street. The long building across the street, extending to your right, is the side elevation of a former Wertheim department store built in 1903 by Alfred Messel. (The Rosenthaler Strasse front has been altered beyond recognition.) Messel and Wertheim invented modern Berlin department-store design with their flagship store on Leipziger Platz. This one is less impressive, but it is the only original Wertheim still standing, and here one can see Messel's typical use of full-length pillars and recessed windows, a simplified rendition of classicism that lent the old street some metropolitan grandeur.

As you walk to the left down Sophienstrasse you may see old-fashioned lettering painted on some storefronts. This is a remnant, not of 1900, but of the 1980s, when the East Germans selected this street for one of their rare inner-city renovation projects. Here they installed their best handicraft shops, some of which (or their successors) have survived unification. Number 18, on the right side, stands out for its ornate Gothic brick entrance. This building, with its attractive brick courtyards, was erected for the artisans' association (Handwerkerverein) in 1905.

A plaque recalls the radical political meetings held inside, as well as the fact that foreign slave laborers worked here under atrocious conditions during World War II. The next few buildings boast attractively redeveloped courtyards with cafés and galleries. Number 21, a late nineteenth-century building, has three yellow-brick courtyards (called the Sophie-Gips-Höfe – they connect through the block to Gipsstrasse) that originally housed a sewing-machine factory. The first courtyard is prominently decorated with a conceptual-art installation, a hint of the presence of the Hoffmann collection (**Sammlung Hoffmann**), which occupies the top three floors sprawling around several wings of the building. It is the private home of a West German textile magnate (recently deceased) and his wife, who have amassed a stunning collection of contemporary art since the 1950s. Every year she installs a new selection of their works in their spacious loft, which can be visited by appointment on Saturdays (English tours are sometimes available). The courtyard at number 28–29 houses expensive shops with understated decor – where, for example, women can buy the kind of shoes they would be ill advised to wear on the cobblestone courtyard.

Across the street, the burial ground of the **Sophienkirche** is visible, with the church itself behind. Both are entered from around the corner on Grosse Hamburger Strasse. There the Sophienkirche is set back from the street and nicely framed by a pair of neo-Baroque apartment buildings from 1905. These buildings, like so many around here, were peppered with bullet holes in 1945 and not repaired for decades afterward. Recognizing that these traces of history would disappear in the whirl of post–1990 renovations, an artist mounted a metal frame, labeled 'Pax', on the right façade: the smidgen of stucco within the frame will remain in its unrenovated condition as a memento of the destroyed city. The church was built in 1712 as a gift from Queen Sophie Luise. It has Berlin's only remaining Baroque church tower (1734), but otherwise the building's modesty seems more of a piece with Christopher Wren's London than Hohenzollern Berlin. The interior was redone in 1892 in neo-Baroque style. The most famous men buried in the churchyard are the historian Leopold von Ranke and the head of the Singakademie, Carl Friedrich Zelter.

The church tower may have underscored Prussia's Protestant identity, but **Grosse Hamburger Strasse** more clearly embodies Berlin's religious diversity, its tolerance, and also the shocking end of that tolerance. (The street derives its name not from any commentary on fast food but rather from the fact that the military road to Hamburg followed this route out of the medieval town.) On the other side of the street, between Sophienstrasse and Krausnickstrasse, stands the first Roman Catholic hospital in this Protestant capital, St Hedwig's, its various wings built in red-brick Gothic styles between the 1850s and 1920s. (The oldest part faces the courtyard.) More notably, the rest of the street echoes with memories of Jewish Berlin. Around the corner in Krausnickstrasse, at number 6 a plaque marks the former home of the world's first female rabbi, Regina Jonas (born in Berlin in 1902, murdered in Auschwitz in 1944). A few doors down from the church, the engraved stone façade of Grosse Hamburger Strasse 27 (1906) still identifies the building as the 'boys' school of the Jewish community'. The school was founded in 1778 by the Enlightenment philosopher Moses Mendelssohn, who sought to combine Jewish tradition with secular subjects. Mendelssohn, a poor immigrant boy from Dessau, became a scholar of the Torah and then a major contributor to the Berlin Enlightenment as well as a respected champion of religious toleration and legal equality. He was the model for the title character in his friend Gotthold Ephraim Lessing's celebrated drama *Nathan the Wise*. His children became wealthy and prominent citizens, and one of his grandsons was the composer Felix Mendelssohn-Bartholdy.

A Jewish school was once again opened here in 1992, fifty years after the Nazis closed its predecessor. Across the street, at number 15–16, stands a subtle but moving memorial to Berlin's vanished Jews. Here is a gap where a building was destroyed by a bomb in 1945. The cafés on either side, with their outdoor tables, may obscure this void; it is apparent only in the blank fire walls of the adjoining buildings, set back from the street. In 1990 Christian Boltanski created the installation 'The Missing House'. On the two blank walls he mounted small signs with the names, occupations and dates of residence of the vanished building's residents. Everything else is left to the imagination (Boltanski included photographs and archival records in his original installation, but they are no longer here). Some of the names look Jewish, others do not. Boltanski found the names in old town directories; we can only guess at their fates.

More ghosts linger down the street. Next to the Jewish school is a vacant lot, the former site of a Jewish old-age home where thousands of Berlin Jews were imprisoned by the Gestapo before being sent on to the death camps in 1942 and 1943. The scenes that played out in this building (destroyed before the war ended) made the street a place of terror – and no one who lived or worked in its narrow confines could have failed to notice the men, women and children herded in and out. The bronze plaque commemorating these deeds dates to the GDR, as do Will Lammert's statues of helpless people. These thirteen female figures, originally designed in 1957 for the antifascist memorial at Ravensbrück concentration camp, were cast in bronze and erected here in 1985, arranged in a wedge inspired by a design of the prewar artist John Heartfield. Just past them is the entrance to Berlin's original **Jewish cemetery**, where three thousand people were buried between 1671 and 1827, when a new cemetery on Schönhauser Allee replaced this one. The Gestapo destroyed the cemetery in 1943; since the war its site has been maintained as a quiet place of contemplation. One grave marker, Moses Mendelssohn's, has been replaced. A few other gravestones can be found along the inner wall.

Across the street, two two-story buildings extend a few feet forward of their neighbors. They are the oldest buildings on the street, dating to about 1800, when the street was narrower. Like their neighbors, they have recently been restored after long decay. Just beyond, Grosse Hamburger Strasse returns you to Oranienburger Strasse, the Spandauer Vorstadt's main artery. If you turn right, across the street you will see **Monbijou park**, extending to the bank of the Spree opposite the museum island. The destroyed Monbijou palace served as a summer residence for more than one Hohenzollern queen. Facing the west side of the park across Monbijoustrasse, and extending along Oranienburger Strasse, is a massive sandstone building from 1913 that long housed the main telegraph office, a busy place in its day. The entire block once belonged to the post office; the far side, facing Tucholskystrasse, became the telephone office, housed in a red-brick expressionist building from 1926. Also incorporated into the complex is the oldest building on Oranienburger Strasse, the former freemasons' lodge from 1791, designed by Langhans (the third story was added in 1839). The building was taken over by the post office after the Nazis banned masonic activities.

Back on the north side of Oranienburger Strasse we reach the new center of Jewish cultural life. A new corner building, Oranienburger Strasse 26 (at Krausnickstrasse) houses several Jewish institutions. (Among the Jewish institutions gathered in this building and neighborhood are several restaurants.) Next door, number 27, the

Kunsthof, is among the oldest of the restored courtyard complexes in the neighborhood. The courtyard buildings, like the delicately detailed street façade, date from the mid-nineteenth century and have been turned into galleries (and a café). The neo-Renaissance building at number 28 houses offices of the Jewish community, as it did before 1933. The magnificent gold cupola of the **New Synagogue** (Oranienburger Strasse 30) is visible from far away, but when you approach the building, it is integrated into the street wall in such a way as to make its presence on the street more modest. When the building was opened in 1866 it heralded acceptance and respectability for Berlin's Jewish community. Eduard Knoblauch and August Stüler's building, with a sanctuary that seated three thousand, was a far grander presence than any synagogue before it. (The nearby eighteenth-century synagogue is long gone; the building you see is, despite its name, now Berlin's oldest synagogue.) Its brick and terracotta façade reflects the influence of Schinkel (Knoblauch's and Stüler's teacher) but displays a colorful version of the orientalizing Moorish style then often used for synagogues. Bismarck himself attended the building's opening. (The king and queen had already toured the unfinished structure.) Services were held in German, and the building dispensed with ritual baths. Concerts were held here, including one in 1930 by the amateur violinist Albert Einstein.

The building's survival is something of a miracle. On the night of 9 November 1938, the notorious Kristallnacht, or 'crystal night' (the name may refer to the reflections of broken glass, but no one seems to know why the ugly events have been graced with such a pretty name), the New Synagogue, like nearly all others in Germany, was attacked by a well-organized mob, plundered and set ablaze. However, the precinct police commander, Wilhelm Krützfeld, obeyed his sense of duty rather than the Gestapo's orders not to intervene: he hurried to the site, ordered the marauders out, and called the fire brigade, which doused the fire before the building was badly damaged. Krützfeld was reprimanded and later forced into retirement, but the Berlin police (who can boast no surfeit of heroes in their ranks) have recently erected a plaque in his memory.

In 1943, however, bombs destroyed most of the building, and it long remained in ruins. A plaque put up on its hundredth anniversary records the East German government's decision to keep the damaged façade as a memorial. A second plaque from 1988, however, declares the same state's plans to restore the building. That decision was part of the Honecker government's attempt to improve relations with Jews at home and abroad. Restoration began before the Wall came down and was completed in 1995 – restoration of the front part of the building, that is: the main sanctuary has not been rebuilt. The building has been restored not as a synagogue, but rather as Centrum Judaicum, a cultural center, with space for temporary exhibitions on the Berlin Jewish community, past and present. Up the elegant iron staircase from the ground-floor rotunda, you reach the grand hall where Jewish community leaders met. Here, as in other parts of the building, the colorfully painted walls have been partly restored. Farther up the stairs, the interior of the tower is accessible. Out of the rear windows of the building you see an empty space, with the dimension of the destroyed sanctuary marked in the ground. The Jüdische Galerie, next door at number 31, also houses display space. Here, after lengthy planning, Berlin's first Jewish museum opened on 24 January 1933 – six days before Hitler assumed power. You will always see police officers patrolling in front of these and other Jewish institutions. German officials believe that anything Jewish offers too tempting a target to people determined to do something outrageous. (Neglected Jewish cemeteries, especially in smaller towns, are often vandalized.)

Oranienburger Strasse 32 is another restored court-yard complex of late nineteenth-century buildings, the Heckmann-Höfe, named after a machinery firm that once had its offices here. Some of these buildings were stables: see the bust of a horse's head. It is possible to walk through these courtyards all the way to Auguststrasse. Alternatively, you can take Tucholskystrasse. This was Artilleriestrasse until 1951, when, in the course of the GDR's purge of Prussian militarist symbols, it was named after the passionate satirist Kurt Tucholsky, whom Erich Kästner described as 'a fat little Berliner trying to stop a catastrophe with a typewriter' and whose words animated Berlin cabaret. Just one sample: 'This continent is proud of itself and has a right to be. What they are proud of in Europe: Of being a German. Of being a Frenchman. Of being an Englishman. Of not being a German. Of not being a Frenchman. Of not being an Englishman.' Tucholsky finally succumbed to despair and killed himself in 1935 in Sweden.

At the corner of Oranienburger Strasse and Tucholskystrasse is a restored house from 1792 that survived decades of utter neglect under the GDR. At the time of its restoration in the 1990s, its most recognizable feature was the old lettering advertising various kinds of drink once sold here. In a typical Berlin gesture of memory, that lettering has been retained on the restored building. Across Oranienburger Strasse, Tucholskystrasse 9, on the right, was the early-twentieth-century home of the Hochschule für die Wissenschaft des Judentums, an important institution in Reformed Judaism, and thus a counterpart to the Orthodox Adass Yisroel up the street. On the north side of Oranienburger Strasse, the corner is dominated by the neo-Renaissance brick building of the former postal dispatch office (Postfuhramt) from 1881.

Its delicate terracotta decoration portrays allegories of postal services as well as portraits of people important in the development of postal and transport services. Since 1989 the building has housed occasional art exhibitions. The rest of this block of Tucholskystrasse (as well as the next block, past Auguststrasse) boasts a nearly intact row of nineteenth-century apartment buildings. Just past Auguststrasse, on the right side, Tucholskystrasse 40 is the home of the **Adass Yisroel** congregation, founded in 1869, in the wake of the New Synagogue's reforms, to preserve a more traditional Jewish observance. The community was forcibly dissolved by the Gestapo in 1939, but after the fall of the Wall it reestablished itself in its former home. The building facing the street, built in 1904 as a seminary, houses a kosher café. Looking into the courtyard from the street, you can see a portal that marked the entry to the synagogue, crowned by a Star of David. The old synagogue was demolished in 1967; a new one is being built in its place.

If you return to Auguststrasse and turn left (east) you will pass the rear entrance to the Heckmann-Höfe and then the long brick façade of a former Jewish girls' school from 1928. Next to it, number 14–16 was designed by Eduard Knoblauch at the same time as the New Synagogue. It, too, belonged to the Jewish community and housed cooking and sewing schools, child-care facilities and, in the brick courtyard building, the Jewish hospital. Number 69, on the other side of the street, is one of the oldest buildings in the neighborhood, from circa 1800. Its courtyard is home to a gallery (one of many in the area) that hosts large-scale art installations and festive openings. A new glass building here houses a restaurant. Back on the right side of the street, number 25 is the home of Clärchens Ballhaus, a famous relic of the 1920s. In those days some nightclubs placed a telephone on each table, which permitted patrons – women, most definitely, as well as men – to initiate conversations with patrons at other tables. At Clärchens, the arrangement survived through the GDR and beyond; this establishment once associated with daring youth became known as the place where the last survivors of prewar Berlin kept their night lives going.

A little farther on you again reach Grosse Hamburger Strasse, which ends a few steps to the left at **Koppenplatz**, named after Christian Koppe, who endowed a poorhouse and cemetery here in 1705 and who is honored here with an 1855 memorial designed by Stüler. Next to it, number 12 is one of the municipal architect Ludwig Hoffmann's many historicist school buildings (1907), with a Baroque tower and carved doorway. Number 11, on the corner, is the former Hollmann foundation for the widows and daughters of higher officials (1850). The square itself sits atop a World War II bunker, which is, however, invisible and inaccessible. On it stands a recent bronze memorial recalling the loss of Berlin's Jews. It is a product of the GDR's belated attention to the specifically Jewish suffering of the Holocaust. Karl Biedermann's design won a 1988 competition for the project. Several years after unification it was completed according to the original plans: a room-sized parquet floor with an old-fashioned table and two chairs, one of which has been knocked over. The memorial is here because this was a Jewish neighborhood, but Biedermann explained that 'visible signs of Jewish culture are lacking, so that the fate of expulsion may be sensed by all'. The only hint of Jewish identity comes in a reference to 'Israel's body' in a poem about the 'homes of death' by Nelly Sachs (herself born a Jewish Berliner) that is engraved around the edge of the base.

The far end of Koppenplatz is intersected by Linienstrasse, which derives its name from the palisade line that marked the extent of the city from the 1730s on.

The wooden barrier was later replaced with a massive stone one, just outside it, along the course of today's Torstrasse, which parallels Linienstrasse. (In the 1990s the old name Torstrasse, or Gate Street, was revived, even though the city gates along it are long gone. The city was determined to remove the GDR's name, Wilhelm-Pieck-Strasse – honoring its first president – but the pre–1945 names, Alsace and Lorraine Street – for different segments – proved too controversial to revive, in view of French fears of revived German power.) The oldest buildings here mostly date from the years after the wall was torn down in the 1860s. Several buildings around the intersection of Koppenplatz and Linienstrasse are products of the GDR's belated attempts to redevelop this neighborhood. The standardized, prefabricated panel construction developed for the large housing estates built on open land was adapted for inner-city use by varying the sizes and shapes of the panels; among the results from the 1980s are the buildings you see here (and in several other corners of the Spandauer Vorstadt). At the time they offered modern comforts in a neighborhood of badly deteriorated housing; next to the much more expensive construction of the 1990s, they look cheap and shabby.

To the left (west) on Linienstrasse, number 101 is the brick expressionist apse of St Adalbert's Catholic church (1933) by the Viennese architect Clemens Holzmeister. Its entrance is at Torstrasse 168, in the courtyard of an apartment building. The courtyards in this area, where accessible, are the best places to glimpse original architecture as well as the ways new Berliners have nested in remnants of the old city. Linienstrasse 155 is one example; another is number 89, the former Royal Loan Office which opens to several courtyards lined with elegant brick buildings, extending through the block to Torstrasse 164.

Bergstrasse runs north from Torstrasse. By the beginning of the new millennium the trendy nightlife that had established itself around Hackescher Markt and Oranienburger Strasse had trickled north into this row of old buildings and courtyards. Behind the 1878 apartment house at number 22 was a brewery, with stables and other facilities as well as a grand neo-Gothic building from 1894, recently restored for an expensive restaurant. A right turn on Invalidenstrasse then takes you past the fountain across the street on Pappelplatz, with its muscular limestone figure that might be mistaken for a Third Reich sculpture; it dates to 1912, however. Near the next corner is an old market hall built into the interior of the block, still in use and accessible from both Invalidenstrasse and Ackerstrasse. The Ackerhalle (1888) was one of fourteen such buildings designed by the municipal architect Hermann Blanckenstein in an attempt to provide a more orderly and sanitary environment for retail food sales, previously concentrated in outdoor markets. Of the four halls that remain, this one most resembles its original appearance, with its brick and terracotta façade, cast-iron columns, and segmented ceiling. Most of the floor space is now used by a supermarket, however, leaving only a few shop stalls to hint at the sights, smells and bustle that once reigned here.

Across Invalidenstrasse, set back from the street, is Karl Friedrich Schinkel's **St Elisabeth's church** (1832–35). In his capacity as architect for King Frederick William III (who was head of the Prussian Protestant church) Schinkel drew a series of different designs for small churches in Berlin's new northern industrial suburbs. (The other three are in Wedding and Moabit.) This one is a simple rectangle, with a pillared portico in front and a round apse at the back. Both the portico and the main façade have gables with Greek-style decoration. The building has been in ruins since 1945 – a neglected masterpiece indeed – but its restoration is planned.

A few more steps along Invalidenstrasse bring you to Brunnenstrasse, one of the major thoroughfares of industrial Berlin, which grew from the old northern gates out to the suburb of Wedding. This is an area of large old buildings with (in many cases) multiple courtyards, some residential, some industrial. The most prominent building at the intersection is a former department store (1904) with vertical stone ribs and Jugendstil decoration. It once housed the GDR's Institute of Fashion. More than a block up Brunnenstrasse, to the left, a courtyard building at number 33 was built in 1910 as a small private synagogue. Its interior was ravaged in 1938, but the exterior survived and was restored in the 1980s. The name of the Volkspark am Weinberg recalls the Wollank family vineyard (Weinberg) on this sloping ground, one of Berlin's few natural hills. After the 1860s the vines gave way to tenements, which were destroyed by Allied bombs, after which East Berlin created this park. In it stands the original Heinrich Heine memorial, banished here in 1958, a new copy of which now stands on Unter den Linden (see Chapter 1).

Continue up Veteranenstrasse (the extension of Invalidenstrasse), across Fehrbelliner Strasse, and you reach Zionskirchplatz, a surprisingly quiet square at the intersection of five streets. On this high point, once the site of the Wollank windmill, the **Zion church** was completed in 1873 according to August Orth's design, a combination of classical and Gothic forms, with a tower that dominated the city's northern edge. This was one of several churches that played an important role in the 1980s GDR dissident scene. The Protestant church, as virtually the only institution permitted to organize its affairs independent of state and party control, became a haven for dissidents and social dropouts, some of whom used Church buildings and services to organize opposition to state policies. Among the galvanizing issues for dissidents was the environmental devastation of the country, and they opened an independent Environmental Library in a church-owned building across from the Zion church. The police raided and closed it in 1987, sparking a deep crisis in church-state relations.

The tradition of Protestant dissent here runs deeper. Nestled close to the church is a gleaming bronze sculpture, a partly abstract kneeling human torso. This is a memorial to the theologian Dietrich Bonhoeffer, who served as pastor here shortly before the Nazis came to power (and just after his American sojourn at a Harlem church). Karl Biedermann designed the memorial in 1987, but amid the controversies over the church's opposition activities, the Stasi prevented its completion. It was finally erected in 1997.

A left on Fehrbelliner Strasse and a right on Choriner Strasse takes you through rows of hulking tenements and back to Torstrasse. Just to the right, at Torstrasse 85 and 87, two simple façades mark Berlin's first attempt at tenement reform. Concerned about the dismal housing conditions of the burgeoning working-class population, particularly here in Berlin's north, Carl Wilhelm Hoffmann founded the Berlin Charitable Building Society in 1847 and designed these, its first buildings, without the usual cellar or courtyard apartments. Gormannstrasse, the southern extension of Choriner Strasse, takes you to the **Garnisonfriedhof**, an army officers' cemetery established in 1722, at the corner of Linienstrasse. (The entrance is on the opposite side, on Kleine Rosenthaler Strasse.) Many of the nineteenth-century grave markers display characteristic cast-iron decoration. The most recent burials date from the 1920s, except for a mass grave of victims of the 1945 street fighting.

The cemetery ended up at the edge of Berlin's most notorious slum, the Scheunenviertel (shed quarter). Only a few of its buildings remain, and even they barely survived the GDR's demolition plans in the 1980s. Farther down Gormannstrasse, you pass a school built in a peculiar style reflecting the ideological uncertainties of the early GDR. The main building (1954) was constructed in an unadorned modernist style but then given pillars and other adornments in the briefly ascendant Stalinist fashion. The only remaining part of an older school is around the corner at Weinmeisterstrasse 15, a richly decorated brick building from 1867. Down this same block of Weinmeisterstrasse, you come to the corner of Alte Schönhauser Strasse (to the left) and Neue Schönhauser Strasse (right).

The architectural riches of **Neue Schönhauser Strasse** begin with the large 1892 building on the southeast corner. Unusually, even its courtyard façades are richly decorated. Just beyond, Neue Schönhauser Strasse 19 is an example of modern Berlin commercial architecture from the first decade of the twentieth century (although the upper stories housed apartments), with its wide bays, large windows, and Jugendstil flourishes. Numbers 14 and 12 are much older, dating to the late eighteenth century, with neoclassical façades from circa 1850. Number 12 long housed a brewery in its second courtyard, with an accompanying pub facing the street. Number 13, between those two, displays yet another style. This 'Volkskaffeehaus', commissioned by a private social-service organization, is an early work of Alfred Messel (1891) in German Renaissance style. Typically for him, the façade is asymmetrical and embellished more by varied bays than by pasted-on detail. Although the apartments on the upper floors were upscale, the ground floor housed a simple restaurant intended to provide cheap meals and coffee (rather than schnapps) to ordinary workers. The two ground-floor archways opened into its two parts: the smaller left side, for women, was walled off from the right side, for men, which extends into the rear courtyard. The fact that a fashionable restaurant took over this attractive space a century later is illustrative of the neighborhood's transition. Across the street, number 8 is a rare example of an intact eighteenth-century façade. It was built around 1780 for the gardener Mollard. It is known that Mollard owned a vineyard, which was probably behind the house. The façade is decorated in the delicate Rococo style favored by King Frederick the Great. It predates the practice of numbering houses and was called the 'house with the six girls' heads' after the keystone sculptures over the ground-floor windows. Its circular Baroque stairway is intact.

Neue Schönhauser Strasse brings you back to **Rosenthaler Strasse**, the street that led from Hackescher Markt to the Rosenthal gate and on toward the village of Rosenthal. At the corner (Neue Schönhauser Strasse 10) is a building from 1887 that was stripped of its original ornament in 1929 and, in the new style of the time, given horizontal bands of color that curve around the corner. Inside the ground floor, however, a pharmacy preserves its original ornate wooden decor. Across Rosenthaler Strasse, only the delicate spiral staircase in number 36 betrays its eighteenth-century origins. You pass the staircase on your way into a garish new complex of courtyard shops which connects to the Hackesche Höfe. Number 37 is another altered eighteenth-century building. A GDR plaque on number 38, a commercial building from the early twentieth century, tells you that the Communist party was headquartered here (in the courtyard) from 1921 to 1926. This building, like number 39 next door, extends deep into the block, with large courtyard buildings that have become artists' lofts. Off the courtyard of number 39 was **Otto Weidt's workshop** for blind people. During World War II the brave and brash Weidt gathered a large staff of Jewish workers and long outwitted the Gestapo by arguing that they were essential to his production of brooms and brushes. The site now belongs to the Jewish Museum and is open to the public. Also in the building is the Anne Frank Zentrum, which hosts an internationally reproduced exhibition about the significance of Anne Frank's life. Next door is the Hackesche Höfe: you are back at Hackescher Markt.

8

Friedrich-Wilhelm-Stadt

IN THE NORTHWESTERN CORNER of the eighteenth-century city, between the new government quarter and the gentrified Spandauer Vorstadt, you can still experience some of the quiet (and neglect) of its years in the shadow of the Wall. Here, a short walk from Friedrichstrasse or the Reichstag, many an odd fragment of the past remains, even as new urban pleasures enliven the neighborhood.

On the north side of Friedrichstrasse station, you can cross the river on the Weidendamm bridge, which dates to 1897. Here, on 2 May 1945, the Red Army came upon a tank barrier that marked the outer limit of Hitler's once-mighty Reich. In the wee hours of that day, a remarkable demonstration of the power of a Prussian uniform played out directly below. After Hitler's and Goebbels's bunker suicides, the motley crew of Führerbunker survivors tried to elude the Russian vise. One group crawled this far through the subway tunnel. The leader, an SS General, recalled: 'The one organization we were not braced for was the BVG, the Berlin Municipal Transport Company. We came on a huge steel bulkhead, designed to seal this tunnel at the point where the subway starts to run under the Spree. Here – and I could not believe my own eyes and ears – we spotted two stalwart, uniformed BVG guards. I ordered them to open the bulkhead forthwith. The guards categorically refused. Not only were these stubborn fellows going by the book; each had a copy of the book and began reading from it. The regulation *did* clearly state that the bulkhead was to be closed every evening after the passage of the last train. No trains had been running here for at least a week, but these two dutiful characters had their orders, and that was that.' The soldier later had ten years in Soviet prisons to curse his reluctance to pull his pistol at that moment. He respected men who respected orders, and an SS general had no authority over Berlin transit workers. The SS is long gone, but the BVG still runs the trains and buses; the next time a driver or conductor treats you with contempt, try not to take it personally.

The general and his group did make it across the bridge, where they found little but ruins and Russian soldiers. Your experiences will be different. Turn left across the bridge, and you are at Bertolt-Brecht-Platz, created by the GDR in 1988 to honor the bohemian communist playwright. The Brecht memorial is a typical work of late GDR sculpture, including a statue of Brecht by Fritz Cremer as well as stone pillars displaying various of Brecht's pronouncements. Next to it stands the **Theater am Schiffbauerdamm** (1892) with its sober exterior (a row of buildings originally blocked the view of it from the Spree) and typically extravagant interior. In 1928 it hosted the sensational premiere of *The Threepenny Opera*, Brecht's first collaboration with the composer Kurt Weill. (It and the other Brecht–Weill play, *Mahagonny*, must be viewed in part as allegories of Berlin.) Since 1949 the theater has been the home of the Berliner Ensemble, the stage company founded by Brecht after he left his California exile for the new East German state. For decades after his death in 1956 the theater subsisted on Brecht's postwar stagings of his prewar plays, in which Brecht juggled his talent for dazzling entertainment with his intermittent desire to preach Marxist doctrine and to make the audience aware of the artificiality of the theater through his use of the 'alienation effect'. Since 1990 the theater has revived its reputation. Behind Bertolt-Brecht-Platz, on the street Am

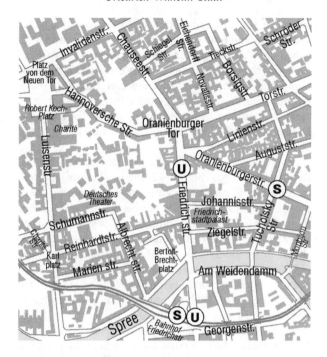

Zirkus, stood another important theater, the enormous old Friedrichstadtpalast (not to be confused with the new one across Friedrichstrasse). It was established in a former market hall that the architect Hans Poelzig remodeled in 1919 for the director Max Reinhardt. Its expressionist interior, famous for its stalactite forms, fell into disrepair, however, long before the building was razed in 1985.

Schiffbauerdamm along the quay was originally built 300 years ago as a path for horses pulling the royal barges to and from Charlottenburg palace. Because this was the downstream edge of town, tanners and butchers settled here, where they could pollute the water with impunity. They were joined by boat builders (Schiffbauer). The arrival of the new rail station in 1882 brought upscale apartments and hotels as well as theaters to the riverbank. When the Wall was built in 1961, this became a very quiet corner of the city, off limits to most people. Downstream along the river, various nondescript buildings have recently been converted into studios by media companies seeking proximity to the Reichstag. Across the river, the large expanse of mirror glass marks the new home of the Federal Press Office.

At the Albrechtstrasse corner, under the rail bridge, the riverbank has become a little 'Rhenish quarter', favored by government employees transferred here unwillingly from Bonn. On weekends, many return to their Rhenish suburban houses; on weeknights, they gather at pubs such as Ständige Vertretung, a kind of shrine to the Bonn Republic. If you turn away from the river into Albrechtstrasse, you find a quieter corner of the area once known as Friedrich-Wilhelm-Stadt. Since the demise of the Wall, its proximity to Friedrichstrasse and the Reichstag has attracted small hotels and restaurants in renovated nineteenth-century buildings. **Marienstrasse**, the first cross street north of the river, is a rare example of a nearly intact street of early nineteenth-century apartment buildings, most of them built in the 1830s and restored by the East Germans during the 1970s. Their neoclassical simplicity contrasts with the more elaborate decoration typical on the far more numerous buildings put up later in the century. Their delicate friezes show that less could be more.

One block farther north along Albrechtstrasse, at the corner of Reinhardtstrasse, stands a concrete air-raid bunker left over from World War II. Bunkers have limited uses, and its fate is uncertain. During the 1990s it briefly housed a techno dance club; more recently it has been used for art exhibitions. Turn left into Reinhardtstrasse (named for the renowned theater director Max Reinhardt);

among the new buildings on the left side, number 29 is set back behind an old portal, all that remains of an army drill house, built in 1828 from a sketch by Schinkel. Cross the park on the other side of the street and you reach Schumannstrasse and the neighborhood's other famous theater, the **Deutsches Theater**, in an 1850 building. Max Reinhardt took it over in 1905, and turned the neighboring building into the smaller Kammerspiele. In the German-speaking lands, unlike France and England, plays rather than novels shaped modern consciousness, so the theater has long been a very important institution. When the Viennese Reinhardt arrived in Berlin, he developed a style of emotive acting and elaborate stage design that revolutionized German theater.

Farther west down Schumannstrasse, past buildings from the 1830s similar to those on Marienstrasse, number 18 offers a fine early twentieth-century stone and brick façade with reliefs of a nursing mother and of one woman examining another. This was obviously a gynecological institute, the first sign that we are entering a neighborhood long dominated by medicine, specifically by the royal hospital, the **Charité**, founded in 1710 by King Frederick I as a plague and military hospital, on a site then outside the city walls. The Charité, now attached to Humboldt University, has long been an important center of medical research. Here in 1896 Wilhelm Röntgen conducted the first demonstration of X-rays. In 1945, the renowned surgeon Ferdinand Sauerbruch stayed at his operating table until Russian soldiers, including a medical officer who had been his student, took control. Several monuments in the area honor medical researchers. At the corner of Schumannstrasse and Luisenstrasse is a bronze statue of the pioneering ophthalmologist Albrecht von Graefe set in a neo-Renaissance stone wall (by Martin Gropius and Heino Schmieden, 1882). Just to the south, on Karlplatz, a muscular limestone statue (1910) honors the nineteenth-century pathologist, archaeologist, politician and public-health reformer Rudolf Virchow. (From here, Reinhardtstrasse leads under the rail line to the new government quarter – see Chapter 3). The main Charité complex lies to the north along Luisenstrasse, the northern extension of Wilhelmstrasse. On the west (left) side, stretching back to the rail line and a canal, a large complex of modern buildings is interspersed with red-brick Gothic structures dating from a major expansion of the hospital at the end of the nineteenth century. The buildings facing Luisenstrasse were supposed to shield the generously spaced pavilions behind them, creating a park-like oasis for patients. You enter from the south end, at Schumannstrasse 20–21. Several buildings back is the Berliner Medizinhistorisches Museum, a medical-history collection founded by Virchow.

More of the Charité's campus, and its oldest buildings, are found on the right side of Luisenstrasse. The broad neoclassical building at number 56 (1840) was built for the veterinary school. Behind it, medical students still have the run of a surprisingly vast and little-known warren of old buildings, forgotten monuments and pleasant gardens along the tiny Panke river. Most notable is the round lecture hall of the Anatomy Theater, a simple neoclassical building (1790) that Langhans designed at the same time as the Brandenburg Gate. The garden is sometimes accessible via the veterinary school, especially the gate at its northern end; other points of access include Philippstrasse and the distant corner of Reinhardtstrasse and Friedrichstrasse.

Luisenstrasse 57 has a plaque noting that the renowned medical researcher Robert Koch worked here from 1879 to 1897. A plaque on the next building recalls that here the East German parliament elected Wilhelm Pieck as GDR president in 1953 and 1957. Until the Palast der Republik opened in 1976, the GDR's obscure parliament met in this obscure building. Number 60 has been much altered, but when it was new in the 1830s, the student Karl Marx lodged here, as a now-vanished GDR plaque recalled. Just beyond looms a twenty-story hospital tower built by the East Germans in 1981, one wing of which bridges the street. Past it, you reach **Robert-Koch-Platz** and its northern extension, **Platz vor dem Neuen Tor**. The two were once divided by the 'new gate' placed here when the old customs wall was extended in the 1830s. Schinkel designed a pair of guardhouses flanking the gate, which were destroyed in the war but have recently been recreated in a modern form by Josef Kleihues – a controversial attempt to compromise between historical imitation and ahistorical modernism. The southern square, inside the gate, was renamed in 1916 in honor of the discoverer of the cholera bacillus. A marble monument to Koch faces a bronze sculpture of the Nobel-winning chemist Emil Fischer, a new copy of a limestone statue destroyed in the war. Two Kleihues buildings on the east side of Platz vor dem Neuen Tor flank the national headquarters of the Green Party, a restored building from 1880. The southerly Kleihues building extends along the north side of Hannoversche Strasse, which follows the course of the old wall. In fact, the new building incorporates a small segment of the wall, which was razed in the 1860s. (Across the street is another relic of old Berlin, an ornate iron water pump, of which only a few remain.)

Across Invalidenstrasse to the north is Invalidenpark (see Chapter 9) and, to the right, a large complex of nineteenth-century buildings, constructed shortly after the royal iron foundry was shut down here in 1873. The architect, August Tiede, designed a matched pair of broad structures flanking an even larger one. The nearest one, at the corner of Invalidenstrasse and Schwarzer Weg, housed the Geological Institute. Like the others, it displays generous proportions and massive neo-Renaissance features: pillars, pilasters, arched windows and fortress-like corners. Nevertheless, it is relatively modest compared to the later neo-Baroque style of the former medical academy across the park (see Chapter 9). It is now the home of the federal ministry for transport, construction and housing. Its more richly decorated neighbor was built a little later (1889) as the **Museum of Natural History**. Its glass-roofed interior court houses the museum's biggest attractions, its large dinosaur skeletons. The museum's fabulous collections largely date to nineteenth-century explorers such as Alexander von Humboldt, but they are not well preserved or displayed. The museum has been scarcely changed since East German times, or indeed since the war: one wing remains in ruins. For all its dinginess, however, and the absence of the sort of interactive displays now typical of such museums, it remains a treasure house filled with rocks and minerals, skeletons and stuffed animals, parents and excited children.

Past the third building in the complex, built for the university's agricultural academy, is an imposing 1955 Stalinist building at the corner of Chausseestrasse, the northern extension of Friedrichstrasse. Turn right; a few steps down on your right is a fine mid-nineteenth-century neoclassical apartment house where the playwright Bertolt Brecht lived with his wife, the actress Helene Weigel, from 1953 until his death. Brecht arrived from southern Germany in the early 1920s and quickly made his mark by outraging patriotic audiences with his 'Legend of a Dead Soldier':

> And when the war reached its fifth spring
> with no hint of a pause for breath
> the soldier did the obvious thing
> and died a hero's death.

His ballad gets even more subversive, as doctors examine the corpse and pronounce it fit for combat. Brecht thrived in the hubbub of Weimar Berlin, happily borrowing phrases and ideas from his illustrious table companions, who found him a brilliant cypher: an abrasive man of the people, a militant proletarian who cherished money and fast cars. (That combination was unusual in the 1920s; in postwar East and West Berlin there were many such men.) His version of dialectical materialism was summed up in a famous line of *The Threepenny Opera*: 'First comes feeding, then comes morality.' After leaving the United States during the postwar red hunts and moving to the new East German state, he was given control of the Berliner Ensemble stage company along with many privileges in return for lending the new state the prestige of his presence. The GDR turned this building into a museum and archive honoring its most famous writer.

Next to it is the entrance to a cemetery – actually several **cemeteries** that have shared this site since 1762. In front is the French cemetery, the burial place for the French community that played such an important role in Berlin after Huguenot refugees brought their technical and entrepreneurial skills to this small and remote town. Farther back is the Dorotheenstadt cemetery, the traditional burial place for Berlin's cultural elite. The most important graves date to the neoclassical period of the early nineteenth century, and include most of the leading artists of that age. There are many early nineteenth-century cast-iron grave markers, but the most common neoclassical form was a standing stone. A simple example is the grave of the philosopher G.W.F. Hegel, a little to the left of the main path. On the right side, by contrast, it takes a more elaborate form on the grave of the chemist S.F. Hermbstaedt, designed by Karl Friedrich Schinkel. Schinkel's own grave, farther back on the left side, is similar. Another typical neoclassical grave marker is a square pedestal supporting an urn or statue. An example, in the back left corner, is Gottfried Schadow's design for the grave of his wife Caroline. Another, next to it, is Schadow's own grave. Nearby, the grave of the industrialist August Borsig takes the form of a temple-like baldachin on four Doric columns, sheltering a bust and other statuary. Yet another form found in the cemetery is the obelisk, such as the grave of another famous philosopher, Johann Gottlob Fichte, who lies near Hegel. Postwar graves here include those of the GDR's cultural elite: Brecht and Weigel, the writers Heinrich Mann, Johannes R. Becher and Arnold Zweig, the composer Hanns Eisler, and the artist John Heartfield.

Across the street, number 13 was built as the headquarters of the **Borsig** machinery company, which once dominated the neighborhood. Number 8, a few buildings down, also remains from the Borsig complex. The street façade is new, but connected courtyards, reaching all the way through the block to Novalisstrasse, are lined with century-old industrial lofts, most now in the hands of software companies, Chausseestrasse being an address favored by high-tech entrepreneurs. Amid all the changes, the combination of cutting-edge technology and cutthroat competitiveness are neighborhood traditions. In 1837, when August Borsig established his locomotive factory here, just outside the city gates, he became the most important single figure in Berlin's early industrial revolution, and this neighborhood became Berlin's first industrial slum, as tenements sprang up to house the burgeoning population of workers. Well-to-do social reformers came here to be appalled at the conditions in which recent immigrants from the provinces were living: six or eight to a room, with few sanitary facilities. The reformers went on to establish charitable housing societies and to press for municipal housing and sanitary codes. Little remains from the first generation of tenements or of factory buildings. By the late nineteenth century, this was expensive inner-city land, and there was no room to expand, so the big manufacturers moved out. Borsig was typical, moving its main operations down the river to Moabit, then farther out to Tegel.

Back across the street, at number 128, is the home of the Catholic Academy and German Bishops' Conference, in a large complex of new and renovated buildings dispersed around several courtyards, and intended to give the Roman Catholic Church a visible presence in this largely Protestant city (and in the capital of a country which, since the annexation of the east, again has a clear Protestant majority). Some of the buildings stand atop the site of Berlin's first Catholic cemetery, which adjoined the neighboring Dorotheenstadt cemetery until it was abandoned a century ago. If you pass all the way through the academy's courtyards, you come out on Hannoversche Strasse, which crosses Chausseestrasse at the northern end of Friedrichstrasse, the former site of the Oranienburg Gate (which is still the name of the subway station: Oranienburger Tor).

A few steps down Friedrichstrasse is the western end of Oranienburger Strasse, the main street of the Spandauer Vorstadt, leading to Hackescher Markt. The tract on the far side of Oranienburger Strasse has long been a source of controversy. The massive ruin that faces Oranienburger Strasse was built in 1906 as an enormous store with an internal arcade, and was destroyed in the war. The ruin was still there at the time of reunification in 1990, when it was occupied by young artists, who named it **Tacheles** and turned it into an indoor-outdoor complex of studios, cafés and nightclubs, which became a tourist attraction. Through the 1990s the city and private investors produced plans to renovate and rebuild the site, and the squatters resisted them. The most recent plan, by the Americans Andres Duany and Elizabeth Plater-Zyberk, proposes new offices and apartments on the empty lots extending to Friedrichstrasse and Johannisstrasse, along with renovation of the abandoned buildings, while leaving space for the artists, who after all attract tourists.

The new development is supposed to give the area a respectability that it has never had. In the 1920s, Oranienburger Strasse and Chausseestrasse at night teemed with prostitutes, and since 1990 they have returned, in different but still recognizable costumes. The stretch of Friedrichstrasse north of the river is still dominated by remnants of an uncompleted GDR redevelopment project from the 1980s, a showcase for fanciful versions of their prefabricated concrete panels. A prime example is the **Friedrichstadtpalast**, completed in 1984 just north of the river and quietly nicknamed 'the Damascus opera'. It continues to stage variety shows that attract busloads of pensioners from the east German provinces.

Just past the Friedrichstadtpalast, a left turn into Ziegelstrasse takes you to a complex of medical buildings dating to the 1880s, designed by the team of Martin Gropius and Heino Schmieden, the last prominent representatives of the Schinkel school in Berlin architecture. Some were replaced in the late 1920s; the only building that remains from that era is on the south side of Ziegelstrasse, in a pure modernist idiom, with plain white walls (albeit more brown than white for most of their existence) and horizontal rows of square windows. Its dramatic gesture comes at the eastern end of the building, facing Monbijoustrasse, a curved wing with a glass-walled top story set back under a protruding roof.

Monbijoustrasse takes you to the Spree by the bottom end of the museum island, across from the Bode Museum's dome (see Chapter 1). Across the river is an enormous barracks completed in 1902 in German Renaissance style, a reminder that these streets were crawling with soldiers a century ago. You can follow the riverside path downstream to Friedrichstrasse, or you can walk past the barracks, to the elevated S-Bahn line.

When the line was constructed across the city center in the 1880s, vaulted interior spaces were left underneath the tracks. They were divided into sections marked by broad brick arches and leased for commercial use. In less busy neighborhoods, and in less busy times, many have been devoted to storage and to repair shops. Near here the GDR opened one of its special hard-currency stores, selling goods unavailable in ordinary shops to visitors or residents privileged to possess Western currency. In recent years, antique shops, bookstores and especially cafés and restaurants have taken over the vaults along Georgenstrasse, which offer character to compensate for the limited natural light. Patrons get used to the frequent rumbling of trains overhead. You can eat, drink and shop your way along the rail line back to Friedrichstrasse station.

9

Borderlands

VISITORS SEEKING traces of the Berlin Wall are likely to look between the Reichstag and Potsdamer Platz, and perhaps also a little farther south toward Checkpoint Charlie, places in which the death strip has all but disappeared. To the north, however, in areas that remain more marginal, the desolation left by the Wall has not been so completely obliterated.

Begin, however, at a marginal place on the verge of becoming a central one. Perhaps by the time you arrive the new central rail station (**Hauptbahnhof–Lehrter Bahnhof**) will be in use. It will be Berlin's first central station, a project that eluded planners for the entire twentieth century, thanks to war, economic crises and division. Now it is finally happening. The largest part of the new station is underground, and indeed the largest construction project was not the station, but the north–south tunnel that carries trains under the Tiergarten and Potsdamer Platz. Paralleling it is a second tunnel for automobiles. Just south of the new station, both tunnels cross under the Spree, which had to be diverted temporarily in order to construct them.

The north–south rail platforms are therefore underground. The two sparkling glass halls cover the elevated east–west tracks. (Plans call for an office building to span the opening between them.) Until now the only rail crossing in central Berlin was this east–west line, completed in 1882. Nearby stood the old Lehrter Bahnhof, built in 1870 as the terminal for trains to and from northwestern Germany. It was named after the city of Lehrte, near

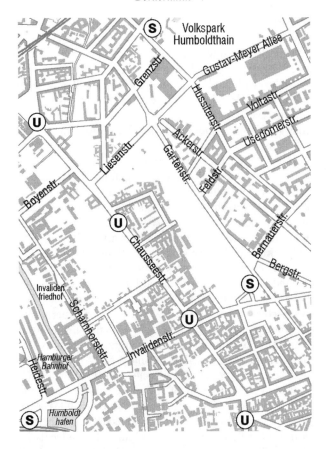

Hanover, and did not survive the war. This was a neglected corner of West Berlin, but redevelopment is
expected to follow the construction of the new station.
For years the view south from the moving trains was a
forest of construction cranes, for the new government
buildings and Potsdamer Platz. Their removal leaves a
clear view of the new Reichstag dome.

The north side of the station has long been desolate as well. Near here in 1972, the skeleton of Hitler's loyal aide Martin Bormann was uncovered, shutting down a lucrative vein of rumors. He had vanished in the chaos after Hitler's suicide, and your local library may still have some of the books detailing his alleged escape to South America or wherever. Construction projects like the rail station may still turn up bodies, but the bigger problem, requiring constant vigilance, is the thousands of unexploded bombs that remain in the ground.

Invalidenstrasse, taken to the right, leads you past an impressive old building at the corner of Heidestrasse, built in 1874 as the headquarters of a railroad company. It stood alone for decades. Past it is the **Hamburger Bahnhof** museum of contemporary art. This is Berlin's only remaining first-generation rail station, completed in 1847. The elegant neoclassical style of the central façade, framed by two towers, recalls an Italian villa – an incongruous image for a noisy and smoky rail terminal. The two archways in the front, now enclosed, once permitted locomotives to pass through to a turntable in the front yard. After a new generation of larger rail stations was built, Hamburger Bahnhof lost most of its traffic to the new Lehrter station, and it was closed in 1884. In 1906 it reopened as a museum of transport, and the two side wings were added in front. The glass shed behind is also a later addition. After the war the building fell into ruin. It lay within West Berlin, barely, but belonged to the Deutsche Reichsbahn, which was controlled by East Germany. Josef Kleihues has given the new museum a white, clean interior that retains the name but not the grit of a rail station. An annex has recently been opened in an old warehouse behind. Many of the museum's works come from the Berlin collector Erich Marx, and they include paintings, sculptures and video and sound installations by most of the big names of late twentieth-century international art, such as the Germans Joseph Beuys and Anselm Kiefer and the Americans Robert Rauschenberg, Andy Warhol and Roy Liechtenstein. Hamburger Bahnhof shows feature the kind of attention-grabbing pieces (from young British artists, for example) that stir up great rows in the United States but receive respectful notices here.

The station stands next to the Berlin-Spandau ship canal, which marked the border between East and West Berlin. Although one of the Wall's official checkpoints was here, not many people used the bridge that you can now so easily cross. Across the bridge, the right side of the street marks the northern end of the Charité medical complex (see Chapter 8). On your left stands the federal economics ministry, completed in 1910 in the style and scale one would expect for something named the Kaiser-Wilhelm-Akademie, an institute of medical research for (naturally) the military. The GDR used it as the government hospital. It is an impressive example of Wilhelmine Baroque, with its massive rusticated sandstone blocks on the ground floor, huge pilasters, varied façade profile, broken gables and a mansard roof topped by a relatively diminutive tower. Follow the building around the corner into Scharnhorststrasse and you come to the two transverse wings that remain from the original **Invalidenhaus**, which dates to 1748. King Frederick the Great established it here, outside the city walls, for soldiers disabled in the first of his many wars.

The open space across Scharnhorststrasse was set aside in the nineteenth century as a park for the residents of the Invalidenhaus. Since its restoration in the 1990s, Invalidenpark is dominated by a pool and a large slanted wall that appears to be rising out of the pool (or sinking into it, if you are a pessimist), intended to commemorate the fall of the Berlin Wall. Behind the park, farther down Scharnhorststrasse, are typical East German apartment blocks. When they were new, the apartments in these bland towers would have been eagerly sought: modern buildings, on a quiet street, but just a short walk from the city center. What made it quiet was the fact that this was the very edge of the GDR. On the corner of Habersaathstrasse once stood a modest stone memorial, accompanied by an eternal flame, honoring a border guard killed in a shootout in 1962 as he tried to stop someone fleeing to West Berlin. After 1989 the offensive memorial was first vandalized and then quietly removed. The actual site of Peter Göring's death was on the other side of Scharnhorststrasse, in an area off limits to the public at the time. But you can now visit it: back on the left side of the street you reach the front wall of the **Invalidenfriedhof**, one of Berlin's most important cemeteries.

It originally served as the cemetery of the Invalidenhaus, then of the neighborhood that grew up around it. Later, heroes of the Wars of Liberation against Napoleon (1813–15) were buried here, and it subsequently became a prestigious burial spot for civilians as well as soldiers such as Manfred von Richthofen, the World War I flying ace known as the Red Baron. The oldest extant graves from the eighteenth century are located near the front on the right side. Farther back are many generals and ministers of war. The most important grave marker is for General Gerhard David von Scharnhorst, creator of the Prussian General Staff. Christian Daniel Rauch's bronze sculpture of a sleeping lion lies atop Schinkel's marble arch, which is decorated with a frieze illustrating scenes from Scharnhorst's career (but with the participants in Roman dress).

A few steps farther back is a wall, with three stone plaques noting that the cemetery contains a mass grave of Prussian, Austrian and Saxon soldiers killed in the intra-German war of 1866; another mass grave of World War II bombing victims; and the unmarked graves of executed participants in the 1944 assassination attempt against

Hitler. Not mentioned is the fact that this was once intended as a cemetery for the elite of the Third Reich, and that Fritz Todt, builder of the autobahns, and the assassinated SS leader Reinhard Heydrich lie in now-unmarked graves. This wall does not actually mark the back of the cemetery; rather, it is a part of *the* Wall. The rear section of the cemetery was bulldozed by the East Germans to create their no-man's-land along this section of the border, which followed the canal and was lined by the more formidable Western-facing Wall, since demolished. The old brick cemetery wall along the canal has been restored, and some gravestones have been re-erected over the graves that remain undisturbed under the ground. Still visible is the asphalt road along which the border guards patrolled the death strip. Here along the canal is where the first East German was killed trying to cross the Wall: Günter Litfin, on 24 August 1961. This is also the spot where the guard Peter Göring died the next year.

The path along the canal, taken to the right, leads to a complex of apartment buildings put up in the 1990s on the former death strip. Their terrace incorporates the canal path. Just beyond, a guard tower from the Wall remains, one of two of its kind still standing, now an incongruous crumbling presence amid the newer buildings. From here you can continue to follow the course of the Wall, first down the pleasant canal path, then turning right on Boyenstrasse, past nondescript East German buildings once used by border troops, and coming out on Chausseestrasse (where you can find a streetcar or the U6 subway – left toward Wedding, right to Invalidenstrasse and Friedrichstrasse). Turn right on Chausseestrasse, following the double row of paving stones that mark the former course of the Wall. Here was another of the official checkpoints. The paving stones soon turn left into Liesenstrasse, lined with cemeteries, but Chausseestrasse takes you back to Invalidenstrasse, past a neo-Renaissance building at number 105, on your right, built in 1892 by Alfred Messel as a Volkskaffeehaus, like the one in Neue Schönhauser Strasse (see Chapter 7). A left turn on Invalidenstrasse will put you in the vicinity of Nordbahnhof. This was another of Berlin's main rail stations, the point of departure for the Baltic beaches and the vast Prussian northeast that now belongs to Poland and Russia. (Before the war it was called Stettin station, after the city that is now Szczecin in Poland.) In 1917 the German army high command, hoping to disrupt the Russian war effort after the tsar's overthrow, secretly arranged to bring a rail carriage with Lenin and other Russian revolutionaries from their Swiss exile across German territory. They arrived at Potsdam station and were hustled across town to Stettin station and a train bound for their rendezvous with destiny at Petrograd's Finland Station. The ruined station was demolished in the 1960s, and only a few buildings remain from the once-bustling quarter of hotels and restaurants. One is the main post office for northern Berlin (1936), facing the side street Am Nordbahnhof, an example of Third Reich modernism: a steel-frame structure with clean lines, colorful travertine facing, deep window openings and a heavy cornice. Also during the Third Reich, the S-Bahn line that ended here was connected to Anhalter Bahnhof, south of the city center, by the tunnel that passes under Friedrichstrasse and Potsdamer Platz. The S-Bahn station Nordbahnhof dates from that time.

Just past the station, Gartenstrasse, taken to the left, will lead you along the disused rail yards, which may soon be landscaped as a park. A short distance up (and across from an entrance to the underground S-Bahn) you reach the corner of **Bernauer Strasse** and, once again, the former course of the Wall. It extended forward along Gartenstrasse, next to the rail line, turning sharply here to follow the entire length of Bernauer Strasse. This was one of the most famous stretches of Wall, certainly the best known outside the city center. Its notoriety arose from a peculiarity of history: the border between the districts of Mitte and Wedding ran along the southern (East Berlin) side of the street. The street was lined with tenements, their front doors standing directly on the border that was closed in 1961. Hence the dramatic scenes of that August, some captured on film: as border troops sealed off the buildings' entrances, residents climbed or jumped from upper-story windows, hindered by guards inside and aided by West Berliners in the street below. It was Bernauer Strasse that made both the pain and the absurdity of the Wall visible to the world.

Over the following months, the buildings were emptied and then demolished, except for their bricked-up ground-floor façades, which remained as the Bernauer Strasse segment of the Wall until the early 1980s, when they were replaced by smooth concrete slabs like those you can see down the street. The wide swath of no-man's-land is still visible along much of the street. Reconstruction since 1989 has been slow, because of uncertainties over property ownership and over incompatible plans for new housing, a widened street, restored cemeteries and a Wall memorial.

Proceeding down Bernauer Strasse, you first walk along a reconstructed brick cemetery wall. Here the Sophienkirche has reclaimed the portion of its cemetery that was bulldozed to create the death strip. A little farther along, however, is a different kind of wall: the 13-foot-high prefabricated concrete segments of the Berlin Wall. The first part you reach retains its 1990 appearance: hacked-up by souvenir-hunters. Farther on, it has been restored to pristine condition. This is the official **Wall memorial**, a controversial design by the architects Kohlhoff and Kohlhoff, completed in 1998. One of the guiding ideas of the memorial, incompletely realized, was to reconstruct the entire complex of border fortifications. The Wall, after all, was not just a wall, although that is what Westerners saw. Behind it were trip wires, dog runs, a patrol road, guard towers, bright lights and above all a wide strip of open space, enclosed on the Eastern side by another, more modest wall. In the memorial, that Eastern wall has also been reconstructed. On both sides of the site are the architects' main contribution: two metal walls that run perpendicular to the original Wall and enclose the space. The metal was supposed to function as a mirror to create the visual illusion of a long and continuous wall, but the effect is lost on most visitors. With the former death strip enclosed on all four sides, you can see it only through the slits in the back wall. There is, in any case, little to see there. The drama of the Berlin Wall lay in the guards' activity (and the decision was made, understandably, to leave that kind of historical reenactment to the movies) as well as in the pervasive atmosphere of fear, something that no memorial can reproduce. A small building across the street (at the corner of Ackerstrasse), the **Berlin Wall Documentation Center**, displays photographs, film, sound recordings and documents from the history of the Wall. As the name implies, it makes the materials available and leaves most interpretation to the visitor. You can also climb to its roof for the best view of the memorial.

You will be aware, then, that the peace and quiet you find on Bernauer Strasse is very different from the quiet that reigned here, most of the time, from 1961 to 1989. The quiet of those days was mixed with tension and, for many people, despair – particularly those whose loved ones were lost to them behind the Wall. The Wall divided families and friends, in part simply because it divided a city, in part because it separated many people from their places of employment. In 1961 thousands of Berliners lived on one side of the Wall (mostly in the East) and worked on the other side. Up to 1961 freedom of movement within the city had been viewed with suspicion by the Eastern police, but had not been impeded. The result was a very strange city, with two different economic and political systems coexisting uneasily. 13 August 1961, for all its obvious brutality, brought clarity and order. From then on East was East and West was West. The case can even be made that the Wall brought security to the entire world, if not for the reasons the East Germans proclaimed. They declared that their 'antifascist protective rampart' (that's really what they called it; they refused to call it a 'wall') had staved off an invasion by the capitalist-fascists. What the Wall *did* make clear was that the Soviet Union would not seize West Berlin, as it had been threatening to do: the Western allies would be permitted to stay there. Although they dared not say so publicly, President Kennedy and Prime Minister Macmillan were relieved that the Berlin crisis had been settled peacefully – albeit at the expense of the Berliners.

A short distance farther along Bernauer Strasse, an oval chapel sits in the former no-man's-land. The moving **Chapel of Reconciliation** replaces the Church of Reconciliation (1894), which, unlike the tenements around it, was not immediately demolished after 1961. It stood unused and inaccessible, however, and in 1985 the East Germans decided to dynamite it to clear their sight lines. The new chapel (2000), designed by Rudolf Reitermann and Peter Sassenroth, is minimally adorned but conceptually complex. It is surrounded by a curved wooden lattice wall whose lightness contrasts with the thick, unadorned clay walls of the chapel itself. The clay is mixed with fragments of red brick, recalling the material of the destroyed church. The chapel takes the form of a circle modified to offer a hint of both an entry and a choir, arranged on an east–west axis, but the building's few details also highlight the northwest–southeast axis of the original building (and the surrounding streets). The interior, lit by a skylight and two high windows, reveals several traces of the past, including a piece of the old oak altar and its sandstone base, set in the floor under the new altar. Through a glass plate in the floor you can see the foundation of the original church, several cinderblocks from the original construction of the Wall in 1961 and an American World War II bomb that was discovered and defused during construction. Outside, gravel covers the entire remaining area of the original church's foundation. Also outside are three bells that were salvaged from the original church, plus the cross from its steeple. When the church was dynamited, the cross fell into a neighboring cemetery (on the Eastern side) and was hidden by care-takers. Another historical trace deliberately left visible is the paved patrol road through no-man's-land, which is still visible along much of Bernauer Strasse.

Along parts of Bernauer Strasse that have not been redeveloped, other traces of the border remain. The over-grown strip of vegetation lining the right side of the street once obscured the Western side of the Wall. This was the tiny strip of land that belonged to East Berlin but lay in front of the Wall and hence was neglected. (Behind the Wall, nothing was overgrown.) Along the Western side, makeshift memorials were put up for those who died trying to cross. Some gave a name; others, just the date of death of an anonymous person whose killing was witnessed from the West. Some of them remain in place.

Other famous events in the history of the Wall occurred farther down Bernauer Strasse. Near Strelitzer Strasse was the most famous of many tunnels that were dug under the Wall in its first years, before the widened death strip and more thorough surveillance made the feat nearly impossible. From the courtyard of Strelitzer Strasse 55, a group of young West Berliners dug a 400-foot-long tunnel that reached into an unused bakery at Bernauer

Strasse 97. On the night of 3 October 1964, 57 people fled through it. On 5 October, an informer revealed the secret to the police and a shootout ensued, at the end of which the 21-year-old border guard Egon Schultz lay dead. Schultz was honored by the GDR as a hero murdered by Western fascist bandits. However, Stasi files reveal that the fatal shot came from a fellow-border guard's Kalashnikov. Another tunnel ran from a now-vanished factory building at the corner of Wolgaster Strasse to a cellar at Schönholzer Strasse 7; through it 29 people fled in 1962. At Ruppiner Strasse, on 15 August 1961, the border guard Conrad Schumann fled to West Berlin over the newly strung barbed wire, with a leap captured in a famous photograph. Bernauer Strasse continues to where it becomes Eberswalder Strasse, which belonged to Prenzlauer Berg (see Chapter 10). If you turn north before that, you remain in the old West Berlin district of Wedding.

In 1961, despite all the wartime damage, this was still a densely built-up neighborhood of nineteenth-century tenements. Little trace of that remains on Bernauer Strasse: the East cleared its death strip, and on the Western side urban renewal replaced most of the old buildings. However, a few steps up Hussitenstrasse, opposite the chapel, number 4–5 is the remnant of an enormous apartment complex built in 1904 by a charitable building society, with six courtyards extending all the way through the block to Strelitzer Strasse. It became home to about a thousand people. Through their various architectural styles, the sequence of courtyards was supposed to illustrate the development of Berlin: Romanesque, Gothic, Nuremberg style, Renaissance, Baroque, Wilhelmine. The front façade on Hussitenstrasse is gone, but the foremost remaining part belonged to the Romanesque courtyard. Behind it is an elaborate red-brick Gothic court, followed by one in the style associated with the late-medieval glory days of Nuremberg. The rest of the complex has been destroyed.

A short walk up Hussitenstrasse brings you to the former **factory complex of AEG** (the German General Electric Company). Along with Siemens, this was the major firm in the new electrical industry in which turn-of-the-century Berlin led Europe. AEG was founded by Emil Rathenau, an assimilated Jew, who was succeeded by his son, Walther Rathenau, an intellectual and supporter of cultural life, who later put Germany's economy on a wartime footing during World War I and enabled it to hold out against the British blockade. He was foreign minister of the Weimar Republic when he was assassinated by anti-Semitic nationalists in 1922. The Rathenaus were determined that their industrial architecture would be distinguished, and to that end they hired prominent architects. For its first buildings in this complex, in the 1890s, AEG turned to Franz Schwechten, architect of the Anhalt rail station and the Kaiser Wilhelm memorial church. His main work was on the left side of Hussitenstrasse, beyond Feldstrasse. The Hussitenstrasse side of that block was mostly destroyed; the best view is from Ackerstrasse. Here you see a brick façade in the tradition of Schinkel's Bauakademie, with pilasters, arched windows and terracotta decoration. It faces Gartenplatz, once the site of the town gallows, now of a Roman Catholic church built in 1893 for the many Catholic workers moving here from the Rhineland.

More important was the work of Peter Behrens, hired by AEG as chief designer in 1907. His first and most famous building was the turbine hall in Moabit (see Chapter 11), but the largest concentration of his work is here. Schwechten, a typical architect of his time, designed façades, leaving the factory interiors to others and making no attempt to coordinate his work with theirs. Behrens was a pioneering modernist in his attempt to make the appearance of entire buildings express their industrial functions. Unlike later and purer modernists, however (such as his young assistants during his AEG years, Walter Gropius, Le Corbusier and Ludwig Mies van der Rohe), Behrens did not entirely dispense with recognizable historical styles. Instead, he updated them.

At the corner of Hussitenstrasse and Voltastrasse (one block beyond Feldstrasse) stands Behrens's large factory hall from 1911–13, resembling the Moabit turbine hall but larger and even more austere. Originally it had a glass roof. Next to it, on Voltastrasse, the building with a clock tower predates Behrens's tenure, although his first job for AEG was an alteration of its façade. Behind it, in the middle of the block (accessible from Voltastrasse) is Behrens's high-voltage factory (1910), an irregularly shaped building (fitted around railroad tracks), complex in its massing, and recalling Egyptian motifs, yet virtually without ornament. Also facing Voltastrasse is Behrens's small-motor factory (1911–13), an enormous example of Greek classicism stripped to its essence. The 190-meter-long, seven-story façade, of glass and glazed brick, is punctuated with pilasters which have neither base nor capital. This building, along with a similar one in an entirely different genre, Behrens's German Embassy in St Petersburg, established models for the classical purity aspired to by high modernists like Mies van der Rohe but also for the oversized, stripped classicism of Hitler's, Stalin's and Ulbricht's architects and perhaps of American, British and French official buildings in the 1930s as well.

Beyond the far end of the small-motor factory, Voltastrasse reaches busy Brunnenstrasse. Most of the Brunnenstrasse end of the complex was demolished after AEG ceased production here in 1978. Between new office buildings there remains an ornate archway designed by Schwechten, which originally served as the entry for AEG's white-collar employees. At the far corner of the AEG complex, Brunnenstrasse crosses Gustav-Meyer-Allee. Down the latter street, a plaque commemorates the many foreign laborers compelled to toil here during World War II.

Near Brunnenstrasse, a simple modern church designed by Otto Bartning (1956) sits at the edge of **Humboldthain**, a park laid out in 1869 in the rapidly growing industrial city. It still provides a pleasant green space, but it changed dramatically after 1941. Here stood one of the three massive flak towers built during World War II (the others were at the zoo and in Friedrichshain park). These nearly indestructible concrete behemoths offered air-raid shelters, housed critical functions (including hospitals) and above all bristled with anti-aircraft guns that took an enormous toll on the British and American bombers that appeared in the skies almost daily from 1943 on. This one, built in 1941 by Italian 'volunteers', Soviet POWs and other forced laborers, could shelter 10,000 Germans. In 1948 the French occupiers tried unsuccessfully to blow it up. After that it was partly buried by the rubble hill that now dominates the park. However, it remains visible – and accessible on foot – on the far side of the park, facing the S-Bahn.

Brunnenstrasse takes you across the rail line to the U-Bahn and S-Bahn (and perhaps soon, long-distance rail) stations at Gesundbrunnen, also the site of a 1990s shopping mall. Here, too, are underground **bunkers** from World War II. Such bunkers exist all over the city; here, however, they have recently been opened to Saturday tours organized by Verein Berliner Unterwelten, a group of amateur explorers who have charted many forgotten man-made structures in underground Berlin. Most date from a crash program of bunker construction begun by the Third Reich in 1940. There was never nearly enough space for everyone during the nightly bombing raids, but thousands did come regularly. After 1943 people bombed out of their homes moved into the bunkers. This only worsened the sanitary and emotional problems that arose with so many people crammed into small, dark spaces. After the war the victorious Allies, facing the possibility of atomic warfare, learned all they could about German bunker construction, the world's best. They also resolved to destroy the bunkers, something the Russians did quite thoroughly (so there are few in the former East Berlin and East Germany). In the West, the Allies gave in to protests from homeless people living in the bunkers, and merely weakened the bunkers enough to make them militarily useless. The very last bunker residents in Germany, in the city of Braunschweig, did not move out until 1973. One of the Gesundbrunnen bunkers was adapted for Cold War use as a fallout shelter and contains the detritus of the 1980s. The other, attached to the U-Bahn station, still displays original signs and phosphorescent wall paint as well as objects found in it and other bunkers: compost toilets, beds, spoons, watches, binoculars, helmets, guns and much else.

The name **Gesundbrunnen** ('fountain of health') recalls the spa established here in the eighteenth century, of which no trace remains. As industrial Wedding encroached in the nineteenth century, the bath houses became dance halls. A few blocks (or one U-Bahn stop) up Badstrasse (the continuation of Brunnenstrasse) stands one of Schinkel's suburban churches. Like the others, St Paul's (1835) is a simple rectangular structure with an entrance hall in front and a rounded apse behind. Its decor is that of a Greek temple. A sacristy and bell tower were added in the 1880s. After wartime damage the building was restored with a modern interior. Just across Badstrasse, Prinzenallee 87 was the site of the synagogue of Wedding's small Jewish community, which was plundered but not (because of the proximity of other buildings) burned in 1938. The synagogue stood in the courtyard, where a plaque recalls it.

10

Prenzlauer Berg

THE NAME PRENZLAUER BERG has acquired an aura in recent years. Like Kreuzberg, this was the name of an unimposing hill that became applied to a city quarter only when the consolidated city was carved into districts in 1920. And like Kreuzberg, Prenzlauer Berg's crumbling tenements became the center of alternative politics and culture during the 1980s. The difference was crucial, however: Prenzlauer Berg belonged to East Berlin, and the social dropouts who gathered there were correspondingly fewer in number, less visible to the casual visitor, and far more daring in every act of nonconformity, since the secret police watched everything and frequently cracked down. What drew the dropouts here were the many rundown and abandoned apartments, unwanted by those who wished to live in comfort (and who moved to the new satellite cities as soon as they could). Here the scruffy noncomformists had a feeling of being among their own kind and also not quite so visible to the authorities, as they conducted their salons with cheap wine, poetry and folk songs.

After the Wall came down, Prenzlauer Berg changed dramatically. Westerners – from West Berlin but especially from West Germany and abroad – came in search of cheap rents and excitement. Prenzlauer Berg's population is now a mixture of established residents who were here when the Wall stood, and a growing proportion of wealthier and more fashionable newcomers. Tensions have accompanied gentrification, even if it has not been as far-reaching as in the Spandauer Vorstadt. By the end of the

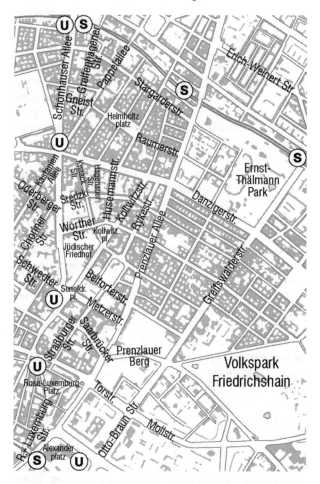

1990s, the self-conscious avant-garde of the Berlin 'scene'
had declared Prenzlauer Berg hopelessly bourgeois and
had sought out more obscure (and cheaper) neighborhoods, mainly in Friedrichshain. Tourists will certainly

encounter others of their kind here, but most will not find the area as staid as those condemnations might imply.

Although Prenzlauer Berg is farther from the city center than the Spandauer Vorstadt, it can still be reached in a comfortable walk, so Alexanderplatz makes a good starting point for a tour. (If you prefer to start your walk at the heart of Prenzlauer Berg, take the U2 train to Senefelderplatz.) If you cross the wide Karl-Liebknecht-Strasse next to the S-Bahn, you will be on Dircksenstrasse, which follows the S-Bahn toward Hackescher Markt. The unremarkable building on your right, extending around the corner of Rosa-Luxemburg-Strasse, was a strikingly modern steel-frame structure at the time of its completion in 1930 as the headquarters of the newly established public transport authority. Its architect, Alfred Grenander, also designed many subway stations, including those of the U8 line, built at the same time, which runs directly below it.

To your right, up Rosa-Luxemburg-Strasse, you are looking into what was once the heart of Berlin's most notorious slum. The 'shed quarter' (**Scheunenviertel**) got its name from the animals' stalls that were concentrated here after a 1672 fire code banished them beyond the town walls. In the nineteenth century they were supplanted by tenements. Middle-class Berliners felt ill at ease in the teeming streets and courtyards, and the area acquired a reputation as dangerous. That reputation was inseparable from the fact that it attracted many poor Jewish immigrants from eastern Europe who came here fleeing persecution. Their distinctive dress, customs and Yiddish language made them easily recognizable. Even many assimilated Berlin Jews openly shared the disdain for these strangers, fearing that they (the 'respectable' Jews) might be grouped with these targets of anti-Semitism. These days many people come looking for the Scheunenviertel, and some even think they've found it.

Today the name is often applied to the Spandauer Vorstadt just to the west (see Chapter 7), which, however, was somewhat wealthier, its Jewish heritage both older and more German. The real Scheunenviertel's reputation made it the target of Berlin's most ambitious slum-clearance project before the Second World War. The heart of the slum was demolished in the first years of the twentieth century to build the street and square now named after Rosa Luxemburg. Further demolition was undertaken by the Nazis, who justified both slum clearance and expulsion of the Jews as public-health measures. Only a few traces of the old quarter can be found in Almstadtstrasse and Max-Beer-Strasse, which run parallel to Rosa-Luxemburg-Strasse.

Rosa-Luxemburg-Strasse opens into the triangular space of **Rosa-Luxemburg-Platz**. After some controversy, unified Berlin agreed to keep this GDR name. Rosa Luxemburg was a cherished figure for West German leftists as well as for East German dissidents, who protested official policies by citing her statement that 'freedom must always mean freedom for those who think differently'. Despite those words, directed against Lenin's repression in revolutionary Russia, she remains an object of suspicion because of her role in founding the German Communist Party and in supporting revolution rather than parliamentary democracy in defeated Germany (until her murder in January 1919). Nevertheless, her supporters continue to push for an official memorial to her, something the ambivalent East Germans never managed. Such a monument would probably be placed here.

In the center of the square is the only building put up before World War I in the newly cleared slum. The Volksbühne (1914) was built as the home of a theater company founded in 1890 to produce serious drama for a working-class audience. First Max Reinhardt ran it, staging the naturalistic, socially engaged drama of Ibsen and

Gerhart Hauptmann, and the radical Erwin Piscator worked here in the 1920s. The grand façade, in the simplified classicism of the time, signified the theater's high-cultural ambitions for its mass public. After World War II, only the walls stood, but the GDR, in the course of establishing its own strong socialist theatrical system, was proud to continue the tradition here, after its own fashion, and it rebuilt the theater. Since 1990 it has been home to renewed attempts to produce artistically ambitious theater for a broad public.

During the years of war and inflation, the theater stood alone in the cleared slum. Construction resumed in the late 1920s, producing the apartment buildings that line both sides of the square, designed by Hans Poelzig and distinctly modern with their horizontal lines and rounded corners. In the building at Rosa-Luxemburg-Strasse 30, at the corner of Hirtenstrasse, Poelzig designed a spectacular cinema. Unfortunately, little remains of the original interior. On the right side of the square, at the corner of Kleine Alexanderstrasse, is a building that the Communist Party took over in 1926 as its national headquarters, naming it Karl-Liebknecht-Haus after the party's murdered co-founder (with Rosa Luxemburg). Old photographs show it adorned with militant slogans. As the republic declined and Nazi support grew during the Great Depression, this (along with many other places in Berlin) became the scene of violent clashes. Among the most shocking was the ambush and murder of two policemen in 1931. One of the perpetrators, a Communist who escaped at the time, was Erich Mielke, later the head of East Germany's dreaded secret police, the Stasi. In the 1990s he eluded prosecution for his work there, but was convicted of the 60-year-old murders. When Hitler became chancellor in 1933, he banned the Communist Party and gave this building to the SA brownshirts. Both it and the square were subsequently renamed after Horst

Wessel, the Nazis' favorite martyr, who had been murdered by a Communist in 1930. After the war, the Communists retook and restored the building. It remains the national headquarters of their successors, the Party of Democratic Socialism.

Torstrasse crosses behind Rosa-Luxemburg-Platz, and from it Strassburger Strasse takes you into the sooty vestiges of industrial Prenzlauer Berg. The next street, Saarbrücker Strasse, was once dominated by breweries. The remnants of one are on your left; to the right is another, the former Bötzow brewery and its extensive beer garden. If you turn left on Saarbrücker Strasse, number 15 on the right is a richly decorated apartment house from 1876, an early example of the extravagant façades that soon became common, as the more restrained classicism of the Schinkel school went out of fashion. The apartments here were intended primarily for army officers stationed nearby. Contrary to much recent mythology, Prenzlauer Berg was by no means a thoroughly proletarian district. Indeed, the typical mammoth Berlin apartment block was a diverse neighborhood all by itself, with larger apartments facing the wide streets (this was before car noise) and smaller ones on the courtyards behind. The next street is **Schönhauser Allee**, the main artery of Prenzlauer Berg and, before that, the road linking Berlin to the villages of Pankow and Niederschönhausen. Across the street is yet another former brewery, Pfefferberg, with buildings and cellars dating as far back as the 1840s. Among the new cultural facilities here is the **Vitra Design Museum Berlin**, a branch of the well-known museum in Weil am Rhein. It offers temporary exhibitions on design, architecture, and fashion.

Pfefferberg faces **Senefelderplatz**, a triangular space named for Alois Senefelder, the inventor of lithography. The 1892 marble monument to him, the first in Berlin honoring an artisan, was sponsored by Berlin's printers and lithographers. Beneath the statue of Senefelder are two putti: one is writing Senefelder's name backwards, while the other holds a mirror to show the name correctly (if that arm has been restored: it was broken off recently). Also in the square is an eight-sided green cast-iron enclosure. 'Café Octagon' is what Berliners dubbed these public pissoirs, found all over the city from the late nineteenth until the late twentieth century. This is one of a few that have recently been restored. Most of the side streets are lined with their original apartment buildings from the 1870s. As you proceed northward, you follow the march of five-story buildings outward during the following decades. These massive and absurdly ornate structures bear witness to the mighty industrial city of a century ago. Prenzlauer Berg lost relatively little to wartime bombing, but it suffered from postwar neglect, as the GDR concentrated its resources almost entirely on new construction. In 1990 Prenzlauer Berg was a vital place, but its life played out behind endless rows of gray, crumbling façades. Since then the number of decayed façades has dwindled, amid a frenzy of subsidized renovation, but they continue to exude an old-fashioned dignity.

Just past Senefelder Platz, Schönhauser Allee 22, a yellow brick building, was constructed in the 1880s as an old-age home for the the Jewish community. Next to it is the entrance to the **Jewish cemetery** that was opened here in 1827, replacing the one on Grosse Hamburger Strasse. The cemetery is open to visitors on weekdays; you can wander among the densely packed, overgrown graves and get some sense of the nineteenth-century Jewish community. Along the exterior walls are larger markers for family plots. Among those buried here are the composer Giacomo Meyerbeer (near the north wall), the publisher Leopold Ullstein, and Bismarck's banker Gerson Bleichröder. After a new and larger Jewish cemetery was opened in 1880,

only a few burials took place here. Among the last was that of the painter Max Liebermann (1847–1935), in a family plot near the southeast wall. Next to him is buried his wife, Martha. In March 1943 she had the good fortune (if one dares call it that) to be warned that the Gestapo was coming to deport her to Theresienstadt, and she took her own life. The East Germans mounted a plaque at the cemetery entrance recalling the Nazis' 'destruction' of it. However, the dead Jews and their graves came out much better than their living descendants. Another East German plaque, inside the cemetery, recalls that men who sought to evade military service during the last months of the war hid in this neglected spot, but were found by the SS and hanged from the trees.

The cemetery is surrounded by apartment buildings. However, it once had a much-used rear entrance. According to unconfirmed legend, King Frederick William III, on his journeys to and from Niederschönhausen palace, was disturbed by the frequent sight of Jewish mourners, who were then ordered to enter the cemetery from the rear. Whatever the reason, burial processions long used the Judengang (Jews' walk). It is closed and inaccessible, but you can glimpse it if you return to Senefelder Platz and head up Kollwitzstrasse behind the cemetery. Past a remarkable playground built with leftover construction materials, you reach the apartment houses that stand between the cemetery and the street. If you can find an open doorway to a courtyard, you should be able to see the cemetery's rear wall and the former land of the Judengang alongside it. (It ends at a gate – open on rare occasions – in a narrow space between two buildings on Knaackstrasse.)

If, however, you cross Kollwitzstrasse and take Belforter Strasse away from the cemetery, the next corner brings you to a park that contains the remnants of Berlin's first municipal waterworks. In the 1850s the city contracted with the English firm of Fox and Crampton to build a much-needed system of piped water, replacing the increasingly contaminated water drawn from wells and from the Spree within the city. This site lay high enough above the city to supply water to the tall buildings down the hill. Water was pumped from the upper Spree to a reservoir dug here, and its discharge was regulated by a minaret-like brick standpipe, which still stands. After the city took over the waterworks in 1873, it covered the reservoir and added a massive brick water tower, necessary to provide water pressure to the buildings rising on higher ground nearby. Six stories of apartments (recently renovated) line the exterior of the round tower. In 1888 a second underground reservoir was added. The covered reservoirs, long empty, have recently been used for concerts and exhibitions. In 1933, however, they served other purposes. Here as in many other places, the brownshirts of the SA, operating with impunity under the new Nazi government, imprisoned and tortured their opponents.

Rykestrasse runs northward in the axis of the water tower. In the courtyard of number 53, the second building on the left, you will find a grand synagogue, a neo-Romanesque building from 1904. It was typical to place synagogues in inconspicuous locations. This one was looted but not destroyed on Kristallnacht in 1938. Authorities did not permit it to be burned, presumably because of its proximity to other buildings. It was restored after the war and served as the synagogue for East Berlin's tiny Jewish community. Rykestrasse is a typical Prenzlauer Berg street, lined with intact rows of ornate apartment houses. They were badly deteriorated by the 1980s, when the East Berlin government decided that the only economical solution to its housing woes was demolition of these buildings and their replacement by new, prefabricated ones. One of the first projects was planned for Rykestrasse. Tipped off about the plans, residents organized opposition (secretly, they thought, although they later learned that the Stasi knew everything) and presented a counterproposal to renovate the existing buildings. This was a brave act in the GDR, and even more remarkably, it succeeded, as in early 1989 the government agreed to fund their renovation rather than demolition. Unfortunately for this project (if for little else) that regime collapsed shortly afterward and the ownership of the buildings passed to previously expropriated Westerners. The new owners have indeed renovated the street, as you can see, and the local residents managed to organize a housing cooperative that acquired two of the buildings (numbers 13 and 14, including a popular café).

In the 1990s, Knaackstrasse, which divides Rykestrasse from the water tower, attracted a row of trendy cafés and restaurants. In good weather, tables spill all over the wide sidewalks, typical of Berlin's older districts with their large granite slabs surrounded by small paving stones tapped into the Brandenburg sand. If you take Knaackstrasse one block west, back to Kollwitzstrasse, you reach **Kollwitzplatz**, the center of the Prenzlauer Berg scene. On your right at the corner of Kollwitzstrasse and Knaackstrasse stands a new apartment building. In its predecessor, from 1891 until its destruction in 1943, the artist Käthe Kollwitz lived with her husband, a physician who treated the neighborhood's poor residents. Since 1947 the street and square have borne her name. Her observations of the children on the square, particularly in the hungry years during and after the First World War, inspired some of her most famous graphic work. In the center of the square is a statue of a mournful Kollwitz, a 1958 work by Gustav Seitz based on a Kollwitz self-portrait. She sits, appropriately, at the center of a popular neighborhood playground.

Husemannstrasse runs for two blocks north from the square, lined with grand apartment houses from the 1890s.

East Berlin selected this street for a showcase project and renovated all the buildings in time for the city's 750th anniversary in 1987, installing old-fashioned shops and cafés. It was an odd sight at the time, since visitors had to traverse many blocks of crumbling buildings to reach this gleaming showcase. Much of the renovation was shoddy and has since been redone. Halfway up, Husemannstrasse crosses Sredzkistrasse. If you turn left here, you will next pass Hagenauer Strasse, which displays a restored row of distinctly less fashionable apartment buildings, lacking the balconies and wide bays of Husemannstrasse. At the next corner (this is Knaackstrasse again) you see a massive yellow-brick tower typical of Berlin's neo-Romanesque churches. This church, however, was actually a brewery. From Sredzkistrasse you can enter the lively complex that sprawls across several large court-yards. (Another entrance is on Knaackstrasse near Danziger Strasse.) This became the main home of the Schultheiss brewery in 1864; these buildings date to circa 1890. The **Kulturbrauerei** (culture brewery), as it is now known, houses artisans' studios and concert rooms as well as a multiplex cinema and restaurants, including 'Soda', known for its audacious insect cuisine. (Try it, if you dare.) The building at the corner of Sredzkistrasse and Schönhauser Allee, topped by an even taller tower, originally housed the brewery's restaurant. The towers deliberately recall medieval churches and castles, whereas the massive arched entrances echo nineteenth-century rail stations – and in fact the architect, Franz Schwechten, is best known for his Anhalt station and for the Kaiser Wilhelm Memorial Church. Many of the old painted signs have been restored: for example, 'Maschinenhaus' and 'Flaschenbierabteilung' (bottled-beer department, where once some 30,000 bottles were filled daily).

If you cross Schönhauser Allee at Sredzkistrasse, you reach Oderberger Strasse on the other side. A short distance up the street, on your left, is the grand façade of Ludwig Hoffmann's 1902 bathhouse. The municipal architect Hoffmann mastered several historical styles and has left examples of each. Here he chose German Renaissance, recalling old German town halls. Behind the row of arched windows were the bathtubs (something found in few apartments) that patrons could use for a small fee. Above them were apartments, mainly for employees of the school built at the same time in the interior of the block. The arched entries at each side of the building lead there: one for boys, one for girls. At the rear of the building is the swimming pool, in a church-like vaulted hall. The ruinous bath has been closed since 1986, but there are plans to reopen it.

Oderberger Strasse, like Rykestrasse, boasts intact rows of apartment buildings that were threatened with demolition in the 1980s. Here, too, residents organized to defend their homes. In those days, the street ended at the Berlin Wall (this is the eastern end of Bernauer Strasse). Just beyond, a stretch of the Eastern-facing wall has been left in place, gaily painted, and incorporated into the Mauerpark (wall park), along with the adjoining stadium originally built by the GDR for the Third World Youth Games in 1951. If, however, you turn right on Kastanienallee before you reach the end of Oderberger Strasse, you remain in the intact nineteenth-century confines of Prenzlauer Berg. This was the city of stone, as Berlin was then known – although, as is most apparent on unrenovated façades, it was actually a city of brick buildings faced with stucco carved to look like stone. One face of the city of stone was the view from the wide streets lined with these ornate façades; its other face, the one most poor people saw from their windows, was the dark courtyard. Kastanienallee 12 is a notable example of a very deep Berlin lot. Enter the first courtyard and you can look through the archways of successive transverse wings back through three more courtyards behind it. The last one is wide open only because the wing behind it was destroyed in the war. These once hated buildings remain vital places, but courtyards no longer teem with life as they did when peddlers and organ-grinders could count on an audience appearing at the windows of the crowded flats.

Just down Kastanienallee is the Prater beer garden, founded in the 1830s as a country retreat for Berliners able to escape the city for a day. As the city grew up around it, it remained an oasis amid the densely packed tenements. It includes a theater building from 1903 and an outdoor stage from the 1950s. Kastanienallee brings you back to Schönhauser Allee at a major intersection. The ring boulevard extending west is called Eberswalder Strasse, which since the demise of the Wall again connects to Bernauer Strasse. To the east its name is Danziger Strasse, after the Baltic city of Danzig. The East Germans renamed this street after the Bulgarian Communist leader Georgi Dimitroff. After reunification there was some hesitation before restoring the German name of a city that is now in Poland and now called Gdansk.

Dominating the intersection is the overhead U-Bahn. This stretch was constructed above ground to save money, as had been done a few years earlier in Kreuzberg. Just as wealthy Charlottenburg had insisted that its end of that earliest line be put underground, so, too, did bourgeois Pankow, north of here. Alfred Grenander's station platform remains in its original, elegant form from 1913. Underneath the tracks is an unassuming shack widely believed to serve the city's best currywurst. Not many foreigners warm to that distinctly German and proletarian treat, bits of sausage doused in a mysterious red sauce. Tile set into the triangle of pavement between Kastanienallee and Schönhauser Allee spells out the name Skladanowsky. This recalls the fact that in 1892, in the elegant building sandwiched between those two streets,

Max Skladanowsky carried out his first experiments with film projection. Most of the world acknowledges the French Lumière brothers as the inventors of cinema, but the Berliner Skladanowsky has a claim to the honor as well – another case (as with the telephone and television) in which the Germans feel cheated of credit for their technological prowess. Skladanowsky premiered the world's first film (and first chase scene) in 1895 at the Wintergarten theater on Friedrichstrasse.

Across the wide intersection, the direct continuation of Kastanienallee is Pappelallee – that is, poplar boulevard instead of chestnut. Its trees are less impressive than its varied historicist and Jugendstil façades. At the next corner, Raumerstrasse leads to the right to **Helmholtzplatz**, a large and leafy square where development has only recently spilled over from Kollwitzplatz, with fancy drinks at sidewalk tables now outnumbering beer cans at park benches. If you instead turn left into Gneiststrasse and then right into Greifenhagener Strasse, you pass a large apartment complex erected between 1871 and 1914 by a nonprofit society dedicated to improving workers' housing. The glazed-brick façades were not typical of speculative housing, but the most notable difference lies in the interior of the blocks, which were largely left open – a sharp contrast to the tiny courtyards of most tenements. Greifenhagener Strasse 58–59 is one of Ludwig Hoffmann's elegant historicist school buildings (1904). This was a 'double school', meaning it taught both girls and boys, but separately. Boys entered on the right, girls on the left, and the building was divided through the center. Next to it is another important example of reform housing by Hoffmann's friend Alfred Messel, who designed the turn-of-the-century buildings at the corner of Stargarder Strasse. In Greifenhagener Strasse 57, the original entry and stairway have been restored. Across Stargarder Strasse, the west side of Greifenhagener Strasse is lined with particularly grand turn-of-the-century neo-Baroque and Jugendstil buildings. Builders identified this as a high-rent location because of the church that had already been built across the street. The architect August Orth built the Gethsemane church (1893) of Berlin red brick in a style based on the transition from Romanesque to Gothic. Its spacious vaulted interior, capable of holding a large crowd, suited it to its most important historical role, when in 1989 it became the most prominent of a handful of churches that drew ever larger crowds to ever more daring discussions of civil liberties and reform in East Germany.

Just past the church, Greifenhagener Strasse crosses the S-Bahn ring, at one end of the Schönhauser Allee station. At the other end, where the S-Bahn crosses the U-Bahn, a generic new shopping mall has become a popular gathering spot as well as the death knell for many downscale neighborhood shops catering to the former East German population.

Other sights in the northern end of Prenzlauer Berg require long walks or use of other transportation. Among those that lie farther afield are innovative 1920s housing projects. Tenements had barely spread north of the ring railway when the outbreak of war in 1914 halted construction for a decade. When it resumed, Prenzlauer Berg became home to several of Bruno Taut's housing estates. The nearest and best known lies east of Prenzlauer Allee, the next major radial street and the next S-Bahn station. The Carl Legien residential estate, completed in 1930, extends north from Erich-Weinert-Strasse and consists of several large U-shaped buildings punctuated by five-story towers in the clean modernist style. Taut was charged with putting a large number of housing units in a small space, but he managed to create an ensemble that left enough well-situated open space to contrast sharply with the prewar neighborhoods nearby. On the other side of

Prenzlauer Allee is another large project from the late 1920s, designed by Paul Mebes and Paul Emmerich. And a short distance east of the Carl Legien estate is another Bruno Taut project from 1928. It extends east from Hosemannstrasse, but is best approached from the other side, near the Greifswalder Strasse S-Bahn, at the corner of Greifswalder Strasse and Grellstrasse.

On the south side of the S-Bahn, the area extending from Prenzlauer Allee to Greifswalder Strasse (the easternmost of Prenzlauer Berg's radial avenues) was, for a century, the site of the municipal gas plant, where coal was converted into gas for fuel. East Berlin shut down the plant in 1981, thanks to new supplies of Siberian natural gas, and replaced it with a showcase housing estate, but the project was dogged by controversy. Three massive nineteenth-century brick gasometers along the rail line had become neighborhood icons, and original plans called for their conversion to new uses, but suddenly and secretly (as was normal in the GDR) they were condemned. When word leaked out, Prenzlauer Berg erupted in protest. There were arrests, and some people lost their jobs, but the gasometers were dynamited in 1984. The new project, **Ernst Thälmann Park**, honored the pre–1933 leader of the German Communist Party who was murdered in Buchenwald, a man the GDR built into a national icon, the preeminent symbol of working-class militancy and antifascist resistance. (As a result, he still has his admirers, although revisionist historians have dismantled much of the official Thälmann myth.) The project includes a planetarium (on the Prenzlauer Allee side) and a spacious array of residential buildings. Its centerpiece is a grotesquely large, 40-foot-high bronze bust of Thälmann with a raised fist, designed by the Russian sculptor Lev Kerbel in the best Soviet monumental style. It was said to be equipped with a heated nose to prevent snow from marring its appearance. Party chief Erich

Honecker himself apparently commissioned Kerbel (who had sculpted the central figure in the Soviets' Tiergarten memorial decades before) after East German sculptors persisted in proposing modest and human-scaled memorials. The bust, on its massive stone pedestal, still faces Greifswalder Strasse, alone in a vast paved square once used for official ceremonies but now left to skateboarders and people who like to be alone but not invisible. After 1990 there were many calls to remove it, which foundered less on opposition than on cost. Since then the statue has acquired many layers of graffiti, most of it banal, some of it clever. ('Don't you have it in a larger size?' 'Imprisoned, murdered, besmeared'.)

The East Germans had long planned to honor Thälmann with a memorial in the city center. The decision to place the monument here was proclaimed as a tribute to this proletarian district, but its location was important to one other audience. Greifswalder Strasse was part of the route taken every day by the motorcade of party leaders on their way to and from their exclusive residential enclave in rural Wandlitz. All of this 'protocol route' was notoriously well maintained, a Potemkin village through the crumbling city. The leaders saw the sparkling residential towers and the militant Thälmann – their gifts to the people – twice daily. (If the leaders were looking at Thälmann, they did not direct their gaze to the other side of the wide street, where monumental gateways on otherwise ordinary apartment buildings betray the fact that these were Hitler's gifts to the people.)

Greifswalder Strasse also takes you to Europe's largest **Jewish cemetery**. Take one of the frequent trams to Albertinenstrasse, four stops beyond the S-Bahn, and walk back to Herbert-Baum-Strasse, at the end of which is the cemetery entrance. It was established outside the city in 1880, when the one in Schönhauser Allee was running out of space. Its surroundings later became an industrial district, but, partly by design and partly by accident, it remains an isolated spot. Inside the entrance is an ornate neo-Renaissance building and a memorial to the dead of the Holocaust. Beyond them, you can wander through acres of overgrown graves, including many magnificent tombs of wealthy businessmen and professionals. Perhaps this place can help you grasp the dimensions of the act of national self-mutilation that Germany carried out under Hitler. The centerpiece of one well-maintained section is a memorial to Berlin Jews who died for their German fatherland in the First World War. Around it are rows of identical grave markers for the many young Jewish soldiers who fell in places like Verdun and the Somme, spared the knowledge of what their fatherland had in store for their families.

If you wish to follow the Communist leaders' route back toward Alexanderplatz (perhaps by tram, if you don't have a motorcade) you will see increasingly older apartment houses as you go inward. On your left, Greifswalder Strasse 15–19 dates to the early 1860s; just past it, number 9–12 is an elegant row from 1879. The side streets on the left lead into a less trendy but largely intact nineteenth-century section of Prenzlauer Berg known as the Bötzow quarter. Beyond it lies **Friedrichshain park**, the western tip of which nearly touches Greifswalder Strasse at the intersection where its name changes to Otto-Braun-Strasse. This was the first park established on the eastern side of the city, in the 1840s. Just inside its western entrance is Ludwig Hoffmann's amusing 'fairy-tale fountain' (1913), with stone sculptures portraying characters from the tales of the Grimm brothers (themselves eminent Berliners). Behind it, the park slopes upward. It didn't, originally, but this was the site of a pair of massive World War II flak towers. After the war they were partially dynamited, then buried in rubble. Near the top of the higher hill you can still see part of one protruding. The top layer of rubble came in part from the demolition of the royal palace in 1950, and it is said that the hill's sandstone steps and railings were carved from the palace's stones.

Among other things, the park offers a display of the GDR's sometimes bizarre public sculpture. On its left side, at the corner of Virchowstrasse and Am Friedrichshain, the GDR erected a pillar, flag, and wall relief to commemorate the solidarity (real or imagined) of German antifascists and Polish soldiers. It was designed by a team of East German and Polish sculptors (1972), declares support 'for your and our freedom' and includes the obligatory nod to brotherhood with the Soviet Union. On the opposite side of the park, facing Friedenstrasse, are a sculpture (by Fritz Cremer, 1968) and relief wall honoring the Germans who died fighting for the International Brigades in the Spanish Civil War. Beyond it, in the southeast corner of the park, is the Friedhof der Märzgefallenen, a cemetery established for those who died on Berlin's barricades in the 1848 revolution. Victims of the 1918 revolution were later added, and the GDR honored the navy men killed in the street fighting in Berlin with a modest 1960 statue of 'the red sailor'. At the corner of Friedenstrasse and Landsberger Allee is Platz der Vereinten Nationen, former site of the Lenin monument (see Chapter 18).

11

The Industrial North: Moabit, Wedding, and Beyond

MOABIT, once a marshy area downstream from the city, was first settled in the early eighteenth century by French Huguenot refugees. It became the prototypical preindustrial and, later, industrial suburb, a place for vital institutions (and people) unwanted within the town walls – a place of the accursed, like the Biblical kingdom of Moab after which it was probably named. Here were hospitals, cemeteries, drill grounds and barracks, and later factories, breweries, rail stations and a harbor. Most of the remaining land filled up with typically massive Berlin apartment houses and their mostly poor residents. Moabit became a working-class stronghold, a place of hard labor and bitter strikes, and later of Nazi attempts to provoke and destroy the 'red terror', as they characterized the dominant socialist and communist organizations. What remain today are many intact blocks of tenements, mainly from the 1880s and 1890s, plus many old factory buildings. Moabit is one of the poorest parts of the city, home to a wide variety of immigrants, but grimy and run-down only by German standards, which is to say not very. Its teeming streets look quite different from the gentrified quarters to the east or the comfortably bourgeois ones to the west. Its shops and pubs are an interesting mixture, some catering to the dwindling numbers of the old working class, others to immigrants, with others, unique and offbeat, clearly here because of the low rents.

Your starting point, the S-Bahn station Beusselstrasse, sits amid the rail yards that mark the northern edge of Moabit. The street crosses overhead. Your first stop is actually outside Moabit, at the northern end of the bridge, past the wholesale produce market (a busy place at dawn), where Beusselstrasse becomes Saatwinkler Damm. Follow it a short distance past the wide highway, and turn left on narrow Hüttigpfad. It is not a particularly pleasant place to stroll; you are making your way around to the back of Plötzensee prison, built in the 1870s and still in use. The **Plötzensee memorial**, a small enclosed space which you enter through a pillared gateway, commemorates a notorious part of the prison's history: its use as the primary place of execution for Third Reich political prisoners. Once inside, you face a stone wall dedicated to the 'victims of the Hitler dictatorship of the years 1933 to 1945'. Off to the side stands an urn with ashes from German concentration camps. This was one of the first memorials established by the postwar West German government, in 1952. Among the 2500 prisoners killed here were participants in the failed 20 July 1944 assassination plot against Hitler, as well as members of the Herbert Baum group, the Harnack 'Red Orchestra' and the Kreisau Circle around Helmuth James von Moltke. Many foreign prisoners were also executed here, as were ordinary Germans convicted for trivial acts or words classified as defeatist by wartime courts.

Directly behind the memorial wall is a small brick building with two rooms. The first was the execution chamber. It is stark and empty except for metal hooks hanging ominously from the ceiling. These were used for hanging the condemned – although most prisoners were beheaded, at first with an axe, later with a guillotine. On Hitler's personal orders, the 20 July conspirators were strangled, slowly and painfully, and their executions were filmed – until the camera operators refused to continue.

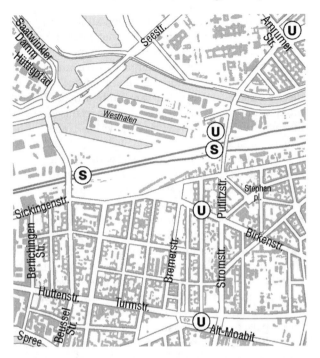

(The executioners apparently had no such qualms.) The second room displays photographs of victims and copies of documents from the Nazi People's Court (Volksgerichtshof) that sentenced them to die here. Here, too, you can pick up an English-language brochure that offers a lengthy description of the site, the Nazi justice system and the resisters who died here.

The memorial's dedication to the Third Reich's 'victims' reflects the mentality of the early Federal Republic, when the minority that had opposed the Nazis and the majority that had supported or tolerated them were able to agree only that Hitler had inflicted a great deal of suffering on his fellow-Germans. Even the courageous resisters of 20 July are not singled out for honor here; in 1952 too many Germans still saw them as traitors. (Their memorial at the Bendlerblock – see Chapter 6 – came later.) Newer memorials in Berlin engage the Third Reich's legacy in ways that are both artistically and morally more incisive. However, this one retains its power through its simplicity as well as the visible traces of the cruelties inflicted here.

You must retrace your steps across the Beusselstrasse bridge, past the S-Bahn station, to see the sights of industrial Moabit. A right turn at the first corner past the bridge takes you to Sickingenstrasse 7–8. This pair of apartment houses from 1893 is the product of cooperation between a nonprofit housing society and the architect Alfred Messel, who broke with the classical symmetry of earlier tenement façades, instead using balconies and gables to vary the profile of the building, in an innovative attempt to design an apartment house that honestly displayed the fact that its façade concealed numerous small apartments, not a palace. Messel retained fashionable Renaissance forms, but used them in ways hitherto reserved for villas. Within a few years nearly all builders were imitating his style. Also influential, but less so, were the building society's provisions for common rooms (for bathing, laundry, reading and meeting), some of them still in use. Messel also left an unusually spacious courtyard.

The heart of residential Moabit lies to the east and south of here. To the west stood the largest factories, and the area remains a neglected museum of industrial architecture. Take Berlichingenstrasse to the left, past a red-brick factory built a century ago by AEG for the manufacture of light bulbs, and you reach one of the world's most famous industrial buildings, another AEG structure. First you must pass a 1939 addition before you come to the original **AEG turbine factory**, at the corner of Huttenstrasse.

Peter Behrens designed it in 1909, and it quickly became acknowledged as the first masterwork of modern industrial architecture. AEG's founder, Emil Rathenau, had hired Behrens to furnish distinctive designs for everything from letterhead to lightbulbs to buildings, in an innovative attempt to link design and corporate identity. Critics hailed this building for its marriage of industry and art, each contributing to the glory of the other. Glass, steel and concrete are the visible materials, and historicizing decoration is completely absent. The slanted glass windows in the long side wall stretch between pillars that openly display their steel bases. Yet the Huttenstrasse front, with its hexagonal gable, recalls a temple. In the following years, Behrens moved on to larger AEG complexes in Wedding (see Chapter 9) and Oberschöneweide. Here, however, credit is also due (albeit rarely given in architecture guidebooks) to Karl Bernhard, the construction engineer who figured out how to make the building stand up without load-bearing walls. Also worth mentioning is the contribution of Behrens's assistant at the time, Ludwig Mies van der Rohe, who worked mainly on the courtyard façade.

The building, now owned by Siemens, remains in use. Next to it, at Huttenstrasse 17–20, stands a more traditional building constructed at the same time, the former headquarters of the Loewe machinery company. The factory buildings behind it have been razed, but diagonally across the intersection of Huttenstrasse and Wiebestrasse are more Loewe buildings from the same era, notably a grandiose 1917 neoclassical factory facing Wiebestrasse. To the right up Wiebestrasse, number 29–39 was built in 1901 as an enormous streetcar depot, and has recently been used by collectors of antique cars.

Both rail and water transportation were important for industrial Moabit. These factories stand just a short distance from the Spree and canals that carry barges in all directions. The nineteenth-century landscape designer

Peter Josef Lenné proposed making the Spree a green corridor, but the industrial era gave the waterfront a utilitarian identity as well as an unkempt appearance. The long-ignored riverfront has recently been beautified, and regular boat cruises will take you through Moabit. Pedestrian paths have also opened up much of the bank to strollers. The southern end of Wiebestrasse will get you to the Spree, near its intersection with the Charlottenburg canal. Back toward the center of Moabit, another convenient point of access to the river (and to the other side) is the elegant sandstone Gotzkowsky bridge from 1911, which is reached by taking either Beusselstrasse or Gotkowskystrasse south (right) from Huttenstrasse. (This brings you near the former site of the Moabit synagogue – see Chapter 13.) Along the bend of the river downstream (right) from the bridge are gleaming Technical University laboratories as well as remnants of the industrial era. The most striking riverfront structure has the address Helmholtzstrasse 42 but is best viewed from the river, past the Technical University buildings or, reached from downstream, near the Dovestrasse bridge. Paul Baumgarten's elegant building in the classical modernist idiom, with a curved shiplike form extending over the riverbank, bears comparison to the finest residential and commercial buildings of the great modernist architects, but it was built and used as a **garbage loading station**: underneath the cantilevered upper story, barges received the city's trash. It was built in 1936, a fact that reminds us of the architectural diversity of the Third Reich. It has been renovated as architects' offices.

Moabit's main shopping street is Turmstrasse, the eastern extension of Huttenstrasse. Near Bremer Strasse is the former district Rathaus, a more typical Third Reich building. Behind it is the **Arminius market hall** from 1891, one of the remaining red-brick municipal market halls, where merchants sell produce, meat, dairy products, and much else. Some of its space has been taken over by larger, newer chain stores, but it has retained many of its pungent stalls staffed by unvarnished Berliners. Just beyond is the Turmstrasse subway station (U9). The area to the south and east, along Alt-Moabit and the river, is the corner of Moabit most directly affected by the new government quarter and rail station (see Chapter 13). A left turn on Stromstrasse, just past the subway station, will keep you in working-class Moabit. Stromstrasse 11–17, on the right, is the remaining wing of a monumental brewery from 1872, which remained in use until 1980. The area ahead and to the right, centered on Stephanstrasse, is known as Stephanskiez, one of the more pleasant residential corners of Moabit, an assemblage of hulking and ornament-laden buildings. Keep going on Stromstrasse, which becomes **Putlitzstrasse**, and you are again on a bridge over the rail yards. The former freight station below was one of the places used by the Gestapo to load Berlin's Jews into boxcars for their miserable journeys to the ghettos and death camps. That unhappy history is recalled by a steel memorial mounted on the bridge in 1987, depicting a Star of David and a twisted stairway. Unfortunately the memorial's location next to a busy roadway makes it both isolated and highly visible; it has often been vandalized by neo-Nazis and others who know their deed will attract attention.

Past the bridge is the expanse of the city's West Harbor (Westhafen), with its mighty brick warehouses from the 1920s. To the right of the bridge is a large power plant from 1900, designed by Franz Schwechten. The U-Bahn and S-Bahn intersect at Westhafen. On the stairway connecting the platforms, an installation in the wall tiles features an extensive quotation (in French and German) from Heinrich Heine, writing from his Parisian exile and recalling how his name, as pronounced by the French, was literally reduced to nothing ('Monsieur Henri Heine' becoming 'Monsieur Rien').

One more stop on the U9, or a further walk, brings you to Amrumer Strasse. On the left side of the street (the open space is named Augustenburger Platz) is the main entrance to the **Virchow hospital**, perhaps the finest work of the longtime municipal architect, Ludwig Hoffmann. It was completed in 1906 in elegant neo-Baroque forms, with a grand palace-like entry and courtyard. The real glory of the hospital, however, lay behind this entrance, with a double row of small pavilions arrayed along a tree-lined path. The facility thus fulfilled physicians' wishes for a place where patients could receive medical care while enjoying the benefits of fresh air, sunshine, and nature. The French visitor Jules Huret, in 1909, was impressed with its cleanliness and order: 'It is the perfect picture of peace and comfort, allowing one to suppress thoughts of the pain contained within these walls. Verily, one wishes that all states would be blessed with such institutions.' Unfortunately, recent additions have wiped out most of the original pavilions and open space. A 1964 statue in the grounds is dedicated to Jewish employees murdered by the Nazis.

Down Amrumer Strasse, toward Seestrasse, is the **Sugar Museum** (Zuckermuseum), dedicated to the history of sugar production and consumption and displaying equipment used in its manufacture and sale. The century-old museum reflects Berlin's importance in the history of sugar. In 1747 a Berlin chemist discovered the presence of sugar in beetroots, opening the way for the first sugar-beet production here, in 1798, production that quickly became important during the British blockade of Napoleonic Europe. Just down the side street Brüsseler Strasse, at number 21 is another venerable if modest Berlin institution, the **Antiwar Museum** (Antikriegsmuseum), which has roots dating to the 1920s but was shut down by the Nazis as soon as they seized power.

Beyond Seestrasse, Amrumer Strasse becomes Afrikanische Strasse. (Note, however, that this end of the

street is far from the Afrikanische Strasse U-Bahn station.)
Numbers 15–41, four similar three-story apartment buildings from 1926–27, are Ludwig Mies van der Rohe's most
important contributions to the innovative social housing
developed by Berlin architects in the 1920s. Their stark
geometric simplicity was far more striking then than
now. Mies varied their cubic forms only with the
arrangement of windows and with the curved balconies
that connect each building to a two-story side wing. All
88 small apartments came with eat-in kitchens and bathrooms, then far from typical for worker housing. This is
Mies's most substantial project from his Berlin years in
the 1920s, and one of his rare contributions to low-cost
housing. Despite the famous simplicity of his style, his
fondness for rich materials made him ill-suited to low-
budget construction.

Seestrasse or Luxemburger Strasse will take you to
Müllerstrasse, the main street of **Wedding**, as does the U9,
which intersects the U6 at Leopoldplatz. In Berlin's industrial history, Wedding overshadows Moabit because it
became larger and more uniformly working class. 'Red
Wedding' was the Communist party's stronghold in the
Weimar years, a center of strikes, demonstrations, and militant opposition first to the 'bourgeois' republic and later to
the Nazis (who had made themselves the beneficiaries of
the Communists' hatred of the republic). Wedding was
also synonymous with overcrowded tenements and, after
the war, even many of its unbombed blocks were leveled by
urban renewal and replaced by blander if more modern
apartments. At Leopoldplatz stands one of Schinkel's four
modest suburban churches, the **Nazareth church** (1834).
The simple brick cube with its low gable is neoclassical, but
the round apse and the façade, with its three arched doorways and rosette window, draw on Romanesque models.
The building has not been used for church services since
the adjoining neo-Gothic church was completed in 1893.

The U6 runs under Müllerstrasse toward the city center as well as outward, to Tegel, a name that outsiders associate with the airport, but the airport takes its name from a nearby village that has long since been swallowed up by the metropolis. Here was the airfield for the French sector (the French army bases were clustered around it). It dates to the Berlin airlift in 1948, when an additional West Berlin landing strip was desperately needed. The site seemed to be a good one, except for Soviet broadcast towers that stood in the way. The Soviets refused to move their towers, so one night French sappers blew them up. Tegel remained an obscure airfield until the 1970s, when a new terminal was built to replace Tempelhof as West Berlin's commercial airport. If and when the long-delayed expansion of Schönefeld airport is completed, Tegel's future is uncertain.

Just past the airport (the subway does not connect to the terminal – only buses do), across Seidelstrasse from the Holzhauser Strasse U-Bahn, stands **Tegel prison**, which dates to the 1890s. After 1933 the Nazis used it for political prisoners and conscientious objectors, including Dietrich Bonhoeffer. Before the Nazis, however (and since), Tegel has had its place on the career ladder of Berlin's demimonde. The most famous convict is probably the fictional Franz Biberkopf: Döblin's *Berlin Alexanderplatz* opens with his release from Tegel and his return to the mean streets of Berlin. On the other side of the U-Bahn, if you take Holzhauser Strasse under the autobahn and turn right into Wittestrasse, you reach the Russian cemetery established in 1894, when Tsar Alexander III sent 4000 tons of soil so that his subjects abroad could be buried in Russian earth. The elegant chapel still serves the local Russian Orthodox community. Along the cemetery's western wall are mass graves for children of Russian forced laborers from nearby armaments plants, victims of starvation and disease during the war. Another indirect reminder of the area's Third Reich industrial heritage is nearby at Jacobsensweg 55–57, once a factory that produced liquid oxygen. In 1931 young Wernher von Braun acquired canisters of it for his experiments with rockets on Tegel field, which he later continued for the Nazis and then for NASA in the United States.

The name of the next station on the U6, Borsigwerke, reflects the dominance of this area by the **Borsig locomotive factory** after it was moved here from Moabit in 1898. Locomotives are no longer built here; it has been redeveloped as a shopping mall and office park. Many of the red-brick façades have been kept, including the main gate. Here, too, is Berlin's first skyscraper (after many earlier, failed proposals for tall buildings), a twelve-story office tower from 1924 in brick expressionist style. On the other side of the U-Bahn, past the S-Bahn line, on Räuschstrasse, the firm built some rows of workers' housing (Kolonie Borsigwalde, 1899–1909) intended to evoke a small-town atmosphere.

The U6 ends at the next station, Alt-Tegel, next to the old village of Tegel, of which little remains – even the village church dates only to 1912. On its far side, the village borders a large lake, Tegeler See. The **lakefront promenade** is much used by strollers and by cruise boats that will take you toward central Berlin or Spandau. The small harbor to the north was a featured site in the 1980s International Building Exhibition (IBA). Its buildings are found just off the main street that parallels the U-Bahn (Berliner Strasse in the village, Karolinenstrasse if you follow it a short distance north). The overall design was the work of the American architects Charles Moore, John Ruble, and Buzz Yudell, and displays their colorful and whimsical postmodernism. They also designed the library at Karolinenstrasse 19 as well as several of the residential buildings along the side street Am Tegeler Hafen (numbers 2, 28, 30–32). The other buildings on that street were designed in the same spirit by many architects, including Robert Stern (number 6), Stanley Tigerman (number 8), and John Hejduk (number 44). From the mouth of the harbor it is a short distance across the water to the Reiherwerder peninsula where the Borsig villa (1913) stands. The Borsigs had watched over their Moabit factory from a grand mansion; in Tegel, too, the lords of the factory maintained their presence, in this neo-Baroque house resembling Sanssouci palace.

A little farther up Karolinenstrasse, number 12 was a seventeenth-century coaching inn and is now a restaurant, 'Alter Fritz'. Before you reach it, however, a left on An der Mühle (named after the nineteenth-century mill that replaced a medieval one) takes you to **Schloss Tegel**, the Humboldt villa. This sixteenth-century country house came into the possession of the Humboldt family in 1766, and in the 1820s the philosopher and statesman Wilhelm von Humboldt hired Schinkel to expand it. Schinkel built three new corner towers to match the existing one, and extended the house between them. Schinkel's forms draw on ancient Greek and Italian Renaissance precedents but have also served modern architects as models of simplicity. The interior, open to the public, retains the furniture, art, and library of Wilhelm and Caroline von Humboldt, and displays their desire to blend modern science and classical humanism in a domestic setting. The building's idyllic setting is a park used for agriculture until Wilhelm had it landscaped. At its far western end, a monument by Schinkel marks the family burial plot, including the graves of Wilhelm and his brother Alexander.

Among the numerous innovative housing estates in the north, the most famous is the so-called **White City** (Weisse Stadt, 1929–30), centered around Aroser Allee and Genfer Strasse, near U-Bahn Paracelsus-Bad. It combines the spacious layout demanded by housing reformers with creative geometric arrangements of the long horizontal blocks. It has been restored to the gleaming white (highlighted by touches of color) that signaled its liberation from the gloom and dirt of the old tenements. Across the U-Bahn to the north (toward S-Bahn Alt-Reinickendorf) is the old village core of Reinickendorf, with its simple fifteenth-century church (to which the tower was added in 1713).

Although thousands of foreigner workers in Berlin toiled in something close to slavery during World War II, there was no concentration camp within the city. One of the most important lay just north of the city, however, and it is a moving experience to visit **Sachsenhausen**, where tens of thousands of prisoners died from cold, starvation, disease and execution. You can reach it via S-Bahn, taking the S1 to the end of the line in Oranienburg. The camp was built on the edge of this quiet town in 1936–37, but most local citizens then and now have tried to ignore its existence. The bus (the 804 to Melz) runs only once an hour; otherwise you can take a taxi or a twenty-minute walk to the northeast (follow the signs). On the way to the camp's west entrance you pass modest brick houses built for SS officers. The SS leadership in nearby Berlin used this camp to train guards for duty elsewhere. Sachsenhausen was also designed as a model camp, in a symmetrical, triangular form. The main entrance faced south; here you find the gate, under a watchtower, with its ominous slogan 'Arbeit macht frei' ('work will make you free'), the cynical façade masking the Third Reich's brutality. Behind the gate is the windswept mustering ground where the thousands of prisoners were lined up for roll call, shivering in their flimsy uniforms. Beyond stood dozens of barracks. A few have been reconstructed. One, housing a display on Jewish prisoners, was firebombed by neo-Nazis in 1992 but has been restored. Elsewhere, near the southwest corner stands the former medical laboratory where doctors carried out gruesome experiments on prisoners, north of it are the pits where prisoners were taken to be shot, and at the center of the camp is an enormous 1961 memorial put up by the GDR.

Current plans call for substantial improvements to make the camp more comprehensible to visitors. Little of what you see is original; the camp was largely destroyed after the war, then restored in the 1960s by the GDR as an 'antifascist' memorial that called attention above all to the heroism of Communist resisters. The GDR barely acknowledged the Nazis' racial persecution. Sachsenhausen was, in fact, a camp for political prisoners, many of whom were Communists, but Jews were also interned here just for being Jews, particularly after Kristallnacht in 1938 and again in the final months of the war, when Auschwitz survivors were force-marched to this and other German camps.

Until 1989 the camp's postwar history was little known. The Russians imprisoned their own opponents here between 1945 and 1950, and although they practiced little of the Nazis' systematic brutality and murder, at least 12,000 died from cold, starvation and mistreatment. Remains of the Soviet camp have been excavated and a commemorative display has been created, but it has been kept separate from the Nazi museum, in order to maintain a distinction between the two regimes and their different brands of dictatorship.

III
The West

12

Around the Zoo

ITS OFFICIAL NAME IS BERLIN-ZOOLOGISCHER GARTEN, but everyone calls it **Bahnhof Zoo**. When Zoo station was opened as part of the new east–west rail line in 1882, it stood in a quiet area at the far western edge of the city. Soon, however, it became the center of the new Berlin West, which within a few decades outshone Friedrichstadt as a center of shopping, entertainment, and elegance. In this sense the postwar division of the city was not a complete break with history: the West had already become the center of wealth and fashion, just as the East's proletarian identity predated the war. West Berlin, extending north, west, and south from the walled-off city center, was in many ways a city without a center, but here, around Zoo station, was the closest thing.

The larger glass shed covers the tracks used for intercity trains; the smaller one, the S-Bahn. As it was during the years of division, it remains Berlin's busiest intercity rail station, pending completion of the new central station. During the 1970s it acquired a dreadful reputation as a gathering place for junkies and homeless youths. The street behind it was known as the place to find male prostitutes. As the departure point for many journeys through the Iron Curtain, it acquired an additional aura. The currency exchange at the corner of the building was one of the few places where you could openly exchange East and West German marks. The GDR prohibited the removal of its currency from its territory, but here no questions were asked of anyone who presented its diminutive bank notes for exchange at the free market rate. Across town the GDR

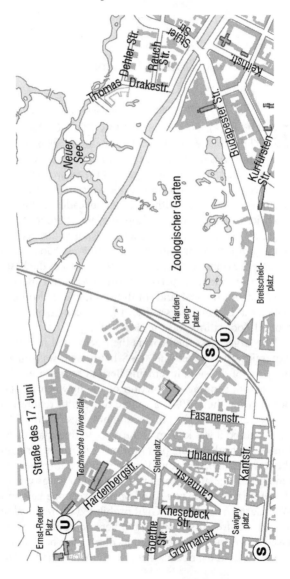

compelled travelers to exchange West marks at the rate of one to one, but around 1980 the free market demanded about four East marks for a West mark. The value of the East mark plunged further in the late 1980s, as mysterious men arrived with suitcases full of Eastern currency. No one knew for sure whether they were black marketeers or GDR government operatives trying to acquire some extra hard currency – something that, as we now know, the GDR was desperate for.

At the time the rail station was built, its name reflected the only major attraction here. Germany's first zoo was opened in 1844 at the southwest corner of the Tiergarten, site of the royal pheasant preserve. The transformation from royal animal collection to public zoo – along with the earlier transformation of the Tiergarten from game preserve to public park – reflected the shift in the city's identity from a royal residence to a commercial and industrial metropolis dominated (in many but not all respects) by a wealthy bourgeoisie that sought its pleasures here. Vladimir Nabokov recalled it as Berlin's 'own man-made Eden. . . . The only sad part is that this artificial Eden is all behind bars, although it is also true that if there were no enclosures the very first dingo would savage me.' One zoo entrance, the Lion Gate, faces the station across Hardenbergplatz, a parking lot that serves as the terminus for many bus and coach lines. The other entrance, facing Budapester Strasse, is the ornate, orientalist Elephant Gate, a reconstruction of a destroyed prewar gate. Although the zoo lacks the spacious habitats typical of modern zoos (that is the strength of the East Berlin Tierpark) it offers an outstanding collection, well displayed. Taken together, the two zoos of reunified Berlin boast the largest number of animals (some 23,000) and of species (over 2500) of any city in the world, and also the largest number of visitors. So it can get crowded, but it remains a place to pass some pleasant hours, and you can count on seeing nearly any zoo animal you might think of. Almost everything here had to be re-created after the war, which left most buildings destroyed and the animals dead or dying. The zoo had continued to function throughout the war, but some beasts had to be killed when their cages were destroyed, and bombs killed others – near the end hungry Berliners feasted on some very exotic meats. The wartime zoo shared its site with a massive flak tower, which the British later dismantled. Some of the current buildings are reconstructions of their fanciful predecessors, folkloric re-creations of the animals' homelands.

Next to the zoo, facing Budapester Strasse, stands the venerable **Berlin Aquarium**, founded in 1869 near Unter den Linden and later moved to this 1913 building, which was built without windows – very odd for its time – but with sculptural reliefs of dinosaurs where windows would be. The first floor is devoted to the world of water, with tanks full of fishes. Above it is the life of the earth, meaning crocodiles, snakes, and other reptiles. The top floor displays creatures of the air: insects and spiders. Little seems to have changed since Nabokov came in the 1920s: 'In the wintertime, when the tropical animals have been hidden away, I recommend visiting the amphibian, insect, and fish houses. Rows of illuminated displays behind glass in the dimly lit hall resemble the portholes through which Captain Nemo gazed out of his submarine at the sea creatures undulating among the ruins of Atlantis. Behind the glass, in bright recesses, transparent fishes glide with flashing fins, marine flowers breathe, and, on a patch of sand, lies a live, crimson five-pointed star.'

If you are not entering the zoo, you might enjoy a walk around its perimeter. North from Zoo station and Hardenbergplatz, you can follow the rail line, with zoo animals visible on your right, into the **Tiergarten** park, where you reach the **Landwehrkanal**. For centuries the flat and marshy Brandenburg countryside has been crisscrossed by canals. This ancient drainage ditch was given its current form by Peter Josef Lenné in the 1840s, at the same time that he laid out the zoo and redesigned the Tiergarten. The canal diverges from the upper Spree and crosses Kreuzberg and the Tiergarten before it rejoins the river farther west. Here you must cross two bridges, since an island divides the canal. Houseboats moor nearby, and tour boats pause to pass through a lock. You may watch them from a grassy spot or from the café by the lock, one of several pleasant establishments around the park. You may also catch sight of a very strange-looking building behind the rail line, with an enormous pipe emerging from each side. This is a laboratory built for Technical University hydraulic engineers in 1976. Since there was no hope of making the building inconspicuous, it was painted in garish colors, which have, however, faded over the years.

'Tier', by the way, means animal, so 'Tiergarten' in fact means the same thing as 'Zoologischer Garten' – but don't confuse the two. The Tiergarten is so called because it was originally the royal game park, but Berliners will laugh at you if you expect to see animals there. The most salient distinction is that the zoo has a fence around it and you have to pay admission. One pleasant walk through the park is along the banks of the canal, on either side, from which you can glimpse some exotic zoo animals without paying the entrance fee. The north side takes you between the canal and the Tiergarten's main lake, **Neuer See**. If you continue north past the lock, however, toward the far side of the lake, you pass through a kind of outdoor museum of ornate cast-iron street lamps, their ages and origins labeled on plaques. You must walk nearly to the wide Strasse des 17. Juni (see Chapter 13) before you come around to the other side of the meandering lake. Your bucolic stroll along the Grosser Weg on the lake's north side is interrupted by the **Karl Liebknecht memorial**, a steel pillar designed by Ralf Schüler and Ursulina Schüler-Witte and put up in 1987. On 15 January 1919, amid the chaos of an abortive communist uprising, nationalist soldiers arrested the new Communist party's leaders, Liebknecht and Rosa Luxemburg, and took them first to the Eden Hotel before packing them into cars. Here, on the bank of the lake, Liebknecht's captors hauled him out of the car and shot him 'while trying to escape'.

At the far end of the Neuer See, a pedestrian bridge takes you to the right on Lichtensteinallee, a pedestrian way. (The same path to the left leads directly to the Victory Column.) Past the bridge you can rent a boat or enjoy Kaffee und Kuchen at an outdoor table, in the company of sturdy old Berlin women. Lichtensteinallee leads back to the Landwehrkanal. The bridge across the canal has two sections, one for zoo visitors and another, outside its confines, which takes you to the path on the far side of the canal. Under the bridge stands the moving **memorial to Rosa Luxemburg**, whose body was dumped in the canal after her murder, at the same time and under the same circumstances as Liebknecht's. Her body was not found until spring, giving her murderers the chance to spread rumors that she had escaped. Because of her left-wing views Luxemburg remains less than universally beloved, but she is now widely honored, not only by leftists who admire her socialism, but also as a Jew and a woman, although her Marxism led her to dispute the significance of both identities. The privately financed memorial, designed at the same time and by the same artists as Liebknecht's, is a steel plate that seems to emerge out of the water, offering a message of hope even as it recalls her shocking fate.

You can follow the canal out of the park, or you can turn back to the vicinity of the café, where the corner of Lichtensteinallee and Thomas-Dehler-Strasse is dominated by the Spanish embassy (1938–43), built in Third

Reich style by the Franco regime. This is one of several grand **embassies** built after the Nazis designated the south side of the Tiergarten as the new diplomatic quarter. After the war, they remained untouched for decades while their owners hesitated to make any commitments in the diplomatic limbo of West Berlin. Among them was this weed-choked ruin, which was restored after 2000, with its destroyed west wing completely rebuilt. Adjoining it is the former Danish embassy (1938–40). In 1987 Denmark, foreseeing no need for an embassy in West Berlin, finally sold the building. On the other side of Drakestrasse, the Norwegian embassy, built in 1940–41 after Norway under Vidkun Quisling became a German puppet state, was converted to residential and commercial uses in the 1980s. Across Rauchstrasse is the former Yugoslav embassy (1938–40) designed by Werner March, architect of the Olympic stadium, with façade decoration by Arno Breker, famous for his sculptures of superhuman heroes at that stadium (and for his many commissions from leading Nazis, although some postwar modernists embraced him as well).

The block on which the former Norwegian embassy stands was otherwise empty for decades until it was chosen as a showcase of the 1980s international building exhibition (IBA). The building at the corner of Drakestrasse and Thomas-Dehler-Strasse was designed by Aldo Rossi to complement the embassy in its outline and to echo old Berlin industrial architecture with its red brick façade and green steel frame. Past the old embassy on Rauchstrasse are more buildings intended to restore the scale of this former neighborhood of grand villas, although the newer buildings each contain several small apartments. The most colorful are by Hans Hollein and Rob Krier. Krier laid out the complex and also designed the front building, facing Stülerstrasse, with a grand arched entry recalling Vienna's 1927 Karl-Marx-Hof housing estate.

The land on the other side of Stülerstrasse was also vacant for decades. Here stand the new embassies of the five Nordic countries – Norway, Denmark, Sweden, Finland, and Iceland – which agreed to a rare compromise in the usually rigid sovereignty of the diplomatic world. Each was designed by a different architect, but all are sheathed in the same distinctive green copper louvers. A sixth building, open to the public (at the corner of Rauchstrasse and Klingelhöferstrasse), includes facilities shared by all five: meeting, reception, and exhibition rooms, a restaurant and a sauna. Across Rauchstrasse to the south, a larger block was redeveloped in the late 1990s. Its most striking buildings face Klingelhöferstrasse on the far side: the dramatic slanted colonnade of the new Mexican embassy and the glass-enclosed national headquarters of the Christian Democratic Union (CDU) political party.

The Stülerstrasse bridge brings you back across the Landwehrkanal. On your right as you cross the bridge you can look back at two odd-looking buildings (Corneliusstrasse 11–12), experimental 1980s 'eco-houses' that incorporate environmentally friendly materials. Their odd forms also, however, reflect the participation of too many architects with insufficiently coordinated ideas, the result being houses that appear (accurately) to have been designed by committee. Down Budapester Strasse, the checkerboard slab of the **Intercontinental Hotel** rises on the right side. It was opened in 1958 by the American Hilton chain, the first luxury hotel built in postwar West Berlin and long the city's largest and finest, a visible symbol of modern design and the Western alliance. Its bar attracted the better sort of spy and other members of the Cold War elite.

If, instead of Budapester Strasse, you take the smaller Keithstrasse from the bridge (this, by the way, the street where Theodor Fontane's fictional Effi Briest lived after her disgrace) you reach Kurfürstenstrasse (not to be confused with nearby Kurfürstendamm). In front of Kurfürstenstrasse 115–116 is the only Berlin bus shelter worth a look. On this site (now a hotel) once stood the building of a Jewish fraternal organization that was taken over by the SS division of Jewish affairs, headed by **Adolf Eichmann**, the dour Austrian who organized the machinery of the Final Solution. Here, that is, was the home of the ultimate combination of bureaucratic routine and genocidal intent. The site remained unmarked until the 1990s, when the city used the bus shelter to install pictures and text (in German and English) explaining what was done here – an admirable step, but one likely to spoil a bus rider's day.

The corner where Kurfürstenstrasse and Budapester Strasse converge is dominated by the curved red sandstone façade of a 1985 bank building with a ground-floor art gallery. On its site once stood the luxurious Eden hotel, where Vicki Baum worked briefly as a chambermaid in order to research a novel later made into the film *Grand Hotel* with Greta Garbo, who had left Babelsberg for Hollywood a few years before. Billy Wilder, fresh from Vienna, first met film people here while he was making use of his dancing skills to work as a gigolo. In 1931, Ernest Hemingway came to town for the German premiere of a play adapted from his *A Farewell to Arms*, but understood not a word spoken on the stage and retreated to the Eden bar to spend the rest of his stay drinking. The hotel has gone down in history, however, as the place where right-wing soldiers imprisoned and beat Karl Liebknecht and Rosa Luxemburg, and from which they were hauled away and murdered.

Across the street is the aquarium and, next to it, the zoo's Elephant Gate. From here you can return to Zoo station and, if you wish, continue your walk on the other side of it. Its neighborhood displays only a little of the sleaze typical in the vicinity of European rail terminals. A recent, more self-conscious addition is just south of the station, at Joachimstaler Strasse 4, at the corner of Kantstrasse. The Beate Uhse Erotik Museum (open to all over 18 years old) displays sex toys (and, perhaps, art) old and new. It is both a commercial enterprise and a fitting memorial to the war widow who built a huge company that operates a chain of shops and cinemas devoted to erotic products.

Turn the corner right into Kantstrasse (named, for no particular reason, after the philosopher) and you reach the back of Helmut Jahn's Ku'damm complex (see Chapter 14) and then pass under the S-Bahn. On the right side stands the grand **Theater des Westens** (1896), decorated with allegorical sculptures representing the cities of Berlin and Charlottenburg. The façade's eclectic Renaissance style contrasts with the pseudo-medieval rear section of the building. The theater has long specialized in popular musicals and revues. Attached to its west side is a cinema which, together with the jazz cellar underneath, filled an important niche in postwar West Berlin's cultural scene.

Across the street stands a recent building by Josef Kleihues with a tower topped by an odd triangle resembling a sail, a weathervane, or a cockscomb. The far side of the building faces Fasanenstrasse, across which, next to the S-Bahn, is a red-brick building bursting with charming historicist detail. It was designed in 1890 by Bernhard Sehring, the architect of the Theater des Westens, for artists' apartments and studios. The façade, forecourt and courtyard display many sculpted human and animal figures; note the Berlin bear in the entry. Pass under the S-Bahn tracks (toward Kurfürstendamm) and on your left is the Jewish Community House, opened in 1959 on the site of a 1912 synagogue that was sacked on Kristallnacht in 1938. Congregrants had a frightening taste of things to come on 12 September 1931, when worshippers leaving

Rosh Hashanah services were attacked and beaten by hundreds of Nazi youths. A Romanesque portal and a carved pillar from the old building have been incorporated in the new one. In the forecourt stands a memorial to the ghettos and concentration camps. This building became the administrative center of West Berlin's Jewish community, which numbered about 5000 (compared to 160,000 before Hitler) but grew rapidly after reunification.

Fasanenstrasse on the other side of Kantstrasse offers a very different sight. A rare Berlin example of British 'high-tech' architecture is Nicholas Grimshaw's **Ludwig-Erhard-Haus** (1998), home of the small Berlin stock exchange. The building clearly and proudly displays its structure: the upper floors hang from a row of fifteen massive steel arches that form a kind of ribcage. Inside, therefore, the building is open, airy, and bright, although perhaps not warm and inviting. The arches narrow as you move from the center toward each end, giving the building its characteristic form and reminding many people of an armadillo. Unfortunately, the city authorities wanted buildings that look like buildings, not armadillos. They stuck to their post–unification guidelines intended to restore urban form, dictating that the upper stories on the front side protrude from the arch to form a vertical street wall. That spoils the elegance of the building's arched form. Proponents of Berlin's conservative architectural rules argue that high-tech monuments like this do not offer the harmony and intimacy that Berlin needs. Having permitted this building, however, little has been gained by turning it into a poor imitation of traditional Berlin architecture. The result shows why architects like Grimshaw felt unwelcome in the new Berlin. By contrast, an office building across the street at Fasanenstrasse 7–8 does conform to the nineteenth-century scale of Berlin architecture, although it was built in 1938, during an era dedicated to creating a new Berlin.

Continue west on Kantstrasse, and at number 152, on the left side, you pass the Paris Bar, a favorite watering hole for the old West Berlin cultural scene, with a reputation as a place of cultivated (or perhaps snobbish) eating and drinking. Just beyond is **Savignyplatz**, the center of a comfortable but lively Charlottenburg neighborhood. Along its south side runs the elevated S-Bahn; the arched vaults underneath contain shops, including Bücherbogen, a leading art and architecture bookstore. More shops and cafés line the narrow passage leading west to Bleibtreustrasse and the S-Bahn station. On many side streets, particularly to the west, the original turn-of-the-century bourgeois apartment blocks are largely intact. In the 1960s rebellious students and artists found grand and cheap apartments here and made this the center of their alternative scene. Many of them have remained through middle age and professional success, making this once again, as it originally was, a comfortable bourgeois neighborhood filled with extravagantly decorated high-ceilinged apartments and interesting shops and restaurants. Kantstrasse itself features more prosaic appliance and furniture stores that attract many Russian customers. The parallel street to the right is Pestalozzistrasse; down at number 14 is a 1912 courtyard synagogue that survived Kristallnacht.

Carmerstrasse, the diagonal street at the northeast corner of the square, offers some particularly grand apartment houses as well as a shortcut to Steinplatz (see below). If you instead take Knesebeckstrasse north from the square, you pass many restaurants, bookstores, and upscale shops on your way to Hardenbergstrasse, two long blocks ahead. At that diagonal intersection the unusual-looking Renaissance Theater (1927) is on your right; to your left, Hardenbergstrasse ends in a vast circular plaza, dominated by many lanes of endlessly circling automobile traffic. This authentic creation of postwar urban planning is named **Ernst-Reuter-Platz** after West Berlin's stead-fast postwar mayor. Before the war it was called 'the knee' because, with one exception, all the streets passing through it bend at odd angles. After the war the square was expanded to its current dimensions and surrounded with solitary towers rather than a wall of buildings. The result may look impressive from the air, but the combin-ation of traffic, distance, and winter winds make it an ordeal for pedestrians. The fountain and flower beds in the center are too remote to enjoy. They are, however, accessible through a pedestrian tunnel; any other route to the center is suicidal.

The tallest building here is the slender, curved 22-story Telefunken tower on the west side, built for that electron-ics firm but now used by the Technical University. Several other buildings around the square also belong to the uni-versity, notably the architecture faculty at the corner of Marchstrasse, a 1968 structure by Bernhard Hermes (who also designed the square) with a low-rise addition by Hans Scharoun. It is less plain than most of the other towers in sight, with its angular, protruding panels, but it does little to contradict the popular belief that the architecture building is generally the ugliest one on campus. Behind it, protected from the traffic noise, are two villas from circa 1905, the only remnants of the elegant neighborhood that this once was. One of them houses a café far more pleas-ant than those installed in the major university buildings.

The **Strasse des 17. Juni** leads directly past the Victory Column to the Brandenburg Gate. (West of here, its exten-sion is called Bismarckstrasse; a few blocks, or one subway stop, gets you to the Deutsche Oper, one of the city's major opera houses.) The avenue retains the enormous width given it when Albert Speer made it the East–West Axis of Nazi Berlin, and the street lamps designed by Speer still line the street. Most of the buildings along it belong to the **Technical University**, which was founded here in 1878 as the Technische Hochschule. A few of the original buildings survive, including the university's main building, at number 135, which was given a new ten-story front after wartime damage. Its back faces the rear of other university buildings that front on Hardenbergstrasse. In the quiet interior of the block stand Ionic columns from Schinkel's demolished cathedral (1821) and Doric columns from a customs house by Stüler (1859) that once stood at the nearby Charlottenburg bridge over the Landwehrkanal. You can return to Hardenbergstrasse either through the block or via Ernst-Reuter-Platz. Amid modern university buildings on Hardenbergstrasse nestles the fortress-like neo-Romanesque sandstone building of the Institute for Ecclesiastical Music (1903). A short distance beyond stands the turn-of-the-century neo-Baroque home of the Berlin University of the Arts. The music school on the Fasanenstrasse side was where Paul Hindemith taught composition during the 1920s, at the same time that an even more influential modern composer, Arnold Schönberg, was leading the master class over at the Academy of Arts. Schönberg's innovations remain influential but not widely loved, and were probably seldom heard at the glass concert hall at the corner while it served as the Berlin Philharmonic's postwar home, before the completion of its current building.

Across the street is the modest square named for Baron Karl vom Stein, who along with Karl von Hardenberg is credited with the social and political reforms that revived Prussia after its defeat by Napoleon. Steinplatz is marked by a pair of simple memorials. On the right corner of the square (as you look from Hardenbergstrasse) is a rough-hewn stone erected in 1951 'to the victims of Stalinism' – clearly meaning above all fellow-Germans just across town, in the grip of an empire still ruled by Stalin himself. But in the 1950s, as in following decades, some Germans did not want to leave the impression that all evil came from abroad. An organization of victims of the Nazi regime put up a corresponding memorial of similar size at the left corner of the square, built of limestone blocks salvaged from the Fasanenstrasse synagogue and dedicated 'to the victims of National Socialism'. The two similar memorials together make a modest assertion of the widespread postwar belief that the West was threatened by the evils of totalitarianism, a term that emphasized the essential similarity of Hitler's and Stalin's regimes – that is, of the West's enemies both before and after 1945.

At the corner of Steinplatz, the green apartment house at Uhlandstrasse 197, by August Endell (1907), is one of Berlin's most elegant Jugendstil structures. Farther down Hardenbergstrasse, just before Zoo station, a modest postwar building on the right has long been the home of Amerika Haus. This official outpost of American culture, with its library and cultural outreach programs, was an important presence in West Berlin during the years after the 1948 airlift. So, to a lesser extent, was the British Council, which was once next door. Across the street stands yet another grand example of Wilhelmine Baroque, a court building from 1907 in the shadow of Zoo station. Behind it, a stately former Prussian officers' mess at Jebensstrasse 2 houses a new photography museum featuring the collection of the Berlin native Helmut Newton.

13

The Tiergarten

THE TIERGARTEN, BERLIN'S GREAT CENTRAL PARK, covers some four hundred acres, far too much to be taken in at once. Forays into it from several sides (see also Chapters 3, 6, and especially 12) will give you a sense of how Berliners use their park, which bears no trace of its sixteenth-century origins as the elector's hunting preserve. Among the formal axes later carved through the park, the most important was the westward extension of Unter den Linden, built to connect the town with Charlottenburg palace in the 1690s. In the eighteenth century, Frederick the Great opened the park to the public; in the early nineteenth, the royal landscape designer Peter Josef Lenné laid out its meandering paths and waterways. The ancient forest did not survive the bitter postwar winter of 1945–46, when freezing Berliners in search of fuel cut down all but a few hundred of the park's 200,000 trees. Since then the trees have grown back, and much of Lenné's design has been restored.

The park's visual focal point is the 220-foot **Victory Column**, which stands at the Great Star (Grosser Stern), a vast intersection, so named because of the many park paths that radiate from it. It is most easily reached by bus, especially the 100 and 200 buses that connect the zoo at one end of the Tiergarten with the Reichstag and Unter den Linden at the other. The Victory Column (Siegessäule) is the preeminent monument to Prussian military power, although time has softened its meaning. Its origins date to the great revival of Prussian power in the 1860s. Prussia's first military victory in many a year was its defeat of

Denmark in 1864, which gave Prussia and its temporary ally, Austria, control over the northern German duchies of Schleswig and Holstein. In celebration of the victory, Heinrich Strack was commissioned with the column. However, events changed its meaning before it could be constructed. In 1866, Prussia manipulated the breakdown of relations with Austria, the other Great Power in the German lands, and in the ensuing war of seven weeks' duration scored a stunning victory. The result was clear Prussian hegemony in central Europe, but the story was not finished. Emperor Napoleon III's France, worried about Prussian power, was also maneuvered into war in 1870, and it too suffered a quick and crushing defeat, after which Prussia gathered all the German states north of Austria into the new German Empire, an event that began a new era in European history.

By the time the sandstone column was completed in 1873, it celebrated all these victories. Its shaft is lined with the gilded barrels of captured cannons. Friezes around the base illustrate battlefield exploits. They were carted off to France after World War II, but were returned in 1987, after passions had cooled. Above them is a mosaic portrayal of unification by Anton von Werner. At the column's top is its most famous feature, the golden victory goddess. Berliners know her as 'Goldelse' and use her as a point of orientation. You can pay her a visit: the stairway inside the column is open to visitors (summer only), and takes you to an open-air observation platform just below the goddess's feet. The reward for the arduous climb (285 steps – there is no elevator) is a grand view of all those places in Berlin from which the column is visible. To the east, the vista beyond the park is dominated by the Reichstag and chancellery, with the old city and television tower beyond; to the southeast are the new towers of Potsdamer Platz; to the northwest, the older towers of the Hansa quarter.

The column originally stood in front of the Reichstag – or rather, on Königsplatz (now Platz der Republik) before the Reichstag was built. Hitler was responsible for moving it in 1938. Königsplatz was destined to be the ceremonial center of the Third Reich (see Chapter 3), and in preparation for new construction, the Great Star became the designated shrine to the lesser, preliminary glories of Bismarck's Second Reich. At that time the column's height was also increased by adding a fourth tambour to

its shaft. Many people who do not know the city, and many who do, best know the column and especially the goddess from Wim Wenders's 1987 film *Wings of Desire* (the German title is *Der Himmel über Berlin*), in which angels survey the divided city from their perch beside her. There is nothing militaristic about Wenders's image of the goddess; she has become a benign symbol of Berlin. Only hardened polemicists (who are, however, numerous here) care to point out her unfashionable origins. At the time of reunification in 1990, in response to proposals to demolish all the communist monuments of East Berlin, a leftist member of Berlin's municipal parliament introduced a resolution to denounce the Victory Column as a 'symbol of German national self-importance, claims to imperial power, and the glorification of militarism and war'. Another politician of a different bent was in turn moved to defend it as a 'phallic symbol' and 'expression of masculinity in the city skyline'. A decade later, plans for the city's millennium celebration called for a midnight light show here, which sparked controversy because critics said the use of vertical spotlights recalled the work of Albert Speer, who had pioneered the technique at Nazi party rallies.

In addition to moving the column here, the Nazis reshaped the Great Star. They designated the road from the Brandenburg Gate (now called Strasse des 17. Juni) as the grand East–West Axis of the new Reich capital and widened it to accommodate ceremonial parades – a great width it retains. During the war the street then had to be covered with camouflage netting, since otherwise it would have offered an ideal guide to Allied bombers. After the Russians surrounded the city and seized all the airfields in April 1945, a few fanatics, including the test pilot Hanna Reitsch, managed to land planes on it to bring the last visitors to Hitler's bunker. In 1938 the Nazis also expanded the diameter of the Great Star from 300 to 660 feet, creating the formidable roundabout you see today. Don't try to cross the circle to the column; tunnels connect it to the four small ceremonial guardhouses that mark the outer edges of the circle. These small buildings in typical Third Reich style (but one could also call it Schinkel style) are Albert Speer's only intact Berlin buildings. For a few days every summer, the vast space now gets put to a very un-Nazi use, when a million techno music fans dance through Berlin in the Love Parade. Not everyone appreciates that colorful crowd, but it is surely preferable to the goosestepping soldiers for whom the wide avenue was built.

Also moved from Königsplatz in 1938, and completing the memorial to the Second Reich, are three statues honoring the triumvirate of German unifiers. Large as they are, they are easy to overlook amid the overgrown vegetation on the north side of the circle. The most prominent is Otto von Bismarck, the 'iron chancellor' who used diplomatic maneuvers along with battlefield ones to crush liberal opponents at home and military rivals abroad. The grandiose bronze by Reinhold Begas shows Bismarck on a high granite pedestal, surrounded by allegorical figures: a woman with her foot on the neck of a panther that symbolizes disorder; a Wagneresque Siegfried, sharpening his sword; Atlas with his globe, kneeling before Bismarck; and a sibyl on a sphinx. Flanking Bismarck are two colleagues. Helmuth von Moltke was the scholarly chief of the Prussian general staff who, more than anyone else, created the model of the modern general who sits not astride a horse but rather at a desk sorting telegrams and intelligence reports. It was Moltke who first exploited the new technologies of the railroad and the telegraph to race larger armies to more distant battlefields than anyone had thought possible – with devastating results in 1866 and 1870. The least known of the three is Albrecht von Roon, the minister of war who supervised the army's reorganization. Every German city once boasted adjoining streets named Bismarck, Moltke, and Roon. In western towns you will still find them; in the east, the Communists systemically purged these 'militarists' from the map. Berlin's were in the Spree bend near the Reichstag, where the Moltke bridge still bears its old name.

The segment of the park behind the statues – that is, between Altonaer Strasse and Spreeweg – is divided into two parts. Toward Altonaer Strasse is the postwar English

Garden, dedicated in 1952 by Foreign Secretary Anthony Eden and therefore known by Berliners as the Garden of Eden. If you follow Spreeweg to the northeast, you approach **Bellevue palace**, with its garden behind. On the way you pass a dark oval-shaped office building that seems to be trying to hide in the forest. This is the new home of the federal president's office. During the years of division, Schloss Bellevue was the Berlin residence of the federal president. The presidency is a ceremonial office, and a visible presidential presence was intended to emphasize Berlin's links to the federal republic, even though its status as a four-power occupied city left Berlin formally as well as geographically outside the West German state. After reunification, there was talk of giving the president a new, more prominent home, but as money became tight, President Richard von Weizsäcker declared that he would stay where he was, with Bellevue supplanting Bonn's Villa Hammerschmidt as the primary presidential residence. In the end, however, this new building was put up to house the president's staff. Its black granite façade is intended to mirror and thus blend in with the surrounding trees. This is another ecological government building, with thermal façades, solar panels, and natural ventilation to minimize energy use.

Just beyond is the palace itself, built in 1785–90 for Frederick the Great's brother Ferdinand in a transitional style between the fussy Rococo favored by Frederick (who died in 1786) and the simpler neoclassicism that supplanted it. It was located at the end of a *point de vue* reaching to Potsdamer Platz (Bellevuestrasse marks the other end). At first it was primarily used as a summer residence, its rural setting underscored by allegorical sandstone carvings set in the central gable, representing farming, fishing and hunting. It had many noble owners before passing into the state's hands in 1927. During the Third Reich it was renovated first to house the Museum of German Folklore and then as an official guesthouse. It was restored from severe wartime damage in the 1950s. The interior (which you won't see without a presidential invitation) is a mixture of restored 1950s and restored eighteenth-century rooms, among the latter an oval ballroom designed in 1791 by Langhans. Its garden is also no longer open to the public.

Across the Spree you can see a very long building that snakes along between river and S-Bahn, built as apartments for federal employees (1999) on formerly vacant land. Beyond it is the chancellery (see Chapter 3). A footpath will take you along the riverbank past the Bellevue palace gardens. The S-Bahn bridge over the river marks the end of the Tiergarten. Bellevue station (1880), just inland from the river, is one of the best-preserved of the original stations on the east–west rail line. North of it are a few streets still lined with elegant turn-of-the-century apartment buildings. You can follow the riverbank past them. The venerable café at the corner of Bartningallee (by the postwar bridge decorated with cute bear statues) is famous for its Baumkuchen, a honey cake named after its eye-catching treelike architecture.

Across the river is a recently redeveloped industrial waterfront. The most prominent structure, a U-shaped glass office building with two rounded ends facing the river, houses the federal interior ministry. Next to it are other new buildings interspersed with nineteenth-century commercial structures built for the Bolle dairy, which introduced modern milk distribution to Berlin. For decades its milk wagons, based here, were familiar presences on the city streets. Its complex, which stretches back to the street Alt-Moabit, now includes restaurants, shops and apartments as well as offices. If you take Kirchstrasse up to Alt-Moabit you will see one of Schinkel's suburban churches (1835). The Romanesque flavored neoclassical box with its rose window is obscured, however, by several additions by Schinkel's student August Stüler: an entry hall, a loggia, a bell tower, a parsonage and a school, all in the style of the original. To the east of the church stands a large complex of court and prison buildings, including a star-shaped panopticon jail (1882), still in use. Many notable prisoners have been confined or tried here, including Erich Honecker, imprisoned by the Nazis in the 1930s and by the republic in 1992.

Back across the river, the **Hansa quarter** (Hansaviertel) stretches south from the S-Bahn. The bourgeois neighborhood of that name was devastated in the war and its remaining buildings were leveled to make way for the new Hansa quarter, the centerpiece of an international building exhibition in 1957. This grand project must be viewed in its Cold War context, as an attempt to call attention to West Berlin, display the virtues of Western freedom, and provide a visible response to the construction of East Berlin's Stalinallee. The new Hansa quarter promised to renounce not only ornate architectural decoration but also axial orientation, a hierarchical arrangement of buildings, and anything that smacked of regimentation or totalitarianism, in either its communist or Nazi form. In its place came an architecture of freedom, individuality and the nonauthoritarian order of democracy and the free market. These buildings thus had a heavy symbolic burden to bear. Prominent modern architects from many lands were invited to contribute designs. Le Corbusier demanded a separate site for his building, which stands in the western part of the city (see Chapter 16), but thirty-six other designs were built here. Along with the old buildings, the street pattern of the old Hansa quarter was discarded in favor of an informal arrangement of buildings oriented to the landscape and the sun rather than to the streets or each other.

Bartningallee takes you south from the S-Bahn into the Hansa quarter. On your right you see the row of five apartment towers that mark its northern border. To the left, on Hanseatenweg, stands the **Academy of Arts** (1960). Both East and West Berlin claimed succession to this venerable institution, and this building became the home of the West Berlin academy, which hosts many lectures, conferences and art exhibitions, duties soon to be shared with the new academy building on Pariser Platz. In front lies a 1956 Henry Moore sculpture of a reclining woman. A short distance farther down Bartningallee is Hansasplatz. Here were grouped most of the facilities deemed necessary for the neighborhood: a subway station, a small shopping center with a cinema (now a theater for stage productions), a library, a Catholic church (a Protestant church stands on Händelallee) and a kindergarten.

Looking down Altonaer Strasse toward the Victory Column, on the left is a long building resting on dramatic V-shaped columns, designed by the Brazilian Oscar Niemeyer, best known as the chief architect of Brasilia. Across Altonaer Strasse, Klopstockstrasse runs through the southern section of the quarter. Number 30–32, the irregularly shaped white block at the corner of Händelallee, is the work of the Finn Alvar Aalto. Aalto, like Niemeyer, included several communal facilities in his building, but in neither case did residents use them. On the loop of Händelallee are several single-family houses, with the Tiergarten behind them – surely a privileged location. Where Händelallee rejoins Klopstockstrasse stands a curved building designed by Walter Gropius. Beyond it, a single 17-story tower marks the quarter's southern end at the Strasse des 17. Juni. Nestled against the S-Bahn are the only two surviving houses of the old Hansa quarter.

Facing the Strasse des 17. Juni, near the S-Bahn station, is the Berlin-Pavillon, a modest exhibition hall built to publicize the international building exhibition. But the Hansa quarter has ceased to be the center of attention. In the short run, it failed to have the hoped-for influence because its construction costs were too high to use it as a model for publicly subsidized housing. By the 1970s and 1980s, its urban design, even more than its architecture, went entirely out of fashion. With no clear border between the quarter's dispersed buildings and the adjoining Tiergarten, it successfully realized its ideal of urban housing amid quiet and green space, so it continues to be an attractive place to live. However, its abandonment of the street and of the historical urban structure was spurned in later plans that sought to restore the traditional street wall separating the busy street from the quiet courtyard.

From S-Bahn Tiergarten you can catch a train back around the park to the east. In the other direction, the next station is Zoo, which can also be reached by a short walk through the southwest corner of the Tiergarten (see Chapter 12). On the other side of the rail line are also a few sights worth noting, however.

The width of the Strasse des 17. Juni is the clearest reminder that you are back on Hitler's and Speer's East–West Axis. The S-Bahn station itself was remodeled in 1937, and its lower level still displays its Third Reich design. If you proceed directly west you first cross a large open space used on weekends for Berlin's largest flea market, where stylishly aged clothes, books, pictures, memorabilia and battered but intriguing household goods of all kinds, among much else, is offered for perusal and sale, year-round and in all weather. The enormous building behind this open space, one of the few the Nazis completed along their East–West-Axis, is a particularly conservative example of Third Reich architecture. It is now named **Ernst Reuter Haus** after West Berlin's post-war mayor, but the oppressively wide and symmetrical structure was built in 1938–42 for the association of German cities. Note also the street lamps designed by Albert Speer.

Just beyond, where the street crosses the Landwehrkanal, stands a neo-Baroque gate put up by the city of Charlottenburg in 1908 to assert its independence from Berlin, whose more elegant Brandenburg Gate stands at the other end of the Tiergarten. Incorporated in the gate are statues of the city's founders, King Frederick I and Queen Sophie Charlotte. The two halves of the gate were pulled far apart in 1937 when the Nazis widened the street. Along the canal to the right are some fine old industrial buildings, notably a 1926 Siemens factory at Salzufer 6–7. Siemens moved here in 1883, to be near the new technical academy. Hidden behind Ernst Reuter Haus, on Wegelystrasse, is the **Königliche Porzellan Manufaktur** (KPM), the royal porcelain factory originally founded in 1763 by Frederick the Great, who wanted to give Prussian-made gifts as good as those produced by Saxony's Meissen works. It moved here in the 1870s and continues to manufacture and sell all kinds of ornate porcelain objects.

The next side street leading away from the S-Bahn behind Ernst Reuter Haus, Siegmundshof, takes you to the bank of the Spree, where a 1986 memorial, a stylized steel menorah, marks the site of a synagogue of the ortho-dox Jewish community Adass Yisroel. Most of the group's members lived in the east, but in 1924 it opened a small synagogue on the ground floor of a building here. Just across the pedestrian bridge, at Hansaufer 7, since 2001 a plaque has marked the site of the destroyed house where Menachem Schneerson lived from 1928 to 1933. Schneerson, the later Brooklyn-based Lubavitcher Rebbe, fled here from his native Ukraine along with his teacher, the then Rebbe. Schneerson studied mathematics and physics at Berlin University before he had to flee west-ward once again when Hitler came to power.

Another synagogue once stood a little farther into Moabit, at the corner of Levetzowstrasse and Jagowstrasse.

Dedicated in 1914, it was one of Berlin's largest, seating two thousand worshipers, and served the many liberal Jews living in the Hansa quarter. It was damaged on Kristallnacht in 1938, and in 1941 became the first assembly center established by the Gestapo for the thousand or more Jews it was rounding up each night. The Jewish community was given the job of taking care of these desperate people. Despite its efforts, there were many suicides here. Most of those brought here then had to walk through the streets of Moabit to the rail stations at Putlitzstrasse or Grunewald, from which they were deported to the death camps. Since 1960 a plaque has marked the vacant site; since 1988 a massive, rough-hewn marble and steel memorial sculpture partially blocks the sidewalk. It is a stylized representation of a deportation ramp and railway car set onto rails. Behind it a metal screen lists the dates and destinations (in most cases, Auschwitz) of the deportations from Berlin. A plaque set in the ground gives information about 36 Berlin synagogues.

14

Kurfürstendamm

JUST BEFORE THE FIRST WORLD WAR, but especially after it, Kurfürstendamm and vicinity became the center of fashion and entertainment, at a time when much of the world looked to Berlin for the most daring attempts to cast off old rules of propriety. The writer Stefan Zweig arrived from Austria at the height of the 1923 inflation, when the respectable classes, seeing their savings vanish, seemed to flee from the sobriety and discipline that had done them no good. He was scandalized: 'I have a pretty thorough knowledge of history, but never, to my recollection, has it produced such madness in such gigantic proportions. All values were changed, and not only material ones; the laws of the State were flouted, no tradition, no moral code was respected, Berlin was transformed into the Babylon of the world. Bars, amusement parks, honky-tonks sprang up like mushrooms . . . the Germans introduced all their vehemence and methodological organization into the perversion. Along the entire Kurfürstendamm powdered and rouged young men sauntered and they were not all professionals; every high school boy wanted to earn some money and in the dimly lit bars one might see government officials and men of the world of finance tenderly courting drunken sailors without shame. Even the Rome of Suetonius has never seen such orgies as the pervert balls of Berlin, where hundreds of men costumed as women and hundreds of women as men danced under the benevolent eyes of the police. In the collapse of all values a kind of madness gained hold particularly in the bourgeois circles which until then had been unshakable in their probity. Young girls bragged proudly of their perversion, to be sixteen and still under suspicion of virginity would have been considered a disgrace in any school of Berlin at that time, every girl wanted to be able to tell of her adventures and the more exotic, the better.' You will find the street somewhat tamer – or perhaps we are just not as easily shocked. In the Twenties, Joseph Goebbels was neither alone nor original in claiming that 'the German people is alien and superfluous here. . . . Berlin West is the abscess on this gigantic city of diligence and industry. What they earn in the North they squander in the West.' Goebbels and Hitler, of course, managed to persuade far too many people that behind the sin and squalor (but not the diligence and industry) stood Jews like Zweig. The Nazis never succeeded in erasing the life of the street, however, and since the war this part of West Berlin has remained synonymous with shopping, strolling, and (sometimes outrageous) entertainment. From its origins, just over a century ago, it has been a fashionable neighborhood for the wealthy bourgeoisie, largely free of the aristocratic presence so obvious and oppressive in the city center. The Weimar-era critic Siegfried Kracauer saw it as a whirlwind of change, a 'street without memory', where businesses appeared suddenly and then vanished without a trace, as if in a gold rush: 'If some streets seem to be created for eternity, then the present-day Kurfürstendamm is the embodiment of empty flowing time in which nothing is allowed to last.' Grand public buildings are lacking, and first-rate architecture is a rarity, but the crowds have kept coming – to shop, to visit the theater and the cinema, to dance and drink all night long and to linger in the sidewalk cafés.

Wittenbergplatz was created as part of the grand boulevard built according to James Hobrecht's 1862 city extension plan. This western part of the boulevard

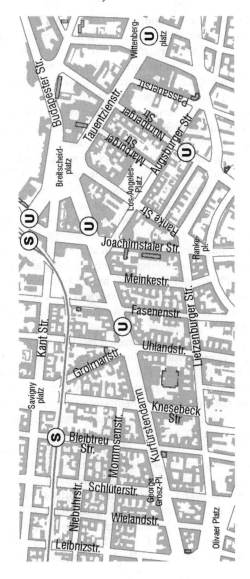

273

became even more important in 1902 when Berlin's first subway line followed it. After additional lines were added in the following years, the station in the center of the square was rebuilt in its current, elegant form in 1913 by Alfred Grenander, Berlin's premier subway designer. The American journalist Howard K. Smith lived on the square during the early years of the Second World War, and he recalled eating dubious concoctions at a restaurant run by Alois Hitler, the dictator's half-brother. No trace of it, or of much else from earlier years, remains. However, on the west side of the station, the newcomer is pulled up short by a sign reading (in German): 'Places of horror that we must never forget', with the names of twelve concentration camps attached below. This arbitrarily placed sign, put up by the district of Schöneberg in 1967 but easily ignored by passers-by, illustrates an early phase of postwar Holocaust remembrance, compared to the more sophisticated (or at least more obtrusive) projects that came at the end of the twentieth century. In 1967, unlike today, visible reminders of the Third Reich's crimes were rare.

A photographic motif favored by the cynical situates this 'places of horror' sign in the foreground of a picture, with the unmistakable **KaDeWe** department store looming behind it. The monumental building at the intersection of the square and Tauentzienstrasse has long been Berlin's preeminent place of tasteful consumption. Its construction in 1907 marked a decisive change in the development of Tauentzienstrasse, which was then a row of grand apartment houses. Johann Emil Schaudt designed the building to resemble such an apartment house, with small windows and articulated stories instead of large pillars, but he remodeled it himself in 1930, adding two more stories. After severe wartime damage it has seen several more renovations. The Kaufhaus des Westens (Department Store of the West, always referred to by its

German initials 'KaDeWe', pronounced Kah-Day-Vay) was built by the Jansdorf department store chain, which was absorbed by its rival, Tietz, in the 1920s. It was the only one of Berlin's grand department store buildings to survive the war, and it quickly became West Berlin's showcase. Not to be missed is the enormous food department on the sixth floor, the Continent's answer to Harrod's. Its selections reflect German tastes – the sausage case seems to have no end – but its vast selection of meats, cheeses, baked goods and delicacies, interspersed with counters for sampling all of them, promises everyone (everyone with a little money to spend, that is) the kind of harmless pleasure that hungry postwar Germany craved.

After KaDeWe's arrival, the short stretch of Tauentzienstrasse from here to Kurfürstendamm became a major shopping street. It was, however, utterly devastated by wartime bombing. Elderly Berliners remember one morning in 1943 when the entire street seemed to be on fire. Your view up the street is of postwar buildings framing the broken tower of the Kaiser Wilhelm Memorial Church. A favorite postcard image is a picture of the church tower framed by the shiny, twisted metal tubes of the sculpture standing in the street's median, *Berlin* (1987) by Brigitte and Martin Matschinsky-Denninghoff. Tauentzienstrasse is still filled with shops and shoppers, and several of its large stores were rebuilt during the 1990s. The most important prewar building in the area, after KaDeWe, stands at Nürnberger Strasse 50, just to the left off Tauentzienstrasse. Its long travertine façade from 1931 manages to combine the simplicity of modernism with an imposing grandeur.

Tauentzienstrasse ends at **Breitscheidplatz**, the heart of West Berlin. Auguste-Viktoria-Platz (after William II's wife) was renamed after World War II in honor of Rudolf Breitscheid, a Social Democratic government minister murdered in Buchenwald. It has been closed to cars since

1980, when a fountain became its central feature. It is usually crowded with passing shoppers, fast-moving commuters, and loitering tourists and vagrants. In the last month of the year it hosts one of Berlin's several outdoor Christmas markets, a place to buy handicrafts and to ward off the cold with a cup of hot mulled wine. Few buildings in the area survived wartime bombing, and it became a showcase for postwar reconstruction, particularly on its north side.

Originally, the square was framed by a pair of neo-Romanesque commercial buildings. The one on the eastern side became home to the most famous of the new neighborhood's gathering places, the cavernous Romanisches (Romanesque) Café, a favored haunt of 1920s writers and artists, and, soon, of tourists and wannabes hoping to glimpse or meet bohemian celebrities. The savvy proprietor knew that artists lingering all day over a cup of coffee would not keep him in business, but he left them undisturbed while cycling tourists through the terrace in front. Max Slevogt presided over the artists' *Stammtisch* where Max Liebermann, Otto Dix and Max Pechstein sometimes came by. George Grosz and John Heartfield (both had anglicized their names in protest against the war) were among the regulars at the Dada table, the nerve center of a movement that arrived here in 1918 with draft dodgers returning from Zurich. For a few frenzied months, the fashionable Dada evenings featured performances of gibberish, abuse, pornography and anything else that passed as anti-art – a strange amalgam of ecstasy and rage provoked by the war that had shattered bodies in the trenches and starved them on the streets of Berlin. Dada soon faded, but its attitude fed the famous wit of Berlin cabaret and theater. Vienna's coffeehouse culture may be better known, but in the 1920s even the Austrians flocked to Berlin cafés. The talent gathered at the Romanisches encompassed provincial Germans like

Brecht as well as German speakers from Czechoslovakia, Austria and Hungary and others from the entire world. The Romanisches was the 'idea exchange' where writers, composers, producers, publishers and gallerists could hatch schemes and make deals. So they kept coming, although everyone seems to agree that the decor was ugly and the food was bad. In 1928, Erich Kästner was struck by the crowds of hangers-on and the concentration of unkempt hair and unwashed undergarments. The Nazis put an end to all that. Since 1965 the café's site has been occupied by a prominent symbol of postwar West Berlin, the 22-story black box of the Europa Center, with a rotating Mercedes-Benz star on top and a shopping mall on its lower floors.

At the center of the square is West Berlin's most famous monument, the ruined tower of the Emperor William (or Kaiser Wilhelm) **Memorial Church**. At this intersection of four major streets, the last emperor decreed the construction of an enormous church in memory of his grandfather and namesake. The choice of architectural style, Rhenish Romanesque, proclaimed both the geographic and historical extent of German power. The architect, Franz Schwechten, created an impressive historicist monument, but it was completed in 1895, shortly before historicism went out of fashion, and the building was widely scorned as a monument to nothing but imperial pomposity. Wags have long opined that destruction improved its appearance. After the war, the church was just another Berlin ruin. In the late 1950s, however, when time came to choose between demolition and reconstruction, the shattered tower was instead preserved as a memorial recalling the war's destruction. The 'hollow tooth' was a suitable memorial for the time: the Western occupiers, as well as many Germans, could see it as a warning about the destruction Germany had called upon itself, while most Germans thought above all of their own suffering in the bombing, not their possible guilt. Indeed, a salvaged statue of Jesus seems intended to suggest that the guilt is shared equally: 'Forgive us our sins, as we forgive those who have sinned against us.' You can enter the interior of the church's stump, which is intended as a place of contemplation but where you can also view the entrance hall's grandiose mosaics, portraying William I and his Hohenzollern predecessors under God's protection. The stone wall reliefs offer some rather shocking juxtapositions of scenes from the life of Christ and from the military victories of William I. Along with the preservation of the ruin came the construction of a new church with two parts, a hexagonal tower east of the ruin ('lipstick') and an octagonal sanctuary on its west side ('compact'). While the ruin has maintained its iconic power, the modern church is little noticed, and the base of the tower bears a fatal resemblance to a public toilet. The sanctuary's interior is well worth visiting, however, to experience the intense blue light created when sunlight passes through the colored glass windows.

The curved façade of Kurfürstendamm 237, at the corner of Rankestrasse and facing the Memorial Church, marks both the spatial and historical beginning of **Kurfürstendamm** as a commercial avenue. The row of grand commercial buildings begun with Schaudt's KaDeWe turns the corner from Tauentzienstrasse with this building by the same architect, completed in 1915 with arched windows that echoed the Memorial Church in a simpler neoclassical form. The street's name reveals the aristocratic origins of this bourgeois stronghold, the ruler of Brandenburg having been one of the seven electors (Kurfürsten) of the Holy Roman Empire. For centuries this was the path that led from the city and Tiergarten to the elector's hunting lodge in the Grunewald forest. It was reborn as an urban boulevard thanks in part to the only town-planning initiative of Chancellor

Otto von Bismarck. Bismarck's interests were strictly rural and aristocratic: he loved to ride horses, and proposed in the 1870s to upgrade the route to the Grunewald. It was in this sense that he envisioned Kurfürstendamm as the new Reich capital's Champs Elysées, leading to its Bois de Boulogne. His intervention, however, coincided with growing interest on the part of real estate developers, and the widened and paved street opened the way to the new Grunewald mansion district. Beginning in the 1880s, new buildings sprang up at the Berlin end of the boulevard (which originally included the eastern section that was renamed Budapester Strasse in 1925); by 1914, it was solidly developed down to the Grunewald. Even the name of the elector disappeared: everyone calls the street Ku'damm.

Ku'damm is usually choked with cars, but it remains attractive to strollers and shoppers because its great width is not entirely given over to motor vehicles. It has kept its broad sidewalks and rows of shade trees; in addition, in recent years one traffic lane in each direction has been reserved for buses and taxis. Another Ku'damm trademark is the row of freestanding glass display cases on the sidewalk. In the 1960s and 1970s, radical Berlin youths protesting capitalist excesses regularly marauded down the bourgeois Ku'damm and found these cases irresistible targets, smashing them along with shop windows. Keen as they were to equate capitalism with fascism, the protesters probably did not know that the display cases have their origin in a 1936 Third Reich beautification program.

The cinema was the greatest of Ku'damm's attractions for most of the twentieth century. Ku'damm's first cinema was Marmorhaus (1913) at number 236, which took its name from its façade of white Silesian marble. The growth of Ku'damm coincided with that of the cinema, and the grand movie palaces clustered here. After the war, many were rebuilt, but at the end of the century most closed (including Marmorhaus, in 2001) in the face of competition from the numerous small screens of the multiplexes. Even the Berlin Film Festival has moved to Potsdamer Platz. Mass entertainment on the Ku'damm somehow coexisted with quiet literary cafés. Down the street at number 217, Robert Musil was working on his novel *The Man Without Qualities*. Number 14–15 was the home of Mampes Gute Stube, which attracted a literary crowd including another transplanted Austrian, Joseph Roth, who wrote his novel *The Radetsky March* during breaks from conversation at its tables. Roth also read the papers and wandered the streets to produce the newspaper essays with which he supported himself, filled with laconic but bitter descriptions of poverty, hatred and violence. (From a report on election violence, for example: 'Three proletarians died from the effects of universal suffrage.') His Berlin was not that of any Golden Twenties, but he returned again and again.

The next cross street is Joachimstaler Strasse, which leads to Zoo station. During the years the Brandenburg Gate was inaccessible, this is where crowds gathered spontaneously on such important occasions as soccer championships. On the southwest corner stands one of the more elegant relics of the 1950s, the offices of the Allianz insurance company, including a six-story building at the corner and a fourteen-story tower behind. It might not catch your eye, but its design became fraught with political significance. In order to look nothing like a Nazi monument, it is curved and asymmetrical and lacks any classical ornamentation. Critics noted that it was clad in stone, however, like Third Reich buildings; soon thereafter stone went completely out of fashion. It was the simplicity of the design, by contrast, that piqued Communist critics across town, who described it as an exemplar of capitalist brutality and compared it unfavorably to the ornate Stalinallee buildings going up at the same time.

The corner on the other side of Ku'damm has been home to many generations of Berlin café life. The ground floor of a new apartment house at number 18 was taken over in 1894 by a café that attracted the most ambitious members of the artistic avant-garde, so that it soon became better known by its nickname Café Megalomania (Café Grössenwahn) than by its official name, Café des Westens. The brief flowering of literary Expressionism was a Berlin phenomenon, and its center was here. At its peak, in 1912, Rupert Brooke became one of the first of many famous twentieth-century Englishmen who sought out this reputed capital of mindless hedonism as a refuge from their own emotions (later arrivals ranged from W.H. Auden to David Bowie). He soon discovered this café with its newspapers and view of the street, where he composed 'The Old Vicarage, Grantchester', in which he idealized everything the bustling city wasn't, but did so with a dose of irreverent good humor – thus proving himself a passable Berliner: the countless German paeans to rural life, penned by sworn enemies of Berlin, are invariably humorless. Brooke, finding here shows of French and Italian art he had already seen in London, quickly decided Berlin was '*frightfully* out of date'. Obviously he had not discovered the recently arrived expressionists of the Brücke group. By the 1920s, not many visitors shared his view.

In 1932 the café was taken over by Kranzler as a branch of its well-known Unter den Linden establishment. The building was destroyed in the war, but Kranzler reopened afterward, first serving ersatz coffee amid the ruins, then constructing a garishly furnished 1950s building. In later years it became known both as a tourist trap and as a stronghold of stout old ladies determined to spend their remaining years recuperating from the traumas of the 1940s. Kranzler still exists, but has recently been banished upstairs to the tower. The other cavernous coffee-and-cake establishments have yielded in recent years to new shops and cafés that, unfortunately, encourage you to quickly rejoin the moving crowd rather than to linger and observe it. The redeveloped block is now dominated by an angular glass tower designed by Helmut Jahn (2000), with one corner reaching Ku'damm and another cantilevered ostentatiously over the department store facing Joachimstalerstrasse. Jahn's complex is centered on the interior of the block, a small plaza dominated, oddly, by a large cage of exotic birds. The birdcage takes the place that might typically be occupied by an artwork – and in fact it is supposed to be a work of art.

The odd architectural melange at Ku'damm 25, just beyond, is an apartment house designed by the young Alfred Messel in 1892, converted to a hotel in 1910 (Joseph Roth lived here during his lengthy Berlin stays) and expanded in the 1950s. Number 26 was another early cinema, the former Union-Palast from 1913. Across Fasanenstrasse stands the Kempinski Hotel, an early postwar building (1952) of simple elegance. The Kempinski family had operated a restaurant here since 1926, with quick service and simple, inexpensive fare that attracted a diverse public in effective imitation of the American fast-food model. **Fasanenstrasse** south of Ku'damm, known for its elegant shops, permits a glimpse of the earliest development of the neighborhood. Before large apartment buildings took over Ku'damm around 1890, grand villas were built here in spacious gardens. One remaining example is Fasanenstrasse 23, a red-brick 1890 house recalling a Renaissance palazzo. It is now the Literaturhaus, a favorite gathering place for Berlin's literary establishment. Next to it is a country villa from 1871, which now houses the **Käthe Kollwitz Museum**. Kollwitz (1867–1945) is known for her politically engaged work and for the anguish expressed in her sculptures, drawings, and prints, many of which are on display here. The emotional accessibility, or simplicity, of her work has given her an unusually broad audience for a modern artist.

Past Uhlandstrasse, at Ku'damm 207–8, is '**The Story of Berlin**' (the name is in English, and the exhibition is bilingual), which presents multimedia shows in a 'time tunnel' and 'event rooms' that portray the history of Berlin. It conveys the terrors of the Cold War in an atomic fallout bunker that was constructed along with the building in 1972. The complex also includes many shops on its interior corridors as well as a musical comedy theater, Komödie am Kurfürstendamm, built in 1924 and incorporated into the modern building. Behind this block, on the Knesebeckstrasse side, a rare old-fashioned beer garden has held on in the inner city.

The turn-of-the-century apartment houses in this area were the city's grandest. The ten-room flats boasted enormously high ceilings, rich decor and all the latest conveniences, notably elevators, central heating, electric lights and marble baths. This stretch of Ku'damm has the largest concentration of surviving old buildings. Most have been converted to commercial uses, but here and there you can find a grand vestibule. Slightly less ostentatious apartments lined the side streets, and more old buildings have survived there, for example to the right on Bleibtreustrasse. A little farther down Ku'damm, at Leibnizstrasse, a corner house still retains its original 1907 façade. Typical for the time are the round corner tower, many recesses and bays, and ornate stucco decoration intended to look like carved stone. In this late example the Wilhelmine Baroque forms show the influence of Jugendstil. Behind it is an exemplar of a very different style, extending through the block from Leibnizstrasse to Wielandstrasse. Hans Kollhoff and Helga Timmermann's two long colonnaded structures of severe monumentality (1999) face each other across a sterile plaza that has been given the name Walter Benjamin Platz despite its dissimilarity to the world of the *flâneur* famously evoked by that Berlin writer.

Here at Olivaer Platz you are not quite halfway down the length of Ku'damm, but the rest of it is less fashionable. Ku'damm has seen its ups and downs since the war, with the result being an ever-changing combination of tasteful shops and tourist traps, elegant ladies and ladies of the night. In the 1990s local merchants feared that Friedrichstrasse and Potsdamer Platz would draw away upscale shoppers. That did not prove to be the case. One of the sources of its continued commercial strength, though not one boasted of too loudly, has been an influx of Russians, some of them with a great deal of money to spend. They settled in Charlottenburg, around Ku'damm, in an echo of the 1920s, when a much larger population of anticommunist Russian exiles bided their time in the Russian restaurants and cabarets of 'Charlottengrad'. Berliners enjoyed the perverse pleasure of having their borscht served by a grand duke. Among the exiles was Vladimir Nabokov, who gave tennis lessons nearby and whose early novels are set in Berlin, but entirely within the Russian community. In fifteen years here, Nabokov claimed never to have learned German, which probably meant only that he couldn't write in it – his standards were high. Although he disavowed any debt to the city, his stories betray the impressions left on him by the splendor, squalor and madness of Ku'damm and the Grunewald. In attentive detail, for example, he described the streetcars that once ran down Ku'damm and that, as he predicted, have long since vanished from it.

Adenauer Platz, farther out, is an unmistakable postwar creation, arranged for automobile traffic plus the subway line (the postwar U7). The widening of streets left an extremely narrow lot on the north side, which was finally filled in 1994 with a glass building designed by Helmut Jahn. On the south side of Lehniner Platz, still farther down Ku'damm, stands Erich Mendelsohn's most important extant Berlin building, built as the **Universum cinema** in 1927–31. Unlike earlier cinemas, it does not resemble a theater. Mendelsohn created architectural forms to capture the modern world of dynamic motion apparent in the films playing inside as well as the traffic flowing by. The low, curved brick front, with its horizontal row of windows, contrasts with the narrow slab that rises behind it, which served as the marquee. The decayed building was restored for one of Berlin's major theater companies, the Schaubühne, in 1981. Mendelsohn also designed an adjoining building for the city's preeminent cabaret as well as an elegant apartment house on the Cicerostrasse side.

Ku'damm continues for another kilometer and boasts an impressive variety of buildings but no great attractions. You are near the end when you cross over the S-Bahn ring, near the Halensee station. Ku'damm ends just beyond at **Rathenauplatz,** under which a tunnel carries the city autobahn. Nearby, when the grand boulevard was new, the banks of the Halensee became a place for family outings. Ordinary workers could not afford to dine out, but for a small fee the proprietor of the lakeside garden provided them facilities to make their own coffee and unpack their picnic baskets. After 1909 this modest facility was replaced by Lunapark, Berlin's leading amusement park, with spectacular expressionist scenery and all the sensational rides, amusements and artificial horrors imaginable. In the 1920s its jazz concerts and dances became popular, until the Nazis replaced them in 1933 with proper German musical fare. By the end of 1933 the park was bankrupt, and it was demolished the next year. The apartment houses that frame the corner of Halenseestrasse are a Third Reich contribution, however. At the center of Rathenauplatz is Wolf Vostell's provocative 1987 sculpture consisting of two Cadillacs upended and embedded in concrete.

The mixing of classes so apparent at Halensee ended just beyond, in the exclusive precincts of Grunewald, where, beginning in 1890, the richest of the rich built their mansions – houses so grand that most have long since been converted to apartments, offices or embassies. One of the rich men was Walther Rathenau, the head of AEG, whose work in organizing industrial production contributed mightily to Germany's World War I effort, and who became foreign minister amid the postwar tensions of 1922. His government's decision to abide by the provisions of the hated Versailles Treaty sparked rage from the nationalist right, and Rathenau's Jewish heritage made him a particular target. On 24 June 1922 Rathenau was on his way from his villa at Koenigsallee 65 when right-wing nationalists ambushed his car and assassinated him at the corner of Erdener Strasse. The spot is marked by a commemorative plaque, and Rathenauplatz now bears his name, but at the time nationalists openly celebrated the murder of one of the pillars of German democracy.

If you want to ride back up Ku'damm, no subway is available. Plans to build one never came to fruition, an early line from Wittenbergplatz having only reached Uhlandstrasse. The S-Bahn is nearby, however, and frequent double-decker buses have plied Ku'damm for nearly a century, offering commanding views from high above the street.

15

Charlottenburg

CHARLOTTENBURG BEGAN AS A POOR VILLAGE and finished as a rich suburb, but it acquired its fame, as well as its name, from the royal palace built here in the 1690s. Elector Frederick III (who became King Frederick I in 1701) granted it to his wife, Sophie Charlotte of Hanover, sister of the later George I of Britain. From his father, the Great Elector, Frederick had inherited a state greatly expanded in territory, power and wealth. Frederick was determined to acquire not only the title of king, but also the trappings of regal splendor. He sponsored the Baroque extension of the Berlin palace and made himself a patron of the arts and sciences. Sophie Charlotte is generally credited with promoting those cultural advances, including the establishment of the royal academy of sciences, headed by the philosopher Leibniz. The queen wanted her new palace to become a center of art and cultivation in the benighted East. The royal architect Johann Friedrich Eosander von Göthe drew up a grid plan for the town expected to grow up around it. It remained a quiet country hamlet, however, until nineteenth-century Berlin grew outward to it.

The U-Bahn station **Richard-Wagner-Platz** is the closest to the palace, although it is just as conveniently reached from other directions: from the station at Sophie-Charlotte-Platz, south of the palace, you have a somewhat longer but more elegant approach; and the U-Bahn and S-Bahn station Jungfernheide is near the back of the palace gardens. Richard-Wagner-Platz was once the town's market square. The dominant building,

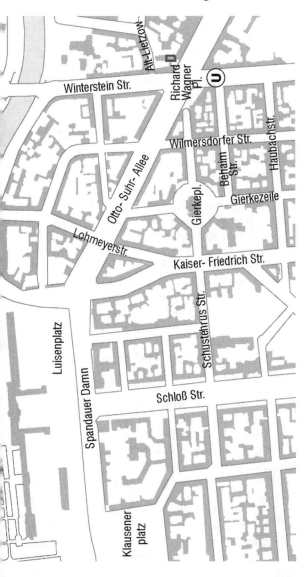

a few steps to the southeast on Otto-Suhr-Allee, is the sand-stone tower of the **Charlottenburg town hall** (Rathaus), dedicated in 1905, two hundred years after the new town had been granted a charter. Originally it was planned in the Gothic style, the typical embodiment of ancient German municipal liberties, but in the end a more modern Jugendstil idiom was chosen instead. If you associate Jugendstil or art nouveau with a light and delicate appearance, as is typical in Brussels, Paris, and Vienna, you will find that things are different in Prussia: rich in organic curves and sculptural decoration, but substantial and weighty, with an obvious debt to the Baroque. Large as it was – it stretches back around three courtyards – it was outgrown almost before it was finished, requiring a new annex, to the right of the main building, built just a decade later in the simpler neoclassical style that had meanwhile come into fashion. The town hall was intended as a display of civic pride and prosperity. At the time, Charlottenburg was Prussia's richest city, and was becoming one of its most populous, as grand apartment houses spread down Kurfürstendamm and engulfed the villas of Westend. Charlottenburg also attracted many Berlin institutions: the zoo in 1844, the polytechnic institute in 1878, major theaters, the municipal opera house in 1911, and later the Olympic Stadium. It remained a wealthy and fashionable district, but not an independent town, after it was absorbed into Greater Berlin in 1920.

The village that predated the palace lay behind where the town hall now stands. You can reach it by taking Wintersteinstrasse a few steps north from Richard-Wagner-Platz, then turning right onto Alt-Lietzow, which takes you behind the town hall (you get a sense of how vast it is) and onto the old square of **Lietzow**. No ancient village buildings remain, just a quiet square with a church and fire station of later date. The oldest and finest structure here is a neoclassical villa from 1866, ornamented with a copy of Rauch's frieze from the Frederick the Great monument on Unter den Linden. On the village square itself is an 1875 memorial, a stone lion asleep atop a classically decorated tomb, dedicated to soldiers who died in the Prussian wars that culminated in German unification, with additional plaques to honor the dead from both world wars.

From Richard-Wagner-Platz, Otto-Suhr-Allee will take you directly to the palace, but a small detour gives you a hint of the original town that grew up around it. Richard-Wagner-Strasse leads you two blocks south to Haubachstrasse, on the right side. In this neighborhood of massive old apartment houses, Haubachstrasse 8 stands out because it has only one story. It conforms to a model house Eosander designed when he laid out the new town in 1705. Houses like it lined most of these streets until the mid-nineteenth century; now only three remain. The next cross street, Wilmersdorfer Strasse, still largely maintains the character and scale of a prewar shopping street with its modest shops. A few blocks to the left, however, past Bismarckstrasse, it becomes the axis of one of West Berlin's major shopping centers, lined with ungainly department stores. At Bismarckstrasse is also the Deutsche Oper, one of the city's three opera houses, in a graceless modern building with its own station on the U1. At the corner of Haubachstrasse, Wilmersdorfer Strasse 18 is another one-story house remaining from the eighteenth century. Just past it, Haubachstrasse 15, a two-story house from circa 1880, shows the kind of building that replaced the older houses. It represents a brief transitional phase in the rapid urbanization of Charlottenburg, however, soon supplanted by the likes of the neighboring four-story buildings, number 17 from 1883 and number 19 from 1888. By the time numbers 21 (1897) and 23 (1900) were built, five-story houses just like Berlin's were the norm here.

If you turn right onto Gierkezeile at the next corner, you pass a salmon-colored building on your left, number 39. This was Charlottenburg's first schoolhouse. It was part of Eosander's original plan from 1705, but lack of money delayed its construction until 1786 (so much for Protestant Prussia's supposedly exemplary schooling). Just past the school, the street opens onto the round Gierkeplatz, centered on Charlottenburg's original church, open by royal decree to both the Reformed and Lutheran denominations. Eosander designated this site, the highest in the area, for a church, which was designed by Philipp Gerlach and completed in 1716. Schinkel remodeled it, and added the tower, in the 1820s, which is also when it acquired its name, Luisenkirche, after Queen Luise. It takes the form of a Greek cross, with arched windows. It was gutted by fire in 1943 but was rebuilt in the 1950s with a modern interior, although some of Schinkel's interior was later restored.

Schustehrusstrasse 13, just east of the square (exiting by the church's apse), is Charlottenburg's oldest house, from circa 1712, built according to Eosander's simple model, with two main rooms on either side of a central entrance hall. It has been restored to its appearance as of 1800 and now houses a ceramics museum (Keramik-Museum Berlin). Schustehrusstrasse in the other direction, west from the church entrance, takes you toward the palace. The large school that faces the park on the left side incorporates the 1881 Villa Oppenheim. Past it you reach the corner of Schlossstrasse which, like Otto-Suhr-Allee, was designed by Eosander as an axis oriented to the palace dome. It has better maintained its character as a grand avenue.

A right turn will take you past several museums before you reach the palace. The palace and its outbuildings were, after Dahlem, West Berlin's second museum complex during the years of division. Since reunification, some collections have moved away, but others have arrived. The former barracks at Schlossstrasse 1A, on the left, is now the **Bröhan Museum**, opened in 1983 to house the collection left to the city by Karl H. Bröhan. The museum focuses on the years 1889–1939, and more particularly on objects in the Jugendstil, art deco, and functionalist styles. In addition to many craft items – glass, ceramic, and metal objects, furniture, carpets, and lamps – highlights are graphic works and paintings by Hans Baluschek, a politically engaged painter of Berlin working-class scenes, and landscapes by Karl Hagemeister.

Just beyond, a pair of identical buildings on either side of Schlossstrasse frame the view from the palace. These officers' barracks were designed and built in the 1850s by August Stüler, based on a sketch by his boss, King Frederick William IV, who took a great interest in architecture. They are square neoclassical buildings framed by pilasters and crowned with high, narrow domes echoing the palace opposite and the twin churches of Gendarmenmarkt. Both are now museums. The one adjoining the Bröhan formerly housed Greek and Roman antiquities, which have been moved back to the museum island. It is now the Heinz Berggruen collection (**Sammlung Heinz Berggruen**), comprising paintings from 'Picasso and his age' recently donated to the city. Some seventy Picassos form the heart of the collection, but other classical modernists are also represented, including Giacometti, Klee, Cézanne, Matisse, Braque, and van Gogh. Berggruen was a native Berliner who, as a Jew, had to flee the Nazis for the United States, from which he returned as a U.S. army staff sergeant. After the war he became a Paris art dealer, meanwhile acquiring one of the world's finest collections of modern art. It was previously on loan to the National Gallery in London, but in 1995 Berggruen brought it to his home town, so that the 'degenerate art' purged by the Nazis could be displayed in their former capital. As part of the deal acquiring the art, the city renovated this building for the collection, and also included in it an apartment where Berggruen and his wife could live next to their art.

The building across Schlossstrasse is the **Egyptian museum**. When the museum island is fully renovated, this collection too is destined to return there. In the meantime, a small sample of an extraordinary hoard may be viewed here, including many pieces excavated by German archaeologists a century ago. The collection ranges from 5000 BC through the Roman period, but its greatest strength is the era of Queen Nefertiti, and by far the most famous work here, perhaps the most famous in the city, is the painted stone bust of that queen, with her ornate necklace, high headdress, long neck, and above all the face that has long set a standard of female beauty, even if one eye is damaged. Another stunning piece, of later vintage, is a green stone head of a man whose face is notably realistic rather than idealized. There are also mummy masks and carved architectural pieces, as well as a papyrus collection. The museum extends into the adjoining building of the former palace stable.

Before there was a town, there was **Charlottenburg palace**, whose yellow expanse extends far to the left and to the right, half a kilometer in width. It was built over the course of a century, quickly repaired after being pillaged by Austrian soldiers in 1760, then all but destroyed in a few bombing raids. The building was nearly given up for lost, but after the East Germans dynamited the main Hohenzollern palace in 1950, Charlottenburg offered the West a chance to distinguish itself from the Communist vandals, and the decision was made to restore it. From the head of Schlossstrasse, you enter the main gate and proceed into the court of honor, which is framed by two side wings. At its center stands Andreas Schlüter's bronze equestrian statue of the 'Great Elector' Frederick William, the prince who made Prussia a force to be reckoned with. It was cast in a single piece in 1700 and has long ranked as the greatest Baroque exemplar of the ancient tradition of the equestrian statue. The elector, more than life size, wears ancient armor but a contemporary wig. His head, turned to the left, was modeled from busts made during his lifetime. The pedestal is a copy; the original has long been in the Bode Museum. The sculptures of slaves sitting upon it (drawing on another Roman tradition) were probably made by other artists working from Schlüter's models. Bronze reliefs on the pedestal portray the electorate, with an allegory of the Spree and muses of history and peace. The west side represents the kingdom, with allegories of strength (Hercules), courage, and faith. The statue originally stood outside the city palace on the Lange Brücke (which is portrayed on the bronze pedestal relief), now the site of the Rathaus bridge between the Nikolai quarter and the royal stables, and Schlüter designed it to be viewed from its elevated position on the bridge. During the war it was taken down and moved to safety. A barge bringing it back in 1947 sank in Tegel harbor in northwestern Berlin. By the time it was salvaged, Berlin was divided and the main palace was gone, so it was placed here in 1951.

Sophie Charlotte's original palace consisted of just the central pavilion and two short side wings, designed by Arnold Nering and built in 1695–99. After Elector Frederick acquired the title of king in 1701, he sponsored a large extension. (He persuaded the Habsburg emperor to let him have the title of king for his territory outside the borders of the Holy Roman Empire. He could not even be the King of Prussia, however, merely 'King in Prussia', because part of that duchy belonged to the Polish crown.) His architect Eosander von Göthe had seen Louis XIV's Versailles and knew that this was the kind of royal grandeur a king would want. In the following years,

Eosander designed the side wings that frame the cour d'honneur as well as the high dome on the central pavilion. The gold-leafed statue of Fortuna atop it is a modern copy. Eosander also designed the Grosse Orangerie, the one-story wing that extends far to the left. His additions maintained the deceased Nering's style, a rhythmic façade of many bays, with ornamented pilasters and window frames.

Frederick's son grew up in the palace, but when he assumed the throne in 1713, he was determined to break with his father's extravagant habits: Sparta this would be, not some foolish Athens. The pious 'soldier king' Frederick William I lavished his money and attention only on his army, which he loved so much that he generally refrained from sending it to war. Otherwise he cut royal expenditure, winding up work here as well as at the Berlin palace, promoting growth and economic development in Berlin and Potsdam, mainly for the good of the army, and building up a surplus in the treasury. This did not endear him to nobles hoping to live off crumbs from the royal table. The king's habit of beating recalcitrant subjects with his own cane did not endear him to the masses, either. His son resembled him only in his distaste for parental ways. Frederick II, Frederick 'the Great', was interested in philosophy and art and saw himself as the enlightened philosopher-king envisioned by some contemporary thinkers. Frederick lived at Charlottenburg until Sanssouci in Potsdam was ready, and he commissioned his architect Knobelsdorff to build the long right wing of the palace in the 1740s.

The final addition to the main building was the theater added at the left end, next to the orangerie, designed by Carl Gotthard Langhans and built in 1787–91. It, too, blends with the Baroque façade of the rest, but also displays the newer, more stringent neoclassical style that characterizes Langhans's most famous work, the

Brandenburg Gate. This addition was commissioned by Frederick William II, a great lover of the theater, but above all a great lover of actresses. Its modern interior houses the recently renovated museum of pre- and early history (**Museum für Ur- und Frühgeschichte**), with its large collection of artifacts documenting human evolution and early Eurasian civilizations. Part of its most famous collection, the treasures gathered in the nineteenth century by Heinrich Schliemann in Troy, can be seen here, but the rest vanished in 1945 (some objects have surfaced in Russia). Built at the same time as the theater was the Kleine Orangerie (which, despite its name, is not at all small), a separate building that stands in front of the Grosse Orangerie. The former gardeners' lodgings at its near end now house a café, with indoor and outdoor seating.

The palace became state property when the monarchy was abolished in 1918. Much of it housed museum collections that have since been moved to the Kulturforum or museum island. The royal apartments, however, are open for tours. Few of the furnishings are original; what you see are careful reconstructions intended to fit the eras of the different royal inhabitants. The main entrance leads you through a pillared rotunda into an oval room that opens onto the gardens. Adjoining it are the best-preserved rooms. To the left are the private apartments of Frederick I and Sophie Charlotte; beyond them, a porcelain collection, and the restored glory of Eosander's chapel. To the right of the entrance are the royal couple's reception rooms, including Eosander's oak gallery. Beyond it are Etruscan and Chinese rooms from the era of Frederick William II (1786–97). A reconstructed grand staircase leads upstairs to the apartments of Frederick William IV and Queen Elisabeth. His library has recently been reconstructed, the furnishings having been stored in Potsdam for decades. To the east, reaching into

Knobelsdorff's wing, are Frederick the Great's rooms, as well as his collection of paintings, which includes two Watteaus, *Embarkation for Cythera* and his famous shop sign for the Parisian art dealer Gersaint. Beyond are a grand dining room, where the original ceiling painting has been replaced by a modern one inspired by Baroque color composition; and the Golden Gallery, with its restored Rococo decoration.

A good place to enter the gardens is at the eastern end of the palace (just across the street from an interesting complex of 1980s buildings, notably a brick apartment house by Hans Kollhoff). Here, by the bank of the Spree, stands a separate building put up in 1825 as a summer residence for Frederick William III and his second wife, Auguste of Liegnitz. It is known as the **Schinkel Pavilion** after its architect. It may seem odd to imagine this small and unpretentious building as a royal residence alongside the vast Baroque palace, but that contrast gives you some sense both of Schinkel's style and of the Biedermeier world reflected in Frederick William III's modest tastes. Schinkel based his design on the Villa Reale del Chiatamone in Naples, where the king had stayed in 1822. Like much of Schinkel's work, it is a simple building – in this case a cube – given elegant touches. The opposite sides are identical, so the building has no identifiable main entrance. The recessed central bays on each side leave the building with four corner rooms on each of its two floors, all accessed from a central stairwell. The sandstone structural elements – columns, pilasters, cornice, window frames – are distinguished in color from the rest of the walls. A cast-iron balcony runs all the way around the building. It was badly damaged in the war but has been carefully restored inside and out, and is open to the public, with a collection of art and crafts from Schinkel's time.

Toward the riverbank rest two Corinthian sandstone capitals from Schinkel's long-vanished Berlin cathedral.

On the west side stand two granite pillars with a pair of gold-leafed bronze victory goddesses (Christian Daniel Rauch, 1840). The pillars emphasize the orientation of the building to the Baroque axis of the palace and its **gardens**, which are a pleasant place to stroll at any time of year, as long as the weather is bearable. The garden was originally laid out formally in the French style; in the 1780s, Frederick William II had it changed to an English landscape garden, crisscrossed with picturesque waterways. Beginning in 1818, the royal landscape architect Peter Joseph Lenné changed the landscaping and vegetation once again. After the war, the front portion was reconstructed in an approximation of the original Baroque formality, with parallel axes and carefully trimmed plants, extending from the central section of the palace back to the large carp pond (Karpfenteich). From there back, a more informal, picturesque design has been restored. If you follow the right bank of the pond, you reach the **Belvedere**, a tea house designed by Langhans for Frederick William II in 1788, and deliberately placed off the axis of the palace. This green and white building, rising up three stories, takes the form of an oval with a square extension on each of its four sides. The structure is thus distinctly Baroque in form, but its decoration is more neoclassical. The exterior was carefully restored from wartime damage, while the modern interior houses a porcelain collection.

The far northwest corner of the gardens, west from the Belvedere, includes a playground. If, however, you return from the Belvedere a short distance toward the Karpfenteich, you reach an arched red cast-iron bridge (1800) that affords a view of the palace. At its other end you are on the Luiseninsel, 'Luise island'. Here and elsewhere stand a large number of eighteenth- and nineteenth-century statues, some of them copies of the originals. Schinkel designed the cast-iron benches. The path across the Luiseninsel leads you back toward the formal garden and the palace. If you turn right (west) at the outer end of the formal garden, just after crossing the footbridge off the Luiseninsel, you can find your way to the elegant **royal mausoleum**, half hidden in the woods, which can also be reached by following a path directly back from the theater wing of the palace. The original sandstone building (1812) was designed by Heinrich Gentz in the form of a Doric temple, as prescribed by Frederick William III after the death of his wife Luise. In 1828, its sandstone portico was removed to the Pfaueninsel, and Schinkel supervised its replacement in polished granite. After the king's death in 1840, the building was extended to the north, with a round apse, according to a design by Schinkel. Half a century after that, it received a larger extension for the tombs of Frederick William's son, William I (the first emperor of unified Germany), and his queen.

Here began the posthumous cult of Queen Luise, which was promoted by Frederick William. Not only the course of modern German history, but also the nature of the Prussian monarchy has left Berlin with only the smallest traces of royalist nostalgia, nothing like what you find in Munich or Vienna. Queen Luise, however, remains the most revered figure in the Hohenzollern pantheon. The former princess of Mecklenburg-Strelitz (its coat of arms, along with Prussia's, decorates the wall here) married the future king in 1793. She developed a reputation as open, friendly and modest – aided, no doubt, by the frugality of her husband. The silk scarf she typically wore around her neck established a new fashion. After Prussia's crushing defeat at the hands of Napoleon in 1806, the royal couple worked quietly with German nationalists to rally support for the monarchy. Ten births in her sixteen-plus years of marriage destroyed her health, however, and she died in 1810 at the tender age of 34, leaving a permanent image of her youthful beauty in the form of paintings and sculptures.

The focal point of the mausoleum is the sarcophagus carved for her in Rome by Christian Daniel Rauch (1811–14), one of the best-known works of Berlin's school of Romantic classicism. Rauch began as a servant to the queen, before he studied sculpture in Berlin, with Schadow, and then in Rome. The queen, greater than life size, is portrayed sleeping, with her arms crossed, covered by a draped fabric. Next to her is the later tomb of her husband (1841), also based on a design by Rauch. The tombs of Emperor William I and Empress Augusta, from the 1890s, also follow Rauch's model. Marble candelabra flanking the later tombs were probably designed by Schinkel in 1812 and originally stood near Luise's tomb. Also designed by Schinkel is a bronze lamp with kneeling cherubs.

When you have had enough royalist nostalgia, you can be confident of avoiding it after you slip back into the city in any direction.

16

The Far West

THE EAST–WEST AXIS BEYOND the Tiergarten is named Strasse des 17. Juni as far as Ernst-Reuter-Platz, after which it is called Bismarckstrasse and then Kaiserdamm. The U1 runs under it as far as **Theodor-Heuss-Platz**. This square, laid out a century ago, was originally named Reichskanzlerplatz in honor of the recently deceased chancellor Bismarck. Later it was named after another chancellor, Adolf Hitler, and now it bears the name of the Federal Republic's first president. To its north is the once exclusive villa quarter of Westend, founded in the 1860s and home to many British officers a century later. By the early twentieth century, suburbs and vast industrial complexes had spread from Berlin as far as the band of forests and lakes stretching from Spandau down to Potsdam. The area subsequently became home to such major public facilities as the broadcast center, the convention center, and the Olympic grounds.

Take Masurenallee from Theodor-Heuss-Platz and you see, on your left, the elegant **Haus des Rundfunks**, completed in 1931 for German state radio, which had begun its broadcasts a few years earlier from Potsdamer Platz. The acoustics of the largest studio make it a favored site for concerts. The architect Hans Poelzig used horizontal ceramic bands to lend visual unity as well as color to the façade, and even more to the entrance hall. The Georg Kolbe sculpture there is a new casting of one removed by the Nazis, who made good use of the building, as Goebbels broadcast Hitler's speeches, set up a comprehensive entertainment program, and sold cheap receivers to make radio available to the masses. In 1945 the Soviets seized the building and began their own broadcasts, refusing their erstwhile allies any access to it until they moved out in 1956, after which it was turned over to West Berlin radio and television.

Across the street rises the radio tower (**Funkturm**), a Berlin landmark since its completion in 1926. The steel latticework resembles Paris's Eiffel tower, but at 150 meters is only half as tall, and in fact was obsolete soon after it was opened. It has remained popular, however, for its observation platform as well as the restaurant halfway up. It stands amid the sprawling **trade fair centre** (Messe) created at the same time. The oldest extant buildings, apart from the tower, are starkly colonnaded Third Reich structures. On the left side is the striking (and little admired) aluminum-clad convention center from the 1970s, its entrance marked by Jean Ipoustéguy's enormous sculpture of a quasi-human figure. The far side of the convention center faces the autobahn that extends north to Tegel airport and south through the Grunewald. The southern stretch was originally built as an auto-racing course, completed just after the First World War, which is why spectators' bleachers stand beside it. Until recently it was still closed occasionally for races. The circular tower in the nearby rest area was originally built in 1936 as a viewing platform.

Scattered sites beyond Theodor-Heuss-Platz offer a rich mixture of twentieth-century art, architecture, and history. From the square, Pommernallee takes you to nearby Karolingerplatz, where number 5 is a pair of attached houses, Berlin's first flat-roofed modernist dwellings (1922), with dynamic horizontal forms typical of the architect, Erich Mendelsohn, who originally intended to live in one of the pair. From Heerstrasse, the extension of the east–west axis beyond Theodor-Heuss-Platz, Sensburger Allee leads to the right just past the

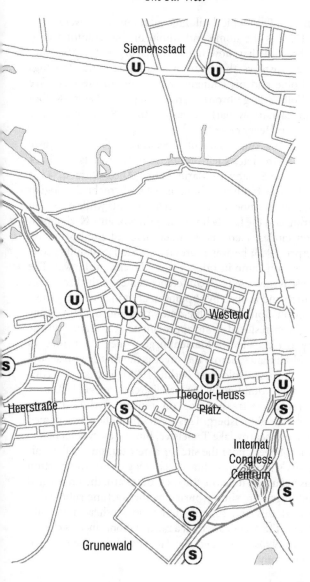

S-Bahn. The cubic buildings at number 25 were built in 1929 as the home and studio of the sculptor Georg Kolbe, and they now house the **Georg Kolbe Museum**, which displays the figurative sculptures and drawings of Kolbe and his contemporaries. Just to the west, five of Kolbe's large bronzes are displayed in Georg-Kolbe-Hain, a narrow park extending from Sensburger Allee south to Heerstrasse.

On the other side of Heerstrasse, Teufelsseestrasse leads to the left. A left on Soldauer Allee leads you back along the S-Bahn to Marienburger Allee. Number 43 is the **Bonhoeffer house**, built in 1935, where the theologian Dietrich Bonhoeffer lived with his parents while he was in Berlin, and the family hosted meetings of anti-Nazi opposition circles. Here the Gestapo arrested Bonhoeffer on 5 April 1943; he was murdered in the Flossenbürg concentration camp just days before the end of the war. The house is now used as a conference center by the Protestant church and is open by appointment. It includes an exhibition on Bonhoeffer's life and work, and his attic study has been restored to its approximate appearance on the day of his arrest. Marienburger Allee continues to Waldschulallee; across the street is the first Jewish school built in post–Holocaust Berlin (1995), a striking deconstructivist building by the Israeli architect Zvi Hecker.

Teufelsseestrasse leads on toward Berlin's highest point, the **Teufelsberg**. This 'devil's mountain' was named after the nearby lake Teufelssee, but it deserves its name. Albert Speer chose the site for a new campus of the university's faculty of military technology, and construction was begun on it before the war. Afterward, the unfinished buildings were simply buried by the wartime rubble that created this and several of the city's other main hills. Atop it, the Americans built a radar station. Since its closure in the 1990s, developers have planned homes and a conference center here.

Several S-Bahn lines pass by the trade fair centre. Nearby is the western crossing of the ring and the east–west trunk line. Although Westkreuz is not as big or busy as Ostkreuz across town, a ride through it on a train affords many glimpses of a neglected landscape of bridges, sidings, signals, and blind tunnels. Here one can get the rare impression that little has changed from the metropolis seen in the introductory shots of Walter Ruttmann's classic 1927 film, *Berlin, Symphony of a Great City*. The first station beyond Westkreuz on the east–west line is **Grunewald**, which affords access to the exclusive suburb of that name. It is also the site of memorials that recall grim events. A freight siding by the station was the place from which most of Berlin's Jews were deported. From 1941 on, thousands of Jews forced out of their homes were compelled to walk through the streets to this station and board trains bound for Auschwitz, Theresienstadt, or the Polish ghettos. Few survived. The site stood neglected for decades, although since 1973 a plaque by the station has recalled its history. If you exit the station via its eastern (front) door, follow the path that slopes upward to your left. On the way to the freight siding, you pass a 1991 memorial sculpture by Karol Broniatowski, a concrete wall with impressions of human forms. Shortly after its dedication, the German railways decided that the inaccessible and rotting freight ramp would be a good site for a new maintenance facility, but public protests forced a change in plans and led to a memorial on the siding itself, completed in 1998. The design by Nikolaus Hirsch, Wolfgang Lorch, and Andrea Wandel comprises 186 steel segments set in the ground, each one engraved with the date, number of passengers, and destination of a trainload of Jews that departed from here. Beyond the Grunewald station, the S-Bahn travels a long distance through the Grunewald forest, offering rapid passage to Wannsee (see Chapter 17) and Potsdam.

Another notorious place in western Berlin is the **grounds of the 1936 Olympic games**, where Nazi Germany temporarily put on a tolerant face for the benefit of world opinion, convincing some (but not all) visitors that Hitler's new Germany was really quite an admirable place. Throughout the city during those weeks, anti-Semitic slogans and 'no Jews allowed' signs temporarily disappeared. In his last novel, published after his death in 1938, Thomas Wolfe evoked the ominous sense of excitement that gripped the entire city. 'The sheer pageantry of the occasion was overwhelming. . . . And the thing that made it seem ominous was that it so evidently went beyond what the games themselves demanded. . . . It was as if the games had been chosen as a symbol of the new collective might, a means of showing to the world in concrete terms what this new power had come to be.'

You can arrive as the sports fans did (and do), by either U-Bahn or S-Bahn. The S-Bahn is nearer to the stadium, but from the U-Bahn station Olympia-Stadion (Ost) you can best appreciate its grand ceremonial entrance. On this ill-fated site, in 1913 the Germans had completed a stadium for the 1916 Olympic games, which were canceled on account of war. For the 1936 games, awarded to Berlin before the Nazis came to power, they decided on a completely new stadium (designed by Werner March, son of the man who built the razed 1913 stadium) as the centerpiece of an ensemble of architecture, sculpture, and landscape intended to serve the new state long after the games. From the east, you approach the stadium through a monumental gateway in the same limestone and oversized classical forms as the stadium and the other buildings. Inside and out, the oval stadium, designed to seat 100,000, exudes an impressive grandeur, which, one hopes, will remain after its renovation for the 2006 World Cup. Here top Nazis and ordinary Germans found plenty to cheer about in 1936, although the world remembers the triumphs of the African-American sprinter Jesse Owens. (The world also remembers a famous story about Owens being personally snubbed by the Führer. Unfortunately, this parable directed against Nazi racial theories is not true. What happened was that Hitler personally congratulated some German winners early on, but was then advised that as the host head of state, he had to remain neutral, so he ceased the practice.)

The grounds are still graced by their original sculptures, including some by the Nazis' favorite sculptors, Arno Breker and Joseph Thorak, accomplished neoclassicists whose muscular Übermenschen exude either a terrible beauty or a terrible ugliness. (The games are also well known through the ravishing film directed by Leni Riefenstahl, who lived until 2003 insisting improbably that she made the film independently of Goebbels's Propaganda Ministry and that she cared only about beauty, not politics.) On the far side of the stadium is a vast Champ de Mars, intended for mass demonstrations, and beyond it the broad Langemarck Hall, built as a World War I memorial, part of the Nazis' elaborate cult of the dead of that conflict. The central tower was destroyed in 1945 but, remarkably, rebuilt in 1962. The entire complex was carefully sited to take advantage of its topography, most impressively at the Waldbühne, just beyond the Langemarck Hall (and not far from S-Bahn Pichelsberg). This amphitheater, modeled on those of ancient Greece, was built into a deep ravine and remains a marvelous site for outdoor concerts. The larger ravine beyond, the Murellenschlucht, had its moment of grim fame in the final days of the Second World War, when hundreds of deserters were summarily shot here. At the same time, Hitler youth, mostly boys of twelve and thirteen, assembled at the Olympic grounds for a futile last stand against the Red Army; two thousand were slaughtered in a pointless battle. Soon after, the British army took over the grounds, making its headquarters in the administrative buildings to the north. The spies of MI6 were based here as well, in this notorious but nearly invisible place. The stadium was returned to civilian use, but most of the grounds remained off limits until the British departed in 1994.

Flatowallee leads south from the stadium to the S-Bahn. The large apartment building just past the station is Le Corbusier's contribution to the 1957 architectural exhibition. It is a version of the '**unité d'habitation**' model that he had previously built in Marseille and Nantes. The seventeen-story building on stilts includes some 500 apartments reached via nine internal 'streets'. The architect envisioned a self-contained city, with shops, a theater, and child-care facilities on the internal corridors. To his disappointment, few of those facilities were built. A short distance farther on, Flatowallee returns you to Heerstrasse. To the west (right), Heerstrasse 107, on the left side, is an elegant 1924 villa by Erich Mendelsohn. Farther down, past the bend in the street at Scholzplatz, is the British military cemetery, laid out in the 1950s, and the adjoining Jewish cemetery established in 1953 for West Berlin. At the next corner on the left, Am Rupenhorn, where the land drops off to the Havel river, are a pair of revolutionary modern steel-framed houses from 1928 by Hans and Wassili Luckhardt, which display dramatic vertical and horizontal forms. Farther back, Am Rupenhorn 6 is the house Mendelsohn built for himself in 1929.

Heerstrasse continues along the southern edge of Spandau. More direct routes to Spandau include the S-Bahn and the U7. On the way, the U7 takes you to **Siemensstadt,** the largest of the industrial colonies built by Berlin's major companies a century ago. Werner Siemens founded his telegraphy firm in 1847 near Anhalter Bahnhof, where he could cultivate the army contacts that brought him his first jobs. In 1883, having established his company as an international leader in electronics, he moved it to Salzufer, near the new technical academy; in 1898, the company began building the first of its factories on the swampy land between the Spree and the Spandau ship canal. Amid the 1920s housing crisis, the fact that 57,000 jobs were located here led the city to choose neighboring land for one of its showcase housing estates.

The Siemensstadt estate, built in 1929–32 to an overall design by Hans Scharoun and Martin Wagner, spreads out north of U-Bahn Siemensdamm. The long V-shaped building between Jungfernheideweg and Mäckeritzstrasse was designed by Scharoun, who used its angles and curves to give it unique detailing that has always reminded viewers of a ship. Scharoun, who also designed the straight row placed at an odd angle on the other side of the Jungfernheideweg, lived here for many years, at Jungfernheideweg 4. Past the closed S-Bahn line (the postwar U-Bahn made it redundant) is the rest of the estate. A very long building on the south side of Goebelstrasse, by Otto Bartning, takes advantage of the street's curve to avoid monotony. Across Goebelstrasse, each side of Jungfernheideweg is lined with a long row by Walter Gropius. Parallel to the right one, extending north from Goebelstrasse, are nine more short parallel rows by Hugo Häring, enlivened by curved brick balconies. The north–south rows follow the modernist belief in the desirability of maximizing sunlight in every apartment rather than building street fronts and closed courtyards, as was the practice up to 1914, and again at the end of the twentieth century.

On the other side of the U-Bahn and of the main street Siemensdamm, along Wernerwerksdamm, one large group of Siemens factory buildings is dominated by a 1920s clock tower, which disguises a chimney and a water tower. A larger complex is past Rohrdamm (the next U-Bahn stop), where Siemensdamm becomes Nonnendammallee. Here, on the right side, is the Siemens administration building (1913), which ceased to be the company's head-quarters in 1957, when management chose Munich over divided and threatened Berlin. In front of it is a 1934 World War I memorial, whereas in the courtyard a plaque recalls the slave laborers who worked for Siemens during the Third Reich – although the plaque stops short of assigning Siemens any responsibility for their suffering. (Siemens was in fact known as one of the more humane employers that profited from forced labor.) Behind it looms the masterpiece of the Siemens architect Hans Hertlein, a massive 11-story factory from 1928. Across the street are older buildings. In the largest, the 1906 dynamo factory, Hitler gave a speech on 10 November 1933, broadcast to all German homes and factories, in which he proclaimed his allegiance to German workers.

The U7 continues into Spandau. The **Zitadelle** station is named after the nearby citadel, one of Berlin's most impressive early monuments, which you reach by following the street Am Juliusturm west past the station. The citadel, surrounded by a moat, stands just outside the old town of Spandau, at a strategic point in the watery Brandenburg landscape, near the confluence of the Spree and the Havel. You enter it across a bridge from the south. (To the north, a large new residential development represents a more contemporary attempt to exploit the waterfront site's advantages.) There was a Slavic settlement here as early as the eighth century. Around 1200, the German conquerors built a castle. Most of what you see is one of Europe's best-preserved sixteenth-century fortresses, a massive brick and stone square with protruding corner bastions, after the fashion of the most up-to-date Italian military architecture, designed to withstand cannon fire.

The ornate entry is largely a nineteenth-century design, with some Baroque decoration. Once inside, you can wander along the walls and bastions. The oldest structure is the high round Julius tower from the thirteenth century, with its ten-foot-thick walls. The foundation of the adjoining fourteenth-century building was constructed in part with thirteenth- and fourteenth-century Jewish gravestones, apparently looted from a local cemetery – evidence of the pogroms that swept Europe after the Black Death. The citadel saw military action only once in its long history, in 1813, when it was held by the army of Napoleon's France, while Prussian and Russian troops attacked. In the battle, the powder magazine exploded. Much of the interior was subsequently rebuilt by Schinkel (who gave the Julius tower a new crown) and others. Since then the fortress has seen many uses, some of them military (a prison, a Third Reich nerve gas laboratory), some not. The nineteenth-century arsenal now houses Spandau's local history museum. The buildings and grounds are also used by local artisans and for fairs and concerts.

The street Am Juliusturm leads across the Havel (where a lock has lifted barges since the sixteenth century) into the old town of **Spandau** (by the U-Bahn station Altstadt Spandau). Like Köpenick on the other side of Berlin, Spandau was one of the earliest and most important German towns in the area, commanding a strategic position, but in later centuries it stagnated as Berlin came to dominate the region. Only at the beginning of the twentieth century did Berlin's expansion transform the town into a suburb, dominated by the many armaments factories that sprang up around it. Also like Köpenick, it retains a recognizable and occasionally quaint old core. Most of the old town stands to your left, but the quiet streets to your right, Kolk and Möllentordamm, are lined with rows of renovated eighteenth- and nineteenth-century houses, with an 1848 church on Behnitz and a piece of the fourteenth-century town wall on Hoher Steinweg. Carl-Schurz-Strasse, left from Am Juliusturm, takes you to the church of

St Nikolai, a building from the fourteenth and fifteenth centuries, with a Baroque tower and numerous other renovations, including many by Schinkel and others in the 1830s. Inside is a large altar from the late sixteenth century, with a painting of the Last Supper and a relief of the Last Judgment. Other notable furnishings are a medieval baptismal font and a Baroque pulpit that originally stood in the Potsdam town palace. The name of the square outside, Reformationsplatz, is illustrated by the most prominent of several sculptures here, an 1889 statue of Elector Joachim II, commemorating the arrival of the Reformation in Brandenburg 350 years before. Following the elector's conversion, the first Protestant service was held in this church in 1535. The base of the statue includes reliefs illustrating, among other things, a conversation that in fact never occurred, between Joachim and Luther. Another sculpture here is Schinkel's 1816 cast-iron memorial to those who fell in the Wars of Liberation against Napoleon. There is also a marble statue of the reformer Baron vom Stein, a fragment from William II's dismantled Siegesallee in the Tiergarten.

Surrounding the central Markt are quiet shopping streets. Carl-Schurz-Strasse, Breite Strasse, Marktstrasse, and Fischerstrasse boast renovated houses from many centuries, some of them half-timbered. Much of the small-town atmosphere is intact, including its discordant notes. A plaque and a 1989 memorial at Lindenufer 12, near Kammerstrasse, recall the Spandau synagogue that was destroyed in 1938. A few blocks away, at Am Wall 3, another plaque honors all who resisted the Nazis, without any reference to local events or to the significance of the site. In fact, part of this town hall annex was taken over in 1933 by the Spandau SA, which incarcerated and tortured its opponents here, before sending them off to concentration camps. Spandau's small-town atmosphere extended to the effectiveness with which the Nazis held it in thrall.

Around the block, the tower of the huge 1913 **Rathaus** faces away from the old town and dominates the square beyond. Here is the end station of the U7, and just beyond is the rail and S-Bahn station, with a new shopping mall that may spell doom for many shops in the old town.

In the wider world, the name Spandau was long associated with the prison specially opened for Nazi war criminals sentenced at the Nuremberg trials. As it turned out, there were only seven who were convicted but not executed, and after 1966, when Albert Speer and Baldur von Schirach were released, the odious but harmless Rudolf Hess was the sole inmate. Absurdly, the entire prison continued to operate under rotating four-power control until his death in 1987 (a suicide, although conspiracy theorists insist he was murdered), after which the British demolished the former military prison, with what some saw as unseemly haste, to make way for a shopping center. It stood a mile to the south of the old town, on the west side of Wilhelmstrasse, just where Gatower Strasse diverges.

A much more pleasant corner of Spandau is **Gartenstadt Staaken**, to the west, at Am Torweg and Am Heideberg. This variant on the English garden city model was built under state sponsorship during the First World War to house munitions workers. The architect Paul Schmitthenner created a small-town setting, with rows of gabled houses (recalling Potsdam's Dutch Quarter) surrounding a central square with a church, a school, and shops. It is a distinctly anti-modern, anti-urban, and anti-industrial vision of modern industrial city life. For decades it stood at the edge of the world: just beyond, Nennhauser Damm and Finkenkruger Weg marked the course of the Berlin Wall, West-Staaken and its unfortunate residents having been traded to the Soviets after the war for a corner of Gatow needed to expand the British landing strip.

17

The Southwest: Lakes and Villas

IN BERLIN, as in so many European cities, wealth migrated westward. The fashionable West moved in the course of a few decades from Potsdamer Platz past the Tiergarten to distant railroad and automobile suburbs, stretching to Potsdam and laced with lakes and forests. Their fortuitous inclusion in the western, capitalist half of the divided city meant that they could retain their cachet, although West Berlin's bourgeoisie was a pale shadow of its prewar predecessor. Since 1990, such neighborhoods as Grunewald, Dahlem and Wannsee have attracted a new generation of the rich and powerful. Meanwhile, lesser mortals have long flocked to the woods and beaches on weekends and holidays.

One of the primary approaches to the southwest is the U1 subway line, which linked the city to Wilmersdorf and Dahlem already before the First World War. **Fehrbelliner Platz**, where the U1 crosses the U7, remained unimportant until the 1930s, when the Third Reich's overscaled neoclassicism gave the square its character. Several office buildings from that era form a curve around the intersection. Fehrbelliner Platz 1 was built for a department store chain. Across Hohenzollerndamm to the south, number 2 housed an insurance company; number 3, a government agency; and number 4, the German Labor Front, the Nazi party's substitute for labor unions. Municipal offices now fill these buildings as well as some postwar additions that manage to make the Nazi buildings look almost graceful by comparison. The square remains overscaled and unfriendly. In fact, it was intended as a place of regimented mass assembly, with its focal point a monument to the brownshirts of the SA, erected in 1933 and removed after 1945.

The stations of the U1, built after 1910, display more creative adaptations of neoclassicism, including the ceramic tiles at Fehrbelliner Platz and the massive columns at Heidelberger Platz. Next to the **Rüdesheimer Platz** station, the square of the same name is the finest example of the upscale apartment projects put up by Georg Haberland, Berlin's most successful developer of the prewar era. Around the pleasant landscaped square, and set back behind garden terraces, the buildings (1910–14) project grace and comfort without being laden with the historicist ornament typical of earlier years. Their half-timbered exteriors and elaborate gables are intended to evoke English cottages.

Farther out the U1 is **Dahlem**, which offers some odd juxtapositions. It became a fashionable suburb in the early twentieth century, but because the manor had belonged to the crown since 1841, it also became home to important state institutions, notably the Kaiser-Wilhelm-Gesellschaft, the elite royal academy for scientific research (now the Max-Planck-Gesellschaft, with institutes all over Germany). That, in turn, made it a logical place to house the Free University in 1948, when students protesting Soviet censorship left the old Humboldt University and founded a new one in the American sector. Today parts of Dahlem are crowded with students making their way from the subway to their classrooms and laboratories, while some quiet streets are still dominated by grand villas, including the official residences of ambassadors and the highest government officials. The combination of city crowds and a bucolic setting have made the vicinity of Podbielskiallee and Dahlem-Dorf subway stations a good place to find leafy beer gardens.

The Dahlem-Dorf station stands near the center of the old village, and is supposed to look far older than it is.

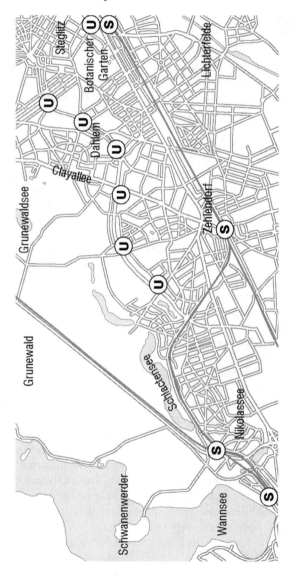

The emperor decreed that the station (1913) and an adjoining kiosk resemble peasants' huts, with thatch roofs. Nothing could have been a greater contradiction to the modernists' belief that a building for modern purposes (a rail station!) should reflect its uses – and yet the building works just fine. On the west side of the rail line (to your left as you exit the station) is the center of the old village. Across Königin-Luise-Strasse, **Domäne Dahlem** is a museum of traditional village agriculture, which includes the old buildings of the manor, displays of tools and artifacts, periodic open-air markets and an actual working farm that practices old-fashioned agriculture. Among the buildings open to the public is the manor house from 1680, which incorporates parts of its predecessor from 1500. Just beyond is **St Anne's**, one of the finest village churches in Berlin, a fourteenth-century building with a fifteenth-century apse and medieval wall paintings. The parsonage, across the street, has been dedicated to the memory of Martin Niemöller, who became pastor here in 1931. At the time he was an enthusiastic Nazi, but in 1934 he organized the Confessing Church in protest against the Nazis' takeover of the Protestant state church. Later he survived eight years in concentration camps.

On the other side of the rail line are the Dahlem museums. Archivstrasse follows the rail line to the old building of the Geheimes Staatsarchiv (Secret State Archive), which, despite its name, has long been open to researchers; it is the main repository of Prussian records. Next to it, the side street Im Winkel leads to the **Museum of European Cultures**, devoted to the prehistory, folklore and customs of European peoples. It was founded as the Museum of German Folklore, and its collections reflect its heritage, although it was recently renamed in a post–national spirit.

From the station, little Iltisstrasse leads a short distance to Lansstrasse and the entrance to the main museum complex. Museum construction began here in 1914; later, in divided Berlin, these buildings housed West Berlin's main art museums. Since reunification, the European collections have been moved to the Kulturforum and museum island. Long-term plans for the Dahlem complex remain uncertain, and much of it is being renovated. However, the fabulous holdings of the **Ethnology Museum** are being displayed in rotating shows focusing on different regions, including entire collections that have been in storage for decades. The museum holds rich collections of art, textiles and ceremonial and household objects from North America, Mesoamerica (including notable Maya and Aztec stone sculptures), Africa (sculptures from Nigeria and Benin are the highlights) and the Pacific islands (the boats are a favorite). Among the treasures of the **Museum of East Asian Art** are calligraphy and archaeological finds from China, Japanese woodcuts, and a recently acquired Japanese tea room. The **Museum of Indian Art** is misnamed: although it boasts a rich collection spanning the entire history of South Asian civilization, southeast Asia is represented as well, and the museum's most renowned works are Buddhist sculptures and wall paintings excavated by German archaeologists a century ago along the Silk Road in central Asia.

The museums are surrounded by buildings of the Free University, which are scattered across much of Dahlem, particularly toward Habelschwerter Allee and Garystrasse. The sprawling 1960s megastructure between Fabeckstrasse and Thielallee is being renovated, with a new library designed by Norman Foster inserted into it. Some university buildings were originally built as research institutes of the Kaiser-Wilhelm-Gesellschaft, which was founded here in 1911. At the Kaiser Wilhelm Institute for Chemistry, Thielallee 63, in 1938, Otto Hahn's lab split uranium atoms for the first time, an experiment that would change the world, although only after correspondence with his former Jewish colleague Lise Meitner, in Swedish exile, did Hahn realize what he had accomplished – and historians are still arguing about why the Germans did not manage to build an atomic bomb. Another legacy of the Kaiser-Wilhelm-Gesellschaft is recalled at the former institute for anthropology, genetics and eugenics at Ihnestrasse 22, near the Thielplatz U-Bahn. The most famous student and wartime correspondent of this institute was the notorious Auschwitz doctor, Josef Mengele, whose experiments on helpless prisoners were planned here. As a plaque on the building notes, the wartime director of the institute, Mengele's teacher Otmar von Verschuer, remained a genetics professor in West Germany until 1965. The 1988 plaque marks an era in which postwar silences about the Nazi era were being challenged. A different postwar history was enacted in the brick building at Kaiserswerther Strasse 16–18, at the corner of Thielallee, home of the Allied Kommandantur, where the military commanders of the four occupying garrisons met after 1945. After 1948, meetings continued, but without their earlier significance, since the Soviet commander no longer attended.

Königin-Luise-Strasse, a few blocks east of U-Bahn Dahlem-Dorf, takes you to another major institution brought to Dahlem, the **Botanical Garden**, which was moved here from Potsdamer Strasse in the 1890s. Greenhouses, administrative offices and a museum are housed in grand turn-of-the-century buildings, and 42 hectares of artificial landscape recreate the flora of several continents. Summer concerts are also held here. Nearby, at Peter-Lenné-Strasse 28, the German Archaeological Institute is housed in Peter Behrens's Wiegand house (1912), the most notable villa built in the simplified neo-classical style Behrens developed.

Just past the main Free University buildings, the U1 crosses Clayallee at the Oskar-Helene-Heim station. The

street honors General Lucius D. Clay, the U.S. army commander in postwar West Berlin, and the man credited
with the firm American response to the 1948 Soviet
blockade. This intersection was the center of American
Berlin. A complex of grandiose buildings on the northeast corner of Clayallee and Saargemünder Strasse (which
parallels the U-Bahn) was built in the 1930s as the
regional headquarters of Göring's air force. After the war
it became U.S. army headquarters. All foreign troops
pulled out in 1994, but one building still houses the U.S.
consulate, pending completion of the new embassy on
Pariser Platz. Across Clayallee was Truman Plaza, the
main shopping and entertainment center for U.S. soldiers
and their families, where the currency was the dollar and
the sights and smells were American. It has been demolished, except for the 1953 movie theater just up the street
at Clayallee 135, which in the 1990s was converted into
the **Allied Museum** (Allierten-Museum), a display of artifacts from the Cold War presence of the American, British
and French forces in Berlin, including, outside the building, a British Hastings plane from the airlift and the
American hut from Checkpoint Charlie. Nearby, a sculpture celebrates 'the day the wall came down'.

A short distance to the west, along Argentinische Allee,
stands one of the largest and finest of the Weimar era's
social housing projects, the **Waldsiedlung Zehlendorf** – a
'woodland estate' because the forest trees were retained
wherever possible. It is centered around the U-Bahn station Onkel Toms Hütte, which includes a shopping center
built as part of the project. (The station's odd name,
'Uncle Tom's Cabin', comes from an old country inn.) An
earlier experiment with social housing took the form of a
row of four houses built in 1923 at Onkel-Tom-Strasse
85–91 by Erich Mendelsohn and Richard Neutra, just
before the latter moved on to his more famous career in
California. After the postwar inflation was overcome, work

began on the larger project in 1926, under the leadership of Bruno Taut, who designed many of the buildings himself. The complex extends from Am Fischtal north to the edge of the Grunewald, on both sides of Onkel-Tom-Strasse. Simple forms and materials and standardized floor plans were intended to keep costs low, but they also gave Taut the chance to create comfort and beauty by manipulating simple forms and colors.

As in Britz (see Chapter 19), the neighborhood gives you the chance to compare architectural styles once in fierce competition with one another. Across Am Fischtal, along the southern edge of the Waldsiedlung, a conservative housing society commissioned a row of houses intended to demonstrate traditional architectural principles. Heinrich Tessenow led a group of architects who produced houses with steep roofs, shutters and other decorative elements. These larger dwellings in small houses became a showcase of upper-middle-class comfort at the onset of the Depression. Still another vision took form a decade later just west of the Waldsiedlung, between Argentinische Allee and Quermatenweg, where the SS built a housing estate for its members. Notable modern villas nearby include Wilskistrasse 66 (1932) by Ludwig Hilbersheimer, Fischerhüttenstrasse 106 (1929) by Walter Gropius and one of Ludwig Mies van der Rohe's first commissions, Haus Perls at Hermannstrasse 14 (1911).

Many points in Dahlem and elsewhere offer access to the vast expanse of the **Grunewald**, the royal hunting ground that has long been a public park. Much of it is flat and monotonous, and its ancient trees were cut down for firewood after the war, but it offers a great deal of open space and lake frontage. You are not actually required to bring a dog along when you go for a walk here; it only seems that way – cramped Berlin apartments shelter an immense population of (often enormous) canines, which are unfailingly well behaved but leave the sidewalks a mess. The most important relic of the forest's earlier use is the **Jagdschloss Grunewald**, which sits framed by out-buildings on the shore of the Grunewaldsee. (The most direct access from the Dahlem side is via Pücklerstrasse, Königin-Luise-Strasse or – by car – Hüttenweg.) Elector Joachim II had it built as a hunting lodge in the 1540s, and it was rebuilt in the late 1600s. Inside, you can see part of the original Renaissance interior, along with furniture and art from the royal collections. Just to the southwest along the lake, and near Hüttenweg, is the Forsthaus Paulsborn, a restaurant since it was built in 1905, shortly after the royal hunting preserve was opened to the public. Another striking presence in the forest, far to the west, is the Grunewald tower, a 55-meter-high neo-Gothic extravagance designed by Franz Schwechten in 1897, with an observation platform above and a restaurant below.

On the Dahlem edge of the forest, at the end of Bussardsteig off Clayallee, stands the **Brücke Museum**. The museum, and its 1967 Bauhaus-style home, are the product of Karl Schmidt-Rottluff's decision to donate many of his works to the city. The museum specializes in the paintings of the group that called itself 'Die Brücke' (the bridge), formed in 1905 in Dresden by Schmidt-Rottluff, Ernst Ludwig Kirchner and Erich Heckel, who together developed a style that married vivid color to intense emotional expressiveness. All the members moved to Berlin around 1910, soon making the city synonymous with expressionism even as their stunning canvases polarized its art world. The museum's collection also features works of other Brücke members, including Emil Nolde and Max Pechstein. Behind the museum is a studio built in the 1930s for Hitler's favorite sculptor, Arno Breker, and used after the war by Bernhard Heiliger, who produced sculptures of a completely different sort.

Another route to southwestern Berlin is the S-Bahn from Potsdamer Platz. This is in fact Berlin's first railroad line, which reached Potsdam in 1838. Either the S-Bahn or the U9 will take you to **Rathaus Steglitz**. You come out at the southern end of the Schlossstrasse shopping district, one of Berlin's busiest. Titania-Palast, up at Schlossstrasse 5, is a grand (and recently restored) cinema from 1927, which survived the war and in fact hosted the first postwar concerts of the Berlin Philharmonic Orchestra as well as the first Berlin film festival. The most striking sight on Schlossstrasse, however, is a brightly colored 1970s building at the corner of Schildhornstrasse, held far above the street by a single massive pillar. It's the kind of place that beckons you to visit the restaurant inside – either to appreciate the unique structure, or, if you fail to appreciate it, to retreat to the only place around where you don't have to look at the monstrosity.

Schlossstrasse in front of the Rathaus Steglitz station is dominated by the thirty-story Steglitzer Kreisel, one of Berlin's tallest buildings, significant only for the scandals and endless costs that accompanied its construction in the 1970s. Across Albrechtstrasse, the relatively quiet space of **Hermann-Ehlers-Platz** is filled with the stalls of an open-air market on some days. The nearby presence of a former synagogue was long forgotten. It was a courtyard synagogue, and the building (now used for offices) still stands behind a new structure at Düppelstrasse 41. Earlier proposals for a commemorative plaque were ignored, but since 1995 a memorial stands in the center of the triangular plaza. The design by Wolfgang Göschel, Joachim von Rosenberg and Hans-Norbert Burkert takes the form of a long steel wall, set perpendicular to the synagogue's site, and polished to such a shine that it functions as a mirror. On it are inscribed, along with pictures and text about local Jewish life, the names, birth dates and addresses of 1600 former Jewish residents of the Steglitz district. The information has been taken from the Gestapo's careful records of its transports to Theresienstadt, Auschwitz and other camps and ghettos, so the visitor can imagine the fate of these former neighborhood residents. The combined experience of looking at one's own reflection, reading familiar addresses and contemplating the murder of these people seems to have been too much for some people to take: the conservative majority on the district council voted to kill the project after it had been approved, and the Berlin government had to overrule it, to avoid embarrassment. For a moment, people recalled that solidly middle-class Steglitz had been the Berlin district where the Nazis did best in elections. Now most, but by no means all, passers-by ignore the mirror wall.

Across Schlossstrasse is the Rathaus from 1897, with yet another red neo-Gothic tower. A plaque on its façade reads: 'On 24 April 1945 a German soldier was hanged here by inhuman Nazis.' This was one of many such cases in the final days of the Battle of Berlin, as fanatical Nazis punished those who dared to stop fighting. They left the soldier's body hanging from a lantern post, adorned with a sign reading, 'I am a traitor'. The plaque was put up later the same year. (This is a replacement; the original is now in the foyer.) A short distance back down Schlossstrasse, opposite the thirty-story Kreisel, a small park holds a statue of a shackled person with a bowed head, dedicated to 'the persecuted of 1933–1945', and erected in 1960. A more moving sculpture nearby portrays a pathetic human figure clinging to a wall. This statue by Dieter Popielaty, *Suffering at the Wall*, was put up four years after the Berlin Wall was built. Its placement next to the earlier piece reflects a typical (and later controversial) attempt to equate the GDR's oppression with that of the Nazis.

Just across Wrangelstrasse stands a starkly elegant manor house, built circa 1804 by Heinrich Gentz, probably based on plans by his (and Schinkel's) teacher David Gilly. It is often called Wrangel-Schlösschen after a field marshal who later owned it. Up Wrangelstrasse, a plaque in front of number 6–7 recalls the Jewish home for the blind that stood here until 1942, when staff and inmates were deported and the SS took over the building. A few blocks farther down Schlossstrasse is the south entrance to the Botanical Garden (see above).

On the other side of the rail line is **Lichterfelde**, created in the 1870s by the developer J.W. von Carstenn as Berlin's first railroad suburb, a place for suburban villas near the Lichterfelde-West station, still housed in its 1872 building resembling an Italian villa. Only a few houses remain from Carstenn's time; most are a generation newer. The long-standing military presence in Lichterfelde is most visible on Finckensteinallee. Here Carstenn, hoping to raise the prestige of the neighborhood, granted a large parcel to the army for the construction of the royal cadet academy, where twelve-year-old boys, typically younger sons from the rural gentry, came to be reared as future officers. Several buildings from the 1870s still remain, alongside others (including the gatehouses) built after 1934, when SS Leibstandarte Adolf Hitler, the Führer's personal guard unit, established its headquarters here. On 30 June 1934, the so-called 'night of the long knives', neighbors heard shooting all night long. This was the night that Hitler ordered the SS to eliminate the insufficiently loyal leadership of the brownshirted SA, along with Catholic conservatives and army officers who had been erstwhile allies. In 1942, it was Jews who were murdered here, to fill a retaliation quota after the Herbert Baum resistance group firebombed an exhibition. After 1945, the U.S. Army renamed this complex Andrews Barracks and constructed its own buildings. Since its departure in 1994, many of the buildings have been taken over by the federal archives.

Farther out the same S-Bahn line is **Zehlendorf**. The old village core, now a pleasant shopping district, is just north of the rail line at the corner of Clayallee and Potsdamer Strasse. Here stands the village church, an octagonal Baroque building from 1768 which probably replaced one destroyed in the Seven Years' War. Next to it is the old village school from 1828, now the local history museum. A few blocks to the west, on Clauertstrasse, is **Museumsdorf** (museum village) **Düppel**, site of a farming village established around 1200 but abandoned and forgotten soon afterward. On its excavated foundations, old-style village buildings have been re-created, and costumed staff members act out the tasks of medieval farmers.

The **Mexikoplatz** S-Bahn station is a striking round building from 1905, with windows and walls in the heavy organic forms of north German Jugendstil. The square itself (this is also the terminus of Argentinische Allee, not far beyond the end of the U1 line) is spacious and pleasant, with grand apartment buildings from 1905–10 designed to resemble the country villas of the side streets. This is the kind of place where the local bakery's Kaffee und Kuchen is the most visible social event. At nearby Wolzogenstrasse 17 is a Walter Gropius house from 1922, with a striking entrance (which has, however, been altered) and roof lines that betray Gropius's debt to Frank Lloyd Wright.

This S-Bahn line passes Nikolassee, another wealthy suburb, on its way to **Wannsee**; it is often called the Wannsee-Bahn. Another S-Bahn connection to Wannsee (also used by regional trains) is via the east–west line, and is faster because the trains travel a long distance through the Grunewald without stopping. The Wannsee station, a relatively sober expressionist building from 1927, replaced the original station from 1874, when the rail connection stimulated the first wave of suburban construction here. Across from the station, you can descend to the lakeshore, as city crowds still do on warm days. Many board boats here. You can take a cruise of two hours or more on the vast network of lakes and rivers in western Berlin, Potsdam and beyond. The cheapest cruise is the hourly ferry (departing on the hour) across the lake to the former village of Kladow, a quiet place to stroll past old country houses or to linger at lakefront beer gardens. Since ferry service began in 1892, Kladow has attracted grand villas and suburban commuters who go to work via Wannsee. Kladow lies within Berlin, as does Gatow, just to its north. Between the two villages, the Third Reich built the Gatow airfield, which became better known as the British sector's airport. It has been shut down and now houses the Air Force museum (**Luftwaffenmuseum**), reached from either Kladower Damm or Aussenweg, by bus or (more easily) by car via Spandau. It displays dozens of aircraft from the air forces of all of twentieth-century Germany's regimes.

To the right of the Wannsee station and docks, the street Am Sandwerder takes you past the exclusive mansions on the eastern shore of the Wannsee. Number 1, with its tower visible from afar, is one of the earliest villas, a neoclassical house from 1875. The Gothic gatehouse tower of number 10a from 1890, on the inland side of the street, often attracts film crews. Many of the villas, built by the richest of the rich, have been taken over by institutions, for example number 5 (1885), now the Literarisches Colloquium. Number 17–19, originally a neo-Gothic extravagance, was remodeled in a more sober modern form during the 1920s for the family of the banker Hans Arnhold. The Arnholds, like many of their neighbors, were Jewish, and after they fled, well-connected Nazis seized the opportunity to live beyond their means. In this case it was the economics minister, Walther Funk. After 1945, Funk moved to nearby Spandau prison, and the house became the U.S. Army Recreation Center. Now it is the American Academy, which is sometimes open to the public for lectures and performances. Farther up the shore is a much less exclusive destination, the public beach at Strandbad Wannsee, an enormous modernist masterpiece by Martin

Wagner and Richard Ermisch, opened to the masses in 1930 and still a place to see the sun-worshipping Berlin proletariat at play – always an edifying if not an appetizing sight. Just beyond, you once again reach exclusive precincts: the tiny island of Schwanenwerder, connected to the mainland by a bridge, has room for only a few villas. The developers marked its status with high-class booty, obtaining fragments from the Tuileries palace after its destruction in the Paris Commune of 1871, and mounting them at the entrance to the island, along with a few lines of promotional doggerel. Rich Jews owned many of the houses, which were subsequently seized by powerful Nazis, notably Joseph Goebbels.

If you go left instead of right out of the Wannsee station, and do not linger too long at the landmark beer garden, you cross Königstrasse, part of the old Potsdam highway. Its bridge marks the division between the Grosser Wannsee and the much narrow Kleiner Wannsee to the south, also lined with grand houses. A short distance down Bismarckstrasse, on your right are the graves of the writer Heinrich von Kleist and Henriette Vogel, at the bucolic spot where, in 1811, they carried out their suicide pact. In the terminally ill Vogel, Kleist the Romantic had finally found someone to act out the final drama he had long plotted. If you return to Königstrasse and cross the bridge (on foot or on bus 114), a right turn onto Am Grossen Wannsee leads you past the mansions on the western side of the lake. The neoclassical number 5 is one of the earliest villas, from 1875. Most of the others are both newer and less visible from the street, including number 39 (1902) by Alfred Messel, and number 42, at Colomierstrasse, built in 1909 for the painter Max Liebermann, and now being renovated as a **Liebermann museum**.

The mansions and their owners made Wannsee synonymous with wealth and privilege, but the world now associates the name with the house Am Grossen Wannsee 56, built in 1914. It became an SS guesthouse and was used by Reinhard Heydrich to convene a meeting of bureaucrats from many agencies on 20 January 1942. Adolf Eichmann's minutes surfaced after the war, as scholars were just beginning to reconstruct the bureaucratic organization of mass murder, and so the **Wannsee Conference** became famous as the birthplace of what the Nazis called the 'final solution to the Jewish question', although experts now agree that the killing had already begun by then. The circumspect minutes never mention killing or even concentration camps, but they reveal a chilling discussion of how to dispose of eleven million European Jews without expelling them or leaving any behind. Exactly half a century later, after years of debate, the house was opened as a memorial center, with a modest display on the history of the Holocaust. Only one day linked this house to the horrific events of the Holocaust, but that momentous day will henceforth define its identity.

Just beyond, a public dock (and café) opens access to the waterfront. Here stands a large statue of a lion, a copy of one dragged back from Denmark by the victorious Prussian army in 1864 (and since returned to Denmark). The statue was a speculator's publicity stunt: he hoped to wrap his new villa quarter in the patriotic aura of the day. Inland, at the edge of the forest that covers the lakeshore to the west, is a complex of brick buildings belonging to a clinic devoted to pulmonary diseases. It was, however, built in the late 1930s as an antiaircraft school.

Königstrasse takes you back to Wannsee station but also on to the palaces on the Pfaueninsel and at Glienicke, and to others on the Potsdam side of the Glienicke bridge (see Chapter 25).

IV
The East and South

18

Stalinallee

BERLIN WAS ONE OF THE MAJOR BATTLEFIELDS of the Cold War. Unlike World War II, however, the Cold War was fought – in Europe, at least – mostly with words and pictures, not guns and bombs. Each side tried to display the superior beauty and comfort of its way of life, and among the most visible means of display was architecture. For one moment in the Cold War, the mile-long row of buildings extending along Karl-Marx-Allee east from Strausberger Platz was the front line in the East's propaganda war. The U5 subway gets you here from Alexanderplatz and continues eastward under the boulevard, offering an alternative to walking its entire length.

This glorious architectural gesture is one of the guilty pleasures of Berlin. Respectable opinion through most of the twentieth century disdained the pointless architectural extravagance that was practiced only by Nazis and Stalinists. The boulevard is in fact the product of a brief and unique phase in East German history. The first post-war plans for the area looked very different, as you can see farther down the street. Most of the buildings that survived the bombing here on Frankfurter Allee (as it was then called, since it led toward the eastern city of Frankfurt an der Oder) were smashed by the Red Army as it fought its way into the city. This once densely populated proletarian district was thus an obvious choice for a project that would showcase the new Soviet workers' paradise. In 1949, on Josef Stalin's seventieth birthday, the street was renamed Stalinallee in the Soviet dictator's honor, and work began on new apartment buildings amid the rubble.

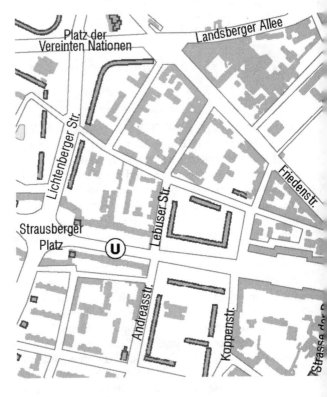

After Hitler's demise, progressive Berlin architects had returned to the unadorned modern style they learned in the 1920s. However, by 1950 that style was being denounced as inhuman and (what amounted to the same thing) capitalist, with the denunciations led by the East German Communist boss, Walter Ulbricht, who took a keen interest in architecture. He told architects to adopt ornate, classicist designs inspired by those that had prevailed in the Soviet Union since the 1930s. The style of Stalinallee reflects Soviet precedent but also displays

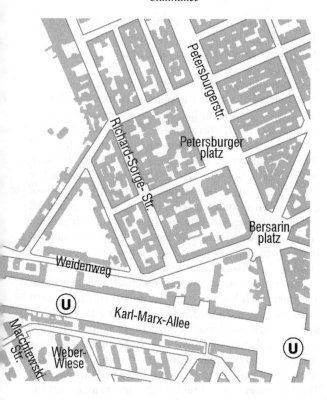

the local traditions of Prussian neoclassicism – that is, of Schinkel. The most prominent architect involved was Hermann Henselmann, a late addition to the project who managed to grab the commissions for the most prominent sites, including the buildings at **Strausberger Platz**. The beginning of the grand boulevard is marked dramatically by a pair of thirteen-story towers and attached lower buildings that curve around the square, with its traffic circle surrounding a large central fountain. While the scale of the square suggests Baroque precedents, the architectural details are freely adapted classical motifs. Richly decorated columns and arches fill the ground-level arcades connecting the buildings around the square.

Before you proceed down the former Stalinallee, you may want to cast a glance in other directions. You may, in fact, choose to walk the half-mile from Alexanderplatz to Strausberger Platz. This segment of **Karl-Marx-Allee** displays the phase of East German architecture that followed that of Strausberger Platz. By the mid-1950s, following Stalin's death, the new Soviet leader Nikita Khrushchev was calling for a thoroughgoing industrialization of construction in order to efficiently meet the great need for new housing. In this, as in nearly all things, East Germany followed the Soviet lead, if somewhat hesitantly. It finished the construction already begun from Strausberger Platz eastward, but then built nothing more in that style, instead devising methods of constructing apartment buildings from prefabricated concrete panels that could be assembled on site, requiring far less labor and skill than traditional construction methods. (In 1961 came a final step: overnight all the the street signs were changed from Stalinallee to a new name, Karl-Marx-Allee, and a Stalin statue was removed, pedestal and all.) The first major project built in the new manner was the segment of Karl-Marx-Allee from Alexanderplatz to Strausberger Platz, begun in 1959. The façades of these apartment buildings lack the classical decoration as well as the varied profiles of their predecessors. Nor do they line the street in an unbroken row. Rather, in the modernist manner, each ten-story slab stands alone. They are purely residential buildings, with shops placed in separate two-story pavilions along the street. The most notable building is a large cinema, Kino International, which remains (inside and out) a showcase of 1960s elegance that stands comparison to anything in the West.

A later showcase project is visible north of Strausberger Platz, up Lichtenberger Strasse toward Friedrichshain park. At the corner of Landsberger Allee is the **Platz der Vereinten Nationen**. This name, 'United Nations Square', supplants a name that stood for a different international piety: Leninplatz. The curved apartment buildings here (1970), also by Hermann Henselmann, were a relatively flamboyant design intended to frame the sixty-foot-tall Lenin statue erected here in 1970. In 1991 the western leaders of Berlin's newly unified government removed Lenin. To their surprise, what they intended as a gesture of triumph over communism met with protests from East Berliners who saw the granite Lenin not as an oppressor but as a familiar neighborhood icon. The reorganized communist party, the Party of Democratic Socialism, effectively exploited the widespread unhappiness with what many newly unemployed Easterners saw as Western highhandedness in this as in many other matters. The quarrel over Lenin's removal marked the end of the honeymoon of German reunification. Where Lenin once stood, tall and militant, there is now a gently trickling fountain constructed with boulders collected around the world.

Leaving these distractions aside, turn your attention to the grand boulevard that extends eastward from Strausberger Platz. It is three hundred feet wide, leaving room for many lanes of traffic carrying commuters to and from the eastern suburbs. Before 1990, however, there were no parking spaces along the street, a fact that reveals how much it differed from Western boulevards. It is well suited, rather, for military parades, especially the big ones formerly staged every May Day. And the street's width extends far beyond the lanes of traffic, especially on the north side, where a wide swath of green space, now shaded by mature trees, separates the buildings from the roadway. A nearly unbroken row of buildings frames each side of the boulevard, with archways and covered passages linking them across side streets. The buildings' profiles are varied horizontally and vertically, including wings that extend forward to punctuate the architectural drama of the street. In comparison to their height and width, however, most of them are relatively shallow, as you can discover by walking through the passages to the rear of them. The effect is thus something like a Potemkin village. This arrangement of buildings, designed to maximize the architectural effect of 'Berlin's first socialist street', was decreed by the Politburo, East Germany's ruling council. It was assumed that later projects would fill in the side streets with similar buildings, but that happened in only a few places.

Each segment of the boulevard was assigned to a different team of architects, all adhering, however, to the style agreed upon by the time construction began in 1952. As intended, the result is considerable architectural variation contributing to a harmonious whole. The buildings are rigidly symmetrical, with clearly differentiated lower, middle, and upper floors. In some of the blocks, entrances, bays, and windows seem to be drawn directly from Schinkel's Prussian neoclassicism; elsewhere, it is mixed with more modern (or inconsistent) details. The eldest of the supervising architects, Hanns Hopp, learned his neoclassicism before the First World War. Some of the others had experience in Stalin's Soviet Union, either before or after 1945, or had worked on Third Reich projects. The buildings' lower stories are mostly faced with stone; upper stories, with ceramic tiles. Carved reliefs decorate the façades, most of them portraying people at work on Stalinallee: removing wartime rubble, designing and building. These may in a vague way recall neoclassical precedents, but they more clearly exemplify the style known as socialist realism, with portraits of workers that might be described as either heroic or naive.

Amid the unsettled political situation in Berlin, this project was a dramatic political gesture, displaying the East's superior commitment both to German tradition and to the comfort of the working masses. Apart from the shops and restaurants at street level, these are indeed residential buildings. The apartments were allocated to those deemed to have provided valuable services to the state, which meant that some went to prominent cultural figures, but many others went to construction workers and other ordinary proletarians. The apartments were roomy and comfortable, and they remained among East Berlin's most desirable. However, construction costs were far above what was sustainable for the broader project of rebuilding the city. Pressures to cut costs and to speed construction were thus inevitable, even as labor and materials were requisitioned from throughout the GDR. In June 1953, when construction workers' daily production quotas were raised, they responded by laying down their tools. Their strike was soon joined by others across the city and country. By the next day, 17 June, the GDR faced a nationwide uprising, with crowds demanding not only better working conditions but also democracy and German reunification. Soviet tanks and bloodshed were required to restore order, and the Communist leaders subsequently avoided any comparable challenges to their authority until 1989 – but at a considerable cost. Their fear of another revolt led them to promote labor peace and consumer satisfaction above class solidarity and proletarian militancy. In fact, it took until 1958 to complete this segment of Stalinallee, and by then, with new architectural and housing policies prevailing, it was clear that it would remain one of a kind.

A short distance east of Strausberger Platz, the row of Stalinist buildings is interrupted by newer structures, put up after the change in architectural style. The one on the north side replaced a demolished athletic arena; on the south side is where the Stalin monument stood until 1961. Across Koppenstrasse, at Karl-Marx-Allee 72, a small exhibition on the street's history was opened in 2002 in a café. Its centerpiece was Stalin's bronze ear, which had been secreted away by a construction worker. However, someone promptly stole the ear from the exhibition, and its fate is unknown. The exhibit was part of the new Stalinallee nostalgia. During the 1990s the street was not fashionable, as its apartments were still filled with pensioners who had lived there since the beginning. As they have died out, a stylish scene has moved in, and it favors the handful of shops and cafés that retain their original 1950s decor.

At the Strasse der Pariser Kommune (which connects to the East rail station) you are halfway along the mile-long stretch of Stalinist boulevard. Just past this intersection, it displays some unexpected variation. Two unadorned modernist apartment blocks on the right side, numbers 102–104 and 126–128, are easy to overlook. These are not later additions; they are the first buildings that went up on Stalinallee, in 1949–50. These five-story buildings lined with recessed balconies are recognizable products of the 1920s housing reform movement, as are several more buildings behind them. This was the normal idiom of non-Nazi German architects in 1949, but when these buildings were completed in 1950, Ulbricht himself denounced them as unworthy of Berlin's dignity, as 'appropriate to the South African landscape', and as bastard offspring of both the Nazi 'bunker style' and American capitalist exploitation. Trees were planted to obscure them. What followed was the style you now see all around.

The first Stalinist building, however, stands behind the modernist houses. Here you will find a small park, the **Weberwiese**, 'weavers' meadow', so called because weavers once bleached their fabrics here. Facing it is the nine-story Hochhaus an der Weberwiese. Its architect was

Hermann Henselmann, who in 1950 was as much a modernist as his colleagues, but who proved more adept at learning the party's new architectural line, producing this design with great dispatch. It displays the vertical and horizontal articulation, stone and ceramic materials, and classical decoration that set the style for Stalinallee, and it was dedicated with great fanfare in 1952, the same year construction began on the boulevard. Henselmann also designed the long building facing the park across Marchlewskistrasse. Note the sculptural reliefs over its entrances, portraying the socialist unity of work and play, men and women, and intellectual and physical labor. Note also, among the male construction workers, the portrait of a woman cleaning bricks. This is a monument to the brigades of 'rubble women' who were the most visible presence in postwar Berlin, East and West, removing rubble and cleaning bricks by hand. Marchlewskistrasse 6, a rebuilt 1884 fire station across from the corner of the park, houses a district history museum.

Amid the Stalinist architectural riches along the rest of the former Stalinallee, the one other building that clearly represents a different style is the Kosmos cinema (1962) on the north side of the street, designed in a dramatically simple circle-and-square form just after the surrounding buildings were completed. The outer end of Stalinallee is marked by another pair of towers by Henselmann, at the intersection known as **Frankfurter Tor** (Frankfurt Gate – although when there was a city wall, it and the gate of that name in fact stood some distance to the west). Each of the towers is topped by a slender dome, clearly intended to echo the pair of eighteenth-century churches on Gendarmenmarkt. Stalinist buildings continue for another block east on Frankfurter Allee (it retains its old name east of Frankfurter Tor).

For decades this unique stretch of boulevard fell into neglect. Most of the original residents, artists and workers alike, held onto their comfortable apartments, but what was supposed to be the beginning of the new Berlin soon looked to most people like the last gasp of a bygone era. Encouraged by party leaders, architects embraced the technological optimism that had been formulated in the 1920s and revived in the postwar West. Eastern propagandists turned their spotlight on new projects, beginning with the western stretch of Karl-Marx-Allee. Many of the ceramic tiles had fallen off by the 1980s and (as was typical in the East) no money was available for repairs. In the West, Stalinallee never had a good press. It was denounced as the embodiment of Communist regimentation and, because of its similarities to some Third Reich projects, as proof of the essential similarity of the totalitarian regimes of Hitler and Stalin. (Consider, for example, the resemblance between Karl-Marx-Allee's street lamps and those designed by Speer on the Strasse des 17. Juni.) Around the time of German reunification, however, the tide of fashion was turning. Western postmodernist architects, notably Aldo Rossi and Philip Johnson, praised its grandeur by contrast to the dismal products of Eastern and Western modernism – and thus made it respectable for people to admit they shared Ulbricht's opinions. As one of its last acts in 1990, the East Berlin government declared the entire street a protected landmark, and its crumbling façades have since been renovated.

The former Frankfurter Allee, taken as a whole, is a museum displaying the entire history of East German architecture and urban planning. In addition to the 1950s and 1960s phases between here and Alexanderplatz, the stretch extending outward from Frankfurter Tor reveals the regime's attempts to redevelop the existing urban structure during the 1980s. After building little other than prefabricated high-rise housing on vacant land (many examples are visible farther down the street), in its last years the GDR tried to renovate a few of the pre–World

War I neighborhoods it had long neglected. Along Frankfurter Allee, and on some side streets, stand turn-of-the century apartment houses renovated in the 1980s, alongside new, prefabricated buildings designed to fit the scale of the old street. Another example of 1980s redevelopment is Bersarinplatz, just up Petersburger Strasse from Frankfurter Tor. This square, by the way, was named for General Nikolai Bersarin (or Berzarin), the first Soviet commandant of the occupied city, who became a surprisingly popular figure among Berliners, credited with helping to bring the city back to life. In 1990, when Westerners proposed that his name, like that of all other Soviet Russians, be purged from the cityscape, protests blocked the renaming of the square.

South of Frankfurter Allee and east of Warschauer Strasse is a largely intact neighborhood built up during the decade before World War I. At the end of the 1990s, as Prenzlauer Berg became too gentrified for some tastes, many 'scene' cafés and nightclubs began moving to Simon-Dach-Strasse, Wühlischstrasse and vicinity. The streets north of Frankfurter Allee are of similar provenance. Here are two of Alfred Messel's turn-of-the-century model tenement projects, on Proskauer Strasse (between Bänschstrasse and Schreinerstrasse) and between Weisbachstrasse and Ebertystrasse.

19

Luisenstadt and the Kreuzberg Mixture

DURING THE EARLY NINETEENTH CENTURY, the only large undeveloped area within the city customs wall was the southeast corner, Luisenstadt (named after the popular Queen Luise), which later became the eastern part of the district of Kreuzberg. Whereas the large new factories at mid-century were built outside the wall, this area attracted smaller-scale production. Typical Luisenstadt buildings included apartments, for proprietors and workers, along with industrial lofts, usually in the deep courtyards. This combination of work and residence, as well as the proximity of different classes, made the area both architecturally and socially diverse. In the drastically changed circumstances of postwar West Berlin, the solidly built, varied structures attracted new but equally diverse groups: immigrants, students, artists, social dropouts and the poor. The term 'Kreuzberg mixture' came to describe both the mixed-use buildings and the mixed-up population.

If you want to plunge into the center of the Kreuzberg scene, take the U1 or U8 to one of the squares mentioned below. Otherwise you can begin across the river from Luisenstadt at the East rail station (**Ostbahnhof**). Across the Strasse der Pariser Kommune to its east (and on the river side of the tracks) stands a complex of buildings built a century ago for the post office's freight station. In one building, which has recently been used for exhibitions, you can still see the tracks that brought the rail cars inside, where packages were loaded and unloaded. These buildings are scheduled for redevelopment. Just beyond them, a large new arena is planned for concerts and sporting events. Meanwhile, this area has nurtured Berlin's thriving techno music scene, with its huge parties that drift from one abandoned warehouse to another.

Toward the river is the busy Mühlenstrasse and, on the far side of the street, a colorful concrete wall. This is one end of the so-called **East Side Gallery**, a preserved section of the Berlin Wall. From here upstream, the river marked the border, and the riverbank on this, the Eastern side, was a no-go area. What you are looking at, therefore, was the unapproachable Eastern side of the Wall, the one that separated East Berlin from no-man's-land. Until 1989 this wall remained utterly blank, with none of the graffiti that made the Western wall so famous. In 1990, however, a group of artists divided this nearly mile-long stretch of Wall into segments and painted it, as a celebratory and commemorative gesture, or perhaps just to take advantage of free outdoor gallery space. Most of the 106 paintings are figurative and easily comprehensible, and many address political topics. Many of the artists were from the Soviet bloc, and their works typically sound the notes of East European dissidents chafing under censorship and oppression. Others address the traumas of German history, notably Kristallnacht and the Holocaust. Still other works portray the fantasies (then well known from the now-vanished art on the Western side of the Wall) of breaking down, bursting through or leaping over the Wall. Perhaps the most famous image was painted by a Russian, Dmitri Vrubel, an enormous portrait of (a real event) the Soviet leader Leonid Brezhnev smothering his GDR counterpart Erich Honecker with a brotherly kiss on the lips. In the early 1990s, as the Wall was quickly dismantled all around Berlin, tourists came here to see the Wall and its graffiti. They treated it like the Western side, which is to say that they contributed their own graffiti – to the displeasure of many of the artists. By 1993, when

the East Side Gallery (the name is in English) was placed under landmark protection, it was ceasing to be as much of an attraction, and the wind and rain were wearing off much of the paint. Meanwhile, however, much of the art has been restored.

At the downstream end of the rail station, to the west, you can cross the Spree on the Schilling bridge, a stone structure from 1873 that affords a view of the post–industrial landscape of the river. A short distance downstream, on the right bank, is a sewage pump station, built in 1880 as part of the city's original sewage system – a crucial event in the history of public health and public works – and in use until replaced by the new structure next to it in 1999. On the other side of the river, you reach Köpenicker Strasse, an important nineteenth-century commercial corridor with massive old office and ware-house buildings. Here the fictional industrialist Treibel lived, next to his factory, in Theodor Fontane's novel *Jenny Treibel.* If you proceed forward, you are following the former course of the Berlin Wall and, long before that, of the Luisenstadt canal, built from the Spree to the Landwehrkanal as a public works project that employed discontented workers after the 1848 revolution. It soon silted up, however, and was landscaped as a park during the 1920s. The green strip has been recently restored, after having served as no-man's-land while the Wall was up. When Kreuzberg was in its heyday, you could not enter it this way. Many Kreuzberg streets ended at the Wall, and the most imaginative Wall art was to be found along its zigzag course here. Fragments of Kreuzberg wall, with their colorful paintings, have been put on display all over the world, but none of it remains in situ.

The former course of the canal curves to the right, but straight ahead stands the brick apse and dome of the church of St Thomas, an 1860s neo-Romanesque struc-ture with elegant terracotta detailing. The rear of the church faced the canal, and later the Wall. Its entrance, framed by two towers, faces the long, shady expanse of **Mariannenplatz**, in which Lenné's original landscaping from 1853 was restored in 1980. In the public toilet on this pleasant square, a retiree named Wilhelm Lehmann scribbled on the wall: 'Hitler, you mass murderer, you must be murdered, so that the war can end.' The year was 1943, and Lehmann was quickly apprehended and executed.

Along with the church, the other main building here, on the long right side, is the former **Bethanien** hospital, built in the 1840s according to a design by Schinkel's pupil Ludwig Persius. It is an austere yellow-brick structure with its entrance framed by two slender octagonal towers. The two-story vestibule is also nicely detailed. It served as a model of hospital construction and was also long seen as a model of patient care. However, it suffered from the same inadequacies as most nineteenth-century medicine, notably ignorance about sanitation, with dirty canal water used for laundry, for example. In 1869, a single year, 991 patients died after surgery. After the Wall went up, the hospital lost many of its patients and its dedicated nurses, and it was closed in 1970. Citizens' protests prevented its demolition, and it was turned into a community arts center, providing space for visiting artists and becoming a major Kreuzberg attraction. Inside the right front corner of the building, the former hospital pharmacy has been recreated, partly as a memorial to Theodor Fontane, who worked here as a pharmacist during the revolutionary year of 1848–49, long before he wrote the novels that made him famous. The pharmacy displays a large collection of nineteenth-century medicine bottles, some originally from Bethanien.

The southern end of Mariannenplatz is marked by a curved row of mid-nineteenth-century apartment houses, echoing the church's round apse across the square. The restoration of these buildings in the 1970s was one of the first projects to restore rather than replace nineteenth-century tenements. Up to then, the hulking old buildings had merely been tolerated where they were intact. The prevailing view was expressed with particular disquiet by Stephen Spender, who recalled that 'the architecture terrified me by the monotonous repetition of extravagant mouldings all emphasizing the same crude conceptions of war and fertility. Nothing has ever given me such a sensation of loneliness, bareness and anxiety, as some long Berlin streets of grey houses, covered from top to bottom with carving and figures, all of them the same on each house.' When the ornate stucco façades were repaired, owners were encouraged to strip off all the decoration and replace it with a flat plastered surface that was supposed to look more modern but in fact ill suited the proportions of the old buildings. (You can still see thousands of these stripped façades.) Here, in the 1970s, the decoration was restored in simplified form, in an attempt to compromise between the fading ideal of modernist purity and the growing interest in the old, absurdly laden façades. Since the 1980s, façades have been more painstakingly restored – no one seems to fear them any longer. A missing building at Mariannenplatz 5 was replaced with a new one (1985) that respected the size and shape of its neighbors but called attention to itself by replacing traditional outward-reaching bays with 'negative' versions cut into the façade.

Mariannenstrasse, continuing the axis of the square, takes you past Naunynstrasse, lined with apartment houses from the 1860s and 1870s. In the courtyard behind number 27, to the right, is a Ballhaus from 1876, a remnant of an earlier era of proletarian amusements. In recent years, reflecting the changing culture of Kreuzberg, it has been used less for balls and more for avant-garde theater and dance performances. Continuing on Mariannenstrasse, the next corner is **Heinrichplatz**, surrounded by 1870-era buildings with squat corner towers. Here, and along the cross street, Oranienstrasse, was one of the centers of the 1980s Kreuzberg scene. Most of the old tenements in this area survived the bombing but were considered inferior housing, with their densely built-up courtyards lacking the 'light and air' that reformers sought. Most apartments were small – as measured by the number of rooms, though not by square feet and certainly not by cubic feet, given their high ceilings. Most also lacked modern conveniences – baths in most cases, toilets in many (these were located down the hall or on the stairwell, and shared with neighbors). After the Wall went up, the area was further devalued by its location in a dead end of West Berlin, with the Wall on two sides. As the old working-class inhabitants moved out, to West Germany or to modern apartments, they were replaced by the foreign 'guest workers' being recruited in the face of labor shortages, and by students, artists and social dropouts, including many young men who came to West Berlin because its residents were exempt from military conscription.

Life in the pubs and galleries of this alternative scene was typically tinged with radical politics. Kreuzberg became associated with several subcultures of militant (and sometimes violent) opposition to capitalism, bourgeois culture, American imperialism and German authority. Kreuzberg-based groups delighted in provoking the police, particularly on the occasion of demonstrations called for any number of purposes. Too often the police, determined to impose order, took the bait, and pitched battles ensued. After the Wall came down, artists and others in search of run-down digs and cheap rents moved East, to Prenzlauer Berg and Friedrichshain, but remnants of the alternative scene remain, including militant as well as pacifist elements, both visible in Heinrichplatz cafés. Now that Kreuzberg has lost the allure it had in the 1980s, however, the downside of its social mixture is more apparent. Kreuzberg has Berlin's highest concentrations of poverty and social pathology, and it still attracts the poorest and most troubled immigrants.

Oranienstrasse, to the right, takes you past a variety of offbeat establishments lodged in solid old buildings typical of the old 'Kreuzberg mixture': residential buildings facing the street and industrial lofts on the courtyards. In many of the wide doorways, you can still see the metal tracks in the ground that guided wagons into the courtyard. Where the doors are open, or at least unlocked, you can explore the courtyards, still home to a mixture of residential and commercial uses. The brick façade of number 26, on the right, is typical for a nineteenth-century school, built in 1863 and expanded in 1892. In 1902 it was taken over by the state school for the blind, a royal institution dating to 1806. Blind boys and girls were trained in industrial skills, and so this, too, was an industrial courtyard, where they produced goods for sale.

The next cross street, Adalbertstrasse, still displays most of its original buildings from the 1860s. Looking left, you will see the forbidding back wall of what might by some measures be considered the center of eastern Kreuzberg. The square at Kottbusser Tor, a former city gate, was completely rebuilt with an enormous apartment complex completed in 1974, intended as an improvement on the old tenements and a model for what would replace them. Within a few years, that kind of urban renewal was out of favor, however, in part because of the unpopularity of this megastructure. Here, from the outside, it looks particularly forbidding, because it blocks the street (and several other streets as well) with a blank wall intended to face a highway that would have obliterated the surrounding neighborhood. Fortunately the highway was canceled soon afterward. Most residents and businesses have preferred to seek out and renovate spaces in the old buildings, leaving the 1970s shopfronts empty and the apartments with a reputation as a high-rise slum. Their concrete walls seem best suited for graffiti expressing anger and despair in German, Turkish and Kurdish. The adjoining U-Bahn station has long been known for its lingering groups of punks, with their fiercely styled hair and studded leather outfits. They are usually harmless, even gentle, in their request for a handout, but their apparent obliviousness to the world of employment leaves most passers-by less than sympathetic to their plight.

The planned highway aided, paradoxically, in the rediscovery of Kreuzberg. With redevelopment on the horizon for many uncertain years, many landlords let their buildings deteriorate and even stand empty, anticipating either expropriation or an opportunity to replace them with lucrative new structures. The low rents attracted students and artists who fell in love with the dilapidated buildings, and their political views led them to condemn the capitalist speculation they saw as their enemy. In the 1970s many abandoned buildings were occupied by squatters, some of whom set to work making them liveable, while others concentrated on establishing authority-free zones to pursue their revolution. Most of the squatters were ultimately driven out amid violent clashes with the police. However, in some cases the city government agreed to let squatters take title to buildings they were renovating, and it went on to promote its own renovation efforts.

Beyond Adalbertstrasse, Oranienstrasse leads to the wide but usually lively expanse of **Oranienplatz**, once bisected by the Luisenstadt canal. Most of the buildings here remain from the original construction boom of the 1860s, several with their distinctive corner towers. Here and there you can see where some were replaced in the years just before 1914, when the demand for commercial space was creeping outward from Friedrichstadt. A department store's 1904 building was incorporated into one of the few Kreuzberg buildings from the Weimar era, which encloses the southwest corner of the square. This exemplar of the sober modern style by Max Taut was completed in 1932 as a department store for a consumer cooperative.

From Oranienplatz you might explore in several directions. Continuing on Oranienstrasse, just past the square, you see the mixture of buildings from the first and last years of Berlin's great boom. On your left, numbers 163, 162 and 160 are finely detailed neoclassical apartment buildings from the 1860s. The ground floor of 162–163 was renovated as a restaurant in 1903, and much of its original decor remains. Numbers 161 and 159 stand out, by contrast, as newer commercial buildings built after 1910, with stone façades, extravagant detailing and designs that emphasize their vertical dimensions. Oranienstrasse continues to Moritzplatz, an intersection that offers a subway stop but little else. Once it was a major commercial center with department stores, but they were destroyed in the war, and the site's proximity to the Wall kept new development away. Just north of Moritzplatz was a border crossing. Beyond Moritzplatz, between Oranienstrasse and the former Wall, the Otto-Suhr-Siedlung was postwar West Berlin's first major housing project, one of many that demonstratively broke with the old pattern of streets and courtyards. Its neighbor and counterpart on the other side of the Wall is a large complex of 1960s modernist slabs along Heinrich-Heine-Strasse. Recent plans have proposed infill development to restore the prewar streetscape there.

Returning to Oranienplatz, you might choose to head north up Leuschnerdamm (the name on the right side) or Legiendamm (the name on the left) along the former canal, which has been landscaped as a park and playground. At the next corner, Waldemarstrasse, you reach the site of the Wall, which followed the former canal from here to the Spree. This part of the canal bed has been restored more recently and more formally, as has the **Engelbecken** (Angel Pool) just ahead. This was a decorative pool created as part of the canal and then left as part of the park, until it ended up in no-man's-land and fell into neglect. The Legiendamm side of the pool was the East Berlin side of the Wall, where all structures were leveled by the East Germans. Facing the pool on the Leuschnerdamm side, in the former West Berlin, most of the original buildings from circa 1870 remain, with their delicate neoclassical detailing. A later, taller addition is number 13, an ornate 1904 apartment building with a tall gable. Behind it is an extensive industrial courtyard – a typical Kreuzberg combination, but in this case one that suffered greatly for a typical feature: access to the entire complex only through a single entry. For years that entry was all but blocked by the Berlin Wall.

Dominating the view from the pool is the tower of St Michael's, one of Berlin's largest Roman Catholic churches, built in the 1850s in a post–Schinkel mélange of historical styles. Since 1990 services have been held in the restored transept, but the main part of the building has remained a ruin since the war. At the corner of Michaelkirchplatz and Engeldamm, next to the church, stands an elegant modernist building from 1930, built by Max Taut based on a design by his more famous brother Bruno, with horizontal bands of windows forming continuous lines around a rounded corner. It was built for a labor union, but was soon taken over by the Nazi Party's German Labor Front and then, from 1949 to 1990, by the Communist Party's labor federation. After many years facing the Wall, it has recently been renovated.

If instead you follow the former course of the canal in the other direction from Oranienplatz, to the south, you reach **Wassertorplatz**, the 'water gate' where the canal crossed the old customs wall. When that wall was demolished in the 1860s, it was replaced by the boulevard that has, for the past century, been in the shadow of the elevated U-Bahn. Continuing along the former canal on

Erkelenzdamm (that is, on the left side) you reach number 59–61, the sprawling Elisabethhof (1898). Facing the street are, as was typical, the larger and better apartments. Pass through to the the first courtyard, and you find more residential wings, less well lit and lined with smaller apartments. Farther back are more courtyards and industrial buildings, built with large windows to bring maximum light into the confined spaces. In them you may find traces of three different generations of uses: the initial, low-tech industrial operations, which are a shadow of their prewar selves; the artists who later took over many of these spaces; and white-collar and high-tech firms that moved after the demise of the Wall unleashed a real estate boom in Kreuzberg.

Just beyond, Erkelenzdamm curves leftward into **Fraenkelufer**. This is where the Luisenstadt canal joined the Landwehrkanal, which remains wide here because of a harbor built for the once-important barge traffic. The canal bank has long been an attractive place to live, stroll and linger in outdoor cafés. The attraction of Fraenkelufer was restored by one of the more successful 1980s redevelopment projects. Amid the row of old façades, numbers 44 and 38 stand out. Their extravagantly shaped, and yet not wholly alien, gables and balconies are the work of the architects Inken and Hinrich Baller, whose forms have been compared to indigenous Jugendstil and expressionist precedents as well as the work of the Catalan architect Antoni Gaudí. They renovated the old buildings and filled gaps left by the war. Enter the gate at number 44 and you find a large courtyard with another Baller building at the rear. You can stroll past it and the older buildings and come back out to the street at number 38. The spaciousness of this complex is partly a product of wartime destruction, which thinned the dense rows of courtyard buildings here as elsewhere in Berlin. It also helps, in this case, that several courtyards have been merged into one.

Note that the rear of this courtyard abuts the industrial courtyards of Elisabethhof, but, as was typical, you can only walk from one courtyard to the next by exiting to the street. Each parcel was developed separately and designed with continuous blank firewalls facing its neighbors. Because so many buildings, and wings of buildings, were destroyed in the war, those huge, blank brick walls became a familiar sight in postwar Berlin.

In the next block, Fraenkelufer 10–16 is the site of an orthodox synagogue completed in 1916, damaged on Kristallnacht in 1938, and later demolished. However, one wing, originally a synagogue for young people, was spared and remains in use. By now you may have stumbled upon other reminders of a vanished Jewish population: the district of Kreuzberg-Friedrichshain has recently sponsored the installation of engraved stones in front of the former homes of residents persecuted by the Nazis, recalling them in the pavement. Those honored include, in addition to Jews, political opponents, gays, Sinti and Roma, Jehovah's Witnesses and disabled people.

The next intersection is Kottbusser Damm (to the right) and Kottbusser Strasse (left), the main commercial street leading south from the Kottbus gate. The shops here reflect the low incomes and the large immigrant population in the neighborhood. On Kottbusser Damm are two of the earliest buildings by the architect Bruno Taut. After World War I, Taut became famous first for his ecstatic visions of the future city and then for his elegant social housing projects. Here, before the war, he was working within the established system of apartment construction. That meant, among other things, that he was responsible for designing only the façades at Kottbusser Damm 2–3, just around the corner, and number 90, across the street. (The latter is best viewed from its side façade on Bürknerstrasse.) In both places his five-story façades display the standard bays, arches, and surface decoration, but

Taut avoided historicist imitation and gave the façades a horizontal rhythm. His use of brick bands anticipates his postwar apartment houses at the Horseshoe Estate (see below). Kottbusser Damm 2–3 was long a ruin; its rear elevation was replaced in 1982 by an Inken and Hinrich Baller design.

Across Kottbusser Damm, on the south bank of the canal, Maybachufer hosts Berlin's largest outdoor **Turkish market** every Tuesday and Friday. Its customers are not tourists but rather Berlin's Turkish families. There is a great deal of attractive produce and other food for sale, along with clothing and, even more, fabrics for making clothes at home, something obviously done by many of the Turkish women, who are generally recognizable by their head scarves. Most of the Turkish immigration to Germany came in the 1960s and early 1970s, when, facing labor shortages after the Berlin Wall cut off the flow of German migrants from the east, the German government began to recruit foreign workers – first in Italy, Spain and Portugal, then in Greece and Turkey. Turks became Berlin's largest minority. Their numbers diminished somewhat after government incentives amid the persistent unemployment of the 1980s drew some back to Turkey, but well over 100,000 remain. Few moved to the east in the 1990s, in part because of neo-Nazi attacks on foreigners there. They remain most visible in the old West Berlin working-class neighborhoods of Kreuzberg, Neukölln, Moabit and Wedding. (However, the Turkish *döner kebap* – meat grilled on a skewer and served with yogurt sauce and bread, by now one of Berliners' indispensable fast foods – is now available at every busy corner in the city.) Most Turks and Germans alike regard even members of the third generation, who know little of Turkey, as Turks, and while peaceful coexistence is the rule, ethnic interaction is not. Acquiring German citizenship has been difficult and generally discouraged, although that has changed a little in recent years, and Berlin's naturalization program has been more ambitious than the rest of Germany's.

If you follow Maybachufer to the end of the Turkish market, the next bridge takes you across to Paul-Lincke-Ufer, named after the most celebrated of Berlin's operetta composers (and a Luisenstadt resident) a century ago, whose song about the 'Little Glowworm' became an international hit. Most of the buildings in this area are either from the 1870s or the 1980s, when the city supported innovative efforts to build new apartment houses that preserved the character of the traditional streets and courtyards. At the intersection of Ohlauer Strasse and the canal stands a large electrical substation, a fine example of 1920s red-brick industrial architecture with expressionist flourishes. Next to it at Ohlauer Strasse 39–41 was, as you can read on the façade, a municipal 'Desinfektions-Anstalt' – an important institution in the industrial city. The bacteriological discoveries of Robert Koch, at the Charité across town, began to offer some answers to the pressing question of how to combat the recurring epidemics of cholera, typhus and other diseases that spread so rapidly in the crowded cities. This facility was built in 1886 after Koch developed disinfection procedures. (The buildings you see date from 1893.) Contaminated clothing, mattresses and furniture from the homes of the ill were brought here in special wagons, driven in on one side (from the canal) and disinfected with steam produced by the machinery of the sewage pumping station then located in the center of the block. The cleaned items were removed on the other side. Formaldehyde and other chemicals came into use a few years later, and this center continued in operation for a century.

A different part of Berlin's rich musical history is represented by Ohlauer Strasse 5–11, in the next block, built in 1907 as the factory of the famed Bechstein piano company. Just past it, Ohlauer Strasse ends at Wiener Strasse, a street with a dubious history even by Berlin standards. Number 45, to the right, was the headquarters of Berlin's tiny Nazi party branch after its official refounding in 1925, upon Hitler's release from prison following his failed Beer Hall Putsch. A pub at number 25 was the local hangout for SA members until it was destroyed in a fierce fight with communists. The brownshirts subsequently assembled at number 10, to the left. When the Nazis came to power in 1933, and the SA street fighters could operate with impunity, they hauled their communist and demo-cratic opponents here for spontaneous detentions and beatings. Much later, this area was also a center of the 1980s Kreuzberg scene. At the corner of Manteuffelstrasse, next to the elevated U-Bahn, once stood a supermarket. The 1987 May Day riots, instigated by the violent ele-ments of the anarchist scene, culminated in the smashing, looting, and burning of the supermarket. The looting, joined by many neighborhood residents, including (according to witnesses) some of the normally law-abiding Turks, was a rare outbreak of mundane material greed amid the typically more abstruse discontents of the late West Berlin era. Recently a mosque has been planned on the abandoned site.

The park across Wiener Strasse occupies the former yards of the vanished Görlitz rail station. In the 1870s, many immigrants from Silesia disembarked here and moved into the new tenements. Since the war Silesia has belonged to Poland (except for the city of Görlitz); if any migrants still come from there, they take a different route. Görlitzer Bahnhof is now just the name of the elevated U-Bahn station. Behind the church on Lausitzer Platz, across the tracks, Eisenbahnstrasse is still the home of one of the surviving municipal market halls, which has offered alluring sights and smells since 1891 and fills the center of the block between Muskauer Strasse and Wrangelstrasse.

To the right of it down Wrangelstrasse, number 97–99 is a typically grand army barracks from the 1870s, later restored and incorporated into a new school. Just past the barracks you once again reach the elevated U-Bahn tracks. This area is not as quiet as it was before 1989. When the Wall followed both the Spree and the Landwehrkanal, which diverge just ahead, these streets took you nowhere. The U-Bahn ended at the next station, **Schlesisches Tor**, named for the 'Silesian gate' in the old customs wall. The 1901 building is one of the most elaborate, and best preserved, of the original U-Bahn stations. It is thoroughly historicist in that it does not look like a rail station, and its iron construction is largely concealed under its stone facing, designed in the 'German Renaissance' style – that is, the combination of Gothic and Renaissance forms associated with fifteenth-century Nuremberg. Köpenicker Strasse, with its ramshackle commercial buildings, ends on one side of the station. Its continuation on the other side, Schlesische Strasse, leads to the upper end of the Landwehrkanal, which once marked the border. In the former no-man's-land stands one of the two remaining square watchtowers, preserved after a group of artists took it over for exhibitions. This **Museum der verbotenen Kunst** (Museum of Forbidden Art) displays works of artists whose work was suppressed in East Germany, as well as material on the history of the Wall.

The elevated tracks, as well as tiny Bevernstrasse, lead you from Schlesisches Tor station to the nearby Spree. The riverside park is populated with sculptures produced by a cooperative effort of artists from several countries in 1985, when this was the end of the world. Another trace of that vanished era is a memorial stone dedicated to 'the unknown refugee', recalling the anonymous victims of the Wall. Much of the riverbank is open for strolling. If you walk a short distance downstream to Pfuelstrasse, however, your way will be blocked by a grand commercial building that extends to the river's edge. This 1908 ware-house built for the Bissinger seed company hints at both Baroque and Jugendstil influences in its carved stone and blue glazed-brick decor. Pfuelstrasse, by the way, is named for a general who, in 1817, established a military swimming facility in the river here. It was later opened to civilians and was one of several popular places to swim in the Spree. Pollution and the availability of cleaner alternatives put it out of business long before the construction of the Wall made swimming here acutely dangerous.

After the Wall severed the U-Bahn line in 1961, trains no longer used the battered **Oberbaum bridge**. It did serve as a border crossing after the resumption of East–West cooperation in 1972, but only for pedestrians. The red-brick Gothic bridge, with its twin towers, has marked the upper end of the inner city since 1896. (Its name, 'upper tree', derives from the tree trunk that was lowered across the river to regulate boat traffic in the days of the customs wall. The 'lower tree' was near where the Reichstag now stands.) From the U-Bahn, or from the roadway below, the restored bridge affords impressive views of the industrial riverfront. On the downstream side of the far bank stand the last of many grain mills and warehouses that dominated this stretch of riverbank as far back as the seventeenth century: hence the name Mühlenstrasse (Mill Street) for the street on the land side. The area upstream was the East Harbor (Osthafen), which has recently been moved farther upstream, with its remaining buildings converted to offices, including a 1928 refrigerated egg warehouse, once capable of holding 75 million eggs. It is to be opened up with a new glass façade.

Once across the bridge you are at the outer end of the East Side Gallery, the painted stretch of Wall (see above). Just beyond is the reopened **Warschauer Strasse** U-Bahn station. Its ornate Baroque stairway tower at the rear leads down to a once-mighty lightbulb factory, shut down in

1990 and now being converted to new uses. The U-Bahn line ends here. It is possible to transfer to the S-Bahn, but to do so you must cross the long bridge over the rail yards, which affords an impressive, if perhaps not at all beautiful, view of the workaday side of industrial Berlin.

The ornate Berlin tenement façades are now much loved. It is possible to share that affection without failing to recognize how preposterous they really are. Foreigners have long wanted to see in them some kind of essential national character. Stephen Spender, for example, believed that even the meanest of them 'never yet quite lost some claim to represent the Prussian spirit, by virtue of their display of eagles, helmets, shields and prodigious buttocks of armoured babies'. However, by the time he arrived in 1930 it was just as plausible to see something essentially Prussian in the clean lines of modernism. During the 1920s German architects offered a vision of the new city that would replace the tenements. Berlin's projects set a model for the world, and the most famous was the Britz estate, better known as the **Horseshoe Estate**, worth a detour to the south. It is best reached from the Parchimer Allee station on the U7, although it extends north nearly to Blaschkoallee. Bruno Taut designed most of it in the mid-1920s as a modernized version of the Garden City ideal. Its centerpiece is Taut's three-story horseshoe-shaped building, facing Fritz-Reuter-Allee and enclosing a large open space, landscaped, serene and seasonally brightened by Japanese cherry trees. The modern simplicity of the buildings and their small apartments is enlivened by the curve of the horseshoe and by Taut's palette (his color scheme has been restored), which includes deep reds and blues, as well as lines of decorative brick. Taut also designed the terraces surrounding the horseshoe, as well as the buildings south of Parchimer Allee. Martin Wagner, the city's building director, contributed the row on Stavenhagener Strasse that marks its northern end. The houses on the east side of

Fritz-Reuter-Allee, facing the horseshoe, were built by a rival housing society and display a more conservative style. The juxtaposition reveals how Taut's lack of commitment to traditional forms like gabled roofs and enclosed blocks gave him more freedom to take advantage of the modern materials and open spaces. By the late 1920s the politics of architecture – and especially of flat roofs – led to nasty polemics between radical modernists and their conservative opponents, arguments that, in different forms, still continue.

20

From the Jewish Museum to Tempelhof

THE JEWISH MUSEUM, the most talked-about building in Berlin, is located on Lindenstrasse, a little way (but only a little) off the beaten path. Buses do run down Lindenstrasse, and it is only a few minutes' walk from the subway stations at Kochstrasse and Hallesches Tor. A tour that begins at the museum might well end there, but if time and energy permit, from the museum you can walk beyond the edge of the eighteenth-century Friedrichstadt, where the museum is, through Kreuzberg's more upscale western end.

The museum is housed in two buildings that could hardly be more different. The elegant Baroque one is a rare relic of King Frederick William I's expansion of Friedrichstadt, built by Philipp Gerlach in 1735 and long the home of Prussia's highest court. Its burned-out interior was rebuilt as a history museum after the war. The Jewish museum was originally planned as an annex to the history museum, and the design competition for it was won by Daniel Libeskind in 1989, after which political and financial complications delayed the new building's completion for a decade. Then for two years the empty building was open to visitors who flocked here just for the stunning experience of walking through its tilted and angled spaces. In 2001 the museum (now an independent institution in possession of both buildings) opened its permanent exhibition on two millennia of Jewish life in Germany.

Libeskind was already known as an architectural theorist, but this was his first building, and it made him a star,

367

despite its complexity. Few visitors will be enlightened by his explanation of the building's form with reference to Walter Benjamin's essay 'One-Way Street' and to Arnold Schönberg's opera 'Moses and Aaron', with its speaking and non-speaking parts corresponding to the building and its voids. The voids are a crucial part of the design, but are visible only in occasional glimpses. They cut through the entire building, from basement to roof, the zigzag of the building crossing the voids again and again. Libeskind has also explained that the building's many angles are intended to point to different parts of the historical city around it. From the outside, it presents a forbidding face, with its zinc façade (intended to darken as it weathers) and angular slashed windows.

Nor does the building have an entrance. You enter the older one to buy your ticket. Here too are the restaurant and shop, segregated from the hermetic experience of the exhibition. From the ground floor, you descend a staircase into an underground passage that leads to Libeskind's building. At the bottom of the stairs you are at the beginning of one of three intersecting axes, the **Axis of Continuity**. It probably makes sense to go through the exhibition upstairs before concluding your visit down here. This main corridor leads you to a stairway (elevators are available, not far away) up to the two exhibition floors. Partway up, you can step into the largest of the voids – otherwise you can only glimpse them through windows. Several works of art have been commissioned for spaces in and around the voids. Here, the floor is covered with the 10,000 tiny metal faces of Menashe Kadishman's *Fallen Leaves*.

The exhibit begins on the higher floor, snaking along its length and then back across the lower floor. Its sections are both thematic and chronological, tracing Jewish life and relations with other Germans from 'the medieval world of the Ashkenaz' through court Jews and the Enlightenment,

nineteenth-century families, struggles for civil rights, modern art, urban life and religious practice, and the last two segments, on the Third Reich and 'the present'. All the texts are in German and English. The recently founded museum does not have a large collection of historical artifacts. Although many pieces have been loaned for the exhibition, including some fine artworks, the display remains in the service of story-telling rather than the other way around. Biographical information, supplemented by documents and everyday objects such as Moses Mendelssohn's eyeglasses, puts an emphasis on particular people in order to make the story more vivid, whether the people are obscure German Jews or famous ones such as Mendelssohn or Einstein. This kind of exhibition is very American and is new to Europe. It has the potential to attract many people, particularly young ones, who do not think of themselves as museum-goers; but it runs the risk of dumbing-down difficult material. There is no danger of an excessively upbeat exhibition, when so much of it is devoted to persecution and genocide, and yet the emphasis on historical personalities is ill-suited to explanations of anti-Semitism as well as intra-Jewish conflicts. It may be indicative that the troublesome German Jew Karl Marx doesn't merit a mention anywhere.

Most of Libeskind's spaces are quite narrow, which limits the scale of the displays. However, the high, white spaces with their occasional windows are light and airy. Visitors are led down a narrow, twisting, corridor-like path, which is easy to lose track of. Detours from the main path lead into corners and lofts with additional displays. The exhibition is hands-on to an extreme degree: beyond the interactive computer simulations and touch screens, texts that might elsewhere be mounted on a wall are placed in distinctly low-tech pull-out drawers. Visitors are encouraged to be so busy picking their way through the clutter of exhibits that the emotional power of Libeskind's spaces will be lost on them. Back in the basement, however, you can explore the intersecting corridors, with little to distract from the odd angles and slanted floors that make this an extraordinary building. Crossing the Axis of Continuity is the **Axis of Exile**, which slants upward to a door that leads outdoors (in all weather) to the Garden of Exile, where you can wander among forty-nine tightly spaced concrete pillars topped with willow oaks (supposed to look like olive trees, which cannot survive in Berlin). Ironically, it is here, outside the building, that the visitor can most fully experience the physical sense of disorientation that defines Libeskind's design. The confined spaces and the tilted floor of the garden disrupt one's sense of balance (even to the point of nausea) in a way intended to reproduce the experience of exile.

Display cases along the **Holocaust axis** exhibit documents and artifacts from victims. The corridor leads downward to a heavy door. When you pass through the door and it slams shut behind you, you are in the bare and unheated Holocaust tower, barely lit through a slit high overhead. Surely it is impossible to simulate the experience of a Holocaust victim, but here you are invited to contemplate that experience. If that purpose is not clear, quotations from Libeskind and references to his intentions are posted along this and the other basement axes – a tactic that penetrates the mystery of the architecture, which is not entirely a good thing.

This neighborhood was devastated in the war. There are scattered 1960s buildings in the area, but much of it remained vacant for decades, with the nearby Wall and a planned highway dampening investors' interest. Only around 1980 did the West Berlin government promote redevelopment here. Adjoining the old museum building on its north side is one of the largest complexes of showcase apartment buildings from the 1980s **International Building Exhibition** (IBA). (Across Lindenstrasse are more IBA buildings.) Around a 1913 office building that remains at Lindenstrasse 20–25, they fill a hitherto largely vacant block with a pleasant variety of shapes, sizes and colors. Rob Krier provided the site plan for this complex as well as another one across Ritterstrasse to the north. The latter includes Krier's postmodern re-creation of Schinkel's famous Feilner house (1829), which stood approximately on the same site until its destruction in the war. (Visitors to the Jewish Museum may wish to take Lindenstrasse yet farther north, to the memorial to the former synagogue at Axel-Springer-Strasse 50 – see Chapter 4.)

Lindenstrasse in the other direction (south from the museum) leads you beyond the eighteenth-century city and toward more intact remnants of intervening eras. At the sharply angled corner of Lindenstrasse and Alte Jakobstrasse stands one of Erich Mendelsohn's best Berlin buildings, put up in 1930 for (and still used by) the steelworkers' union. Mendelsohn took advantage of the triangular site to combine the simplicity and sobriety of the new modernism (evident in the horizontal lines of the two side façades) with the more exuberant, expressionist forms he was known for, including a concave glass front as well as a glass stairwell on the rear. Just beyond, at the corner of Lindenstrasse and Gitschiner Strasse, the enormous home of the patent office, a 1905 building in German Renaissance style, overlooks the elevated U-Bahn and the Landwehrkanal. Brandesstrasse, on the other side of Lindenstrasse, is little more than a tunnel leading to the formal southern terminus of Friedrichstrasse, the circular plaza of **Mehringplatz**. After Friedrichstadt was extended in the early eighteenth century, this became the counterpart to the new square at the end of Unter den Linden (Pariser Platz) and the octagon of Leipziger Platz. All were originally military parade grounds, that being the only kind of ceremony that mattered to King Frederick William I.

This circle was long known as Belle-Alliance-Platz in honor of the 1815 defeat of Napoleon (also known as the Battle of Waterloo) by a Prussian army under Blücher and a British one under Wellington (although to this day the British – and Americans – tend to give exclusive credit to the British general).

Little that is old remains here, just two statues from the 1870s in addition to the sixty-foot-high granite 'peace column', put up in 1843 to honor the 1815 victory, and crowned by a bronze victory goddess, the work of Christian Daniel Rauch. Nothing else survived the war, not even the name, which was deemed too militarist – Franz Mehring, by contrast, having been a turn-of-the-century socialist. The original shape was restored by a circle of bland 1970s apartment buildings, which block the view northward into Friedrichstrasse and leave the plaza free of traffic but also of life. Originally the diagonal Lindenstrasse and Wilhelmstrasse also converged here, but they have been rerouted. Just west of the circle, where Wilhelmstrasse and Stresemannstrasse now converge, the Social Democratic party has built its new national headquarters in a building that deliberately echoes Mendelsohn's. Across Stresemannstrasse from it, at number 28, stands an imposing Jugendstil theater from 1908. The proprietors made the mistake of naming it after the street, which follows the course of the old customs wall from here to Potsdamer Platz. First it was Theater in der Königgrätzer Strasse, after the devastating military victory over Austria in 1866; then the street, and, necessarily, the theater, were renamed in honor of the Weimar Republic's greatest leader, Gustav Stresemann, after his untimely death in 1929; then the Nazis, who despised Stresemann, changed the name to Saarlandstrasse after the province they succeeded in taking back from France. After the second war the theater was sensibly renamed Hebbel Theater after the nineteenth-century dramatist.

The main exit from Mehringplatz is to the south, where a bridge crosses over the Landwehrkanal and under the elevated U-Bahn. The station retains the name **Hallesches Tor**, the outer end of the circle having been the Halle Gate in the customs wall. Across the canal is the green expanse of Blücherplatz. Standing alone in its center is the curved façade of the American Memorial Library (Amerika-Gedenkbibliothek), so called because the 1954 building was an American gift. It was placed in the axis of Friedrichstrasse so that it would be visible from the Soviet-occupied city center. That visual connection was broken with the reconstruction of Mehringplatz, but by then the Wall had stopped East Berliners from coming here to borrow books. This remained West Berlin's central public library, and after 1990 it was administratively united with East Berlin's.

To your left, the eastern end of Blücherplatz is dominated by the massive dome of the Church of the Holy Cross (1888), a particularly grand example of the many red-brick Gothic Protestant churches put up under royal sponsorship in the growing city. In the 1990s it was remodeled as a community center. The south side of the square is lined with several church burial yards. After the new customs wall was built in 1735, all burials had to be (for a time) outside it, and this site was chosen for new cemeteries. Here you can find many eighteenth- and nineteenth-century grave monuments, especially in the cemeteries entered from Zossener Strasse, around the corner to the left. Felix Mendelssohn-Bartholdy and E.T.A. Hoffmann rest here. Otherwise this area was once known for its tough working-class gay bars, such as the Cosy Corner at Zossener Strasse 7, frequented in the 1920s by the young W.H. Auden and Christopher Isherwood. (For all that Isherwood has contributed to our image of Weimar-era Berlin, it is worth recalling his later admission that for him 'Berlin meant Boys'.) Today you will probably have better luck finding used bookstores here.

On the western side of the cemeteries and of Blücherplatz, Mehringdamm is the main street leading south. Across it looms a vast medieval-looking building with crenellated towers, built in the 1850s as a barracks for the First Dragoon Guard Regiment. The building appears to be constructed of massive stone blocks, but that, too, is an illusion: like so many nineteenth-century Prussian buildings, it was built cheaply with a stucco façade squared to look like stone. The small arched windows reinforce the impression of age; they were kept small to save on heating costs. Inside, seven soldiers were housed in each room. Some of the former stables are still behind the building. Since the post–World War I demilitarization, it has housed the Kreuzberg district finance office.

Just beyond, Mehringdamm intersects the wide east–west boulevard laid out by the 1862 Hobrecht plan that drew the street grid for Berlin's subsequent expansion. Unlike many of the spacious boulevards and squares foreseen by the plan, this one was in fact built: it extends all the way to Breitscheidplatz and the ruined Memorial Church. However, just west of here it deviates from its planned course. The enormous growth of the rail yards south of the Potsdam and Anhalt stations forced the boulevard to bend southward, as Yorckstrasse does, and to pass under many railroad bridges. The segments of the boulevard, including Yorckstrasse (west from Mehringdamm) and Gneisenaustrasse (to the east) are named after generals active in the Napoleonic wars. At Gneisenaustrasse 2 is the entrance to Mehringhof, a warren of courtyards that have long housed a colorful mixture of leftist political organizations and multicultural nightlife.

Crossing Yorckstrasse and then taking it to the right, you reach the red-brick Gothic façade of the Roman

Catholic church of St Boniface (1907). Rather than a free-standing building (as was typical for Protestant churches, which were granted public land), this church takes its place in the continuous street wall of apartment buildings. In fact, the church built a Gothic apartment complex around its hall of worship, accessed via the archways on each side of the church. Just beyond, at Yorckstrasse 83–86, stands one of Berlin's best-known apartment complexes, **Riehmers Hofgarten**. Its genesis was typical for speculatively built Berlin apartments. Wilhelm Riehmer was a master mason who acquired a tract of land at this booming edge of the city in 1871. From 1880 to 1899 he employed other artisanally trained builders – not architects – to design and construct ornate apartment houses. Riehmer broke with precedent in developing his properties as a unit rather than as individual, unconnected parcels. The main entrance on Yorckstrasse (1892) is a typically grand street façade decorated in the then-fashionable combination of Renaissance and Baroque. You enter the courtyard through a massive archway under a balcony that appears to be held up by sculptures of Atlas and Hercules. In the typical Berlin building, the largest and finest apartments faced the street, with the smaller apartments facing dark and bare courtyards. Here, however, the courtyard is a pleasantly landscaped park stretching through the block, a pedestrian street lined with ornate façades. Riehmer identified a substantial market for middle-class apartment dwellers: officers from the nearby guard barracks, government officials from Wilhelmstrasse and prosperous artisan masters like himself (although he kept his home around the corner at Mehringdamm 50, in an attractive neoclassical building that he built earlier). Although few army officers remain in the area, Riehmer's buildings still attract other middle-class residents. When they were renovated in the 1980s, a cinema replaced the one wing destroyed in the war.

Riehmers connects through the block to Grossbeerenstrasse (via a side passage to the right) and Hagelberger Strasse. The latter street is lined with slightly older buildings displaying the neoclassical style of the 1870s. Where you can find open doorways, you will see (here as in other neighborhoods) more typical Berlin courtyards.

Hagelberger Strasse, taken to the right, connects with Grossbeerenstrasse, which affords a surprising view of a waterfall just one block farther down. Unlike most of Berlin's prominent hills, this one is not a pile of wartime rubble but is in fact natural (although the waterfall isn't). This is the **Kreuzberg** (cross hill), which took its name from the monument at its peak, and in turn gave that name to the district. Once in Viktoria Park (honoring military victory, not a queen) paths lead you up the hill to the monument, resembling the top of a Gothic church tower, placed here by order of King Frederick William III to commemorate the victory over Napoleon. It was designed by Schinkel and completed in 1821 in the Romantic Gothic style he had cultivated up to then (but subsequently abandoned). Its use of cast iron was innovative, and both the top of the monument and its ground plan used the distinctive shape of the Iron Cross, with each of the four points curving outward to a broad tip. This Schinkel design became the form of Prussia's highest military medals, making it notorious in later wars, and indeed has been out of use since 1945. Niches are filled with neoclassical (rather than Gothic) allegories of the Wars of Liberation, sculpted according to Schinkel's instructions. From a distance this hill scarcely dominates the city, but Berlin's natural hills are few and small, and in the 1820s it stood prominently above the countryside south of Berlin, which is why the king placed the monument here. A few decades later, it had been engulfed by the city, and buildings as well as trees obscured the view. In the 1870s the monument was hydraulically raised 26 feet upward and a new stone pedestal was inserted. Since then it has again afforded an impressive view.

Before the monument was built, this was known as Round Vineyard Hill. Since the late Middle Ages grapes have been grown and wine produced on these slopes. A tiny vineyard remains, its annual production reserved for those who absolutely must drink a Berlin wine. However, wine long ago yielded to beer as the locally produced beverage of choice, as is apparent on the south slope of the hill, visible from the monument, and reached from Methfesselstrasse, which passes by the eastern side of the park. The new Kreuzberg monument and its environs quickly became a popular destination for Berliners' country outings. In 1829, the Gericke brothers opened the Tivoli amusement park just below it (Tivoli was becoming a generic term for amusement parks). Its property was taken over in the 1850s by a newly founded brewery, which kept the name Tivoli. It expanded up to the turn of the century, particularly after Tivoli, then Berlin's second-largest brewery, was acquired in 1891 by its larger rival, Schultheiss, which at that point became Germany's largest brewer. The earlier buildings were constructed in a sober industrial style; the later ones, in a more fanciful neo-Gothic.

By the mid-nineteenth century many Berliners had abandoned their weak, sour top-fermenting brews in favor of distilled spirits. (Tourist pubs will, however, serve you an authentic 'Berliner Weisse'.) In the second half of the century, though, northern Germans discovered the light, smooth 'Bavarian' beer hitherto produced only in the south. Industrial steam power, plus underground storage, enabled breweries to maintain the cool temperatures necessary to produce the more popular bottom-fermenting beers. The breweries' large banquet halls also became centers of social and political life, rented out to political parties of all stripes, including the socialists, who apparently bought enough drinks to keep themselves in good favor with the presumably more conservative proprietors. Air-raid bunkers were built into the Tivoli cellars in the late 1930s, and bombs destroyed parts of the complex, but production continued until 1993. Schultheiss even used horse-drawn wagons until 1981. (It still produces beer, but connoisseurs will steer you away from Berlin brews in favor of Frisian or Saxon imports.) Long-delayed plans call for conversion to new uses, including exhibition space in the large underground storage areas as well as a museum of brewing.

If you continue south past the brewery on Methfesselstrasse, you reach its end at Dudenstrasse. At the corner is a 1955 apartment complex designed by Max Taut, tailored to fit with the older building next door, Dudenstrasse 10, also by Taut and completed in 1926. This was one of Taut's labor union projects, the headquarters of the association of book printers. An apartment building faces the street, with a print shop on the courtyard. That combination of uses fits the pattern of prewar mixed-use Kreuzberg buildings, but its sober style is distinctly modern, with its façade enlivened not by historicist decoration but by a rhythmic arrangement of loggias and by bands of colored brick and ceramic tile.

Dudenstrasse marks a clear transition in the city. Only a few buildings across the street predate World War I. Into the early twentieth century this all belonged to Tempelhof Field, a large army drill ground. Years of dispute accompanied plans to close the drill ground and open the land for development. Housing reformers hoped to stop the outward march of the 'rental barracks' and mandate a less dense pattern of construction. They were disappointed at the plans unveiled in the last years before the war. All that came of those plans, however, are a few buildings, notably the pair whose curved and colonnaded façades face the corner of Dudenstrasse and Tempelhofer Damm (the southern extension of Mehringdamm). The outbreak of war halted further development. After the war, the 'rental barracks' was dead, and a new plan, drawing on English Garden City models, laid out curved streets south and west as far as the rail lines. Among the new buildings was Schulenburgring 2, which General Vasily Chuikov took over as his forward command post in late April 1945, after the Red Army had conquered the outer parts of the city and before its final assault on the center. Here, on 2 May 1945, General Helmuth Weidling arrived to surrender the city.

Even before the Second World War broke out, Hitler's plans for Berlin changed the course of development in the area. In 1923, the half of the drill ground east of Tempelhofer Damm became the site of **Tempelhof airport**, replacing Berlin's original landing strip at Johannesthal. Soon afterward it became the home of the new national airline, Lufthansa. The leaders of the Third Reich were enamored of flight – not only, as is all too well known, its military potential, but also its civilian uses – and consequently expanded the new airport. Hermann Göring, the Reich minister of aviation, took charge of the project, assigning it to the architect Ernst Sagebiel, who had already designed Göring's enormous new ministry (see Chapter 5). Among the buildings razed for the expansion was one of Berlin's most notorious, the Columbiahaus prison where the SS held its prisoners during the early years of Hitler's reign (not to be confused with Erich Mendelsohn's Columbushaus on Potsdamer Platz).

The open space in front of the terminal is called **Platz der Luftbrücke,** and on your way across you can take a closer look at the monument that accompanies that name. 'Air bridge' (Luftbrücke) is what Germans call the Berlin Airlift of 1948–49. In June 1948, the simultaneous introduction of the new Deutschmark currency in the three Western occupation zones of Germany and the

Western sectors of Berlin provoked Stalin's Soviet Union to void agreements reached in 1945 and cut off all road, rail and canal lines linking West Berlin with the western zones. The new currency was indeed a threat to Soviet economic policies, but the occasion was also a pretext for the Soviets to try to extract concessions by squeezing the Western powers at their most vulnerable point, the isolated island of West Berlin. No one in the East, and hardly anyone in the West, believed it possible to supply the needs of two million West Berliners via the three air corridors across the Soviet zone, the only legally recognized access routes not cut off by the blockade. The Soviets had no intention of letting the Berliners starve, but once they accepted the proffered East bloc supplies, they were expected to submit to Soviet control over the entire city. In 1948 the West, led by the United States, was in the process of formulating the doctrine known as containment, according to which any step backward would have had the effect merely of whetting the Soviets' appetite. Therefore they proceeded with the daunting logistics of supplying West Berlin with all its needed food and fuel via a nonstop air operation. Despite serious difficulties at first, hard work and brilliant operational planning enabled the airlift to succeed by the autumn. In May 1949, after 250,000 successful flights (and some, but remarkably few, crashes) the Soviets quietly reopened the land corridors.

Along with the later construction of the Wall, this was Berlin's contribution to the high drama of the Cold War. It also sealed the division of Germany into two states. And it reshaped the international image of Berlin: the city of Hitler and Göring and murderous Nazi minions became the city of stoic anti-Communists, grateful recipients of American potatoes and chewing gum, and front-line civilian combatants in the new, cold war. You can see the immediate postwar city through American eyes (albeit those of the ex-Berliner Billy Wilder) in the 1948 film *A Foreign Affair*, in which Marlene Dietrich embodies the treacherous German (and memorably sings 'In the Ruins of Berlin'). The painful transition in the American view of Germans is well portrayed in the 1950 film *The Big Lift*, an impressive example of Hollywood's contribution to Cold War propaganda. The soaring airlift memorial was, appropriately, West Berlin's first postwar monument, erected in 1951. The sixty-foot-high white steel tower curves toward the west, its three points symbolizing the three air corridors. (There are corresponding memorials in Hanover, Frankfurt and Nuremberg.) The sharp-witted Berliners, with food still on their minds, may have noted the resemblance to a fork, but the popular nick-name for the monument became 'hunger rake'. A bronze tablet at its base names the Allied and German personnel who died while assisting in the airlift.

Tempelhof was not the only airport used for the airlift, but it was both the busiest and, due to its central location, the most visible. It was thus one of the many ironies of Berlin history that the Nazis' largest Berlin construction project hosted the city's symbolic de-Nazification. Work began in 1936 on Sagebiel's enormous (for its time) air-port and ground to a halt, short of completion, after the war broke out. It is the best example of the Nazi mod-ernism that married technological modernity to architec-tural monumentality. Here, as in his aviation ministry, Sagebiel designed a steel-framed building faced with limestone, sparsely decorated but rigidly symmetrical and lined with endless arcades, simplified pillars and stone-framed windows. The buildings facing the square, which extend across to its north side, have concave façades, framing a wide circular space. The main entrance, and the axis of the symmetrical airport building, is set diagonally to the square as well as the field, facing the Kreuzberg monument. Behind the entrance and its forecourt is the main passenger hall, which at its far end opens onto the airfield. This is the center of the immensely long terminal building that curves around the field for over a kilometer, divided into sections by regularly spaced stairwells.

One more monument here cries out for explanation. Beside the main entrance (to your right as you go in) stands a large eagle's head on a pedestal. This aluminum figure was part of a sculpture that originally crowned Sagebiel's building. It is a good (and rare) example of a martial Third Reich eagle. When the Americans removed it to make way for radar equipment, they shipped it to a West Point museum. In 1985 it was returned and given a place of honor here as a symbol of German-American friendship. The plaque on the pedestal praises that friendship and declares this to be 'Eagle Square' – without losing a word over the statue's (or the airport's) origins.

After 1945, both before and after the airlift, this was the airport in the American sector and therefore largely used for U.S. military purposes. It was also, however, West Berlin's commercial airport until the expansion of Tegel airport in 1974. After 1990, with Tegel overwhelmed, Tempelhof was reopened for use by small commercial jets. It will probably be closed soon, and its land devoted to parks and housing, its building perhaps to an aviation museum. Meanwhile, one of the pricier outings in town is a tour of the city aboard a DC-3 'candy bomber' (a nickname acquired by the airlift planes after some American airmen tossed candy down to Berlin's children).

Sagebiel's airport predated Hitler's and Albert Speer's bombastic plans to rebuild Berlin, but it was supposed to be integrated into the new monumental capital, with Dudenstrasse transformed into a wide boulevard linking the airport to the southern terminus of the grand North–South Axis. That intersection was to be the site of the triumphal arch that would dwarf its models in Rome and Paris: four hundred feet high, and, due to its great width and depth, with 49 times the volume of Paris's Arc de Triomphe – room to carve the names of all 1.8 million German dead from the First World War. Neither it nor (apart from a tiny beginning) the North–South Axis was built, but the planned site of the arch is easy enough to find. If you take Dudenstrasse west nearly to the railroad bridge, and turn left into Loewenhardtdamm, the corner of General-Pape-Strasse, just a few steps away, is where the arch would have stood. What *was* completed here, in 1941, was a test to see if the earth could support the tremendous weight of the arch. And that test remains: a broad, forty-foot-high concrete cylinder, an impressive if not at all photogenic sight. This is not a bunker: it is solid concrete. Decades later, it has crumbled a bit, but obviously the soil passed the test. And just as obvious is the reason it has not been removed: imagine what its removal would entail.

The twentieth century has ensured that the name Tempelhof will long be associated with air power and military force, both Nazi and American. Its origins, however, lie with an older military tradition. This land south of Berlin was settled in the thirteenth century by the Knights Templar, the crusading order of holy warriors. What little remains of the old village center is south of the airport, near the U-Bahn station (and street) Alt-Tempelhof. On nearby Reinhardtplatz stands the Templars' thirteenth-century stone church, the largest of the old village churches around Berlin, with its eighteenth-century half-timbered tower, rebuilt after the war. Other old villages have left their traces farther south, with medieval churches and nineteenth-century village houses to be seen on the appropriately named streets Alt-Mariendorf, Alt-Marienfelde and Alt-Lichtenrade. Other parts of the district, notably along the Teltow canal (east from U-Bahn Ullsteinstrasse), display a more recent history in the form of impressive early twentieth-century industrial buildings.

None of that heritage is within easy walking distance. You can, however, walk back north into Kreuzberg on the eastern side of Mehringdamm. (Visible across the street is one of the few remaining early villas at number 116.) Fidicinstrasse takes you to the right into one of the hilliest parts of the city (which isn't saying much). On the street Am Tempelhofer Berg, parallel to Mehringdamm, numbers 6 and 7 are old brewery complexes, once the site of a popular spring bacchanalia. Continuing on Fidicinstrasse, at the next corner stands a massive neo-Gothic water tower from 1888. From there Kopischstrasse will lead you around a corner into idyllic **Chamissoplatz**. Part of this square's charm derives from its intact and well-preserved buildings; part is due to its location away from thoroughfares – a rarity in Berlin. The sloping terraces around it are also unusual in this flat city. Its façades date to the 1880s, when the Schinkel school's relatively austere neoclassicism was being supplemented with richer Renaissance decor, but before the neo-Baroque explosion of the 1890s. It remains a quieter neighborhood than the more fashionable parts of Prenzlauer Berg. If you don't wish to wander aimlessly, you can take Arndtstrasse (the north side of the square) east (right) and turn left on Schenkendorfstrasse. The next cross street, Bergmannstrasse, the lively neighborhood shopping street, leads right to **Marheinekeplatz**. Here stands one of the four extant municipal market halls. This one may hold little architectural interest, but it is unique in having been reconstructed in 1953 after being shattered by Russian shells in 1945. At that point only its western end and its extensive cellar remained, but neighborhood merchants insisted that they needed it. It remains a popular place to buy food and much else.

At the corner of the square stands the Church of the Passion (1908), built from a design attributed to the last emperor himself, its intact interior making it an exemplary showcase of Wilhelmine church design. From Marheinekeplatz, either Zossener Strasse or Mittenwalder Strasse will take you to Gneisenaustrasse and its U-Bahn station. You can also continue northward through old streets back to the Landwehrkanal and Hallesches Tor.

21

Schöneberg

SCHÖNEBERG WAS ONE OF THE VILLAGES utterly transformed by the nineteenth-century growth of Berlin. The independent town had 7500 residents by 1875; shortly after the turn of the century, there were 100,000, most of them in massive Berlin-style apartment buildings. Like its western neighbors, Charlottenburg and Wilmersdorf, it attracted mainly middle-class residents to its spacious new flats, particularly in the western part of town – first near Nollendorfplatz and Wittenbergplatz, then around such fashionable squares as Bayerischer Platz, Viktoria-Luise-Platz and Barbarossaplatz. However, the eastern part of town was distinctly poorer. That diversity persisted, in a modest way, in postwar West Berlin, with Schöneberg acquiring the reputation as calmer and more comfortable than Kreuzberg but livelier and less bourgeois than Wilmersdorf or Charlottenburg.

After 1902 the first, privately constructed, line of what became known as the Untergrundbahn or U-Bahn ran above the street from Nollendorfplatz east. (The underground platforms were added a few years later.) At Dennewitzplatz it passed *through* an apartment building (now long gone). When the Wall was built, the elevated line was shut down and the stations here and at Bülowstrasse were converted into flea markets, the one at Bülowstrasse specializing in Turkish goods. After 1990, however, the line was reopened.

Nollendorfplatz has long been a center of Berlin gay life. On the south wall of the station is a memorial recalling the homosexual victims of National Socialism.

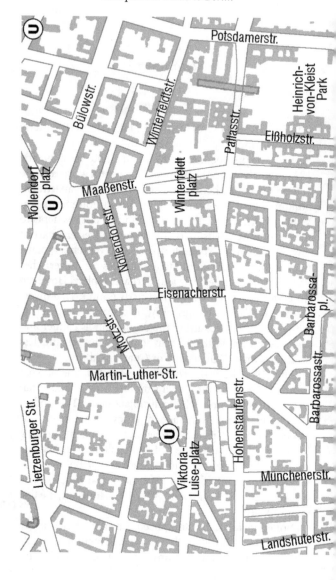

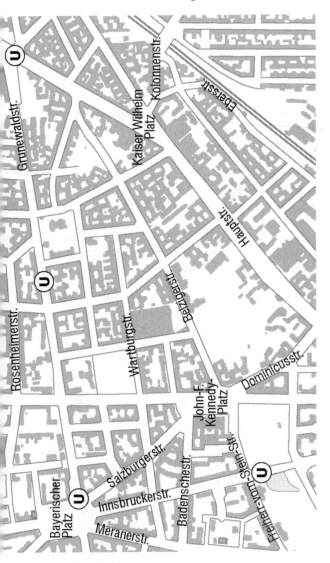

The granite plaque takes the form of the pink triangle insignia that homosexual prisoners in Nazi concentration camps had to wear on their uniforms. Both the culturally conservative and the pro-natalist traditions of the Nazis fed their anti-gay prejudices. On the other hand, within the party's masculine subculture, homosexual bonds were not unimportant. They were tolerated until the purge of the SA, the brown-shirted stormtroopers, in 1934. The marchers and fighters of the SA had played an important role in attracting support to the Nazis, but after taking power in 1933 Hitler cast his lot with the army rather than the sometimes revolutionary-minded brownshirts. On the 'night of the long knives' in 1934 Hitler unleashed Heinrich Himmler's SS to murder SA leaders and other potential rivals. SA leader Ernst Röhm's homosexuality had been an open secret before his murder that night, but it became a pretext for the purge, and thereafter the fanatically puritanical Himmler was freed to persecute gays. Thousands were sent first to prison, then to concentration camps, where many died. Release was only possible for some who agreed to castration.

The area north of the station originally developed as a prestigious residential quarter, but only a few scattered villas remain. On the south side, the façade of Nollendorfplatz 5, built in 1906 as a theater, is still lined with sculptures of classical figures. Its greatest fame came from 1927 to 1931, when the avant-garde director Erwin Piscator experimented with new stage technologies, including the use of film in plays. Piscator was also an active member of the Communist Party, and after the theater's bankruptcy he worked in the Soviet Union, from which he escaped before falling victim to Stalin's purges. Unable to return to Hitler's Germany, he spent the war leading a drama workshop in New York. Later his politics got him into trouble with the Red-hunters of the House Committee on Un-American Activities, and he returned to

Germany, once again directing plays in (West) Berlin. Piscator, however, was not the target of the most notorious demonstration here. In December 1930, this building hosted the Berlin premiere of the Hollywood film based on Erich Maria Remarque's novel *All Quiet on the Western Front*. Joseph Goebbels gathered his Nazis to protest against its antiwar message. Some Nazis bought tickets; then, as soon as the lights went down, they opened boxes of mice they had smuggled in. The ensuing pandemonium accomplished their goal: the film was banned as a public disturbance.

The square itself has lost most of its character, which is probably a good thing if we look at it through the eyes of Stephen Spender, who lived on Motzstrasse in 1930: 'an eyrie of concrete eagles, with verandas like breasts shedding stony flakes of whatever glory they once had into the grime of soot which caked the walls of this part of Berlin'. Maassenstrasse, the street leading south from the square, is lined with cafés attracting a bourgeois-bohemian clientele. The first cross street is Nollendorfstrasse. To the left it offers an intact row of the neighborhood's original nineteenth-century apartment buildings. To the right, Nollendorfstrasse 17 is where Christopher Isherwood lived during the last years of the Weimar Republic. Things have not entirely changed since Isherwood ('I am a camera') looked from his window on 'the deep solemn massive street. Cellar-shops where the lamps burn all day, under the shadow of top-heavy balconied façades, dirty plaster frontages embossed with scrollwork and heraldic devices.' His Berlin stories (later the basis of the play and film *Cabaret*) immortalized fictional versions of his 'middle-class shabby' landlady, ruined by the 1923 inflation, and her colorful and dubious lodgers, notably the one he named Sally Bowles. His fictionalized fellow-tenants included a prostitute, a music-hall yodeler (and ardent Nazi) and a bartender who called himself Bobby because

English names were fashionable. 'And now Frl. Schroeder has not even got a room of her own. She has to sleep in the living-room, behind a screen, on a small sofa with broken springs. As in so many of the older Berlin flats, our living-room connects the front part of the house with the back. The lodgers who live on the front have to pass throught the living-room on their way to the bathroom, so that Frl. Schroeder is often disturbed during the night. "But I drop off again at once. It doesn't worry me. I'm much too tired." She has to do all the housework herself and it takes up most of her day. "Twenty years ago, if any-body had told me to scrub my own floors, I'd have slapped his face for him. But you get used to it. You can get used to anything." ' Spender would wait for him in this room and recalled that 'Christopher lived in this apartment sur-rounded by the models for his creations, like one of those portraits of a writer by a bad painter, in which the writer is depicted meditating in his chair whilst the characters of his novels radiate round him under a glowing cloud of dirty varnish, not unlike the mote-laden lighting of Fräulein Thurau's [her real name] apartment'.

Maassenstrasse ends at **Winterfeldtplatz**, an unre-markable paved square that on Wednesdays and Saturdays hosts one of the most popular of Berlin's many open-air markets. Crowds come in search of the usual market fare – fresh produce, meat and cheese, cheap clothes – along with trendier items. For decades, the ruins on the east side of the square remained largely untouched, attracting a few shady businesses. Only in the 1990s did new buildings supplant them. The southern end of the square is occupied by the Roman Catholic St Matthias church. A plaque at its corner notes that Clemens August von Galen was pastor here from 1919–29. The conservative Galen was sympa-thetic to the new Nazi government when he was named bishop of Münster in 1933, but his growing disenchant-ment culminated in a 1941 sermon denouncing the regime's systematic murder of handicapped people. This rare act of protest actually led the Nazis to stop the killings, if only temporarily.

A left on Pallasstrasse, at the far end of the square, takes you toward a building that extends overhead across the street. As you approach, you will see that it spans not only the street but also an older, concrete structure on the right side. This is a Third Reich bunker, best seen after you have passed under the newer building. It was built to protect the main telephone exchange (itself an interesting 1920s building nearby, at Winterfeldtstrasse 19), but was never completed. Too much trouble to remove, it has remained, designated as a fallout shelter during the Cold War but otherwise of little use, although in the 1970s it was proposed to shelter the West Berlin government here in case of war. In 2002 teachers and students at the adjoining school created an exhibit recalling the hundreds of Russian forced laborers who lived miserably in the school building while constructing the bunker. A low blue metal wall from the school to the bunker serves as a memorial to their suffering.

Across Pallasstrasse once stood the renowned Sportpalast, a popular place to see ice-skating shows, concerts and sporting events, especially the famous six-day bicycle races. It opened in 1910 with a performance of Beethoven's Ninth Symphony conducted by Richard Strauss. Later, Berlin's Nazi masters favored it as a place to rally crowds of up to 20,000. More famous than the many Hitler speeches here was one by Joseph Goebbels on 18 February 1943, when he built up his handpicked crowd to his climactic question, 'DO YOU WANT TOTAL WAR?' To which they dutifully roared, 'YES!' His purpose, after Stalingrad and El Alamein, was to prepare Germans for a degree of sacrifice that they had so far been spared, as the Germans had plundered conquered territories. The Sportpalast was pulled down in 1973 and replaced by the dull complex of subsidized or 'social' apartments that extends over the street. It became known as the 'Sozialpalast' and gradually acquired a dreadful reputation as last-resort housing. Its future is uncertain.

The block on the other side of Pallasstrasse (that is, the block on which the bunker stands) is dominated by relatively unobtrusive Third Reich buildings, built in the conservative, ungainly classical style favored by the many mini-Führers who were building their own bureaucratic empires. Potsdamer Strasse 182 was the headquarters of Robert Ley's German Labor Front, the organization that replaced the banned labor unions and was responsible for keeping workers enthusiastically devoted to nation and race by taking them on cruises and promising them the new 'people's car' (Volkswagen). The building boasts a 'Führer balcony' like the one added to the Reich chancellery after 1933. Hitler himself presumably never stood on this one, but the 'Führerprinzip' dictated that every lower-level leader command his own forces, and a scheming epigone like Ley might have dreamed of being cheered from here. The balcony was originally flanked by two enormous flag masts, and above it perched a huge granite eagle clutching a swastika in its claws. After the war the eagle vanished, and two new windows were punched through the façade, closely matched to their neighbors.

Farther down the block, number 190 housed the administration of the famous Reich autobahn program. Before you reach it, however, you pass one of Berlin's first high-rises, number 186, slightly older (1930) but distinctly more modern-looking than the Nazi buildings. Its entrance is on the side, facing **Heinrich von Kleist Park**, on the site of the royal botanical garden, which was established here in the seventeenth century and moved to its current home in Dahlem around 1900. The park's centerpiece is a colonnade, one of several that once formed ceremonial city entrances across the defensive moat.

This one, designed by Karl von Gontard, stood near Alexanderplatz from 1780 to 1910, when it was moved in order to widen a street. The colonnade leads back to the park's other main structure, built in 1913 as the home of Prussia's supreme court, a Wilhelmine Baroque structure with a grand entry and 500 rooms. Its history mirrors the troubled rule of law in twentieth-century Berlin. The Nazis established a special court, the Volksgerichtshof (People's Court), to deal efficiently with traitors. Its headquarters was on Bellevuestrasse, but its growing caseload during the war led it to hold many of its summary trials (typically culminating in death sentences) here. Many of the conspirators in the 20 July 1944 assassination attempt against Hitler were tried here. The proceedings were filmed, and they offer the best evidence of the character of the court's chief judge, Roland Freisler, who delighted in humiliating his helpless defendants. They, obviously beaten down by physical abuse since their arrests, did their best to maintain a dignity otherwise so lacking in the court. After the war the building was taken over by the Allies for their four-power control council, intended to govern Germany pending a final peace treaty. No treaty was completed, nor was the council dissolved, but after a Soviet walkout in 1948 it ceased to function, leaving this building a ghostly place. The one four-power operation that did continue, and the only use of this building for decades, was the Allied air traffic control authority, responsible for coordinating the use of Berlin airspace, which was shared by Soviet military jets and the airliners of Pan American and British Airways. Now this is once again a court building.

Potsdamer Strasse was part of the old highway connecting Berlin to Potsdam. Here at the corner of the park its name changes to **Hauptstrasse**, reflecting its status as the 'main street' of the village of Schöneberg. It and the side streets have maintained a lively mix of shops and cafés, including the now venerable and low-key gay café Anderes Ufer. Nearby Hauptstrasse 155 was home to the rock stars David Bowie and Iggy Pop for a time in the 1970s. Bowie enjoyed the unworldly anarchy of West Berlin and later recalled that despite his fame Berliners tended to leave him in peace, since they generally ignored everyone around them. Numbers 14 and 15, on the right, remain from Germany's first private psychiatric hospital, the Maison de Santé, founded here in 1862. Its chapel still stands, now in a courtyard. At Kaiser-Wilhelm-Platz, a little farther down Hauptstrasse, stands an early (1967) Holocaust memorial in the form of a sign with a some-what arbitrary list of twelve concentration camps and the admonishment, 'Places of horror that we must never forget'. Like its twin on Wittenbergplatz, it lacks any historical or architectural connection to its surroundings, making it more of an oddity than an effective memorial.

The western parts of Schöneberg gave the then-independent city its bourgeois identity in the years of rapid growth before 1914. The streets off Hauptstrasse have always been more socially diverse, and to the east lies the poorest part of Schöneberg. Kolonnenstrasse leads from Kaiser-Wilhelm-Platz into this so-called '**red island**' – 'red' because it, unlike most of Schöneberg, supported the Marxist Social Democrats at election time; an 'island' because the diverging Potsdam and Anhalt rail lines left it cut off from easy access to the rest of Schöneberg, to the west, and from Berlin proper, to the east. A detour over the railroad bridge will show you that the streets off Kolonnenstrasse have remained fairly quiet and working class, although increasing numbers of students, artists and professionals have found their way into its many old apartments. These days the health-food stores are doing more business than the grimy old pubs.

At Leberstrasse 65, several blocks south of Kolonnenstrasse, the actress **Marlene Dietrich** was born in 1901, child not of a raw Berlin proletarian but of a police officer living comfortably one floor above the street. (The street was then named Sedanstrasse, celebrating Prussia's defeat of the French army in 1870; it has been renamed after a Social Democratic politician killed by the Nazis.) When she was three, the family moved to nearby Kolonnenstrasse 48–49. Dietrich failed to stand out during her first years in the thriving Berlin film industry. Only *The Blue Angel* (1930) made her a star, and she soon decamped for Hollywood. After her death in 1992, the district of Schöneberg discussed renaming a street in her honor, but proved unable to agree on one. It became clear that some Berliners had never forgiven her for her appearances before American troops during the Second World War. In the end, the newly created Marlene-Dietrich-Platz off Potsdamer Platz became her memorial. In accordance with her instructions, however, she was buried in Berlin beside her mother, at gravesite 34/38 in the quiet cemetery on Stubenrauchstrasse, near Bundesplatz.

At the center of Gustav-Müller-Platz, the octagonal Queen Luise Memorial Church (1912) revived an eighteenth-century style of circular church. Its location and its name betray its place in the Hohenzollerns' generally futile efforts to shore up religious faith, or at least church attendance, among Protestant workers. Toward the northern end of the 'red island', near the Grossgörschenstrasse S-Bahn, is St Matthäus cemetery, where the Grimm brothers are buried. Here Claus von Stauffenberg and his co-conspirators were hurriedly buried after they were shot on 20 July 1944, following their failed attempt to assassinate Hitler. Later the SS secretly exhumed their bodies, cremated them, and scattered the ashes. A plaque marks their former burial spot.

Kaiser-Wilhelm-Platz (to return to it) and the northern end of Hauptstrasse originally marked the center of

Neu-Schöneberg, a colony of Bohemian Protestants established in 1750 by Frederick the Great, one of many settlements of Protestant refugees welcomed in Brandenburg. Beyond Kaiser-Wilhelm-Platz was Alt-Schöneberg, the original village, which was, however, destroyed by Russian soldiers in 1760, during the Seven Years' War, and rebuilt thereafter. Hauptstrasse no longer resembles a village, but traces of its transformation do remain. Schöneberg became famous for its 'millionaire peasants', a handful of farmers who got rich selling their land to developers. Several of their villas from the 1860s and 1870s still stand on Hauptstrasse, dwarfed by the apartment houses that soon surrounded them. Just past them stands the 1766 village church in traditional Brandenburg style with Baroque accents, as well as the strikingly angular Paul Gerhard Church (1962).

At the corner of Dominicusstrasse a plaque commemorates an all-too-typical event from April 1945: a soldier was hanged from a street lantern as a warning to all who might hesitate to fight to the bitter end against the Russian invaders. Dominicusstrasse, taken to the right, leads you past the eastern end of a long greenbelt, a former marsh that was filled and landscaped to create a pleasant urban oasis below the level of the surrounding city. The subway station visible in the park (Rathaus Schöneberg station, 1910) forms a bridge across it. Across from the park is **John F. Kennedy Platz**, thus renamed shortly after the U.S. president's assassination. Kennedy had endeared himself to Berliners with the speech he made here on 26 June 1963, five months before his death, a speech given in English but made famous by a German phrase that Kennedy did his best to pronounce. That line concluded his ringing affirmation that the fate of the free world was inseparable from that of walled-in Berlin: 'All free men, wherever they may live, are citizens of Berlin. And therefore, as a free man, I take pride in the words, Ich bin ein

Berliner.' This being Berlin, though, pathos soon yielded to bathos. 'Ein Berliner' is what most Germans (although not Berliners) call a jelly doughnut, giving rise to endlessly repeated jokes about what the president had in fact proclaimed himself to be.

Kennedy spoke here because the building that looms behind the square, the **Schöneberg Rathaus**, was the seat of West Berlin's government. The wealthy city of Schöneberg completed its enormous town hall in 1914, six years before it lost its independence. At one corner is the entrance to the inevitable Ratskeller. By long-standing tradition, a German town hall must devote its cellar (in this case, a small part of it) to a traditional restaurant and beer hall with heavy wooden tables set under the cellar vaults. Even Berlin's modern district Rathäuser uphold the role, as you may notice all over town. The main entrance to the building, at the base of the tower, takes you past a small exhibition on the life of Willy Brandt, who worked here as West Berlin mayor (1957–66) before he went to Bonn as foreign minister and then chancellor. Beyond that are a spacious entrance hall, ornate reception areas and the chamber where the West Berlin municipal parliament sat. If you follow the signs 'Zum Turm' around many twists and turns and up many, many stairs, you can climb all the way up the tower. On the way you pass a small exhibition on the history of the building and of local politics, consisting mainly of German documents with German captions, but also including information about American support for West Berlin. A little higher up you reach the symbol of that support, a replica of Philadelphia's famous Liberty Bell that was an American gift to Berlin: 450,000 Berliners attended its dedication in 1950. From the top of the 230-foot tower (which was originally topped by a dome but was rebuilt after the war in a square form) you have a view in all directions. The view offers fewer landmarks than you can see from the Victory Column, the TV tower or Potsdamer Platz. If you didn't want the exercise, it may not be worth the climb.

Just north of the town hall is a building of the same age but a more modern form. The former office of the Nordstern insurance company (1914) forms a dramatic curve from Salzburger to Badensche Strasse. As a stone-clad structure with recognizably historicist pilasters and window frames, it conforms to the style of the Wilhelmine age. However, the architects, Paul Mebes and Paul Emmerich, kept those ornaments rather flat and thus subordinate to the sweeping horizontal emphasis of the entire façade, thus anticipating the postwar modernism of Erich Mendelsohn. Its steel frame and open interior spaces also mark it as a modern structure.

North of the town hall is also one of the most interesting of the memorials to Berlin's murdered Jews. In keeping with the desire to integrate remembrance into the cityscape, this one is not found in a single location; rather, it consists of eighty small signs mounted on lampposts throughout the neighborhood centered on **Bayerischer Platz**. Maps of the neighborhood, showing the location of the signs, stand on that square as well as outside the town hall. This area was developed during the first decade of the twentieth century as an upper-middle-class residential district. The new buildings conformed to the standard Berlin pattern: massive five-story structures with side wings extending back around courtyards. The varied rhythm of the façades – bays, balconies, picturesque gables – displayed both the latest fashion and the neighborhood's high status. Monumental stone entrances and landscaped forecourts also set many of these buildings apart from proletarian tenements. The large apartments attracted prosperous renters, many of them Jewish, which meant that Nazi policies in the 1930s had profound if not always visible effects here.

The memorial project, dating to 1993, was chosen by the district of Schöneberg to commemorate this lost Jewish presence in the Bayerisches Viertel, or Bavarian quarter, so called because its streets were named after south German towns and its central square after Bavaria (Bayern, in German). The design by Renata Stih and Frieder Schnock dispenses with the traditional memorial intended for pious, passive observance. Instead, they have filled the neighborhood with reminders of how the Nazis made ordinary life difficult and ultimately impossible for its many Jewish residents. Each of the eighty signs displays a simple, colorful icon on one side, and the other side quotes or paraphrases a related Third Reich decree. (It is possible to buy an English version of a brochure that identifies each sign.)

There are one or two signs per block. From the town hall, Salzburger Strasse is the most direct route to Bayerischer Platz. However, you will find signs by wandering any of the streets west from Martin-Luther-Strasse and north from Badensche Strasse (as far as Kufsteiner and Bamberger Strasse to the west, Hohenstaufenstrasse to the north). Just as the signs are located arbitrarily along the streets, to be encountered in the course of ordinary events, many of their themes emphasize the disruption of Jews' lives by petty but growing harassment. For example, a sign with a picture of a cat explains, on the other side, that after 1942 Jews were not permitted to own pets. A sign picturing a telephone dial explains that Jews were forbidden first to own telephones and then to use public phones. A clock face (just outside the Bayerischer Platz U-Bahn) illustrates a curfew imposed on Jews; a bench, the rule that Jews could use only the park benches painted yellow. Many other signs recall prohibitions on professional activity: for veterinarians (a dog), musicians (a violin case), physicians (a thermometer), state officials (a rubber stamp). The earliest of the decrees date to early

1933, just after the Nazis took power. Among the latest, some from 1942 and all from 1943 deal with deportation to the death camps. The last, dated 16 February 1945, declares that 'documents relating to anti-Jewish activities are to be destroyed'. These signs are now a part of this pleasant neighborhood of shaded streets, comfortable apartments, cheerful playgrounds and attractive shops and restaurants. Attentive visitors will find the signs to be a bracing presence. Some residents may come to ignore them, but these signs would seem to resist fading into the background more effectively than a single plaque or sculpture. They are more likely to be misunderstood than overlooked: when they were being mounted, residents called police to report that someone was putting up anti-Semitic signs.

An older memorial recalls the neighborhood's syna-gogue at München Strasse 34 (at Westarpstrasse), which stood largely intact, but unused, until it was demolished in 1956. The abstract stone sculpture from 1963, with its relief of a menorah, was in fact the first postwar memorial to Berlin's destroyed Jewish commu-nity. As elsewhere in the city, plaques here and there recall distinguished former residents. Here, many were Jewish. Certainly the most famous was Albert Einstein, who lived from 1918 to 1932 at Haberlandstrasse 8 (at the corner of Aschaffenburger Strasse). The young Einstein's theories were making him famous by the time he was named director of the new Kaiser Wilhelm Institute for Physics in 1914. His fame always attracted the venom of anti-Semites, a problem that became intolerable with the rise of the Nazis. He was a visiting professor at Princeton when the Nazis took power, and he never returned. A second plaque at the same address recalls another former resident, Rudolf Breitscheid, a prominent Social Democrat caught by the Gestapo in 1940 in his French exile. He died in Buchenwald in 1944.

Georg Haberland, after whom the street is named, was a controversial real estate developer responsible for some of the most attractive neighborhoods in Schöneberg (including Bayerischer Platz) and then, after a falling-out with the local government, in neighboring Wilmersdorf (notably Rüdesheimer Platz). Haberland, in fact, boasted that his influence was responsible for the fact that Wilmersdorf's subway line (now the U1) was extended conveniently outward to Dahlem and inward to central Berlin, whereas Schöneberg's (the U4) remained a stump. Because he was Jewish, the Nazis changed the name of the street that honored him (as is explained by one of the memorial signs); his name was restored only in the 1990s.

Other pleasant squares nearby include Viktoria-Luise-Platz and Prager Platz. From Bayerischer Platz, two subway lines will take you in any direction.

22

The Communist East

BERLIN'S EAST has never been fashionable. Communism and the Wall merely reinforced older divisions: long before, the monied classes drew wealth and fashion ever farther west, and for most visitors, the vast reaches east of Alexanderplatz remained as remote as the steppe. Since the Wall's demise, money has reconquered the old center and Prenzlauer Berg, but Alexanderplatz still marks the beginning of a proletarian Berlin largely undisturbed by tourists. Lichtenberg and other eastern districts attract attention only when skinheads and neo-Nazis commit violent acts against foreigners. These are far from daily events, and daytime visitors need not be deterred. The highlights of the east include traces of the Communist era that were not intended for public viewing, as well as monuments the Communists were proud to display, such as Stalinallee (see Chapter 18) and Treptow.

The Treptow district, on the left bank of the Spree, belonged to East Berlin but is not far east. From the S-Bahn station Treptower Park, Puschkinallee takes you into the spacious old park of that name. The observatory at the far end dates to 1896, when it opened with the world's longest telescope. On the left side of the street is a riverfront garden, in good weather a popular East Berlin spot, with sausage stands and docks for tour boats. Farther upriver is an amusement park. On the right side of the street is the quieter part of the park, including one of the city's essential sights, the extraordinary **Soviet war memorial**, completed in 1949 by Soviet artists, using granite that had been quarried by concentration camp prisoners and stockpiled for the construction of Hitler's new capital. For forty years, the East Germans and their Russian protectors staged regular ceremonies here. Now it attracts much smaller crowds of the curious and the reverent, including many Russians. From the street, you enter the memorial through a massive stone arch. There is another one on the other side, on the once elegant street Am Treptower Park. Those two side paths converge at a granite statue of a female figure, representing the homeland. This is only the beginning of the vast memorial landscape that now opens before you. Next you pass between a pair of gigantic red granite pylons, each accompanied by a bronze figure of a kneeling soldier. From here you look down a stairway into the central field of the cemetery, the burial place for five thousand Red Army soldiers who died in the Battle of Berlin. Each side is lined with large tomblike stones, carved with reliefs and with quotations (in Russian and German) from Stalin, banal profundities about the soldiers' courage and the motherland's glory. At the far end, a staircase brings you up a tall burial mound to the base of an enormous bronze statue of a soldier who is trampling a swastika while gripping a sword with one hand and nestling a baby with the other. At the top of the stairs you can look into an enclosed mausoleum beneath the statue, lined with glittering mosaics. It pays to linger at this awe-inspiring place, whether your thoughts turn to the soldiers buried here, the many other people who died at the hands of Hitler's Germany, or the irony of this memorial built to glorify another mass murderer.

The GDR's most notorious institution was its secret police, organized in the ministry of state security (Staatssicherheit), or **Stasi** for short. Its headquarters was a sprawling complex of anonymous buildings off Frankfurter Allee. The complex remains but is easily overlooked. To

find it, take the U5 east to Magdalenenstrasse, then walk back west along Frankfurter Allee. The buildings you pass on your right, standard-issue GDR prefabs, all belonged to the Stasi. At the corner, turn right into Ruschestrasse, then follow the driveway into the courtyard. A sign identifies the location of the dozens of buildings once used by the Stasi: all those you can see, and more, where thousands of bureaucrats toiled to protect German state socialism from enemies, real and imagined, at home and abroad. Some buildings belonged to the foreign spy service, long headed by the charismatic Markus Wolf, which scored notable successes in infiltrating West German government offices, sometimes by planting dedicated communist moles, more often by employing Lotharios who seduced lonely secretaries and then kept them happy for years while they worked their way up the hierarchy. But most of the Stasi was devoted to tracking domestic enemies: reading mail, tapping telephones, recruiting 'unofficial agents' in nearly every office, social club and neighborhood – and then recording the often mundane details of people's private lives, in endless detail, on reams of paper. At its peak the Stasi had 90,000 employees, in addition to the 170,000 'unofficial collaborators' who more or less voluntarily informed on their friends and colleagues. In a land of 17 million people, they were nearly everywhere. The Stasi also held thousands of political prisoners, but West Germany quietly bought the freedom of many, the two Germanies having negotiated the hard-currency price of a person's freedom.

Most of these buildings are now leased to businesses and government agencies. The one to visit is Haus 1, the oldest building, and the one you reach if you continue directly across the courtyard from Ruschestrasse. This was the headquarters, stormed by GDR dissidents on 15 January 1990, because they feared, correctly, that the Stasi was frantically shredding documents while its agents stalled discussions about reform. The dissidents seized the building and soon opened it to the public, displaying the spies' paraphernalia. They continue to maintain this modest **Normannenstrasse Research and Memorial Centre** (Forschungs- und Gedenkstätte Normannenstrasse), although the national government may take it over. Its centerpiece is the office of Stasi chief Erich Mielke, preserved with its bland 1950s-modern furniture and numerous telephones. In the museum you can also see such disturbing Stasi relics as electronic surveillance devices and bottles containing personal items stolen from dissidents. These were collected so that if arrests were ordered, Stasi dogs would have a scent to work with. Films and documents reveal more Stasi secrets that emerged after 1989. We now know that even the smallest and least militant dissident circle (GDR dissidents were uniformly nonviolent and generally pacifist) nearly always had a member who had been persuaded to give regular reports to a Stasi officer. As these revelations trickled out of Stasi files after 1990, they destroyed friendships, families and marriages: a few people discovered that their informers were their spouses. The mountains of Stasi documents were transferred to a special agency that continues to sort through them, and even to reassemble shredded files. Individuals are permitted to see the files kept on them, something many former East Germans have done – with at times devastating consequences – while others have chosen not to. Foreigners, too, can see their files, if only for the less painful experience of finding out how important the Stasi judged their activities on GDR soil. (Some of us were disappointed to learn what a feeble threat we posed.) Poisonous revelations from the Stasi files have had political as well as personal consequences: many East Germans who entered politics in 1989 were soon forced out by revelations of their Stasi contacts. Compromises with the Stasi were a normal part of life for clergy, professionals, artists and bureaucrats, in ways that westerners fail to comprehend.

The **Friedrichsfelde cemetery** was a place the GDR was proud to display. It dates to 1881, and became important to communists when the murdered Karl Liebknecht and Rosa Luxemburg were buried here in 1919. For them the otherwise apolitical Mies van der Rohe designed a brick memorial wall (1926) intended to evoke the walls against which earlier revolutionaries had been shot (Paris 1871, for example). The Nazis destroyed the memorial in 1935. The cemetery is near the Lichtenberg rail station (U-Bahn and S-Bahn). From the north side of Frankfurter Allee, follow Gudrunstrasse northeast, keeping the rail line on your right. The cemetery will be on your left. Inside its entrance is the GDR's open-air pantheon dominated by a granite slab inscribed with the words, 'the dead exhort us'. Here the GDR buried the politically prominent (if they died while still in favor) and reburied earlier socialist leaders. It was also a site of solemn ceremonies, for example on the anniversary of Liebknecht's and Luxemburg's murders. A stone now marks the site of Mies's monument, which stood back in the northern part of the cemetery, the city having denied the Communist party a more prominent spot in the 1920s.

One of the more pleasant legacies of division is the presence of two zoos in Berlin. The old zoo ended up in the western sector, so the East Germans created the new **Tierpark** during the 1950s in the grounds of Friedrichsfelde palace. The two zoos are now under common management, sharing the unparalleled riches of Berlin's fauna collection. U-Bahn Tierpark deposits you at the zoo's entrance. The Tierpark has the advantage of being less visited and thus less crowded than the western zoo, all the more so because it possesses far more land for inmates and visitors alike to wander. In the southeastern part, by the Alfred Brehm house for tropical animals, a stone with attached plaques was erected in 1985 to recall the site of the Wuhlheide work camp, where the Gestapo processed slave laborers from eastern Europe as well as POWs, political prisoners and Jews. Between 1940 and 1945, 30,000 prisoners passed through the camp, of whom at least 2000 died from hunger, exhaustion, disease and mistreatment.

At the northern end of the zoo grounds is **Friedrichsfelde palace**, originally built in the 1690s (probably by Nering) as a country house for Benjamin Raulé, director general of the elector's navy. After his fall from grace a few years later, the house passed through several noble families. It was expanded to its current dimensions in 1719, and in the late eighteenth century the Baroque roof was rebuilt in neoclassical form, with a triangular center gable, as was the interior. The East Germans restored the interior with the addition of neoclassical furnishings from other sites.

Not far to the south is the former army school that the invading Soviet army made its headquarters in 1945 and where, by some accounts, the Second World War ended. This is now the **Deutsch-Russisches Museum**, at the end of Rheinsteinstrasse, near Zwieseler Strasse. The nearest S-Bahn station is Karlshorst. On 7 May 1945, the Western allies summoned German commanders to Eisenhower's headquarters at Reims to sign the unconditional surrender. A Soviet representative was present; nevertheless, the Russians wanted their own ceremony, so Western representatives hastily flew to Berlin. Late in the night of 8 May, a second ceremony took place in the Karlshorst officers' mess. General Georgi Zhukov presided, as Field Marshal Wilhelm Keitel, along with navy and air force commanders, signed the surrender documents, in the presence of Air Marshal Arthur Tedder, General Carl Spaatz and General Jean de Lattre de Tassigny. The building then became the first command post of the Soviet military administration in occupied Germany. By 1949 headquarters had already been moved to Wünsdorf, south of Berlin, when the Soviets used this site to grant sovereignty to the newly founded GDR. In 1967, the Soviets opened the 'Museum of the unconditional surrender of fascist Germany in the Great Patriotic War', displaying weapons, uniforms, flags, and other objects from the Red Army's campaign against Germany and especially Berlin. When Russian troops withdrew from Berlin in 1994, Germans and Russians worked together to arrange the handover of the museum and its reopening as the German-Russian museum. You can still visit the surrender room as well as Zhukov's restored office and see many of the artifacts of the old museum, including a diorama, 'Storming the Reichstag'. Instead of serving up antifascist inspiration, however, the new museum emphasizes the suffering of civilians as well as the experiences of soldiers on both sides.

The upper Spree is part pastoral and part industrial, with enormous old factory complexes like the one along Wilhelminenhofstrasse in Oberschöneweide. Two S-Bahn stops beyond Karlshorst is the **Köpenick** station. From there, Borgmannstrasse leads you past a new glass-roofed shopping mall toward the old town. Borgmannstrasse becomes Puchanstrasse, and the former jail at number 12, on the right, houses a memorial to the 'Köpenick Blood Week'. This jail became the local SA headquarters in the months after the Nazi takeover, and in May and June 1933 they systematically brutalized their local opponents, mostly socialist and communist activists they had long been at odds with. In late June they rounded up hundreds of them and beat many to death. An exhibition in some of the former cells was opened by the GDR in 1980 and has since been revised. Puchanstrasse merges with Bahnhofstrasse, and before you reach Lindenstrasse, a park on the left side opens a view of the upper Spree, a mixture of urban and suburban vistas typical for the Brandenburg fringes of Berlin. This park is named Platz des 23. April, commemorating the Red Army's liberation of Köpenick in 1945, and here stands a 1970 memorial to the Blood Week: a pillar in the form of a raised and clenched fist. Such a symbol of proletarian militancy was typical of the GDR's antifascism and far different from Western commemorations of Nazi victims. Although the memorial remains, its eternal flame does not.

Lindenstrasse, to the left, takes you across a bridge into the old island town of Köpenick, an obscure gem of a place engulfed but not obliterated by the big city. A Slavic fortress is known to have stood on this strategic spot as far back as the ninth century. It was replaced by a German one in the thirteenth century, around the time that Köpenick was losing its commercial strength to Berlin-Cölln, although it remained an independent town until 1920. The church you see here is an early nineteenth-century replacement for a thirteenth-century building. Past it on the right, the grandest of several eighteenth-century houses on the street Alt-Köpenick is number 15, the Anderson palace from 1770. Looming above it is the tower of the Rathaus (1904), a typically grand red-brick-Gothic suburban town hall from the boom era. On its steps you are greeted by a life-size statue of the **Captain of Köpenick**, and inside is a small exhibition on the history of the building and the captain. It does not tell the story, however: you are expected to know it.

In 1906, an unemployed shoemaker, Wilhelm Voigt, just released from prison, wanted to emigrate (according to his own later account) but became frustrated when he could not obtain a passport. He bought an old Prussian captain's uniform in a second-hand shop, donned it, stepped outside, and hailed some passing soldiers, who obediently followed the 'officer' to this town hall, where he announced that he had orders to clear up irregularities. When he learned that no one here could issue the papers he wanted, he commandeered the city treasury from the mayor, who meekly handed it over. After marching out, Voigt dismissed the soldiers and vanished. He was soon apprehended, but this vivid illustration of the power of the army uniform in Prussia made him a celebrity, and the sensational story has long been known to every German, especially through Carl Zuckmayer's 1931 play. The GDR, happy to mock Prussian militarism, re-enacted it annually. At the time, though, the emperor was pleased to learn that his subjects offered such unquestioning obedience to an officer's insignia, and he later pardoned Voigt.

Alt-Köpenick leads past Müggelheimer Strasse to the bridge across a moat that is the only entrance to **Köpenick palace**, one of Berlin's earliest and best preserved Baroque buildings. Here in 1730 a court martial deliberated the fate of the unhappy crown prince, the later Frederick the Great, after his father caught him trying to flee and accused him of treason. The elector's sixteenth-century hunting lodge was replaced in the 1670s by a Dutch Baroque palace designed by Rutger van Langervelts, facing west toward the water. It was the home of Prince Frederick, the later King Frederick I, until the death of his father in 1688. During the 1680s Nering drew up plans for a grand expansion of the palace, of which a few parts were built, including the arched entrance gateway, the two-story gallery at the northern end of the palace, and, on its eastern side, a chapel with attached outbuildings. The interior of Langervelts's palace still has its original ceiling paintings from the 1680s by Jacques Vaillant as well as original stucco decoration. The freshly renovated palace is now a branch of the applied art museum, displaying state collections of Renaissance and Baroque furnishings.

Back across the moat, Müggelheimer Strasse leads east (right) across a short bridge, after which the first right turn takes you into **Kietz**, which is the name of the street as well as the former fishing village that stood here, just off the island, since the thirteenth century. Several four-story apartment buildings from the early 1900s betray the arrival of the big city, but otherwise the street, lined with one-story houses from the eighteenth and early nineteenth centuries, retains its village character like few places in Berlin. Returning across the bridge into the old town, bear right to the street named Alter Markt. Number 1 at its southern end, near the canal you just crossed, is a large half-timbered house from 1665 that houses the local history museum (Heimatmuseum), with displays on topics such as Köpenick's once thriving laundry business, which exploited the relatively clean river water upstream from Berlin. On Alter Markt and the next street over, Katzengraben, stand several other seventeenth-century houses, most of them with stucco covering their half-timbered construction.

Köpenick may seem a good place to escape from big-city turmoil, but traces of the wider world are even closer than the Blood Week memorials just outside the old town. Off Alter Markt, Futranplatz is dedicated to local workers who died opposing the Kapp Putsch in 1920, when right-wing officers and civilians tried to topple the new German Republic, seizing the centers of power without resistance from a disloyal army, only to be foiled by a general strike that left them helpless in their Berlin offices. Alter Markt ends at Freiheit, across from an eighteenth-century silk factory at number 12. Turn left, and on your left, Freiheit 8 (until recently a vacant lot) was the site of Köpenick's synagogue, destroyed on Kristallnacht.

A few more steps bring you back to the Lindenstrasse bridge leading toward Bahnhofstrasse and the S-Bahn. A tram or the S-Bahn will take you east to **Friedrichshagen**, founded by Frederick the Great in 1753 as a village of Bohemian silk and cotton spinners. The original village street, Bölschestrasse, extending south from the S-Bahn to the waterfront, displays a mixture of nineteenth-century village houses and later buildings of metropolitan scale. The market square halfway down was planted with mulberry trees for silkworms; two of them remain. The silk business did not flourish, however, and after the middle of the nineteenth century the impoverished village became dependent on Berlin tourists and suburbanites. Friedrichshagen borders the **Grosser Müggelsee**, one of Berlin's largest lakes and still the favorite warm-weather destination on the eastern side of town. The main beach, east of Friedrichshagen, is a 1930 product of Martin Wagner and the city's progressive building department. Soon after, the lakeshore sprouted a Depression tent camp of unemployed workers. It was called Kuhle Wampe, and is remembered because of the film of that name, written by Brecht. Hiking paths lead around the lake and into the surrounding woods. To the south, an 82-meter-high tower, the Müggelturm, a 1960 concrete replacement for an old wooden one that burned, is open to those who want to climb 124 steps for the view.

Bölschestrasse ends at Müggelseedamm, which follows the shore. Near the intersection, at Müggelseedamm 164, an old brewery has opened a museum of brewing. A few blocks to the left, at Müggelseedamm 307 on the eastern edge of the village, the old municipal waterworks from 1893 extends inland from the lake, a vast complex of pumping and filtration facilities. It was designed to the most modern standards by the director of the city water department, the Englishman Henry Gill, and built in red-brick Gothic style. Since 1987, it has been a museum, where you can visit the old buildings with their original machinery.

Pankow, just north of Prenzlauer Berg, is a pleasant but obscure corner of the former East Berlin that has, from time to time, attracted its own wealthy and powerful residents, even if it was never a match for the western suburbs.

It was a country village when Frederick the Great offered Jean-Jacques Rousseau a farm here, so that he could adorn the king's court and still have a place to practice the peculiar rural virtues he preached. (Rousseau was not interested.) Pankow displays great architectural variety. The housing developments south of the S-Bahn, for example, are among the city's most interesting from the years both before and after the First World War. The old village core is on Breite Strasse, a short distance north of the Pankow U-Bahn/S-Bahn station. The fifteenth-century village church was expanded in 1859 by Stüler, just as the village was becoming a thriving suburb. Down the street to the left is the grand Rathaus from 1903, built for the substantial town Pankow had by then become; it was extended in the 1920s in expressionist style. Breite Strasse still boasts several one- and two-story houses from the nineteenth century, as well as number 45, down the street to the right, an eighteenth-century Baroque house with an ornate original door. Amalienpark, across the street, is lined with picturesque houses from the 1890s.

It is but a short walk to **Niederschönhausen palace** and park. (The most direct route is Ossietskystrasse from the church.) The Baroque palace, originally built for a Countess Pohna in 1662, was bought by Elector Frederick III, the later King Frederick I, in 1691. In the following years he had Nering and Eosander von Göthe rebuild it. It was damaged by Russian troops during the Seven Years' War and subsequently remodeled in the 1760s into its current form, with a Rococo staircase in front and new galleries at the southern end. The garden was last transformed by Lenné around 1830. In 1740 Frederick the Great gave the palace to his wife, Elisabeth Christine. It might be more accurate to say that he banished her to it: Frederick had little use for his wife, or most other women, and kept her away from his court in Potsdam. The fact that the palace, unlike central Berlin, survived the Second World War intact recommended it to the new East German regime, and President Wilhelm Pieck made it his residence from 1949 to 1959. Thereafter it was an official guesthouse. Western politicians long belittled the GDR as 'the Pankow regime' as if to imply that it had no claim on Berlin. Many GDR leaders, in fact, lived in villas in the vicinity, especially around Majakowskiring, which remained the home of Walter Ulbricht's widow until her death in 2002.

Not far to the west is the **Soviet cemetery at Schönholz**, at the western end of Schönholz park, west of Germanenstrasse. The memorial here, completed in 1949 by Soviet artists, is smaller than its better-known contemporary in Treptow, but is nevertheless grand and glorious. The entrance is flanked by massive red granite pillars with bronze reliefs, dedicated to 'the fighting and the sorrowing heroes of the Soviet land'. The cemetery itself is a rectangular space enclosed by a wall lined with plaques naming the dead. The centerpiece of the memorial is a bronze sculpture of a Russian mother mourning her fallen son, set in front of a 33-meter-high obelisk.

Nearby loom the residential towers of the Märkisches Viertel, which might strike you as a typical socialist housing complex, but it was in fact one of West Berlin's 1960s satellite cities, with 17,000 apartments and a dismal reputation. East Berlin's counterparts are farther east. After the unique experiment of the Stalinallee in the 1950s, the GDR began to build large modern apartment complexes in and around existing neighborhoods. Most were constructed from prefabricated concrete panels, made in factories and assembled on site. By the 1970s, nearly all were built with a single type of panel, and in ever larger complexes, sited on vacant land. Three large new districts dwarfed earlier projects. Few tourists go near them, but those who want to get a feel for post–socialist Berlin should visit one. The first and largest is **Marzahn**, with 57,000 apartments, begun in the mid-1970s and best reached from the S-Bahn stations Marzahn and

Springpfuhl. **Hohenschönhausen**, near the S-Bahn station
of that name, lies to its northwest. Farther east, **Hellersdorf**,
along the U5, was incomplete when the East German construction industry collapsed in 1990. Western visitors are
generally appalled by the sight of these endless rows of mid-
rise and high-rise buildings, but most East Germans were
not. They welcomed the opportunity to move from deteri-
orating inner-city buildings with nineteenth-century
plumbing and heating to centrally heated flats with full
bathrooms, accepting as the cost the longer commutes
(although some worked in neighboring factories). The government was proud of its achievements, which were going
to enable it to declare the housing problem 'solved' by 1990.
The problem was that they defined the housing problem in
strictly quantitative terms – numbers of flats – so that is all
they built. Beyond a few basic facilities, especially schools
and (as always in the GDR) child-care centers, everything
else was put off, including any landscaping of the new districts. Thus they remained ugly and lifeless places outside
the doors of the flats. Since 1990, Western money has given
these satellite towns the centers they never had. Many of the
buildings have also been renovated, including the addition
of new energy-efficient 'skins', which have typically been
painted garish colors, creating a lively contrast with the uniform drabness of the older façades.

One reason Western visitors are repelled by these projects is that they associate such public housing with concentrations of poverty and social pathology. It is worth
recalling that East Germany was different. For all the ways
the communist goal of a classless society was an illusion, it
did have a kernel of truth that is evident in housing pat-
terns: all classes lived side by side in these buildings. After
unification, however, with more choices available, the
wealthier and better educated were the first to move out.
Since then there have been many vacanies here, along with
the problems associated with concentrations of poverty,

unemployment and disaffected youth. Frightening incidents involving skinheads and neo-Nazis make for good headlines abroad, giving a sometimes one-sided impression of life in eastern Germany, but incidents of racist violence in Berlin are indeed concentrated in places like these, and in the long nighttime S-Bahn rides between here and the center.

A far grimmer relic of GDR life is located in Hohenschönhausen at Genslerstrasse 66, near Bahnhofstrasse. A former Soviet prison camp here was taken over by the Stasi and used to detain political prisoners. It is now a memorial; guided tours are available. The GDR was a police state that used physical violence sparingly, but here the Stasi, with its worst enemies in its hands, revealed itself at its most insidious, subjecting inmates to isolation, claustrophobia and deliberate disorientation. The writer Jürgen Fuchs recalled learning how human beings can suffer 'cruelty, humiliation, and barbarity, without a hair on their heads being touched'.

Memories of earlier evil are awakened at a memorial off Wiesenburger Weg, near the Marzahn S-Bahn station. This was the site of the Nazis' 'gypsy camp', where Sinti and Roma (as they prefer to be known) were confined after the Nazis declared that Berlin would be 'gypsy-free' by the 1936 Olympics. Many died amid the dreadful conditions in the camp. In 1943, the 1200 survivors were deported to Auschwitz-Birkenau and gassed. The first memorial here, in the form of a boulder, dates to the late GDR, 1986. An accompanying marble slab and an explanatory plaque were erected in the 1990s. A more substantial national memorial may someday be built here, unless proponents succeed in getting a memorial put up at a more prominent site in central Berlin.

V
Potsdam

23

Potsdam: the Old Town

PRUSSIA WAS FAMOUSLY DESCRIBED as an army with a state (rather than the other way around). This caricature captures a great deal of historical truth, since it was the patient, disciplined creation of military power that enabled this impoverished northern European backwater to become one of the Great Powers. The image of Prussia remained inseparable from its army, in the eyes of Prussia's rivals, but also in the eyes of the monarchs who resided in Potsdam, the city of kings and soldiers, of palaces and barracks. Apologists for Prussia, who dominate Potsdam far more than Berlin, will remind you of Prussia's achievements in the arts and sciences, of its legal system and its religious tolerance. They will tell you that Hitler, that uncouth Austrian who arrived via Bavaria, was the perversion, not the culmination, of Prussian virtues. These apologists have a point, but few foreigners will be inclined to mourn the passing of Prussia – which does not prevent us from feeling a certain awe at the sight of its ruins.

Potsdam remains to a great extent an eighteenth-century city – although the clusters of East German high-rises might give you a different impression. Potsdam, that is, saw little of the nineteenth-century industrialization that utterly transformed Berlin. It remained a garrison town, dominated by nobles and state officials along with soldiers. Eighteenth-century Berlin, too, was a garrison town, but it was in Potsdam that Frederick William I housed and marched his bodyguard of 'tall blokes', the prize regiment of giants he gathered at great expense from all over Europe. A century and a half later, the future Kaiser Wilhelm II felt ill at ease in bourgeois Berlin and preferred to spend his time here, in the bosom of the army. Potsdam's other heritage, equally authoritarian and perhaps equally dangerous, is that of enlightened absolutism: it is a town built by royal decree. Already in 1828, Heinrich Heine felt that Berlin had freed itself from 'the shallowness as well as the thoroughness' of Frederick the Great. Not so Potsdam: 'We wander through its deserted streets as we do through the extant philosophical writings of the philosopher of Sanssouci. It belongs with his *oeuvres posthumes*, and although it is now only so much waste-paper in stone, and quite ridiculous, we regard it with serious interest, and now and then suppress the temptation to laugh as if we suddenly feared to feel on our backs the blows from old Fritz's Spanish cane.'

Potsdam remains a world apart, a place many Berliners mistrust because they think it still hasn't cast off the shadow of the monarchy. If you want to see what 'waste-paper in stone' looks like – it's charming, actually – you are most likely to arrive in Potsdam at the main rail station (Potsdam Hauptbahnhof). The S-Bahn (S7) brings you here, as do regional (RE) trains, which run less frequently but get you here quickly from Zoo or Friedrichstrasse. (A local ticket covering zone C is valid on these trains as well.) The station was recently rebuilt amid an ugly shopping mall. The decision to build the mall was controversial because it threatened to suck the life out of the town center and because it created such a monstrous presence on the edge of the old town. The controversy became international, in fact, since UNESCO, which includes the Potsdam palaces on its World Heritage list, feared for the integrity of the landscape.

If you wander through the mall, you may come out on the north side, facing the river. However, the main station

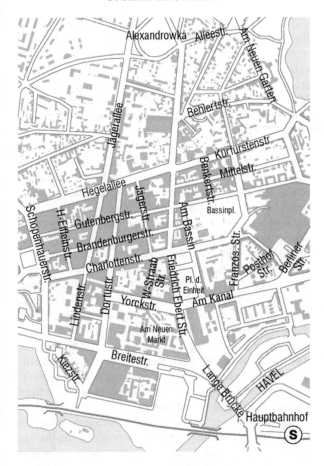

exit is on the south side, away from town, but facing many bus and tram lines that can take you (to the right) into the center. It is not a long walk, although it is a rather long bridge (called just that: Lange Brücke) that gets you there. This narrow point on the Havel, below the expanse of wide lakes that stretches from Spandau past Wannsee, is the reason for Potsdam's existence, ever since a twelfth-century fort was built to guard the ford. The bridge takes you across the Freundschaftsinsel (friendship island), recently landscaped as part of the 2001 Federal Garden Show. Across the water to your left, an eighteenth-century colonnade stands by itself, having been re-erected here in 1970. It once connected the town palace to the stables, extending across the open space now pierced by the street that stretches in front of you. The bridge takes you into the windswept old town square (**Alter Markt**). Potsdam was nearly spared the ravages of World War II, but on 14 April 1945 the RAF laid the old town center to waste, and decades later the results are all too visible. This was the site of the town palace. The palace was largely a product of the seventeenth century, after the Great Elector chose Potsdam as his secondary residence in 1660, although Frederick the Great's architect Knobelsdorff rebuilt much of it in the 1740s. The bombed-out ruins stood until 1960, when the GDR made the controversial decision to level them and make a new start. The problem is that their new start never got off the ground. Although the areas to the north and east of the square were replaced with standard-issue 1960s modernist blocks, the square itself remains largely vacant, a gaping hole separating the old town from the waterfront and the rail station.

Since 1990, as in Berlin, there has been a great clamor to rebuild the vanished palace as a way of making the bad times disappear and making the town whole again. The proposal was approved more readily than in Berlin – Potsdam's identity being more wholly bound up with the vanished glory of Prussia – but the money has not been forthcoming. What was rebuilt at private initiative at the beginning of the 2000s was the **Fortuna portal** at the palace's northern end. It is a carefully constructed copy of the original entrance, designed by Jean de Bodt and crowned with a gold-leafed copper sculpture of Fortuna, put up to celebrate the Prussian royal crown acquired by Frederick I in 1701. For now, it serves as an advertisement for the greater project of reconstructing the entire building.

Obviously something is needed to fill this open space. The GDR finally began its redevelopment in 1989 with the construction of a large theater near the river. After the Wall fell, protests halted its construction; ever since, a tent roof has permitted its temporary use, pending final plans for the square. The square's dominant structure remains the massive dome of Schinkel's **Nikolaikirche** (St Nicholas church). This elegant neoclassical study in cubes and spheres was completed in 1835, but with a gabled roof, at the insistence of King Frederick William III. It thus resembled Schinkel's modest suburban Berlin churches until 1843, after the king's and the architect's deaths, when Ludwig Persius supervised the construction of the high dome Schinkel had planned, dramatically changing the building's appearance. St Paul's in London was obviously a model for Schinkel, but he also borrowed from Florence, Rome and Paris to distill his Prussian classicism. The GDR restored the badly damaged church, along with two other old buildings on the square. The former Rathaus by Johann Boumann dates to the mid-eighteenth century and is based on an unbuilt design for Vicenza by Andreas Palladio. The GDR connected it to the so-called Knobelsdorff house from 1750, named after its architect. Knobelsdorff also designed the obelisk that remains at the center of the square.

The rest of the old town, behind these restored buildings, is a showcase of crumbling Soviet-bloc prefabs (an information office can be found in the one next to the church). However, the bombers largely missed the eighteenth-century extensions to the north and west, and they are what make the town worth visiting. The nearest escape from the twentieth century (for that is what most visitors to Potsdam seek) is across the wide Friedrich-Ebert-Strasse. The long, narrow building extending westward is the former royal stables (**Marstall**), but its shape as well as its broad arched bays betray its original function as an orangerie, built in 1685 by Nering. It was converted to stables in 1714 and then renovated, extended westward, and given its upper story (and horse-themed statuary) by Knobelsdorff in 1746. The GDR opened the **Film Museum** here in 1981, and it remains a place for changing displays about German film history, so much of which took place in nearby Babelsberg (see Chapter 25). Films are also screened here regularly.

Behind the museum stands a statue of Baron Friedrich Wilhelm von Steuben, the Prussian officer who (as generations of American schoolchildren have learned) aided General Washington in his famous revolution. He has long been honored with a statue in Washington. In 1911 the U.S. Congress gave a copy of it to the German emperor and people, which was destroyed in 1945; what you see is a 1994 copy of the copy – a suitable emblem of German-American relations. Next to Steuben, a narrow street leads away from the stables into one of Potsdam's little-known gems, the eighteenth-century ensemble of New Market (**Am Neuen Markt**). It survived the war nearly intact, but by 1990 was nearly a glorious ruin. Although the buildings have been restored since then, it remains a quiet place, sheltered from busy streets and attracting few visitors. At its center stands the modest 1836 building of the royal (later municipal) weighbridge, now a restaurant. Am Neuen Markt 1–2, on the south side (to your left as you enter the square) dates to 1753 and was the home of the later Frederick William II while he was crown prince. Number 3, on the east side, and 6 through 8, on the north, date to the 1770s. Number 5, in the corner, was a 1755 copy of a Palladio palace from

Rome, which crammed four stories of apartments behind the two grand palace stories visible on the façade. It was the only building on the square destroyed in the war; what you see is a 2002 building that replicates the old façade. The largest structure on the square – now home to an exhibit on Brandenburg history – is the recently restored royal carriage house (Kutschstall) from 1789, broad like the stables, with a grand classical portal, crowned by a sculpture of Frederick the Great's coachman driving the sun god's chariot. Just off the square on little Schwertfegergasse, which connects the square to the wide Friedrich-Ebert-Strasse, a Rococo house from 1771 by Karl von Gontard has an indented corner entry. Originally it was matched by three identical houses on the other corners.

Siefertstrasse leads diagonally out of the square to the broad expanse of **Yorckstrasse** – broad because of the canal in its center. The elegant Dutch-style canal replaced ancient drainage ditches around the old town in 1720. In the 1960s it was filled in but in the early 2000s it is being restored. Along with the canal, Frederick William I sponsored the first Baroque town extension in 1721, northward from here, in order to provide more housing for soldiers in his growing garrison. This street became its showcase. The grandest house is number 20, on the south side, which served as a court building, and looks like one, but was originally built in 1776 as a residence for the obviously successful glassmaker Brocke, whose trade is honored in the retorts held by putti sculpted on the façade. Surviving houses from the 1720s include the rebuilt row on the north side at numbers 5–7. Number 3–4 was built in 1823 to a design by Schinkel. Although the side street Wilhelm-Staab-Strasse presents an intact Baroque appearance, in fact it was all but destroyed in the war and carefully recreated by the GDR in the 1950s, in a rare example of ambitious architectural conservation.

The façades of numbers 7 and 8, for example, are entirely new postwar creations, inspired by, but not copies of, the street's prewar architecture. Another, less subtle kind of Baroque continuity can be found at the end of Yorckstrasse: the massive court building on Dortustrasse is an example of Wilhelmine neo-Baroque from 1907, a reminder that this style (so common in Berlin public buildings) is a grotesque parody of the original.

A short distance to the left down Dortustrasse, at the corner of Breite Strasse, is another large Baroque structure, this one built for an important local institution, the **military orphanage**. Prussia's many wars, plus the ordinary hazards of life in an eighteenth-century garrison town, left many children in the state's hands. Frederick William I founded the orphanage in the 1720s. Children received a modicum of schooling (but, one imagines, little affection) in return for their labor, mostly as spinners of wool and silk. The army also recruited many NCOs among the boys here. Gontard's building from the 1770s incorporates parts of the original structure.

Facing the orphanage across Dortustrasse was once the eighteenth-century garrison church (Garnisonkirche), where the Prussian church blessed the Prussian army, Frederick William I was buried, and, against his will, Frederick the Great, too, was interred. The coffins were carted westward in 1945 to keep them out of Russian hands, but the damaged church remained standing until it was blown up in 1968, a symbolic blow against Christianity and Prussia struck by the ruling Communists. Since the 1990s a private initiative has lobbied for the church's reconstruction as a kind of resurrection of the Communists' enemies, but other Germans are quick to recall what happened here on 21 March 1933, the so-called Day of Potsdam, when the newly appointed Chancellor Hitler and the doddering president and war hero Hindenburg bowed before the grave of Frederick the

Great, a gesture widely interpreted as Prussia's blessing of its newly minted Nazi successor.

Also near this corner are two 1770 buildings by Georg Friedrich Unger that belong to the modest Potsdam Museum. Breite Strasse 13, next to the orphanage, houses natural history collections. Across the street, the richly articulated Hiller-Brandtsche houses at numbers 8–12 are based on Inigo Jones's unbuilt Whitehall palace. This was a double house, with Hiller and Brandt each taking a three-story wing, and the lower central section given over to housing for soldiers, which was mandatory for Potsdam homeowners. Next to it is the oldest house in Potsdam, built in 1674 as a home for clergymen's widows and orphans, and given its neoclassical façade in 1827.

Breite Strasse, which leads east back to the old town square, juxtaposes old buildings and GDR prefab high-rises. South across it, the late-eighteenth-century row of houses on the side street Kiezstrasse replaced the older houses of a fishing village. Just to the west across Lindenstrasse, a lonely obelisk is one of two once incorporated in a town gate that stood here. Farther west, where a bay of the Havel reaches almost to the street, stands an elegant black and white striped mosque. Except it isn't a mosque: it's a **pumping station**, completed in 1843 to power the fountains in Sanssouci park. Frederick William IV directed Ludwig Persius to make it look like a 'Turkish' mosque with a minaret for a chimney – a stunning example of industrial architecture clothed in exotic forms. It is open for guided tours on weekends between mid-May and mid-October, when visitors can see its original Borsig steam engine. Newer pumps still send water up to the park.

If you return to Lindenstrasse and take it north, you pass more old army buildings, including number 26, an officer's house from 1734. The imposing colonnade of the Old Guardhouse (Alte Wache) from the 1790s, crowned with martial-themed sculptures, faces Charlottenstrasse, the border between the first and second Baroque town extensions. The second, begun in 1732, retains far more of its original, modest houses, built with minor variations on a prescribed model: two stories high, five windows wide, with a small central gable. This is truly the town built by royal decree, in which every homeowner had to set aside one upstairs room to house soldiers, two to six in a room (and two to a bed, to help guard against nighttime desertion). It had to be a front room so that the soldiers could hear the alarm sounded by drummers making their way through the streets. Lieutenants were given their own rooms; a captain got two. In return, the king provided homeowners with subsidies and building materials. All the houses were built of pine, the Great Elector having felled Brandenburg's great oak forests and sold the wood to England and Holland to pay his debts. Some houses were given masonry fronts, but the appearance of massive stone buildings was and is an illusion created with the yellow and ochre painted stucco. Where the stucco has fallen off – or rather, where it has not been restored since having fallen off nearly everywhere in GDR times – the illusion is laid bare.

Brandenburger Strasse, the next street north of Charlottenstrasse, has long been a main shopping street. It has also been closed to cars since the East Germans restored it during the 1970s (leaving all the surrounding streets to crumble further). It remains an intriguing mix of shops catering to local residents and to tourists, but it has not thrived since the rail-station mall opened. Most of its houses are from the eighteenth century, either the simple originals or grander ones from Frederick the Great's time. To the west it culminates in the **Brandenburg Gate**, which, like its Berlin namesake, faces west toward the city of Brandenburg. This ornate imitation of a Roman triumphal arch, once part of the town wall but now standing alone, was built in 1770 to a design by Gontard and Unger intended to make it a worthy gateway to Sanssouci park, to which this is the most convenient entry (see Chapter 24).

The red-brick building at Lindenstrasse 54, just north of Brandenburger Strasse, served as the home of the Potsdam garrison's commander after its construction in the 1730s, but in the twentieth century it had other functions, hinted at by its barred windows. From 1935 to 1941 it was a Nazi court that decided matters of 'racial health'; later it housed political prisoners. After the war the Soviet secret police used it for the same purpose, then turned it over to the Stasi. After the prison was closed in 1989, it was turned into a memorial. For a nominal charge you can visit the cell block off the courtyard and get some sense of the conditions in which the Stasi kept its prisoners.

Lindenstrasse leads to **Jägertor** (hunter's gate), the only town gate remaining in its original form from the 1730s. The modest Baroque gate's sculptural decoration depicts hunting scenes. On the way to it you cross Gutenbergstrasse, which, like Brandenburger Strasse, will take you east through the blocks of the second extension. Most of the badly deteriorated houses have been restored since 1990, but on a few side walls you can still glimpse the half-timbered construction of the buildings from Frederick William I's time. When you reach Friedrich-Ebert-Strasse, a shopping street, you can look left at the remarkable Nauen Gate (**Nauener Tor**), the third surviving gate from the eighteenth-century wall. Like the Brandenburg Gate, this one was rebuilt in grander form under Frederick the Great, with a central archway between two fantastic-looking towers. It was the first neo-Gothic structure in central Europe, dating to 1755 and based on a sketch by the king.

The second Baroque extension ends with the four blocks of the picture-perfect **Dutch quarter** (Holländisches Viertel), north of Gutenbergstrasse and east of Friedrich-Ebert-Strasse. It is visual testimony to the mercantilist policies that made Prussia cosmopolitan (in its own limited way) and prosperous. Frederick William I personally recruited Dutch artisans to come to Prussia, among them Johann Boumann, who was given the job of designing this quarter for them in the 1730s. The red-brick houses are of two basic types, with either five bays and an eaves front or three bays and a Dutch gable. The quarter has survived war and other ravages almost completely intact, and most houses have recently been restored.

South across Gutenbergstrasse is the open space of **Bassinplatz**, once a pool of water left after the Dutch quarter was drained, now dominated by the elegant Roman Catholic Church of Sts. Peter and Paul (1868) and, facing it, Gontard's more ornate Dutch-style houses from the 1770s. Behind the church, and easy to overlook, is a small cemetery of Red Army soldiers who died here in 1945, arranged around a central monument. (You will find something similar in nearly every east German town.) Away at the southeast corner of the square stands the peculiar round 'French Church' (1753), built for another important immigrant community, the French Huguenots, by Boumann, following a plan by Knobelsdorff based on the Roman Pantheon – a smaller and more elegant version of the same men's St Hedwig's in Berlin. Around the corner at Posthofstrasse 17 is another queer remnant of the garrison town: the so-called 'actors' barracks' (1796), built along with the garrison theater (now gone) for the actors who, like nearly everything in Potsdam, belonged to the army.

Follow Charlottenstrasse (in front of the French Church) back across the south side of Bassinplatz, turn left past a new shopping center, and you reach the other main inner-city square, **Platz der Einheit**. This, too, remained an open space because it was too swampy to build on. In fact, the eighteenth-century houses around it kept sinking, as the swamp swallowed the piles on which they stood. More recent events have not been permitted to sink from view. Near the southwest corner is a recent white stone sculpture with holes in it, dedicated to 'the unknown deserters' – from, one is to presume, Hitler's Wehrmacht. Its counterpart to the east, a 1975 GDR antifascist memorial, endures in a kind of limbo, having been ignored, but not removed, in the recent landscaping of the square. Across the street from it, next to the post office building (1900), a plaque recalls the site of a synagogue destroyed on Kristallnacht in 1938.

Along the south side of the square, the canal's restoration is planned. Beyond it lies the old town, dominated by 1960s Soviet-style architecture. Friedrich-Ebert-Strasse (and its frequent buses and streetcars) will take you back past the old town square and across the river to the rail station. A few areas beyond the station are worth a look. Leipziger Strasse runs southwest through a tangled mixture of crumbling waterfront warehouses dating back to the time of Schinkel, who helped design one of them. Albert-Einstein-Strasse, which diverges from Brauhausberg just south of the station, takes you up a steep hill. In the woods at the top are an array of scientific laboratories, including an observatory from 1877 as well as a later, better known one. Erich Mendelsohn designed the remarkable **Einstein tower** (1921) as an observatory intended to make astronomical observations to test Einstein's theory of relativity. The astronomy did not work out satisfactorily, but the building became one of the world's most famous monuments of expressionist architecture. It is smaller than photographs might lead you to believe, and with its round tower and protruding base it vaguely resembles a boot, although you are presumably supposed to visualize something less earth-bound. Its peculiar curved forms, notably its drooping windows, were intended to showcase the possibilities of concrete construction, but in fact brick was substituted in places because the the molds proved too complicated.

24

Sanssouci Park

FREDERICK WILLIAM, the Great Elector, pulled both Berlin and Potsdam out of obscurity, and his grandson, the 'soldier king' Frederick William I, made this garrison town the second most important in the kingdom. But it is the latter's son who gave Potsdam its lasting fame. Frederick II, later known as 'the Great', spent far greater sums than his father on ostentatious new buildings in the town and lavished even more attention on the private retreat he established on a barren hill beyond the town walls. Sanssouci is not just another imitation Versailles. Among the many royal retreats of absolutist Europe, this park's generations of construction and landscaping, leavened by the following decades of disorder and decay, lend it a unique charm.

The most convenient access to the park is from the town, specifically Luisenplatz and the Brandenburg Gate (see Chapter 23), although the more formal entrance, through the 1740s Obeliskportal, is a short distance to the north along Schopenhauerstrasse. (Alternatively, if you come from Berlin on a regional train, you could take it past the main station to the Park Sanssouci station – be sure your train stops there – and tour the park from west to east.) Behind the Brandenburg Gate, the Allee nach Sanssouci leads you through a gate near the simple and elegant **Friedenskirche** (church of peace). This end of the park was shaped by Frederick William IV, whose idea for a church modeled on early Christian basilicas was given form by Ludwig Persius and completed in 1854. In the apse is a thirteenth-century Byzantine mosaic that Frederick

William acquired when its home, a church on the island of Murano in Venice, was demolished. The king and his queen are buried in the crypt. A bell tower and cloister complete the original ensemble. Added decades later was the mausoleum for Emperor Frederick III and his wife, Victoria, eldest daughter of Queen Victoria. Around the church is the Marlygarten, a masterpiece of Romantic garden design, laid out in the 1840s by the royal landscape designer Peter Josef Lenné.

On the far side of the garden you reach the park's main east–west path, which brings you to the base of the terraces below **Sanssouci palace**, the park's first and most famous building. During the 1740s Frederick the Great worked closely with his architect, Georg Wenzeslaus von Knobelsdorff, on the palace design. It reflects the king's preference for what became known as Frederician Rococo, with its endless tangle of delicate curls and swirls, inside and out. For a royal palace, Sanssouci is very small: Frederick intended it as a private retreat that left no space for tiresome courtiers or supplicants or even his queen. In 1764, James Boswell cooled his heels for several weeks in Berlin and Potsdam, observing the king on several occasions but in the end departing without having achieved his goal of an introduction. He was told that such an approach to Frederick was not possible in Potsdam, only when the king was in Berlin – and he was hardly ever there. No one would intercede for the frustrated Boswell, leaving him to conclude that 'this king is feared like a wild beast'. It seems that Frederick William I succeeded in molding his recalcitrant son into a worthy successor. We are left to wonder how the 'soldier king's' cruelty imprinted itself on young Frederick. As an unhappy eighteen-year-old, he formed a plan to flee to England, but his father got wind of it and had him arrested, then forced him to watch the beheading of the friend who had aided his escape.

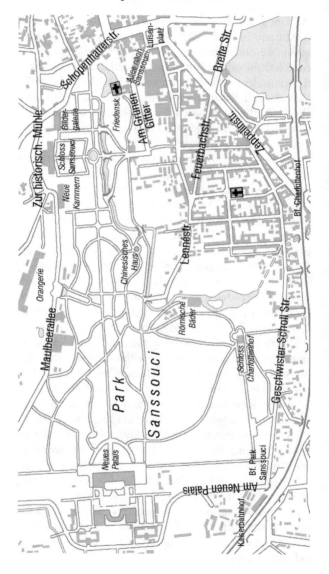

Sanssouci means 'without worry' in French, the language of culture and philosophy for Frederick, who was less than fluent in German and considered it 'crude and still almost barbaric'. (The German nationalists who made Frederick a hero, from Napoleon's opponents to Goebbels and Hitler, ignored this inconvenient fact.) Before you feel secure in your stereotypes, however, consider his view of English: 'Other languages lose something in translation; English alone gains.' This Francophile's wars against the Catholic rulers of France and Austria nevertheless made him a folk hero in England; the apotheosis of that hero-worship was Thomas Carlyle's popular biography a century later. At Sanssouci the melancholic king sought to escape his troubles, taking refuge in music, poetry and philosophical conversation with his intimates. Frederick was a talented flutist and composer and kept a small orchestra, including, for many years, C.P.E. Bach. The king also strove to lure eminent French *philosophes* to his court. Most kept their distance, although the radical materialist Julien Offroy de la Mettrie stayed until his untimely death in 1751, his reputation as a gourmand cruelly enhanced by his fatal food poisoning from a rich pheasant pie. (The king was reassured to learn that the notorious atheist had not summoned a priest for extreme unction.) The most famous of the *philosophes*, Voltaire, lived here from 1750 to 1753, as his difficult friendship with the king deteriorated. The notorious scourge of *l'infâme* proved unable to curb either his greed or his literary malice: the king caught him engaged first in illegal speculations and then in spreading libelous attacks on Frederick. Voltaire probably would have chafed under even a less trying master than this one, who had him detained in Frankfurt after he departed with a confidential edition of Frederick's poems, which contained scurrilous remarks about rival princes that Frederick did not wish to see fall into their hands. Nevertheless the two men maintained a correspondence until Voltaire's death.

The one-story yellow palace hugs the ground and even its central dome barely peeks over the top of the hill. Frequent guided tours permit you to see the interior, which unlike most local palaces has survived virtually intact. Passing along an inner gallery lined with paintings by Antoine Watteau, one of Frederick's favorite artists, you reach Frederick's rooms overlooking the gardens: the cedar-paneled corner library (the bibliophile king had identically stocked libraries installed in five palaces), the concert room with mythological pictures by the court painter Antoine Pesne, the domed marble chamber at the center and the naturalistic carvings of the 'Voltaire room' – all more or less as they were in Frederick's time. Among later kings, only Frederick William IV spent much time here. He was responsible for the east and west wings built in the 1840s, but he concentrated his efforts on transforming other parts of the Schlosspark.

The semicircular colonnade on the entry side (to the north, facing away from the gardens) affords access to a road (and buses) as well as a view of a distant clump of picturesque ruins. These have been ruins since they were built as such in the 1740s. The Mount of Ruins (**Ruinenberg**) conceals a reservoir that feeds the fountains in the park. Below the palace on the garden side, six curved vineyard terraces, with peculiar glassed niches intended to protect rare fruit plants, reach down into a formal French garden. On the side, a stone marks one of the least imposing of royal graves, Frederick's own. Against his wishes, he was buried in 1786 next to his father in the garrison church, and both coffins were hauled off to western Germany in 1945. In 1991, however, Frederick was reburied according to his own instructions: next to his only loyal companions, his dogs. Here it is easy to feel pity for this lonely man who wanted to be the model of a new kind of enlightened monarch, a man of both Athens and Sparta in the age of gunpowder; but there is also good reason to believe that this self-appointed patron of art and philosophy poisoned his own chalice with his military aggression, autocracy and censorship.

A matched pair of buildings flanks the palace. To the east is the picture gallery (Bildergalerie), completed in 1763, the oldest German museum building. It still houses part of Frederick's collection of Flemish and Italian paintings (no German ones, since Frederick scorned German culture). On the opposite side stands the Neue Kammern (new chambers), built in the 1740s by Knobelsdorff as an orangerie, then converted to guest apartments in the 1770s. Behind it stands a recent reconstruction of a 1790 windmill. To the west, Frederick William IV and his architect Persius (Schinkel's gifted but short-lived successor) planned a grand *via triumphalis* along the ridge. What was eventually built instead (in the 1850s, by Stüler and others) was the enormous **Neue Orangerie** (a guest house, despite its name), in Italian Renaissance style, with its centerpiece the Raphael room, filled with new copies of the revered master's paintings.

Behind it, just a short distance up Ribbeckstrasse (outside the Schlosspark) is the former royal manor (Krongut) of Bornstedt. After it was destroyed by fire in 1846, the king had the house and outbuildings rebuilt in Italian villa style by Johann Heinrich Haeberlin, with gardens by Lenné. In the 1860s, it was taken over by the crown prince, the later Frederick III, and his English wife Vicky, who ran it as a model manor. In 2002 the restored complex was reopened for visitors, who will be attracted above all by the traditional artisans working at glassblowing, brewing, baking and other trades. Across the street is the neo-Romanesque manor church, built in the 1850s by Haeberlin according to a design by Persius and Stüler.

At the bottom of the terraces below Sanssouci, you can follow paths west (right) and south past the geometrical garden into the more informally arranged paths of the Rehgarten, laid out in the 1760s. Here you will stumble across the precious **Chinese tea house**, built in the 1750s on Frederick's orders, a colorful Orientalist fantasy complete with sculptures of stereotypical Chinese figures. In later years, the king sometimes dined here with his elderly friend George Keith, the exiled Jacobite Earl Marischal, who had long served him as ambassador in Paris (to the great displeasure of the king's uncle, George II of Britain) and whose house still stands at the south gate of the park. A little farther south and west, across a tiny canal, you reach a southern extension of the park laid out by Lenné for the later King Frederick William IV while he was crown prince. The first cluster of buildings you reach are the so-called Roman baths (**Römische Bäder**), designed mostly by Persius on the basis of suggestions by the crown prince and Schinkel. The informally arranged buildings and gardens in the Italian villa style, intended as a summer retreat with housing for gardeners and for guests, are a marvelous example of Romantic design. The main house with the tower was built first, beginning in 1829, and others were added in the 1830s, including a tea pavilion to the south and, in front of it, a memorial to Frederick William III and Queen Luise. The actual Roman-style baths are on the north side of the garden, behind an arcade by Schinkel.

Just past the Roman baths, the footpath brings you to the garden side of the serenely neoclassical **Schloss Charlottenhof**, one of Schinkel's masterpieces, built just after the crown prince acquired this estate in 1825. In the house's immediate vicinity are formal, Italian-style gardens. The garden adjoining the eastern side of the house, centered around a large fountain, is terraced up to a pergola that encloses its southern end. While the garden faces north, the house faces west, creating an appealing asymmetry. Like so many of Schinkel's buildings, this was a renovation of an existing one, the eighteenth-century manor house that came with the estate. Schinkel kept the house's modest dimensions and turned it into a one-story imitation of a Roman villa with a strikingly simple front façade. It was the crown prince's dream to create his own version of Sanssouci: a house intimately connected to nature in which he would entertain the land's greatest artists and thinkers. Schinkel's richly colored decoration of the interior rooms (open for guided tours) is largely intact. Most unusual is the 'tent room' reserved for the renowned explorer Alexander von Humboldt.

If you walk toward the west, you pass Persius's hippo-drome, and soon catch sight of the 700-foot long façade of the magnificent **Neues Palais**, enclosing the western end of Sanssouci park. This grandiose product of Frederick the Great's later reign is the counterpart to modest Sanssouci. Initial plans in the 1750s were delayed by the Seven Years' War, when Frederick brought Prussia to the brink of disaster before coming out victorious after the tsarina's death permitted a favorable peace settlement in 1763. The Neues Palais then rose as a gesture of tri-umph and as proof of Prussia's continued strength and wealth – even if much of that wealth had to be squan-dered on it.

The palace was intended above all as a guest house – surely the world's most opulent – separate but not remote from Sanssouci, although a suite of apartments was built for Frederick. The architects were Johann Gottfried Büring (who also designed the Chinese tea house and the picture gallery) and Karl von Gontard. From the garden side you see a long, symmetrical façade with a central dome and a low extension at each end. It is a late example of the Baroque in all its laden glory. Twelve sculptors worked for years to produce the 428 allegorical statues that decorate the façade. On the garden side they illus-trate the horrors of war and the deeds of ancient Greek heroes; on the opposite side, other gods symbolize peace. The entirety is to be understood as an apotheosis of the Prussian state. The main entrance was on the western side, where two wings enclose a central court. Tours take you through the long enfilades of cavernous, richly decorated Rococo rooms. Highlights in the center section are, on the ground floor, a grotto room, and, above it, the vast marble hall. In the south wing is a large theater. The palace is outfitted with a collection of Baroque paintings, some of them from the palace's original collection, others brought here after 1945 from destroyed Prussian palaces.

The far side of the rear entry court is enclosed by a matched pair of large domed buildings, connected by a semicircular colonnade. You would not guess that these stately 'Communs' were built (by Gontard, at the same time as the palace) as kitchens and servants' quarters. They were partial ruins until the 1990s, when they were renovated for Potsdam University. Their purpose was to magnify the grandeur of the entry court. With all the pomp, it is not surprising that the last emperor, William II, chose this palace as his main residence. Indeed, he took charge of it in a decisive manner. His father, the tragic Emperor Frederick III, had been born in the palace and chose to return here to die of the throat cancer that ended his long-awaited reign after a mere three months in 1888. Young William attended his father's deathbed, but not out of love. He had the palace surrounded by soldiers to ensure that no liberal orders could be sent out, and the moment Frederick drew his last breath, he ordered it sealed and searched for state papers that (he feared) might be spirited away to England by Frederick's wife Vicky, empress only minutes before and now a prisoner in her room.

Sanssouci differs from many Baroque parks in that its axes, even in its more formal parts, do not lead the eye incessantly back to the royal palace. It is, rather, a delightful place for aimless wandering past lawns, hedges and half-hidden neoclassical statues. Sanssouci palace itself was not designed to dominate the park, but the later Neues Palais does line up with the western end of the park's main axis. Completing the formal composition are two classical temples (1770), set symmetrically on either side of the axis and surrounded by vegetation. Gontard designed both based on the king's ideas. On the south side is the Friendship Temple, probably inspired by Voltaire's poem 'Le temple de l'amitié' and dedicated to the memory of Frederick's sister. Its northern counterpart was originally used to display the king's collection of antiquities, which are no longer here, except for a second-century Roman marble relief of Trajan. Later this became a mausoleum for the last empress, Auguste Viktoria. Here, too, is a copy of Rauch's sculpture for Queen Luise's grave in Charlottenburg.

Off to the north, on the same ridge as the Neue Orangerie, is a Belvedere by Unger (1772) and the Drachenhaus (dragon house), built by Gontard for the keeper of the hillside vineyard, and more recently used as a restaurant. A short distance to the northwest, outside the park, Lindstedter Chaussee leads to **Schloss Lindstedt**. This was another neighboring manor acquired by the crown prince Frederick William, in 1828, and subsequently yet another park landscaped by Lenné. Plans for the manor house originated with Frederick William and then passed through the hands of several architects, with the final product modest and picturesque. In the late 1850s, when the king had slipped into insanity (and his brother William had become regent) this was foreseen as his quiet residence, but it was barely completed before his death in 1861.

You are invited to leave the Neues Palais by the route the emperor took. South from the entry court, the street Am Neuen Palais leads to the main rail line. Here stands the imposing Romanesque pile of the **Kaiserbahnhof**, the station built in the 1890s for the exclusive use of the emperor's train, permitting a quick transfer from Baroque opulence to modern speed for the restless monarch nick-named the Reisekaiser (traveling emperor). At last report the building was still a ruin, no one having come up with an economical use for it. Just across the road at the Park Sanssouci station, you can board a more modest regional train back toward central Potsdam and Berlin, or you can follow Geschwister-Scholl-Strasse east through the Brandenburger Vorstadt, a nineteenth-century quarter on the south side of the Schlosspark that retains much of its East German shabbiness.

Between Potsdam and Berlin: Waterfront Palaces

BERLIN IS SEPARATED from Potsdam by a network of forests and lakes, most of which are actually wide and placid stretches of the Havel river. In the late eighteenth and nineteenth centuries, Prussian kings and princes scattered a remarkable array of palaces along these waterways. The division of Germany left this landscape divided and fortified, since some of the palaces ended up in West Berlin, others in Potsdam, but it can once again be enjoyed in its entirety. Cruise boats take you from one end to the other, a car can get you between them quickly, while a combination of walking and public transportation requires breaking the trip into several segments.

From the Wannsee S-Bahn station, you can take a bus or car (or a bicycle, if you want a serious workout) west on Königstrasse. The A16 bus turns right onto Nikolskoer Weg, stopping at Persius's Moorlake house, built in 1841 as a Swiss-style forester's house with a royal tea room upstairs, since 1875 a restaurant. Even deeper in the woods, you are supposed to think you might have arrived in Russia as you reach the wooden Blockhaus Nikolskoe (1819; rebuilt after a 1985 fire). Frederick William III and his daughter Charlotte were charmed by a Russian farmhouse they visited en route to her wedding to the later Tsar Nicholas I, and the king ordered the construction of a copy here. Its restaurant is said to date back to the time of the king's Russian coachman, who supplemented his income by selling refreshments to visitors. The king also requested that

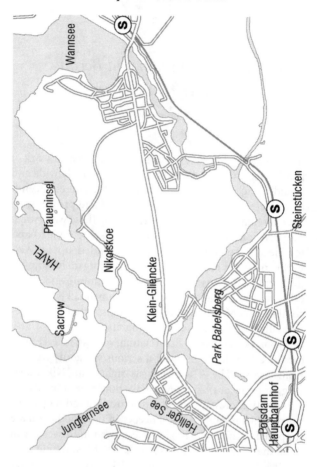

the nearby church be built in the Russian style, but Stüler stuck to his elegant Italian Romanesque for the church of Sts. Peter and Paul (1837), with the onion dome and wooden entry the only Russian details. The interior is the best preserved of any Berlin church of its era.

A short distance farther on, you reach the dock for the ferry to the delightful **Pfaueninsel** (peacock island). The island is kept free of cars, shops and other facilities, even of smoking, so the restaurant and beer garden are here on the mainland side. The ferry ride takes barely a minute; its ticket opens the entire island to you, for as long as you care to wander without the benefit of the buses and cafés that you can rely on everywhere else in Berlin. You may well be greeted by the eponymous peacocks, a small flock of which is maintained here – although the island's original menagerie became the founding collection of the Berlin zoo in 1844. Near the ferry landing is the island's most extraordinary building, the half-ruined castle which is, however, in fine condition, having been built as a ruin, with a fragmentary upper story between two towers connected by an arched bridge. This whimsical house was built for Frederick William II and his mistress Wilhelmine Enke in 1795 and was placed so that it could be seen from the distant Neuer Garten, the king's main home (see below). Guided tours are available through the well-preserved interior. After the king's death in 1797, it became a favored summer home of his son Frederick William III, and the rest of the island reflects his influence. Lenné landscaped the island in the informal English style in the 1820s, and you can wander past woods, meadows and a variety of structures from that period. Near the island's center, the neo-Gothic Kavaliershaus, a gardener's residence, was rebuilt by Schinkel in the 1820s around the original façade of a sixteenth-century house brought here from Danzig. Farther out, the neoclassical Luisentempel uses the original 1812 façade of Queen Luise's mausoleum in Charlottenburg, moved here when the mausoleum was rebuilt in 1828. At the far end of the island is an artificial Gothic ruin intended to look like a dairy, built at the same time as the castle.

If you return to Königstrasse and take it farther out, the Romantic gem of **Klein-Glienecke** park unfolds on your right. Prince Carl, the king's son, bought the estate in 1824 and put Schinkel and his followers in charge of constructing its wide variety of practical and whimsical structures. Lenné had already been hired in 1816 by the previous owner, Chancellor Karl von Hardenberg, to landscape the property in the English style as what was called (in German) a 'Pleasureground'. The main entrance brings you to Schinkel's Lion Fountain (1838) in front of the house. Next to it, near the road, is the 'curiosity' (Neugierde), a 1796 teahouse rebuilt by Schinkel. Artfully placed fragments of classical columns are among the artificial ruins in the Pleasureground, which reaches nearly to the Glienecke bridge, where the corner of the property is marked by an open round temple, sometimes called the 'large curiosity', redesigned by Schinkel as a place from which to view the bridge.

The small and elegant neoclassical manor house (it is sometimes called a Schloss, but it is anything but a palace) was designed by Schinkel in the 1820s. Its side wings enclose a courtyard, used to display the prince's collection of antiquities, and a pergola connects it with a service building behind. Past it is Persius's orangerie (1839) and the 'cloister' (1850), so called because its square courtyard resembles one. A collection of medieval and Byzantine architectural fragments are incorporated into it. Not far from it, standing above the lakeshore, is Schinkel's first building for Prince Carl, the Casino, an older billiard hall that the architect reshaped to resemble a miniature Italian villa. Beyond this row of buildings, the larger park extends far to the north and east along the shore, including a hunters' hall (Jägerhof, 1828) jointly designed by Schinkel and Prince Carl's brother, the later Frederick William IV. The park extends as far as the Moorlake restaurant accessible from Nikolskoer Weg (see above), and it affords a view of Persius's Heilandskirche (Church of the Redeemer), an elegant 1840s reinterpretation of the early Christian basilica, across the lake in Sacrow.

Across Königstrasse is Jagdschloss Glienecke, a hunting lodge that dates to the seventeenth century, but offers little of interest since its reconstruction in the late nineteenth. It does help illustrate the diversity of nineteenth-century historicist architecture, its neo-Baroque contrasting with the neoclassicism across the road as well as with the pseudo-medieval Babelsberg palace visible across the water (see below). It is also possible to walk to Babelsberg from here, if you follow the shore back eastward to the Lankestrasse bridge.

Königstrasse leads to the **Glienecke bridge**, which marks the border between Berlin and Potsdam. For decades it was also the heavily fortified border between the East and West blocs. Among the few who crossed it were spies such as Francis Gary Powers and Rudolf Abel, exchanged here by the United States and USSR. During the years of division, Potsdam's Berliner Vorstadt, on its side of the bridge, was a very quiet place. (The tangled story of the forlorn neoclassical villa just across the bridge is told in Katie Hafner's book *The House at the Bridge*.) In recent years many of the newly wealthy have moved into old and new villas here. Some locals complain that unchecked development on the previously pristine south side has spoiled the waterfront landscape.

Serious walkers can reach the **Neuer Garten** from here by following Schwanenallee along the lake to the right. A pedestrian bridge brings you into the park and on to Cecelienhof palace. The usual access, however, is from the other end of the Berliner Vorstadt, reached via streetcar from the Potsdam side of the Glienecke bridge or, most conveniently, from the center of Potsdam, on foot or via the buses and trams that run north from Nauener Tor. The park's main entrance is on the street Am Neuen Garten, near Alleestrasse (see map on p. 425). This park is the main legacy of Frederick William II, who decided to build his own summer palace away from his uncle's at Sanssouci. As he succeeded Frederick the Great in 1786, the new king was acquiring property along the banks of the Heiliger See, on the other side of Potsdam from Sanssouci – the first of several royal palaces on the interconnected waterways stretching to Glienecke, Babelsberg and the Pfaueninsel.

From the gate you can follow the park's main axis past the palace's service building, on the left, with the orangerie beyond it. Most of the park's buildings date to Frederick William II's eleven-year reign. The centerpiece is the **Marmorpalais** (marble palace). Architectural historians credit Frederick William with bringing the new classicism to Prussia, after Frederick the Great had clung to the increasingly unfashionable Rococo style, but the transition was gradual. Here the architect was the elderly Karl von Gontard, who had long worked for Frederick, and who absorbed many influences – Dutch, French, English – apparent in the square palace built on a terrace above the lake. The interior decoration (largely intact) was in the hands of the younger Carl Gotthard Langhans, best known for Berlin's Brandenburg Gate. (Gontard, by contrast, was responsible for Potsdam's more ornate Brandenburg Gate twenty years earlier.) Langhans also designed the two wings later added to the palace, completed in 1797, the year the king died here. They remained shells until the 1840s, when Frederick William IV put Persius in charge of designing the interiors. Elsewhere in the garden, Langhans is responsible for the Egyptian themes: an obelisk, a pyramid, and a statue of Isis. He also designed the neo-Gothic library that stands at the southern tip of the lake, some distance away from the palace, as well as Palais Lichtenau, across the street at Behlertstrasse 31, an elegant neoclassical residence for the king's mistress. The so-called Green, Red, White and Brown Houses scattered through the park were there when the king acquired it, and were integrated into the new planning. Apart from the main axis, the park's landscaping mainly reflects a reconstruction by Lenné after 1816.

Near the north end of the park stands the very last Prussian palace, **Cecelienhof**, commissioned by the crown prince (William II's son) just before World War I broke out, and completed in 1917. Paul Schultze-Naumburg (who became a Nazi propagandist a few years later) designed an elegant variation on the English country house, with a half-timbered façade and asymmetrical wings grouped around several courtyards. The house is most famous as the meeting place of the Potsdam Conference in July and August of 1945, the last wartime summit of the Big Three Allied leaders. Just weeks after destroying Hitler's Reich, Stalin, Truman and Churchill (the last replaced by Attlee when the British election returns came in) discussed plans for postwar Europe and for finishing the war against Japan. The plans for Europe soon dissolved in rancor, while those for Asia were not given serious consideration, since, after his arrival, Truman received word that an atomic bomb had been successfully tested in the New Mexico desert. The main hall where they met has been preserved and can be visited. The rest of the building has long been a hotel.

Across the Heiliger See are the villas of the newly fashionable Berliner Vorstadt. Just north of Cecilienhof is the Jungfernsee. Boats once carried royal parties from here to the Pfaueninsel. Visible to the west, at the top of the Pfingstberg, is the Belvedere, a fantasy castle (also concealing a water reservoir) planned by Frederick William IV. On the edge of the hill is the recently restored Pomonatempel, Schinkel's first building (1801). Just to the south is Potsdam's old Jewish cemetery.

The surrounding Nauener Vorstadt was long blighted by the presence of the Red Army. A former KGB prison can be visited at Leistikowstrasse 1. Many of the neighborhood's villas have recently been acquired and restored by those some might see as eastern Germany's new occupiers, the capitalists. The Russian presence here long predated the Red Army, as is evident on the hill just south of the Pfingstberg, the Kapellenberg (chapel hill), site of an unmistakable Russian Orthodox church from the 1820s, designed at the Tsar's court and built under the supervision of Schinkel, who decorated the interior, although the icons were painted in Russia. Just south of the church is another, odder Russian presence. (Trams as well as buses from the inner city come out this far, via Friedrich-Ebert-Strasse and Nauener Tor.) In 1826, Frederick William III decreed the creation of a Russian village, **Alexandrowka**, as a memorial to his deceased ally, Tsar Alexander I. Lenné laid out the oval space in imitation of eighteenth-century Russian army villages (of which none remain). Along the two cross streets are arrayed a dozen log houses with overhanging gables and ornate serrated gable ends. They were intended for Russian soldiers on loan to Prussia, and include ample space for gardens. The houses are still lived in.

The S-Bahn stations between Wannsee and Potsdam Hauptbahnhof offer access to the Babelsberg side of the river landscape. If you get off at **Griebnitzsee**, the first station in Potsdam, the main entrance of the station faces you north toward Griebnitzsee, one of the chain of Havel lakes. To your left, you can cross Rudolf-Breitscheid-Strasse and follow a lakeside path (reserved until 1989 for GDR border guards, since the border ran through the lake) around Neubabelsberg, home to film stars in the 1920s and still boasting many tasteful neoclassical villas from the early twentieth century. Among those confiscated by the Russians in 1945, Karl-Marx-Strasse 2, overlooking the lake, was where U.S. President Harry Truman lived during the Potsdam conference that summer.

Farther along, the Urbig house at Virchowstrasse 23 was the conference residence of the British prime ministers, Winston Churchill and (after the 1945 election brought Labour to power) Clement Attlee. The villa is an early work of Ludwig Mies van der Rohe, built in 1915. Still farther down, Karl-Marx-Allee 27 was Josef Stalin's residence. The Mosler house at number 28–29 is another Mies house (1926), as is the nearby Riehl house (1907) at Spitzweggasse 3, designed when the architect was 21 years old.

A little farther on is a gatehouse marking the entrance to **Babelsberg park**, laid out as the summer residence of Prince William, the later king and emperor William I. (This is near the Lankestrasse bridge that connects to the Berlin-Wannsee side, and buses come here from S-Bahn Babelsberg.) The picturesque landscaping was begun by Lenné in the 1830s and continued a decade later by Prince Hermann von Pückler-Muskau. Farther down the shore is what appears to be a small castle, built, in fact, to house machinery driving the park's fountains and waterfalls. Up the hill from it is **Schloss Babelsberg** itself. Schinkel designed it in a Tudor-Gothic style according to the wishes of the prince and princess, drawing on what he had learned in his English travels. Its towers, arches and crenelation, along with its neo-Gothic interior, make it a remarkable specimen of picturesque architecture. Only the east wing and the massive octagonal tower were constructed in the 1830s according to Schinkel's plans. The rest was built in a somewhat different form during the 1840s by his students Persius and Strack, who also designed most of the park's other neo-Gothic structures. These include a nearby kitchen building; the Kleines Schloss, farther down the shore, built to house guests; and, away from the shore, the stables. Also nearby is the Gerichtslaube, a thirteenth-century loggia from the old Berlin town hall, moved here when the new town hall was built in the 1860s (a recent replica stands in Berlin's Nikolai quarter). Farther on is the Flatow tower, modeled on a medieval tower in Frankfurt am Main and incorporating guest apartments and an observation platform. Below it on the lakeshore is the 'sailors' house' where the emperor's boats were docked. Near the park's far end, a bridge across a pond is said to be the place where the desperate king, locked in a constitutional crisis, convinced Bismarck to become prime minister in 1862.

East of here you can exit the park onto Grenzstrasse and take it to the left across Alt-Nowawes, which brings you into the **Nowawes weavers' colony**, established by Frederick the Great in 1750 for Bohemian immigrant artisans. Some of the original cottages survive, albeit in altered form. Take Karl-Liebknecht-Strasse to the right and then Lutherstrasse left into Weberplatz, the colony's center, where its 1753 church stands. A short distance farther down Karl-Liebknecht-Strasse you pass the Babelsberg Rathaus from 1899, a typical suburban Berlin town hall, and reach the S-Bahn station in the center of the formerly independent town. Potsdam Hauptbahnhof is the next station west; to the east is Griebnitzsee and then Wannsee.

The rear exit of the Griebnitzsee station takes you across to the south side of the tracks, past a spacious Third Reich building now belonging to Potsdam University, to Stahnsdorfer Strasse, which taken to the left (east) leads to the bland Bernhard-Beyer-Strasse. It was not always unremarkable. To your right is the tiny exclave of Steinstücken, which by historical accident belongs to Berlin, although it is surrounded by Potsdam. From 1961 to 1989, the Berlin Wall surrounded Steinstücken and lined both sides of Bernhard-Beyer-Strasse, its only link to the rest of the world. (Number 12 is an Erich Mendelsohn house from 1927.)

Stahnsdorfer Strasse taken in the other direction leads to August-Bebel-Strasse, which takes you past the sprawling

Babelsberg film studios, long the German Hollywood. The Unionsfilm-Aktiengesellschaft (UFA) was founded by the German Army high command in 1917 to make film propaganda to counteract sagging morale on the home front after three years of war. In the 1920s UFA continued as a private enterprise, employing directors such as Ernst Lubitsch, F.W. Murnau and Fritz Lang to make memorable films that reached a mass audience. A sound stage remains from the 1920s, an undistinguished building revered as the place where Josef von Sternberg directed Marlene Dietrich in *The Blue Angel*, the film that launched her career, and one of the few international UFA hits in the new era of sound film. By then UFA was owned by the right-wing press magnate Alfred Hugenberg, whose temporary alliance with Hitler smoothed the transition to control of UFA by Goebbels's propaganda ministry, which continued until 1945 to churn out high-quality entertainment along with vicious racist propaganda. Here, near the end of the war, sets were built for the Berlin film *Life Goes On (Das Leben geht weiter)* because most of the buildings on location had been destroyed by bombs. (A comparable but happier case came half a century later, when the Berlin Wall had to be rebuilt on a film set here.) After the war, UFA became DEFA, the GDR's film studio. Since 1990 it has been renovated as part of an attempted revival of the European film industry, and it now houses international co-productions that try to match the high-tech extravaganzas of Hollywood. The land has also recently been turned into Filmpark Babelsberg, more a film theme park than a studio tour, although it includes opportunities to see authentic film studios, costumes, animals and sets. The main entrance is around the corner on Grossbeerenstrasse.

To the south, the Drewitz district includes many GDR-era prefabricated apartment blocks set willy-nilly in the landscape. Just beyond them, the **Kirchsteigfeld** development offers a startling contrast. It was built in the 1990s according to a master plan by Rob Krier and intended to evoke the kind of traditional urban ambience missing from postwar suburbs. Its winding streets and brightly colored buildings in varied shapes are centered around a postmodern version of a village square. Kirchsteigfeld is next to the autobahn but otherwise remote, at the end of tram lines from the center of Potsdam (end station Marie-Juchacz-Strasse).

The neighborhood north of Kirchsteigfeld is known as Am Stern (at the star) because several woodland paths converge. The star is now next to the Babelsberg exit of the autobahn and near GDR high-rises. Nevertheless, **Jagdschloss Stern** still stands alone. Frederick William I had this hunting lodge (and the diverging paths around it) built in 1730. Its walls are decorated with his own paintings, rare evidence of the 'soldier king's' interest in something other than soldiers. To call this a royal palace would be quite misleading. It is little more than a single room, concealed behind a Dutch gable, a lonely relic of a vanished world.

Appendices

Museum Information

Berlin has two hundred museums, in addition to the ever-changing roster of art galleries concentrated in the Spandauer Vorstadt as well as the temporary exhibitions that frequently spring up in parks and lobbies. The most important complexes are the museum island (Museumsinsel) off Schlossplatz and the Kulturforum near Potsdamer Platz. Included here is information on museums described in the text: their addresses, telephone numbers (from overseas, the international dialing code for Berlin is 00 49 30), web sites and hours. (Potsdam telephone numbers include the 0331 prefix required if you are calling from Berlin; if you are calling Berlin from outside the city, you need to dial 030 before the number.) Most of the web sites include a page in English. Note also that admission to the state museums (those run by the Prussian Cultural Property Foundation: www.smpk.de) is free on the first Sunday of each month. Twice a year, all the major museums stay open until 2 a.m., and the crowds flock to them. (For dates, see www.lange-nacht-der-museen.de.)

Allied Museum (Alliierten-Museum), Clayallee 135, 8181990, www.alliiertenmuseum.de
  Thur–Tue 10–18, free

Bauhaus-Archiv, Klingelhöferstrasse 14, 2540020, www.bauhaus.de
  Wed–Mon 10–17

Berlin Wall Documentation Center (Dokumentationszentrum Berliner Mauer), Bernauer Strasse 111, 4641030, www.berliner-mauer-dokumentationszentrum.de
  Wed–Sun 10–17, free

Bode Museum, Museumsinsel, Am Kupfergraben, www.smpk.de
  Reopening 2006

Bornstedt manor (Krongut Bornstedt), Ribbeckstrasse 6–7, Potsdam, www.krongut-bornstedt.de
Daily from 10, free except for special events

Botanical Garden and Botanical Museum (Botanischer Garten und Botanisches Museum), Königin-Luise-Strasse 6, 83850100, www.bgbm.org
Museum: daily 10–18; garden: daily, opens at 9, closes at dusk (between 16 in winter and 21 in summer)

Bröhan Museum, Schlossstrasse 1a, 32690600, www.broehan-museum.de
Tue–Sun 10–18

Brücke Museum, Bussardsteig 9, 8312029, www.bruecke-museum.de
Wed–Mon 11–17

Centrum Judaicum, New Synagogue, Oranienburger Strasse 30, 88028300, www.cjudaicum.de
May–Aug: Sun–Mon 10–20, Tue–Thur 10–18, Fri 10–17; Sept–Apr: Sun–Thur 10–18, Fri 10–14

Charlottenburg palace, Spandauer Damm, 320911 or 0331/9694202, www.spsg.de
Tue–Fri 9–17, Sat–Sun 10–17

Checkpoint Charlie Museum (Mauermuseum Haus am Checkpoint Charlie), Friedrichstrasse 43–45, 2537250, www.mauer-museum.com
Daily 9–22

Deutsch-Russisches Museum Berlin-Karlshorst, Zwieseler Strasse 4, 50150810, www.museum-karlshorst.de
Tue–Sun 10–18, free

Deutsche Guggenheim Berlin, Unter den Linden 13–15, 2020930, www.deutsche-guggenheim-berlin.de
Daily 11–20, Thur 11–22, free on Mon

Deutsches Technikmuseum Berlin, Trebbiner Strasse 9, 902540, www.dtmb.de
Tue–Fri 9–17.30, Sat–Sun 10–18

Domäne Dahlem, Königin-Luise-Strasse 49, 6663000, www.stadtmuseum.de
Wed–Mon 10–18, free on Wed

Egyptian Museum (Ägyptisches Museum), Schlossstrasse, 20905555 or 34357311, www.smpk.de
Tue–Sun 10–18

Ephraim Palais, Poststrasse 16, 24002121, www.stadtmuseum.de
Tue–Sun 10–18, free on Wed

Ethnology Museum (Ethnologisches Museum), Lansstrasse 8, 20905555 or 8301438, www.smpk.de
Tue–Fri 10–18, Sat–Sun 11–18

Filmmuseum Berlin, Potsdamer Strasse 2, 3009030, www.filmmuseum-berlin.de
Tue–Sun 10–18, Thur 10–20

Filmmuseum Potsdam, Marstall, 0331/2718112, www.filmmuseum-potsdam.de
Daily 10–18

Filmpark Babelsberg, Grossbeerenstrasse, Potsdam, 0331/7212755, www.filmpark.de
Mar–Oct, daily 10–18

Friedrichswerder Church (Schinkelmuseum), Werderscher Markt, 20905555 or 2081323, www.smpk.de
Tue–Sun 10–18

Gemäldegalerie (Picture Gallery), Kulturforum, Matthäikirchplatz, 20905555 or 2662101, www.smpk.de
Tue–Sun 10–18, Thur 10–22

Georg Kolbe Museum, Sensburger Allee 25, 3042144, www.georg-kolbe-museum.de
Tue–Sun 10–17

German Historical Museum (Deutsches Historisches Museum), Unter den Linden 2, 203040, www.dhm.de
Daily 10–18

German Resistance Memorial Center (Gedenkstätte Deutscher Widerstand), Stauffenbergstrasse 13–14, 26995000, www.gdw-berlin.de
Mon–Fri 9–18, Thur 9–20, Sat–Sun 10–18

Hamburger Bahnhof, Museum für Gegenwart (Museum for the Present), Invalidenstrasse 50–51, 20905555 or 39783412, www.smpk.de
Tue–Fri 10–18, Sat–Sun 11–18

Heinz Berggruen Collection (Sammlung Heinz Berggruen), Schlossstrasse 1, 20905555 or 32695815, www.smpk.de
Tue–Fri 10–18, Sat–Sun 11–18

Hoffmann Collection (Sammlung Hoffmann), Sophienstrasse 21, 28499121, www.sophie-gips.de
Sat 11–17 by appointment; closed in August

Huguenot Museum, Gendarmenmarkt 5, 2291760
Tue–Sat 12–17, Sun 11–17

Jagdschloss Grunewald, Hüttenweg 100, 8133597, www.spsg.de
May–Oct: Tue–Sun 10–17; Nov–Apr: Sat–Sun 10–16

Jewish Museum (Jüdisches Museum Berlin), Lindenstrasse 9–14, 25993300 or 308785681, www.jmberlin.de
Mon 10–22, Tue–Sun 10–20

Käthe Kollwitz Museum, Fasanenstrasse 24, 8825210, www.kaethe-kollwitz.de
Wed–Mon 11–18

Knoblauchhaus, Poststrasse 23, 23459991, www.stadtmuseum.de
Tue–Sun 11–18, free on Wed

Kunstgewerbemuseum (Museum of Applied Art), Kulturforum, Matthäikirchplatz, 20905555 or 2662902, www.smpk.de
Tue–Fri 10–18, Sat–Sun 11–18

Kupferstichkabinett (Museum of Prints and Drawings), Kulturforum, Matthäikirchplatz, 20905555 or 2662002, www.smpk.de
Tue–Fri 10–18, Sat–Sun 11–18

Lapidarium, Hallesches Ufer 78, 43095333
Sat–Thur 10–18

Luftwaffenmuseum, Kladower Damm 182, 36872605, www.luftwaffenmuseum.de
Tue–Sun 9–17, free

Märkisches Museum, Am Köllnischen Park 5, 30866215, www.stadtmuseum.de
Tue–Sun 10–18

Martin-Gropius-Bau (exhibition hall), Niederkirchnerstrasse 7, 254860, www.gropiusbau.de
Wed–Mon 10–20

Medical History Museum (Berliner Medizinhistorisches Museum), Schumannstrasse 20, 28022542
Tue–Sun 10–17, Wed 10–19

Museum für Kommunikation, Leipziger Strasse 16, 202940, www.museumsstiftung.de/berlin
Tue–Fri 9–17, Sat–Sun 11–19, free

Museum of East Asian Art (Museum für Ostasiatische Kunst), Lansstrasse 8, 20905555 or 8301383, www.smpk.de
Tue–Fri 10–18, Sat–Sun 11–18

Museum of European Cultures (Museum Europäischer Kulturen), Im Winkel 6–8, 20905555 or 83901295, www.smpk.de
Tue–Fri 10–18, Sat–Sun 11–18

Museum of Forbidden Art (Museum der verbotenen Kunst), Schlesische Strasse at Puschkinallee, 5320009
Apr–Oct: Sat–Sun and holidays 12–18, free

Museum of Indian Art (Museum für Indische Kunst), Lansstrasse 8, 20905555 or 8301361, www.smpk.de
Tue–Fri 10–18, Sat–Sun 11–18

Museum of Pre- and Early History (Museum für Vor- und Frühgeschichte), Schloss Charlottenburg, 20905555 or 32674811, www.smpk.de
Tue–Fri 10–17, Sat–Sun 11–17

Museumsdorf Düppel, Clauertstrasse 11, 8026671, www.dueppel.de
Apr–Oct: Thur 15–19, Sun and holidays 10–17, free tours at 11

Musical Instrument Museum (Musikinstrumentenmuseum), Tiergartenstrasse 1, 25481178, www.mim-berlin.de
Tue–Fri 9–17, Sat–Sun 10–17

Natural History Museum (Museum für Naturkunde), Invalidenstrasse 43, 20938591, www.museum.hu-berlin.de
Tue–Fri 9.30–17, Sat–Sun 10–18

New National Gallery (Neue Nationalgalerie), Kulturforum, Potsdamer Strasse 50, 20905555 or 2662651, www.smpk.de
Tue–Fri 10–18, Thur 10–22, Sat–Sun 11–18

Nicolai house, Brüderstrasse 13, 20458163, www.stadtmuseum.de
Tue–Sun 10–18, free on Wed

Nikolai church, Nikolaikirchplatz, 24724529, www. stadtmuseum.de

Tue–Sun 10–18, free on Wed

Normannenstrasse Research and Memorial Centre (Forschungs- und Gedenkstätte Normannenstrasse), Ruschestrasse 103, 5536854, www.normanne.de

Mon–Fri 11–18, Sat–Sun 14–18

Old Museum (Altes Museum), Museumsinsel, Lustgarten, 20905555, www.smpk.de

Tue–Sun 10–18

Old National Gallery (Alte Nationalgalerie), Museumsinsel, 20905555 or 20905801, www.smpk.de

Tue–Sun 10–18, Thur 10–22

Pergamon Museum, Museumsinsel, Am Kupfergraben, 20905555 or 20905301, www.smpk.de

Tue–Sun 10–18, Thur 10–22

Plötzensee Memorial (Gedenkstätte Plötzensee), Hüttigpfad, 3443226, www.gedenkstaette-ploetzensee.de

Daily 9–17 Mar–Oct; 9–16 Nov–Feb, free

Potsdam Museum, Breite Strasse 8–12 and 13, Potsdam, 0331/2896600

Tue–Sun 9–17

Sachsenhausen concentration camp (Gedenkstätte und Museum Sachsenhausen), Strasse der Nationen, Oranienburg, 03301/2000, www.gedenkstaette-sachsenhausen.de

Daily 8.30–18 Apr–Sept; 8.30–16.30 Oct–Mar

Sanssouci palace and other Potsdam palaces, 0331/9694202, www.spsg.de

Sanssouci and Cecilienhof: Apr–Oct: Tue–Sun 9–17; Nov–Mar: Tue–Sun 9–16

Neues Palais: Apr–Oct: Sat–Thur 9–17; Nov–Mar: Sat–Thur 9–16

Most other buildings: May–Oct: 10–17

Stasi exhibition (Informations- und Dokumentationszentrum der Bundesbeauftragten), Mauerstrasse 38, 23247951, www. bstu.de

Mon–Sat 10–18, free

Stasi prison (Gedenkstätte Hohenschönhausen), Genslerstrasse 66, 98608230, www.stiftung-hsh.de
Daily 9–18

The Story of Berlin, Kurfürstendamm 207, 88720100, www.story-of-berlin.de
Daily 10–20 (admittance until 18)

Sugar Museum (Zuckermuseum), Amrumer Strasse 32, 31427574, www.dtmb.de/Zucker-Museum
Mon–Thur 9–16.30, Sun 11–18

Tierpark Berlin (East Berlin Zoo), Am Tierpark 45, 515310, www.tierpark-berlin.de
Daily: opens at 9, closes between 16 and 18, depending on season

Topography of Terror, Niederkirchnerstrasse 8, 25486703, www.topographie.de
Daily 10–20 in summer, 10–dusk otherwise, free

Verein Berliner Unterwelten, 22680535, www.berliner-unterwelten.de
Bunker tours meet at corner of Badstrasse and Hochstrasse across from Gesundbrunnen station,
Sat 12, 14, 16, 18

Vitra Design Museum Berlin, Pfefferberg, Senefelderplatz, 4737770, www.design-museum.de
Tue–Sun 11–18

Wannsee Conference Memorial Center (Gedenkstätte Haus der Wannsee-Konferenz), Am Grossen Wannsee 56–58, 8050010, www.ghwk.de
Daily 10–18

Zitadelle Spandau, Am Juliusturm, 3549440, www.zitadelle-spandau.de
Museum and exhibitions: Tue–Fri 9–17, Sat–Sun 10–17

Zoologischer Garten und Aquarium, Hardenbergplatz 8, 254010, www.zoo-berlin.de
Daily: opens at 9, closes at 17 or 18, depending on season

Further Reading

History and Culture

Beevor, Antony, *The Fall of Berlin 1945* (2002)

Friedrich, Otto, *Before the Deluge: A Portrait of Berlin in the 1920s* (1972)

Friedrich, Thomas, *Berlin: A Photographic Portrait of the Weimar Years 1918–1933* (1991)

Fritzsche, Peter, *Reading Berlin 1900* (1996): the world created by mass-circulation newspapers

Gill, Anton, *A Dance Between Flames: Berlin Between the Wars* (1993)

Gross, Leonard, *The Last Jews in Berlin* (1982)

Hafner, Katie, *The House at the Bridge* (1995); see also www.thehouseatthebridge.com

Jelavich, Peter, *Berlin Cabaret* (1993)

Kaes, Anton, Jay, Martin, and Dimendberg, Edward, eds., *The Weimar Republic Sourcebook* (1994): a large compendium of translated texts

Kramer, Jane, *The Politics of Memory* (1996): superior journalism

Ladd, Brian, *The Ghosts of Berlin: Confronting German History in the Urban Landscape* (1997)

Large, David Clay, *Berlin* (2000): the best general history

Le Tissier, Tony, *Berlin Then and Now* (1992): pairs old and new photos

MacDonogh, Giles, *Berlin* (1997): a chatty and charming account of manners and morals

Richie, Alexandra, *Faust's Metropolis: A History of Berlin* (1998): lively, opinionated, and not entirely reliable

Roth, Joseph, *What I Saw: Reports from Berlin, 1920–1933* (2003)

Snodin, Michael, ed., *Karl Friedrich Schinkel: A Universal Man* (1991)

Taylor, Robert, *Berlin and its Culture: A Historical Portrait* (1997)

Wise, Michael Z., *Capital Dilemma: Germany's Search for a New Architecture of Democracy* (1998)

Wyden, Peter, *Wall: The Inside Story of Divided Berlin* (1989)

Memoirs and Diaries

Agee, Joel, *Twelve Years: An American Boyhood in East Germany* (1981): James Agee's son, whose stepfather was an East German writer

Benjamin, Walter, 'A Berlin Chronicle' and 'Berlin Childhood around 1900' (available in various compilations of his works)

Clare, George, *Before the Wall: Berlin Days 1946–1948* (1990): by an Austrian-born British intelligence officer

Deutschkron, Inge, *Outcast: A Jewish Girl in Wartime Berlin* (1989)

Fromm, Bella, *Blood and Banquets: A Berlin Diary 1930–1938* (1943): a Jewish society columnist watches the Nazis take over

Garton Ash, Timothy, *The File* (1997): what a Stasi file reveals

Kessler, Harry, *Berlin in Lights: The Diaries of Count Harry Kessler (1918–1937)*: he knew everyone

Krüger, Horst, *A Crack in the Wall* (1985): growing up in Nazi Berlin

Neiman, Susan, *Slow Fire: Jewish Notes from Berlin* (1992): a critical view of 1980s West Berlin

Shirer, William, *Berlin Diary* (1941): by an American journalist chafing under Nazi censorship

Smith, Howard K., *Last Train from Berlin* (1942): a young American journalist who remained during the first years of the war

Vassiltchikov, Marie, *Berlin Diaries 1940–1945* (1985): a young Russian who knew all the feckless aristocrats supporting Hitler, but who cast her lot with the honorable few

Walker, Ian, *Zoo Station* (1987): a young Englishman living the 1980s Kreuzberg scene

Fiction

Döblin, Alfred, *Berlin Alexanderplatz* (1929): a rich evocation of Berlin's poor east

Fallada, Hans, *Little Man, What Now?* (1932): a poignant story from the depths of Depression

Fontane, Theodor, *Jenny Treibel* (1893): the most Berlin-centered of his many novels of manners

Grass, Günter, *Local Anaesthetic* (1969): set amid the 1960s student movement

Isherwood, Christopher, *Mr Norris Changes Trains* (1935) and *Goodbye to Berlin* (1939), which have been published together as *The Berlin Stories*

Mann, Heinrich, *The Loyal Subject* (*Der Untertan*, 1918, also translated as *Man of Straw*): a bitter satire of Imperial society

Mann, Klaus, *Mephisto* (1936): a roman a clef about theater and collaboration in the Third Reich (made into a fine 1981 film by Istvan Szabo)

Nabokov, Vladmir, *The Gift* (1938): set, like most of his early works, in Berlin's Russian emigré community

Schneider, Peter, *The Wall Jumper* (1981): the definitive novella of divided Berlin

Timm, Uwe, *Midsummer Night* (1996): adventures in the post-Wall East and West

Wolf, Christa, *Divided Heaven* (1963): division from an East German perspective

Film and Video

Berlin, Symphony of a Great City (1927): a documentary filled with stunning images

Berlin's Hidden History (2002): a modest documentary effort by the author of this book, available at Amazon.com

The Big Lift (1950): Hollywood's take on the Airlift

A Foreign Affair (1948): made by Billy Wilder 'in the ruins of Berlin', as Marlene Dietrich sings

Germany, Year Zero (1947): Roberto Rosellini's story filmed in the ruins

The Last Laugh (1924): F.W. Murnau's classic tale of urban misery

The Legend of Paul und Paula (1973): an East German cult classic about love and conformity

M (1931): Fritz Lang's classic story of crime and the Berlin
   underworld
One, Two Three (1961): Billy Wilder's farce of divided Berlin
Run, Lola, Run (1998): more fun than profound, unlike most
   German movies
Wings of Desire (1987): Wim Wenders' visually arresting film of
   angels in the divided city

Websites

www.berlin.de (the city's official site; click on the Union Jack to
   get to the English page)
www.potsdam.de (official site)
www.btm.de (the Berlin tourist office)
www.berlinfo.com
www.berlin-info.de
www.berlin-stadtfuehrung.de
www.berlin-hidden-places.de
www.bvg.de (transit authority)
www.dailysoft.com/berlinwall (with links to other sites featuring the Wall)
www.berlin-judentum.de (Jewish Berlin)
See also the museum websites listed on pp. 460–466

Index

Index

Index

479

Index